Self

Mary Cassatt, The First Mirror, *captures the shared attention with mother through which infants first distinguish themselves from other people; the mirror adds further self-reference.*

Self

Ancient and Modern Insights
about Individuality, Life, and Death

RICHARD SORABJI

THE UNIVERSITY OF CHICAGO PRESS

RICHARD SORABJI is emeritus professor of ancient philosophy at King's College, London, and fellow of Wolfson College, Oxford. Besides coediting *The Ethics of War: Shared Problems in Different Traditions*, and editing seventy volumes so far of *The Ancient Commentators on Aristotle*, he is the author of *Matter, Space and Motion*; *Animal Minds and Human Morals*; *Emotion and Peace of Mind*; *Aristotle on Memory*; *Necessity, Cause and Blame*; and *Time, Creation and the Continuum*, the last three of which are also published by the University of Chicago Press.

The University of Chicago Press, Chicago 60637
Oxford University Press, Oxford OX2 6DP
© 2006 by Richard Sorabji
All rights reserved. Published 2006
Printed in the United States of America

15 14 13 12 11 10 09 08 07 06   1 2 3 4 5

ISBN-13: 978-0-226-76825-0 (cloth)
ISBN-10: 0-226-76825-2 (cloth)

Library of Congress Cataloging-in-Publication Data

Sorabji, Richard.
    Self : ancient and modern insights about individuality, life, and death / Richard Sorabji.
        p.   cm.
    Includes bibliographical references and index.
    ISBN 0-226-76825-2 (cloth : alk. paper)
    1. Self (Philosophy)   I. Title.
    BD438.5.S67 2006
    126—dc22

                                                            2005038002

To Orde Levinson

CONTENTS

Alc. 1: First Alcibiades
   in Alc. 1: Commentary on Plato's First Alcibiades
An. Post.: Analytica Posteriora (= *Posterior Analytics*)
   in An. Post.: Commentary on Aristotle's Posterior Analytics
An. Pr.: Analytica Priora (= *Prior Analytics*)
   in An. Pr.: Commentary on Aristotle's Prior Analytics
CAG: Commentaria in Aristotelem Graeca
Cat.: Categories
   in Cat.: Commentary on Aristotle's Categories
CCL: Corpus Christianorum Series Latina
CLCAG: Corpus Latinum Commentariorum in Aristotelem Graecorum
CSEL: Corpus Scriptorum Ecclesiasticorum Latinorum
DA: De Anima (= *On the Soul*)
   in DA: in De Anima (= *Commentary on Aristotle On the Soul*)
DK: Diels-Kranz
Dox. Gr.: Doxographici Graeci, ed. H. Diels
EE: Eudemian Ethics
EN: Nicomachean Ethics
GC: On Generation and Corruption
   in GC: Commentary on Aristotle On Generation and Corruption
GCS: Die griechischen christlichen Schriftstellen
Int.: De Interpretatione (= *On Interpretation*)
   in Int.: Commentary on Aristotle De Interpretatione
Isag.: Isagôgê (= *Introduction*)
   in Isag.: Commentary on Porphyry's Isagôgê

LS: A. A. Long and D. N. Sedley, *The Hellenistic Philosophers*, Cambridge
   1987
Math.: Adversus mathematicos
Metaph.: Metaphysics
   in Metaph: Commentary on Aristotle's Metaphysics
Meteor.: Meteorology
   in Meteor.: Commentary on Aristotle's Meteorology
Mixt.: On Mixture
MM: Magna Moralia
PG: Patrologia Graeca
PHP: De Placitis Hippocratis et Platonis
Phys.: Physics
   in Phys.: Commentary on Aristotle's Physics
PL: Patrologia Latina
Quaest.: Quaestiones (plural), *Quaestio* (singular)
Rep.: Republic
   in Remp.: Commentary on Plato's Republic
Res.: On the Resurrection
SVF: Stoicorum Veterum FragmentaI, ed. H. von Arnim, repr. Stuttgart
   1978 from 1st ed. of 1903–5
Tim.: Timaeus
   in Tim.: Commentary on Plato's Timaeus
Trin.: On the Trinity

ACKNOWLEDGMENTS

As well as giving a number of individual lectures on the subject, I tried out some topics at Gresham College as Gresham Professor of Rhetoric. I also had the chance of presenting two term-long seminars in Oxford on the self, one with Carlos Steel and another with Pauliina Remes, Inna Kupreeva, and Jonardon Ganeri. I also benefited greatly from giving a seminar for over a week at Fribourg in Switzerland at the invitation of Dominic O'Meara, with an audience very well versed in medieval philosophy and theology. Another seminar helpful to me was given at the Philosophy Department of the Graduate Center of the City University of New York, and I gave several lectures in the Philosophy Department of the University of Texas at Austin and others at the Higher Institute of Philosophy in Leuven. In the final stages, I was able to try out ideas on Indian thought as a guest visitor in India of the Indian Council of Philosophical Research. Acknowledgments of individuals from whom I have learned particular things are made in the text itself. Finally, I thank my publishers for getting me excellent comments on the submitted manuscript. Those of Christopher Gill, which I was able to identify, were extremely thoughtful and helpful.

Translations are my own unless otherwise indicated. I have used with acknowledgment standard translations for Kant and for most Indian sources. In other cases I have used or re-used, sometimes with small adaptations, the translations of friends who are gratefully acknowledged ad loc. Translations from Greek that are re-used were originally published in the series *Ancient Commentators on Aristotle*, ed. Richard Sorabji, London and Ithaca N.Y. 1987–present, or in the accompanying Richard Sorabji, ed., *The Philosophy of the Commentators: A Sourcebook*, 3 vols., London and Ithaca N.Y. 2004.

I am grateful to Michael Griffin for compiling the index locorum.

INTRODUCTION

The subject of this book is the idea of the Self, and I will start with that. But gradually there will emerge implications for life and death, and how we should view them. Parts of the book are more historical, others largely philosophical, although these categories are never separate.[1]

My original interest in the self stemmed from my discovery at the age of six that mortality applied to me and not just to insects. Initially, that interest led to a focus on certain types of question about the self, particularly whether it made sense to think of the same person as existing again after the interruption of death, and what made people distinct from each other. Those questions of personal identity and difference have indeed provided the main focus for much modern philosophy of the self. But actually the subject is much wider, and even for someone whose interest remains confined to mortality, other relevant aspects of selfhood need to be considered. The process of writing a book on the self and of taking in ancient treatments of selfhood led me to realize that the subject is much wider again. The Greeks from early on were interested in the idea of a human's true self. Later, they became interested in identity in a different sense, the individual's identity or persona. They were also interested in self-awareness, its possibility, its value as a route to the deepest truths, and eventually, but not until much later, its supposed certainty.

These ancient interests created a huge range of conceptions of self, which contrasted with the very minimalist or negative views prevalent in

1. Life: chapters five, eight to ten, thirteen, and fifteen. Death: chapters three, six, eight, ten, and sixteen to nineteen. Largely philosophical: chapters one, end of three, four, eight, nine, end of fourteen, fifteen, seventeen to nineteen. Chapters five and twelve bear on Locke and Descartes.

the tradition stemming from the English philosophers Locke and Hume. The many denials in the current English-speaking tradition that there is any such thing as self seemed wrong to me. And the views of self connected with this denial seemed to me impoverished compared with the rich variety of conceptions in Antiquity. I could not believe all of these ancient conceptions, but some of them seemed to me to contain truth, and I felt something had been lost in neglecting them. There was still more to be gained, I thought, from the separate ancient and medieval controversy on selfhood between Buddhists and Hindus.

In parts II, III, VI, and VII of the resulting book, I focus on the aspects of selfhood that I have described as the most familiar ones: personal identity and difference. Part II is concerned with the question what constitutes the same person at different times, part III with what differentiates people at the same time, or even outside of time. Parts VI and VII return to the question of identity at different times, but with a difference. In these later stages of the book, I am less concerned with introducing texts for analysis and discussion, except for some Indian texts, and more concerned with engaging in philosophical reflection on the issues.

I discuss less familiar aspects of selfhood, particularly in part IV, where I consider the idea of a person's identity in the different sense of a persona in ethics, and in part V, where I deal with questions of self-awareness. These issues are interconnected because to create a persona and act in the light of it, one needs self-awareness. But parts IV and V also connect with the other parts. Already part III introduces Plato's idea of the true self, the same for everyone, reason or intellect. The idea of persona in part IV individualizes that idea. Each individual has a distinct individual persona, which is in some ways like a true self. But there are differences: it is not an essence but at most a nature, something that can be molded and either developed or to some extent opposed. Other parts of the book connect with the theme of self-awareness in part V. Thus the case in part VI against people being no more than embodied streams of consciousness turns on our needing, for purposes of ethics and agency, to be aware of the self-same self at different times.

Chapter two of part I is a special chapter in that it introduces some issues that are not further developed in the rest of the book, and some of these issues connect with self-awareness too. Thus the idea of finding ultimate truths or realities within, discussed in chapter two depends on an intense form of self-awareness. Chapter two also introduces the Stoic idea of the newborn's natural attachment to its own body, an attachment that starts from a self-awareness of one's own body.

Nowadays philosophers tend to separate such discussions up. Charles Taylor's seminal *Sources of the Self*[2] is about something like the personae that people have had at different times in Western history. He does not, like Derek Parfit, discuss metaphysical questions about what sort of self can be supposed to exist in the universe. Conversely, many discussions of the self confine themselves to such metaphysical issues. Marya Schechtman is unusual in her book, *The Constitution of Selves*,[3] in comparing metaphysical ideas about the self with ideas about a person's identity in the sense of persona, and finding the latter more important. Parfit's outstanding *Reasons and Persons*[4] is itself unusual not only in that it is wide enough to draw very interesting conclusions about ethics as well as metaphysics, but also in that it rejects the usual metaphysics according to which it is very important whether a person at one time is identical with a person at another time. Because he rejects the importance of this identity, he is able to take the view that major changes of value can produce a different self.[5] They do this not by changing the metaphysical situation and making a person cease to be identical with a former self. Rather, on Parfit's view, the changes of value can alter the closeness of links in a stream of consciousness, and it is that, rather than identity, that really makes a difference to what self there is. He thus turns out to share a view with those whose interest is in personae, that people can contribute to creating their self, just as they can contribute to creating their persona.

I think there is value to seeing the wider canvas and taking in the wider range of questions that were discussed in Antiquity, both because of their intrinsic interest and because of their interconnections.

I now offer a guide to the structure of the book by providing a summary of the topics to be discussed.

PART I: EXISTENCE OF SELF AND PHILOSOPHICAL DEVELOPMENT OF THE IDEA

In the first chapter, I say what I mean by self, why we need to think in terms of self, and why there is such a thing. Our need is no proof of there being

2. Charles Taylor, *The Sources of the Self: The Making of the Modern Identity*, Cambridge 1989.

3. Marya Schechtman, *The Constitution of Selves*, Ithaca N.Y. 1996.

4. Derek Parfit, *Reasons and Persons*, Oxford 1984, corrected edition 1987.

5. Ibid. (1987 ed.), 327–29.

such a thing, but it creates an onus of disproof. Meanwhile, what I am postulating is not an undetectable soul or immaterial ego, but an embodied individual whose existence is plain to see. This individual is something that *has* or *owns* psychological states as well as *having* or *owning* a body and bodily states. It is not to be thought of either as an *essence*. The idea of self applies to individual humans and higher animals. Each of them needs to relate itself to the world in terms of *me* and *me again*. We could not survive without seeing ourselves in these terms. But the individual can also be referred to in other persons as 'you', 'him', or 'her'. To study the self in this sense is not to study what it is to be a human in general, although if there were not humans and higher animals, there would be no selves. It is to look at the *individual* and the perspective that each individual must take on itself.

There has been much opposition to the idea of self, but often the opposition turns out to be to a particular philosophical idea of self as something disembodied and undetectable, like a soul or Cartesian ego. But this is only one conception of the self. Many have denied that there is such a thing as the self, partly because of their dislike of one particular conception. But I concentrate not on the denials, but on giving a positive account. I consider only one denial in detail, the idea that there is only an embodied stream of consciousness and that there is nothing that *has* the consciousness, no *owner* of it, except as a mere way of talking. I describe in chapter one why I could not even survive infancy, or develop in the direction of being able to learn language, if I did not already see the world in terms of its relationship to me as the owner of properties, including eventually psychological properties. But I postpone to chapters fifteen and sixteen consideration of the rival view that all that is needed is the idea of an embodied stream of consciousness, with ownership a mere mode of speech. And I discuss in chapters seven, fifteen, and sixteen attempts to substitute the idea of *location* for that of ownership.

Given what I mean by 'self', is there an ancient philosophy of self? I argue in chapter two that there is because, contrary to what is sometimes implied, there was an intense preoccupation among ancient philosophers with the idea of *me* and *me again*. This is not to say that ancient philosophers all came up with the same answer as myself, or as each other, about what this *me* consists in. Some of them did indeed think in terms of an embodied individual, but others privileged some *aspect* of the embodied individual, as particularly deserving to be called its self. The Platonists were furthest from the view I have recommended. They did tend to postulate reason or intellect as something that could exist disembodied, and that provided a person's essence, and some of them spoke as if, instead of there being one subject, namely the individual person with a number of aspects, there were instead distinct subjects within a person, different levels of soul, reason, and intellect, any of which might constitute that person's self. The Platonist tradition may in turn have encouraged some of the later conceptions of self as disembodied and undetectable that have made the idea suspect among many modern philosophers.

That the ancient thinkers' views were views about *self* is, I believe, clear both from their intense interest in the first-person 'me' and from their struggle to express the idea of self, as we do, through the use of pronouns and through the use of words like the Greek *autos*, which in some contexts makes sense only if translated as 'self'. I try to bring out the repeated interest in the first person, *me*, by giving over a dozen examples of ancient theories. I then use these examples to oppose the idea that interest in this first-person kind of selfhood is missing from early Greek philosophy.

All the same, different issues about the self had different starting dates in ancient thought, and I distinguish how some questions about the self were raised sooner and others later.

PART II: PERSONAL IDENTITY OVER TIME

In chapters three to five, I discuss ancient views about what makes a person the same person at different times, particularly in the context of death and physical destruction, if it is believed that the original person could come back. In chapter three, I consider three views: the Stoic view that the same people will return when the universe repeats its history exactly in the next cycle, the Christian view that after death people will eventually be restored by God in the resurrection and given their bodies back, and the modern idea of teletransportation, that is, of beaming someone electronically to a distant planet and reconstituting them with a new body after the destruction of their old one. It will emerge that all three discussions have turned on the Aristotelian question of whether same matter or same form is required for having the same person.

The survival of one and the same individual, it has been thought, cannot depend exclusively on the survival of another individual. For survival is not a relative notion like my being taller than someone else, which can depend on his not growing taller than me. This principle has been put to the test by modern discussions of what would happen if a person split into two and whether their survival would depend on one half of the split not surviving. It will turn out in chapter four that the same question was discussed by the ancient Stoics in connection not with the fission of persons, but with their fusion.

Finally, John Locke has been considered with justice the father of modern views of personal identity, which he made to depend on memory. This had the advantage of avoiding dependence on something as undetectable as sameness of soul. For most of the ancients, memory was not the central issue. But there were exceptions. One, Plutarch, is considered in a later chapter, but another was the Epicurean Lucretius, who has been recognized as a probable influence on Locke. I add that Locke's refusal to treat sameness of soul as the central issue, startling as it may have been in the context of the Christianity of the time, looks like a reversion to what Stoics and Epicureans would have taken for granted. And I suggest some possible traces of Stoic as well as Epicurean influence.

PART III: PLATONISM: IMPERSONAL SELVES, BUNDLES, AND DIFFERENTIATION

I believe Plato sowed the seeds of a problem when he made reason the true self. In chapter six, I discuss whether this did not make the true self rather impersonal and whether, consequently, it leaves sufficient room for individuality. This is where I suggest Aristotle diverged from Plato by stressing the role of practical reason. Plotinus, the founder of Neoplatonism, was the one who above all wrestled with the problem. Might not our individuality ideally be merged in the divine Intellect, from which indeed our souls ultimately derived, and did we not lose our true identity by separating out from it? On the other hand, do we not long for some kind of individual identity anyhow? I discuss the ingenious analogy by which he seeks a resolution. His reader, Augustine, felt torn in the same way between an intense sense of individuality and an aspiration for a less individual life after death.

The subject of individuality was continued by other Platonists who saw Aristotle as largely in agreement with Plato, and sought to interpret his short account of different kinds of human intellect in *On the Soul* 3.5. They rejected the view of Alexander, Aristotle's great defender in the Aristotelian school, and took Aristotle's immortal productive intellect to be a human intellect, not, as Alexander said, God resident in us. But this did not automatically give individual immortality to the human intellect. For Themistius regarded the productive intellect, though human and immortal, as shared and not individual. Philoponus and pseudo-Philoponus were to call it immortal only by succession, that is by the unending succession of mortal individuals in the human race. And this was the view of all human intellect that the Islamic philosopher Averroës was to ascribe to Aristotle in the twelfth century, in his *Long Commentary on Aristotle On the Soul*. Hence Thomas Aquinas' need in the thirteenth century to engage in the so-called Averroist controversy and take Aristotle as defending individual immortality for the human intellect. In this he was assisted by the fact that Themistius had allowed individuality to human intellects lower than the productive intellect. But for this, Thomas might not have been able to present Aristotle as a philosophical guide safe for Christians.

The differentiation of individuals was also a problem at the mundane level of embodied individuals in ordinary life, and I discuss in chapter seven the different criteria suggested by ancient philosophers for differentiation. One picture of the individual was that he or she just consisted of properties, being a *bundle* of properties in the same *location* rather than, as I have argued, being an *owner* of properties. I argue that Porphyry took this idea of the individual as a bundle of properties again from Plato, from his *Theaetetus*.

PART IV: IDENTITY AND PERSONA IN ETHICS

In the next three chapters, I discuss not identity, but identities. That is, assuming we have one and the same person living a life, that person may have one identity or persona rather than another. In chapter eight, I discuss the Stoic idea that the decision on how it is right to act depends only partly on how a rational being would act, the criterion that Kant has made prominent in modern times. That may rule out unacceptable conduct, but it leaves too much latitude, and one must also consider, within the constraints imposed by rationality, how to be true to oneself as an individual, to one's own persona. A person may be unique, like Cato, so that when he was on the losing side in the civil war and Julius Caesar became dictator, it was right for him to commit suicide, but not right for any of the others who were in the same circumstances. This sounds opposite to the universalizability that Kant advocated, according to which the test of whether something is right is whether it would be right for everyone in the same circumstances. Kant's view can be made verbally consistent with the Stoic one, but I think the spirit is entirely different, and that this late development in Stoicism attaches a new importance to the individual.

In chapter nine, I consider Plutarch's view that, for the different purpose of achieving tranquility, one must use one's memory to tell a narrative of one's life, because without that one will not have an identity. This is a different kind of identity from the Stoic persona, which was based partly on nature and chance and partly on one's choices. But both views are talking about an identity that you help to create and that is not merely waiting for inspection in the way in which Hume supposed a self should be available for inspection, if it existed. Both views stress the importance of a whole life. Although a persona might be built up unconsciously, that is not what the Stoics are recommending. You will need to reflect even on such things as choosing a career, perhaps against your parents' wishes.

Would it really matter if we did not take Plutarch's advice and look at our lives as a whole? It might matter to something other than tranquility, namely to the subject discussed in connection with personae, the making of decisions. Virtually all the ancient Greek and Roman moral theories assume that for making decisions you will need to take into account your life as a whole, or a large part of it. The chief variation concerns whether they recommend you to consider your long-term future or past or both. I wonder, in fact, how many moral theories there have been that did not expect one or the other, or both. It seems to be sometimes omitted from modern moral discussions. But if so, is this not an oversight?

In chapter ten, I consider Epictetus' narrowing down of his conception of self, and hence in a way of his self, so as to exclude his body and anything a tyrant could control. This too involves *creating* a self. He aspires to be just his rightly directed will, which cannot be put in chains by the tyrant. The word I am paraphrasing very roughly as 'will' is *proairesis*, a term borrowed from Aristotle, whom I see as like Epictetus in identifying the self especially with *practical* reason, in contrast with Plato, who identified it with reason quite generally. For Aristotle the roles of practical as against theoretical reason in selfhood are a serious question, but I do not think it can be assumed he agrees in the end with Plato. Despite the similarities between Epictetus and Aristotle on *proairesis*, I think they come out very different from each other in the end. I also think that while Epictetus does not reject the views of his Stoic predecessors, he too comes out looking very different from them. Non-rejection does not stand in the way of huge novelty.

PART V: SELF-AWARENESS

The topic of self-awareness is not entirely distinct from the topic of self-hood, because the identity of a persona was seen in chapters eight to ten to depend partly on one's *conception* of one's self. But the topic has many other dimensions. Plato started a tradition of doubt about whether self-knowledge is even possible. Would it be contentless? Would it involve an infinite regress? In chapter eleven, I trace how the the doubts were further discussed by Aristotle, the sceptic Sextus, and Plotinus.

But, as I show in chapter twelve, Augustine, who knew of the controversy, stood the subject on its head by saying that the soul is present to itself so that it does not need to seek itself, and the problem is why the soul ever makes any mistake about itself. Augustine formulates in many of his works the Cogito argument that Descartes was to use more than a millennium later. This is designed to show that we cannot consistently doubt out own doubting, thinking, remembering, wanting, and so on. I support the suggestion, recently made, that Augustine could have been inspired to think of this by a discussion in Plotinus.

Augustine, again like Decartes later on, puts his Cogito argument in *On the Trinity* to a second use to show that the body cannot be part of the essence of self. This time there is a striking similarity with the Flying Man argument of the Islamic philosopher Avicenna in the tenth century. Avicenna would certainly not have known a Latin writer such as Augustine. So did these two great minds think alike independently of each other? I suggest that if there is any common source of stimulus, it is likely to be Porphyry.

Plato had started the opposite tradition of thinking that self-knowledge is difficult and one knows oneself best through seeing oneself reflected in another. This view, discussed in chapter thirteen, is used by Aristotle as part of his explanation of the value of friendship. The view that knowledge of self requires knowledge of others features in an entirely different way in Stoicism. I point out in chapter one that modern infant psychology also supports the view that the infant acquires consciousness of self only in conjunction with its consciousness of divergence from another. This is in total opposition to Descartes' view, in his discussion of the Cogito, that I know myself alright, but as regards others, I see only hats and coats and have to make an inference.

Augustine takes the huge step in the direction of Descartes. He denies Plato's view that one gets to know of one's self as mirrored in another. Mirroring would distort. Rather, the soul is directly present to itself. This raises the question that Descartes made so acute, how we are aware of others at all.

And for Augustine it is important to know how we are aware of God in particular. But he says in the *Confessions* that he had learned from the books of the Platonists to find God within himself. Thus the direct knowledge of self need be no barrier to the knowledge of God. This is not to exclude that Augustine may have believed in a two-way relationship, with our learning more about ourselves through our knowledge of God.

Plotinus brings into view a further idea, that other people may enter into one's conception of oneself and hence into one's identity. For people feel a loss of identity if they do not know who their father is. This comes closer to a modern German tradition that sees the self as a relationship with other people.

The idea that knowledge of self is through others contrasts not only with Augustine's idea that the soul knows itself directly, but also with his idea that even in infancy the soul knows itself all the time, at least with a certain sort of knowledge (*nosse*). It is unexpected to find Aristotle combining in one discussion the conflicting ideas that we invariably know our own activities with the idea that we see a friend's activities and see them as ours more easily than we see our own. I consider what made Aristotle think that we are invariably aware of our own activities, something that it is difficult to believe in the wake of Freud.

In chapter fourteen, I discuss the unity of self-awareness, on which Plato and, even more graphically, Aristotle insisted. Sweet and white cannot be compared, says Aristotle, using Plato's example, unless both are presented to something unitary. Otherwise it would be like a case of my perceiving white and your perceiving sweet. But what is this unitary thing? Aristotle is discussing a perceptual example and for that case he is happy to say that the general faculty of sense perception, the common sense, as opposed to the five special senses, is responsible. But Plato had postulated reason. This was to create a debate among the Neoplatonists. For a start, we need to consider that we have other forms of cognition besides sense perception, and not only of cognition, but also several different forms of desire. What unitary thing can give us awareness of this great variety? Some said the highest faculty, reason, would be needed. Others suggested Aristotle's common sense, and others defended this in a way Aristotle would have abominated by permeating the common sense with reason. Yet other suggestions were made, one being the screen of the imagination. The debate has been re-run in modern times. Is self-awareness due to higher-order perception (HOP) or to higher order thought (HOT)? But why should it be due to any one faculty? Are not different faculties at work in different cases? I argue that what needs to be unitary is the *owner* of the faculties.

The most useful of the ancient suggestions, I think, was that we need to postulate a faculty of attention. It is perfectly true, as 'Philoponus' argued, that attention to our perceptions and thoughts need not be an extra piece of perceiving or thinking. Attention does need to be studied as something distinct.

PART VI: OWNERLESS STREAMS OF CONSCIOUSNESS REJECTED

In chapters fifteen and sixteen, I return to discussion of personal identity and whether there is such a thing. I describe and oppose the view that there is just a stream of consciousness and that talk of an owner of consciousness is just a way of talking, but does not add anything, or, according to another version, does not add anything of importance. I propose a little test. If nothing is added, then let us omit talk of an owner and just talk of the embodied stream of consciousness itself. We should be able to say all we need to. But I object that there would in fact be little left of agency or ethics. There would be sufferings, but no sufferers, improvements, but no beneficiaries. Nor could there be any of the many 'I'-thoughts I described in chapter one as essential to us, except by way of an (ownerless) illusion. The best modern exponent of the idea that there are only embodied streams of consciousness, and that ownership is only a way of talking, is Derek Parfit in his challenging book, *Reasons and Persons*. But I believe he is able to go on to discuss agency and ethics only by treating ownership as if it did add something after all, as if there were sufferers and beneficiaries, as well as streams of consciousness.

If indeed there were only embodied streams of consciousness, it would become crucial that all the right activities should be linked into one single stream and that activities belonging to different streams should not be linked in the same way to each other. It is hard to specify the links that would secure the intended result, especially because there are so many linkages connecting the consciousness of different people. But we are not allowed to distinguish streams of consciousness by the people who own the consciousness, if ownership is only a way of talking. The problems of how to define ownerless streams overlap with the problems about how to define bundles which face those who say that individuals are merely bundles of properties. An obvious alternative that has been suggested is that we could define the streams by their location in the bodies on which they depend. But this alternative is not available to Parfit, because he holds that we can make sense of the idea of the very same stream of consciousness being teletransported into a totally different body. The Buddhists would make it even more impossible to appeal to the body as anchoring each stream, since for them, as we shall see in a moment, bodies are themselves merely streams of a different kind. And they may be right that it is hard to see why consciousness should be a stream and bodies not. Indeed, their Nyaya opponents, we shall see, argue that they must think this way.

Others have pointed out that it may be misleading to start with psychological activities as if they were isolated events and then to look for links to link them up with each other. For the majority of psychological activities come already interlinked. What I am adding is that the links may not be the right ones for the tidy identification and distinction of streams without reference to owners.

In chapter sixteen, I consider ancient Buddhist views according to which there are only streams of psychological and physical events. There is one type of view that, like Parfit's, seeks not to deny selves, but to reduce them to the basic simple events in the psychological streams. It compares a chariot, which, it claims, is nothing but the wheels, axles, and other parts. I am uncertain about how this reduction works, but, like Parfit's view, it claims that the person is only a name. It seems to me, therefore, to run into the same problem of eliminating all but the name of person. But this time I have additional difficulties in understanding the view. For example, why should it be thought that a chariot is *nothing but* its simple parts?

There is another Buddhist view that avoids these questions by denying that there are any simples to which selves or bodies could be reduced. But it avoids the questions at the cost of making no attempt to retain selves and declaring that selves and bodies are alike empty. But, as a further subtlety, emptiness is itself empty and is not to be taken as a doctrine, but as a medical purgative, to be purged away with the doctrines of self and body that it was designed to cure. In that case, both the supposed emptiness of self and the supposed emptiness of emptiness will be designed to encourage attitudes rather than to state facts, and this might explain the recommended changes of attitude in another Buddhist thinker. For purposes of compassion it is best to think of there being selves that suffer. For purposes of avoiding selfishness, such thoughts are best avoided. But there remains a difficulty. There must be *some* facts to be expressed, or it will not be a fact that there has been a change of attitude, or that it has promoted compassion or selflessness.

The Hindu philosophers of the Nyaya school made very able replies to the Buddhists. They drew attention to the many activities that require the same person to exist. Even understanding a single sentence requires the same person to engage in many distinct acts. But perhaps the most impressive argument that modern scholars have brought to light is 'I touch what I see'. One reconstruction makes it rather like Kant's argument in *The Critique of Pure Reason* (A 99–110). If one does not think of oneself as a unitary perceiver, one cannot think of the sweet and white qualities that one perceives as belonging to one and the same external object or even, we might add, as residing in the same location. Thus the idea of bodies as unitary owners of multiple qualities depends upon the idea of perceivers as unitary owners of multiple perceptions.

PART VII: MORTALITY AND LOSS OF SELF

In chapter seventeen, I discuss some of the ways in which it has been thought that people might survive death after the destruction of the body. The ways discussed in this chapter go beyond anything known to science. The Christian belief in resurrection was already discussed in chapter three, and it was seen that if a substantial part of our bodies was not preserved intact, we might be faced with a choice between having our scattered particles reassembled from all over the universe or receiving entirely new matter shaped in a photographic likeness of the original body. Either alternative would raise the question of whether there would be enough bodily continuity for the new person to be the selfsame person as the original one.

Reincarnation seems to be treated by Plotinus sometimes as a matter of one person, Pythagoras, being reincarnated as *another*, Socrates. On that view, the soul of Pythagoras would survive, but not Pythagoras himself. On the other hand, Plotinus sometimes speaks as if each of us *is* his or her soul. In that case, Socrates would need after all to be the same person as Pythagoras. It is only on the latter sort of view that reincarnation offers any prospect of survival to Pythagoras. But more needs to be done to show what it would mean for Socrates to be the same person as Pythagoras. I believe that Indian thought does far more to make sense of this sort of idea, and I discuss some of what would need to be done.

A third mode of survival would be disembodied survival. But the range of experiences that could be conceived as occurring without a body is restricted. Some activities, like taking a hot bath, are so bound up with the body that we cannot even make sense of them occurring in its absence. A further question is whether bodiless experiences could be linked up into a stream, but it was found in chapter fifteen that even embodied experiences could not easily be linked into streams, if appeal was not allowed to an *owner* of the experiences. In the present case, it would have to be the same reasons that enabled us to make sense of the idea of there being a stream and of there being an owner of the stream. In thinking about this, I have, like Locke, avoided appealing to the idea of a soul as owner, because making sense of the idea of there being the same soul would be no easier than making sense of the idea of there being the same owner.

There has been a search for activities that we might be able to conceive of as happening without a body, and might be able to ascribe to an owner in the absence of body. Philosophers and theologians have often settled on thinking or contemplation as the activity most easy to conceive as happening, and to ascribe to an owner, when no body is available. But they have therefore thought that we would have to prepare ourselves to enjoy an eternity of this very different diet of activity. That is why Plato called philosophy a preparation for death. It is not an easy prospect to think of abandoning most of our earthly pleasures even in exchange for other pleasures. But if we do not prepare ourselves for the very different kind of life that might be available, that life, if it were to happen, might be a kind of hell.

In chapter eighteen, I consider a way in which people might survive after death naturally. If time were to go round in a circle, then someone on his or her deathbed could reflect that his or her birth lay not only in the past, but also in the future. For everything, as you move round a circle, is both in front of you and behind you. I first discussed this idea in my book *Matter, Space, and Motion* in 1988, but I try here to offer an improved and more streamlined version.

In chapter nineteen, I ask what if we do not survive death? Are those people irrational who, like Plutarch, feel horror at the prospect of annihilation? This too I discussed in an earlier book, *Time, Creation, and the Continuum* in 1983. Here I consider a wider range of ancient passages, but I take the same view as before, that the horror can be shown to be irrational, because we do not feel corresponding horror at the thought of our past non-existence before birth. Nonetheless, although irrational, the horror may be inevitable for those who feel it because natural selection has adapted us to feel anxiety about the future that we do not feel about the past. This raises a question about the limits of philosophy. Can it not calm an emotion by showing it to be irrational? I think that philosophy can achieve different things in different cases. In the present case, it does not get rid of the horror for those who feel it. But it should prevent the horror from growing, as emotion often can, through the belief that it is justified.

PART I

Existence of Self and philosophical development of the idea

CHAPTER I

The Self: is there such a thing?

OPPONENTS OF THE SELF

Is there such a thing as the Self? In analytic philosophy, this has often been denied. In Germany, Nietzsche denied it and gave rise to another tradition of denial. Both traditions have been influenced directly or indirectly by the earlier denial of David Hume. The Buddhists have been in conflict for over two millennia with other Indian schools concerning their view that there is no continuous self. Thus there is skepticism in all these traditions. In psychology and psychiatry too, various schools have fragmented the selves of their patients or of everyone.[1]

Even before Hume, some conceptions of the self available in 17th- and 18th-century philosophy were so thin that one might well wonder what useful work they did. Descartes needed a very thin concept in his *Meditations* of 1641, because he was looking for something about which he could be certain. He could be certain of 'I think', 'I exist', provided that the word 'I' meant very little. For he could be mistaken, if he supposed that a Frenchman existed, whose name was Descartes, and who studied at La Flèche. The word 'I' must not even imply a past history at all, although he may not recognize this. If he was to avoid the possibility of error, it must imply only the existence at that moment, but not necessarily previously, of the thinker of the thought.

In 1694, John Locke, to whom I shall return in chapter five, also en-

---

1. For some 19th-century controversy based on brain studies, see Dan Robinson, 'Cerebral plurality and the unity of self', in his, ed., *The Mind*, Oxford 1998. In psychoanalysis, Melanie Klein sees the self as fragmented. The psychologist Kenneth J. Gergen gives an account of the fragmented postmodernist self in *The Saturated Self*, New York 1991, ch. 6. For the deliberate production by psychotherapists of multiple personalities, see Ian Hacking, *Rewriting the Soul*, Princeton 1995.

couraged a thin conception of the self. In giving an account of what constitutes the same self at different times, he wanted to avoid relying on the soul,
which cannot be inspected. He appealed, therefore, instead to what he called
'consciousness', which can be extended backward to past mental or physical
activities and also, although this is less emphasized, forward to future ones.
Consequently, those in Locke's tradition who expected consciousness and
other such relationships to do all the work were left with a thin conception
of the self. I shall argue that Antiquity provides some corrective to these
thin conceptions.

David Hume notoriously said, in his *Treatise of Human Nature* in 1739,
that when he looked inside himself, he could find many perceptions, but no
self linking them together.[2] Hume granted reality only to what could be inspected. It may be asked why Hume supposed that the Self is something internal and introspectible. And why did he assume that it is something already created, rather than something to whose creation, as Locke allowed,
you might yourself contribute?

Hume's denial of self influenced Kant, who conceded in 1781 in his *Critique of Pure Reason*, as we shall see in chapter five, that we could not tell
whether there was a whole series of subjects of consciousness, rather than a
single self. His strategy was to describe how we have to think, rather than
how things are, and to urge that we have at least to think in terms of a unified
self. Kant's response, and Schopenhauer's response to that,[3] was part of the
background against which Nietzsche denied a self in 1887 in the following
representative statement from *On the Genealogy of Morals* I.13:[4]

> There is no 'being' behind doing, effecting, becoming. 'The doer' is merely a
> fiction added to the deed—the deed is everything. . . . our entire science still
> lies under the misleading influence of language and has not disposed of that
> little changeling, the 'subject'.

Analytic philosophy has often followed Hume. A self has been denied
in the analytic tradition by Wittgenstein,[5] Elizabeth Anscombe,[6] Norman

2. David Hume, *A Treatise of Human Nature*, book 1, part 4, section 6, p. 252, in L. A.
Selby-Bigge, Oxford 1888, repr. 1988.

3. Schopenhauer, *The World as Will and Representation*, trans. R. B. Haldane and
J. Kemp, London 1896, 2, 139–40.

4. Translated by W. Kaufman and R. J. Hollingdale, New York 1967.

5. Ludwig Wittgenstein, *Philosophical Investigations*, Oxford 1953, para. 413, criticizing William James.

6. Elizabeth Anscombe, 'The first person', in S. Guttenplan, ed., *Mind and Language*,
Wolfson College lectures, repr. in her *Collected Philosophical Papers*, vol. 2, Cambridge 1991.

Malcolm,[7] Tony Kenny,[8] and Daniel Dennett,[9] to name a few, while Galen Strawson[10] has allowed only short-term selves. I shall treat Derek Parfit separately in chapters fifteen and sixteen, because it is a more complex question in what sense he denies a self.[11]

Daniel Dennett has argued that the number of different life stories that can be told about someone shows that the idea of a Self is a fiction, albeit a convenient one. But the many life stories might all be true as readily as they might all be false. Their number does not tell us either way.

Elizabeth Anscombe offers perhaps the most formidable attack. She argues that the word 'I' does not even attempt to refer to something. According to Anscombe, 'I' is unlike other referring expressions, and even unlike the demonstrative 'this'. Thus when we say 'Heraclitus', or 'These ashes', we sometimes fail to refer, because no relevant person or ashes are available. With 'I', however, no such possibility of failure exists. However, I think the same is true of 'this time', 'this conscious thought', 'the thinker of this conscious thought'. Reference is guaranteed here, but not by the word 'this' alone. The existence of a time, a thought, and a thinker to refer to are guaranteed by the occurrence of any thought at all. Consequently, so long as no extra information is implied by the use of these expressions, they must succeed in referring.

Tony Kenny has claimed that the notion of Self is a grammatical mistake. We speak of my house, my car, and my self, so we assume it is a thing like a car or a house. But I think we shall see that the ancients had very different reasons for talking about a Self. And I think this cannot in any case be the explanation, since philosophy has been done in English for only 400 years, and the grammatical point would not work in the other European languages used for philosophizing over the last 2500 years. Even in English, Sarah Broadie has suggested to me, the word might origi-

7. Norman Malcolm, 'Whether "I" is a referring expression', in Cora Diamond and Jenny Teichman, eds., *Intention and Intentionality*, Ithaca N.Y. 1979, 15–24.

8. A. J. P. Kenny, 'The Self', the Aquinas Lecture, Marquette University, Milwaukee, Wisconsin, 1988–89, and 'Body, soul, and intellect in Aquinas', in James Crabbe, ed., *From Soul to Self*, London and New York 1999.

9. Daniel Dennett, 'Why everyone is a novelist', *Times Literary Supplement,* 16–22 September 1988, p. 1016, and *Consciousness Explained*, Boston 1991.

10. Galen Strawson, 'The Self', reprinted from *Journal of Consciousness Studies* 4, 1997, 405–28, in Shaun Gallagher and Jonathan Shear, eds., *Models of the Self*, Thorverton, UK, 1999, 1–24.

11. Derek Parfit, *Reasons and Persons*, Oxford 1984, revised 1987.

nally have been 'meself', not 'myself', since after all we say 'himself', not 'hisself'.[12]

WHAT IS THE SELF?

I shall not try to answer the objections to selfhood in detail, except those of Parfit in chapters four and fifteen, and I could hardly do them justice in a short space. Rather, I want to give a positive account. First, what is the Self?

In asking about the self, I am not asking what it is to be a human being or a higher animal in general, but about what it is to be an individual one. Of course, there would be no selves, if the type, the human being or higher animal, did not exist, and so what it is for the type to exist is a prior question. The discussion cannot avoid sometimes talking about that, but it has to assume that the type exists and go on to ask about the individual.

One reason why the notion of self comes in is that humans and animals could not cope with the world at all unless they saw things in terms of *I*. The notion 'I' belongs to the same group of notions as 'now', 'here', 'yonder', 'this', 'that', 'today', 'past', 'present', 'future', 'ago', 'hence'. I have discussed the temporal ones elsewhere.[13] What I would emphasize is that these words and the corresponding ideas have an irreplaceable importance, because they have a unique ability to guide action and emotion. If Adam Smith knows, 'An arrow gets to be fired through the window of Adam Smith's study on May 1 2004', he will have no idea whether precautions are called for, except insofar as he can also judge, '*I* am Adam Smith', and '*Today* is May 1 2004'. Otherwise Adam Smith might be anybody, and 2004 thousands of years into the past or future. These words therefore have a special action- and emotion-guiding force, which can be retained by paraphrasing them in terms of each other, but not by replacing them with terms from outside the group. 'I', for example, has been paraphrased roughly—though not exactly, for there are a number of difficulties[14]—by 'the thinker of this thought', or 'this person'. The terms have been variously called egocentric, or token-reflexives, according to the different analyses that have been given of them.

---

12. My manuscript editor Michael Koplow points out that the *Oxford English Dictionary* (s.v. 'myself') says of the emphatic 'I myself', 'In Old English *ic mē self . . . mē* is perhaps a kind of ethical dative and the uninflected *self* is in apposition to *ic*'.

13. Richard Sorabji, *Time, Creation, and the Continuum*, London and Ithaca N.Y. 1983, chap. 3.

14. See, e.g., Robert Nozick, *Philosophical Explanations*, Oxford 1981.

'I'-thoughts do not postulate an extra entity besides the embodied human with its various aspects. But they do have a meaning additional to that of 'Adam Smith'–thoughts, and a meaning that is essential for Adam Smith if he is to cope with the world. Admittedly, the conditions under which 'I'-thoughts will be *true* can be stated, without using any token-reflexive expressions, just as others have shown to be the case for 'now'-thoughts.[15] For example, an 'I'-thought is *true* if and only if it is true of the thinker of the thought. But nonetheless when all the non-token-reflexive facts about Adam Smith have been stated, there are still some further facts that he urgently needs to know, including, 'I am Adam Smith'. I am speaking of further meaning and further facts, but not of further entities or further truth conditions.

We need to notice the third-person perspective on the individual, as well as the first-person perspective. We talk of *him* or *her,* as well as of *me.* I shall be pointing out shortly that in the order of child development, awareness of *me* as distinct from *her* is all acquired simultaneously as a single awareness. Recognition of a particularly close him or her is also partly based on emotion, it seems. For there is an emotional thump whose absence in adults, it has been suggested,[16] can prevent recognition of one's nearest and dearest in the disease known as Capgras syndrome.

By a 'person' I mean someone who *has* psychological states and *does* things, by a 'thinker' someone who *has* thoughts. This having and doing can be summed up by saying that a person *owns* psychological states and actions. He or she also owns a body and bodily characteristics. A person is not just a stream of experiences and actions, but the owner of experiences and actions, as I shall argue in chapters four, fifteen, and sixteen.

The *meaning* that I have ascribed to the word 'I', though vital, is a thin meaning, paraphrasable, for example, as 'the subject of this awareness', or 'this person'. But since 'I' does not refer to an entity separate from the embodied being that is rapidly acquiring a unique history, the *reference* of 'I' is a thick one. Moreover, the *speaker's* meaning on any given occasion may be much thicker than the strict meaning of the word itself. He or she may in-

15. Hugh Mellor, *Real Time,* vol. 1, Cambridge 1981. The point about Now and I, that 'same truth conditions' does not imply 'same fact', has been made by Thomas Nagel, *The View from Nowhere,* Oxford 1986, ch. 4; and 'The objective self', in Carl Ginet and Sydney Shoemaker, eds, *Knowledge and Mind,* Oxford 1983.

16. William Herstein and V. S. Ramachandran, 'Capgrass syndrome: a neural probe for understanding the neural representation of the identity and familiarity of persons', *Proceedings of the Royal Society of London, Biological Sciences* 264, 1997, 437–44.

tend to draw attention to more or less of his or her personal history and circumstances and of his or her character as an embodied human being. As we
pass beyond infancy, we tend to develop an autobiographical picture or pic-
tures of ourselves. A thicker picture is employed in making decisions and in
reacting emotionally. For decisions and emotional reactions may depend on
one's being aware of oneself as a person with a certain standing, past history,
culture, and aspirations. We thus build up a particular persona or identity,
and this identity is often considered part of the self.

None of this implies that a self is an *essence*. That is not the conception
of self that I am propounding. The thicker descriptions we give of ourselves
may be extremely important to us. We may come to feel that, in an everyday sense of identity,[17] we would lose our very identity if the descriptions
ceased to hold; if, for example, we changed our gender, profession, na-
tionality, or culture. But there is no suggestion that we would cease to exist
without them. And indeed we could come to see a new overarching identity
and unity that embraced the new characteristics along with the old.

Sometimes it is thought that there is no need to mention selves and that
the only question is what it is to be a human or a person. We can now see
why this is wrong. Some modern books about the self are really discussing
the prior question of types, what it is to be a human, or what it is to be a person. But I want to discuss the further question of individual selfhood, even
though it constantly involves the other questions as well.

IMPORTANCE OF THE 'I'-PERSPECTIVE

So much for what I mean by 'self'. But is there such a thing? I shall approach
this question indirectly by arguing that there is a *need* to see the world in
terms of me and me again. This need is no proof of existence, but it does create an onus of disproof on the person who wants to show that something on
which so much of life utterly depends is after all illusory. It is with this onus
of disproof in mind that I shall now focus on the 'I'-perspective and try to
show how essential it is for our very survival from infancy.

I have said that 'I'-thoughts have a unique action- and emotion-
guiding force. But I want to say more. They must enter also into our perceptions. They not only guide, but also help to constitute, many of our emotions, the fear of death being only one. I shall say more in chapters fifteen
and sixteen about how they enter into our intentions and actions. They

---

17. On this, see Marya Schechtman, *The Constitution of Selves*, Ithaca N.Y. 1996, pt. 2.

consequently enter into linguistic communication. This helps to make the many questions that arise in connection with selfhood emotionally urgent for people's lives, rather than being matters of mild curiosity.

The point about perception was made by the psychologist J. J. Gibson and developed by Ulrich Neisser, Colwyn Trevarthen, and a good number of others.[18] Infants do not, and cannot afford to, see the world as mere spectators perceiving patches of color. They need to see the world, if they are to cope with it, in relation to themselves. They have to see things as *within reach* or *out of reach* of themselves, as likely to *support* them or not, as in danger of *colliding* with them or not. And the same applies to higher animals, even if lizards or flies react to perception too automatically to be described that way.

In discussing animal perception in an earlier book,[19] I made use of the seminal idea of Gareth Evans and Christopher Peacocke that the content of perception does not have to require the possession of corresponding concepts. To take an example of Peacocke's, one can see a mountainside as having a distinctive but complicated crinkly shape, without having the concept of that shape. Of course, whether one should be said to have a concept depends on how concept-possession is analyzed. Peacocke has his own analysis,[20] and Aristotle, as I have explained in my book,[21] gives an account of rudimentary concepts in *Posterior Analytics* 2.19 that may extend them to animals. But it is not very plausible intuitively to ascribe concepts to very young infants or animals. So it may be much better to say that they see things as within reach of themselves, without yet necessarily having a *concept* of themselves. I am very glad to find José Luis Bermúdez has defended this non-conceptual view of the infant's awareness of itself.[22] Part of my sug-

---

18. See for example the contributions to Ulrich Neisser, ed., *The Perceived Self*, Cambridge 1993, and Ulrich Neisser's paper, 'Five kinds of self-knowledge', *Philosophical Psychology* 1, 1988, 35–59.

19. Richard Sorabji, *Animal Minds and Human Morals*, London and Ithaca N.Y. 1993, 30, referring to: Gareth Evans, *Varieties of Reference*, Oxford 1982, and to Christopher Peacocke, 'Analogue content', *Proceedings of the Aristotelian Society*, supp. vol. 60, 1986, 1–17; and id., 'Perceptual content', in J. Almog, J. Perry, and H. Wettstein, eds., *Themes from Kaplan* Oxford 1989.

20. Christopher Peacocke, 'What are concepts?' *Midwest Studies in Philosophy* 14, 1989, 1–28.

21. Sorabji, *Animal Minds and Human Morals*, 30–35.

22. See José Luis Bermúdez, *The Paradox of Self-Consciousness*, Cambridge Mass. 1998, which also makes good philosophical use of some of the same psychological literature that I have cited. Pages 54–58 reply to the objection that the perception of the mountain's shape does after all include a concept, namely, the concept *that shape*. So John McDowell, *Mind and*

gestion was that, even though the infants themselves do not have words or concepts, adults may need as third parties to use words and concepts, in order to do justice to the way the infants are seeing things.[23]

A little later the infant can navigate its way back to a recognized place. It then sees the place as one where it has been before, and so is aware of itself as something with a history enduring through time.

At this stage, it is its bodily self of which the infant is aware, and in general the body is very central to how we see ourselves even as adults. Another part of J. J. Gibson's view about perception was that our face, eyebrows, and nose supply a frame by reference to which we perceive how the world is relating spatially to our bodies. As part of the scene before us streams towards the edge of the frame, we see ourselves as about to move past that part, and this keeps us safe by telling us how our bodies are currently related to the world. The Stoics, as I have explained elsewhere,[24] followed by Galen, were very interested in the knowledge that newborn animals have of their bodily parts and of the use to be made of them, whether for attack or defense. A modern version of this interest is supplied by Brian O'Shaughnessy, who describes in his book on the will[25] how, in order to scratch an itch, one must be aware of where the itch is, of where one's scratching hand is in relation to that, and that one has such bodily parts. In his view, one starts with awareness of one's mouth in relation to the breast and expands one's awareness from there.

Not only do we need to see things in the world in relation to our bodily selves, but we also need to know which of the two is doing the moving, or whether both are. Otherwise we shall not be able to make interceptions or avoid collisions. O.-J. Grusser has traced the history of the idea, which, unexpectedly, was stimulated in the 19th century by Aristotle's remarks on after-images that appear to move as the eye moves, producing a false appearance of light or motion derived from what was being looked at before.[26]

World, lecture 3, Cambridge Mass. 1994. Bermúdez replies inter alia that *that shape* is too uninformative to determine how the supposed concept should be applied to subsequently encountered shapes.

23. Sorabji, *Animal Minds and Human Morals*, 22–23.

24. Hierocles *Elements of Ethics*, ed. A. A. Long, *Corpus dei papiri filosofici greci e latini*, vol. 1, Florence 1992, esp. pp. 300–326, discussed in Sorabji, *Animal Minds and Human Morals*, 26, 86–87; Galen *On the Use of Parts*.

25. Brian O'Shaughnessy, *The Will*, Cambridge 1980, vol. 1, ch. 7.

26. O.-J. Grusser, 'Interaction of efferent and afferent signals in visual perception: a history of ideas and experimental paradigms', *Acta Psychologica* 63, 1986, 3–21, refers to Ar-

A common view is that self-generated motion is detected by the feeding in of information about one's intentions to move and kinaesthetic sensations of moving.

But what about awareness of one's *psychological* attributes? A dramatic change, many psychologists say, comes after 9 months. Up to then, the infant has been aware of itself as a material object in relation to which other material objects are seen or felt. But now it begins to be aware of itself as a being with mental activities. And this happens in a way opposite to that which Descartes would lead us to expect. On Descartes' view, we can be certain of our own minds, but as regards other people, he says in the *Second Meditation*, he sees only hats and coats and has to make inferences. What these psychologists find, on the contrary, is that infants become aware of themselves as conscious beings only as they become aware of their carers as conscious beings. What happens is that they notice the divergence between their own attention and their carer's attention. This can happen after 9 months in games of 'look with mother'. The infant wants to align its gaze with its mother's or carer's, so as to be looking at the same thing. The phenomenon is beautifully illustrated in Mary Cassatt's *The First Mirror*, which adds further self-reference through the shared gaze being directed to a mirror. It has been called 'shared attention' or 'joint attention',[27] and it may be unique to humans. For although young chimpanzees have been found to follow a gaze, even into the space behind them, and without any warning shift of gaze, there is said to be evidence that they do not recognize gaze as a sign of attention.[28] On the other hand, observations in the wild may be different. For in the story I shall mention below about a chimpanzee looking away, to conceal its interest in the contents of a banana box, it expected its orientation to be taken by another chimpanzee as a sign of its own attention. For the infant, at a further stage, not only attention to gaze, but also intention and action are involved, as the infant tries to *make* the carer align his or her gaze with its own, and thus experiences the pleasures of successful agency. The pleasures of agency are further developed in other games, and they involve

---

istotle *On Dreams* 459b7–20, and its influence on Jan Evangelista Pukyne. I am grateful to Thomas Campbell for the reference; Campbell tells me that theories on the subject go back at least as far as Franciscus Aguilonius in 1613.

27. Michael Tomasello, 'On the interpersonal origins of self-concept', in Ulrich Neisser, ed., *The Perceived Self*, Cambridge 1993; id., *The Cultural Origins of Human Cognition*, Cambridge Mass. 1999.

28. Daniel J. Povinelli and Timothy J. Eddy, 'Specificity of gaze-following in young chimpanzees', *British Journal of Developmental Psychology* 15, 1997, 213–22.

the idea of one party's action getting aligned with the other party's intention. The alignment and non-alignment of gaze, or intention and action, involves for the infant awareness of its own mental states, but only insofar as they need to be aligned with those of others.

I have seen in a grandchild the following phenomenon. My wife blew a pipe that made an unusual sound that he found very striking. But he looked first to me to see my reaction before feeling able to indulge in pleasure at it. In this much observed sort of case, another alignment is sought, the alignment by the infant of its action or emotion with the *approval* of a carer: 'would this be the right thing to do?'. This too involves the infant in awareness of possible divergence between its reaction and another's. This phenomenon in children has been called 'social referencing'.[29] I suppose that another case of seeking alignment would be crying in order to get attention. Here too, presumably, there is an awareness of the need to align directions of attention. In fact I have seen some of these attitudes in a granddaughter of 8 months, and I suspect that quantitative studies will eventually confirm earlier and more widespread examples. At 8 months, I have seen apparent attitudes not only of 'is this the right thing to do?', but also of 'look at me' and of 'no, I am not going to perform for you'. I am not aware of these latter attitudes having been studied.

In my earlier book on animals,[30] I reported a case in which a chimpanzee in a compound lifted the lid of a box to help itself to a banana. But then it saw another chimpanzee in the compound and hurriedly shut the lid, pretending that there was nothing of interest there. The deceiving chimpanzee then left the compound, but looked back through a crack in the fence to see if the other chimpanzee had discovered the secret. Here was an intense awareness of the need to keep knowledge un-aligned, and a monitoring for possible alignment.

A more austere view might be taken about how we should describe the infant's mental content in some of the first examples I gave. Perhaps the infant should be described as seeing things simply in terms such as 'within reach', 'likely to support', 'likely to collide', without any specification of 'me', since there is no contrast in the infant's mind with somebody *else* who

29. S. Feinman, 'Social referencing in infancy', *Merrill-Palmer Quarterly* 28, 1982, 445–70.

30. Sorabji, *Animal Minds and Human Morals*, 43, reporting Andrew Whiten and Richard W. Byrne, 'The manipulation of attention in primate tactical deception', in their, ed., *Machiavellian Intelligence: Social Expertise and the Evolution of Intellect in Monkeys, Apes, and Humans*, Oxford 1988.

might suffer the collision instead. Similarly, the infant might be more eco-nomically described as seeing a place in terms of 'safe', 'familiar', or 'dan-gerous', rather than in terms of 'where *I* was before'.[31] If so, the need for the infant to see the world in terms of 'I' would first come in with the interaction with other human beings, e.g., in the games of look with mother or carer. But this would not radically affect what I have been saying, especially as the banana-loving chimpanzees would still need to see the situation in terms of 'I'. The shared attention phenomenon has been re-described by John Bar-resi and Chris Moore in terms of 'we', rather than 'I'.[32] The child is thinking in terms of 'have we got we-ness?'. But this too would not affect the spirit of what I am saying. 'We' still belongs in the group of token-reflexive words along with 'I', and my idea is that infants need to see the world in terms of 'we' or 'I'.

At as little as 42 minutes old, babies can perform a nonreflex imitation of seen tongue protrusion, even though they can only feel their own imita-tion. It has been suggested that they sense the likeness of the original ges-ture and their own imitation, and that this is a primitive exercise in see-ing other humans as like themselves.[33] I do not want, however to rely on this interpretation, as the reaction may be too automatic to call for such an explanation.

'I'-thoughts enter not only into perceptions but also into intentions and emotions. Emotions are not only *guided* by 'I'-thoughts; they very often *in-clude* them and involve the idea that 'Harm / benefit is at hand for me / mine; I should react accordingly'. Admittedly, there are helpless spectator emo-tions, in which one thinks, 'Harm is coming to Adam Smith; somebody should help *him*'. These do not so obviously involve 'I'-thoughts as do emo-tions about what is happening to oneself or one's dearest. But even here the thought is likely to involve 'the Adam Smith I know' and 'somebody other than me should help him'.

An intention also involves many 'I'-thoughts. Suppose I intend to shout at someone, in order to draw their attention. Then, to follow an account

31. I am grateful to Mark Sainsbury for the point, who referred me to the plea for aus-terity in a different range of examples made by Crawford L. Elder, 'What versus how in nat-urally selected representations', *Mind* 107, 1998, 349–61.

32. John Barresi and Chris Moore, 'Intentional relations and social understanding', *Behavioral and Brain Sciences* 19, 1996, 107–54.

33. Andrew Meltzoff and M. Keith Moore, 'Infants' understanding of people and things: from body imitation to folk psychology', in José Luis Bermúdez, Anthony Marcel, and Naomi Eilan, eds., *The Body and the Self*, Cambridge Mass. 1998.

once given orally by Paul Grice, I want to shout, because I want to draw their attention. I believe I will shout, and I believe that the shouting will be because of my want. If I carry out the intention, I do so because of these wants and beliefs.

If I am right that 'I'-thoughts enter into intentions, they will enter also into much else that is essential to human life. Much of our agency involves intention. So too, I believe, does our linguistic communication. For I accept Paul Grice's further view[34] that for a speaker to mean something, except in the special case of soliloquy, is to *intend* to produce an effect in the hearer. One intends to produce the effect not by automatic means, as one might intend to make someone jump by shouting 'boo!' in a startling way, but by getting them to recognize one's intention. In Grice's view, the effect intended is always psychological. For example, if one quietly instructs someone to jump, one intends that they shall believe that that is what you require of them. There are many thoughts here about divergence and convergence between what I think and what the other person thinks. But the important point for now is that linguistic communication involves intending, and intending 'I'-thoughts.

Michael Tomasello has argued[35] that children's learning of speech depends on the prior activities of shared attention. In learning of speech, the child sees itself, the adult, and the object under discussion as all being objects of shared attention. In using a novel word, it is trying to direct the adult's attention. This applies not just to naming situations, but to the cases where the object is being manipulated and the manipulation (e.g., picking up, putting away) is the center of interest. Apes are said not to reach this stage because they do not progress in the same way with shared attention activities, and the autistic are very poor at shared attention. I would think a qualification is supplied by the example above of the two chimpanzees at the banana box. Surely one was seeking the non-alignment of attention and the other was trying to get his attention aligned. But the point can still be true that for apes aligning attention is not a part of the parent-child upbringing.

In chapters fifteen and sixteen, I shall consider some ethical concepts that seem to involve the idea of *me*, or of the individual. These concepts are relevant to the view of Buddhism and of Derek Parfit that where we talk of persons, there are only streams of consciousness. I shall ask, and these

34. Paul Grice, 'Meaning', *Philosophical Review* 66, 1957, 377–88; id., 'Utterer's meaning and intentions', *Philosophical Review* 78, 1969, 147–77.

35. Michael Tomasello, *The Cultural Origins of Human Cognition*, Cambridge Mass. 1999, ch. 4.

thinkers themselves discuss, how their view can accommodate compassion, punishment, compensation, relief, commitment, rights, duties, praise, and blame.

The deficiency of autism shows the importance for normal development of acquiring a full sense of *me* and *you*,[36] and some of the evidence concerns the development of a normal moral sense of ownership and responsibility. Autistic children are said not to engage much in activities of shared attention, and correspondingly to be poor at developing language. They tend to have an underdeveloped sense of self. The deficiency is said first to have been described in 1943. In 1945, there was a study of a patient called 'L'.[37] He did not react emotionally when other children removed his toys, evidently not seeing them as '*his*' in a sense that carried its normal emotional implications. He had little sense not only of what he might expect of others, but also of what others might expect of him, as he ran about naked, drumming on his ears. At the age of 15, he could already use the pronoun 'I', but it did not carry the usual awareness of what might be expected of him. Asked what would happen if he shot someone, he made no reference to his own responsibility, but replied that *he* (the victim) would go to hospital.

In her fascinating book, *George and Sam*,[38] Charlotte Moore describes her two autistic children. Their reduced sense of self removes from them pride, embarrassment, shame, humiliation, vanity, feeling sorry for what they did, ambition, emulation, or the idea of reward. Elsewhere she says that her children are not aware of a *past* and *future* self. The self of which they are aware lacks the proper span.[39] She refers to Baron-Cohen's use of the criterion for autism that the autistic have no sense of other people's state of mind. Their unawareness of themselves goes together with their unawareness of the state of mind of others. Her children, like others, never engaged in shared attention. We might expect the autistic at least to see things in relation to a *bodily* self, as normal infants do before they engage in shared attention. But even here she noticed less exploration in the infants of fingers

36. Simon Baron-Cohen, H. Tager-Flusberg, and D. Cohen, eds., *Understanding Other Minds: Perspectives from Autism*, Cambridge 1993; Simon Baron-Cohen, 'Precursors to a theory of mind: understanding attention in others', in A. Whiten, ed., *Natural Theories of Mind: Evolution, Development, and Simulation of Everyday Mindreading*, Oxford 1991; Peter Hobson, *The Cradle of Thought*, London 2002, chs. 7 and 8.

37. M. Scheerer, E. Rothmann, and K. Goldstein, 'A case of "idiot savant": an experimental study of personality organisation', *Psychological Monographs* 58, 4, 1945, 1–63.

38. Charlotte Moore, *George and Sam*, London 2004, 29, 110–11, 124, 139, 240.

39. Charlotte Moore, 'Mind the gap', *The Guardian* June 5, 2002. See also Hobson, *The Cradle of Thought*.

and toes, and reports a case of an autistic woman's unawareness that it was she who was touching herself.[40] Though she cheerfully lives with it, the damage caused is vividly described, and autism could not be the norm. The children would not continue to survive without the devoted attention of nonautistic people, herself first and foremost.

THE SENSE OF SELF AS AN UNRELIABLE GUIDE

My case for a self does not depend on everyone having a *sense* of a single self. I have said that everyone sees the world in terms of self, but they may none-theless not have a strong sense of self. Many people have a weak sense of self, not only the autistic. Yet others have a sense of having more than one self. Multiple personalities can be induced in a single person, as Ian Hacking has described,[41] as a way of enabling people to shift blame from one personality to another. More tragically, a person's different aspirations can so frustrate each other that they feel as if they had been split into two. But the tragedy of this case depends upon there really being a single self that suffers the frus-tration, and in the first case the need to create extra personalities arises only because it is recognized that a single self has done what might attract blame.

My colleague Galen Strawson agrees with me that there is such a thing as self, but he bases his concept on his *sense* of self, which in his case, he re-ports, is a sense of only short-term selves, and accordingly he postulates short-term selves.[42] Admittedly, not all the selves that ancient philosophers postulate are life-long, since those that have to be created or developed take time to produce. But the idea of short-term selves, we shall see in the next chapter, is rare. Moreover, most ancient philosophers do not rely particu-larly on a *sense* of self. Exceptions may include Augustine, insofar as he ap-peals to the soul being present to itself, although he has much more to say, and Plotinus. But Plotinus is rather different, in that he relies on the sense of

40. Moore, *George and Sam*, 29.

41. Ian Hacking, *Rewriting the Soul*, Princeton 1995.

42. Galen Strawson, 'The self', *Journal of Consciousness Studies* 4, 1997, 405–28, and id., 'The self and the SESMET', *Journal of Consciousness Studies* 6, 1999, 99–135, both repr. in Shaun Gallaher and Jonathan Shear, eds., *Models of the Self*, Thorverton UK 1999; id., 'The sense of self', in James Crabbe, ed., *From Soul to Self*, London 1999; id., 'The phe-nomenology and ontology of the self', in D. Zahavi, ed., *Exploring the Self: Philosophical and Psychopathological Perspectives on Self-Experience*, Amsterdam 2000, 39–54; id., 'Against Narrative', *Times Literary Supplement*, October 24, 2004.

self gained from intense meditation, which he considers a better guide to reality than ordinary impressions.

ONUS OF DISPROOF

I have said what I mean by 'self' and argued that we need the concept. But is there such a thing? That does not follow from the mere need. Kant was to agree that the concept was needed, but as to what actually exists, he suspended judgment. We shall see in chapter sixteen that the Buddhist Sânti-deva allowed that for purposes of compassion the thought may be needed that there are suffering selves. But for other purposes he wants to be rid of the concept.

When we ask if there is such a thing as the self, we need to draw a distinction. In chapters eight to ten, I shall discuss the idea of an individual persona. On the Stoic view, we are all endowed by nature with an individual persona, but some people may not develop it strongly. Plutarch is recorded in chapter nine as thinking that some people do not develop a persona at all. Although I doubt his case, what I have been emphasizing in this chapter is two things, the individual embodied owner and the owner's need to see himself or herself as *me* and *me again*. Given the familiarity of the first and the need for the second, the onus should be on the person who attempts to deny that they correspond to reality.

The onus is a very difficult one to take up. Against Parfit's attempt to replace the idea of *ownership* with the idea of *location* I shall argue in chapter fifteen. Against the attempt to replace it with the idea of a *bundle* of properties, or of properties in a *location*, I shall argue in chapter seven, while in chapter sixteen knowledge of location is argued to depend on knowledge of self. Attempts to reject the idea of self are usually directed only against a particular conception of it. Kant, we shall see in chapter five, was suspending judgment on the sort of subject that Locke refused to rely on, a soul, or *disembodied* subject of experience and action that could not be inspected. Similarly, Parfit, we shall see in chapter fifteen, is concerned to dismiss a *disembodied* ego such as Descartes postulated. But what I have been speaking of is an *embodied* subject that is plain for all to see.

CHAPTER 2

The varieties of self and philosophical development of the idea

I have said what I mean by 'Self' and why I think there is such a thing. The next task is to see whether ancient philosophers had accounts of self. I think they most certainly did. Again and again, they show the same interest in the individual person, and especially the individual viewed from the first-person point of view as '*me*'. Moreover, like ourselves, they often express these ideas of self just as we do, by the use of pronouns. They talk of 'I', 'we', 'each', the reflexive 'oneself' (*heautos*), or the emphatic 'himself' (*autos*), or (Plato *Laws* 959B3) 'that which is each of us truly'. Where *autos* is used without an accompanying noun, it sometimes *demands* to be translated by the English 'Self', and *autos* is sometimes combined with *hekastos*, meaning *each self*.

The point is worth making because some accounts appear to deny it. I shall document a little later these apparent claims that there was no philosophical idea of self until much later, or at least no idea of self subjective enough to put stress on the notion of *me* and *me again*.

I do not mean that in giving an account of what is meant by *me*, they all came to the same conclusion as I have, that there is an embodied self plain to see, which *has* or *owns* both psychological and bodily characteristics. The *question* they are asking is about the nature of the individual self, as shown by their interest in the first person. But in their *answers* there is too much variety for consensus. All the same, many of them do take a view like mine. Aristotle, if he can be said to have a view of self, is one. The Stoics, the Epicurean Lucretius, and Christians all take such a view when they consider whether there could be an embodied return of the same person after this life has ended. Others do so when they seek criteria for differentiating embodied individuals. But there is a different approach that seeks to privilege for some purpose not the embodied individual as a whole, but some aspect belonging to the embodied individual as especially deserving to be called self, for example the individual's reason, will, mind, or body. An aspect may be picked out as the true self, or the inviolable self, or the self to be fostered for tranquility, the self to be considered in deciding where your duty lies, the self to which you feel attached, or that feels attachment, the self that you hope might survive in the face of death.

The answers that are furthest from the one I have favored are probably those in the Platonist tradition. Socrates awaiting execution is represented in Plato's *Phaedo* 115C as offering his friends the reassurance, *I* am not my body, but my rational soul, which will continue and flourish better without a body. In his *Republic,* Plato introduces non-rational parts of the soul as well as the rational part, and the parts are sometimes treated not merely as aspects belonging to a single subject, but as subjects in their own right. In the *Phaedo, Republic* book 9, and, if it is his, the *First Alcibiades,* Plato treats reason or intellect as if it constitutes the *essence* of the person. In doing so, Plato can be seen as treating the reason or intellect as the true self. Admittedly, it is only the discussion at *Phaedo* 115C that demands expression in terms of '*me*'. But that discussion is closely related to the one in *Republic* 9, which is couched in terms not of *me,* but of what the inner *human (anthrô- pos)* is. The two discussions, and that in the *First Alcibiades,* are so closely related that it would be artificial to say that the first was about the self, but the others were not. Plotinus, following Plato, also believes in selves that exist, and exist best, disembodied, and he has a series of them that he too treats not as aspects of a single subject, but as subjects in their own right. Much the same is true of Themistius' Platonist interpretation of Aristotle as endorsing the immortality of individual human intellects without bodies, and of Platonist interpretations of the after-life of Homer's Heracles, whose 'I myself' is interpreted as intellect and as a disembodied essence.

To bring out the interest of ancient philosophers in the individual, especially as viewed from the first-person perspective, I shall offer a survey of their very various views. It will be only partly a preview of topics to be discussed in later chapters because a number of topics will not be treated again, and to these I shall sometimes give a slightly fuller treatment here.

When we deal with the self as persona or acquired identity, the self selected can be something that has been deliberately fostered and shaped, rather than being there all ready for inspection in Hume's manner. Even Plotinus has an analogue, for although the divine realities with which we seek to identify ourselves exist independently of us, it is we who work at the process of identification and so achieve a higher self. To that extent, for him too our identity is something we create.

Further, the self selected varies not only according to different purposes and contexts of discussion. Even within a single sentence, there may be radically different aspects selected as self, because one aspect is often seen as working on another, where each is regarded as a self. This means that I cannot agree with any account that says that, for the ancient Greeks, self meant so and so, because the notion can refer to different things in the same sentence.

The self in the ancient philosophers is seldom identical with the soul. Sometimes it is connected with only one aspect of soul, its reason or will, for example, or a part of soul to be distinguished from the shade or ghost. Again, in theories of reincarnation, the same soul may be successively borrowed by entirely different people, and so outlasts any one self and cannot therefore be identical with it. Sometimes the self is the body, or includes the body along with the whole person.

Let us now look at a dozen or more examples of ancient views.

1. We can start with Homer's *Odyssey*, or the possible interpolation at 11.601–3, where it is said of the dead Heracles that Odysseus is talking to his shade while he himself (*autos*) is with the gods.

> Then I spied the mighty Heracles [his shade, but he himself enjoys festivities with the immortal gods].

This led to many Platonist discussions of what his true self was, which I shall discuss further in chapter five.[1] The next two writers, in order of date, that I mention come from the 5th century BC, Epicharmus and Heraclitus. Heraclitus' interest in self is suggested by his saying that he went in search of himself and looked for the *logos* of the soul.[2] I shall also cite both below for the denial of continuous selves. But I shall next discuss Plato in the 4th century BC and subsequent Platonism.

2. Plato held, as we shall see in chapter six, that the true self is the reason or intellect.[3] This raises the worry of whether the true self is sufficiently

1. See Jean Pépin, 'Héraclès et son reflet dans le néoplatonisme', *Le Néoplatonisme*, Colloque du CNRS, Royaumont, Paris 1971, 167–92; Harold Cherniss, note *c* to Plutarch *On the Face Appearing on the Orb of the Moon*, *Moralia* 944F, Loeb vol. 12. Besides the Plutarch reference, see Plotinus 4.3 [27] 27 (1–25); Proclus *in Remp.* 1. 119,23–120,15.

2. Heraclitus, frags. 45, 101, 116, Diels-Kranz.

3. Plato, e.g., *Phaedo* 63B–C; 115C; *First Alcibiades* 133C4–6; *Republic* 9, 589A6–B6.

individual. Do we differ from each other in our reason in distinctive ways? On one interpretation, we shall see, Plato is even conscious of a contrast between the true self and individuality at *First Alcibiades* 130D. In the passage from the end of the *Phaedo*, he has Socrates recapitulate what he has been saying throughout the dialogue about the rational soul by reminding the interlocutors that he *is* that rational soul (115C):

> CRITO: How are we to bury you?
>
> SOCRATES: However you like, provided you can catch me and I do not escape you.

3. As I shall explain in chapter six, I doubt that Aristotle agreed with Plato that our true self was the intellect in quite the way that Plato meant. Each of the four times he reports the doctrine, he reports it as something that is *thought*, rather than as something to which he is committed. He does not believe the doctrine of Plato's *Phaedo*, that Socrates can survive after death. So he does not believe that there will be a time when a human can become a pure philosopher, instead of an embodied social being who has to *eat*. At the very least the human needs the social and practical intellect, along with the theoretical intellect. I think that he puts the case dialectically for Plato's view of the true self as theoretical intellect (*Nicomachean Ethics* 10.7), but then in the next chapter (10.8), puts his case for the human as embodied social being who always needs to eat, although the more he uses theoretical reason, the happier he is. This fits with his view in *On the Soul*, that it is as wrong to say that our soul pities or is angry as it is to say that it weaves or builds. It is the human (*anthrôpos*) who is angry, in virtue of having a soul.[4] It fits too with Aristotle's description of a friend as another self (*allos* or *heteros autos*). The pseudo-Aristotelian *Magna Moralia* also says 'another I' (*allos* or *heteros ego*).[5]

Finally, it fits with Aristotle connecting the human with practical reason, when in *Nicomachean Ethics* 6.2, speaking of practical policy decisions (*proaireseis*), he says, 'such a source [of action] is the human'.

4. It was Plotinus, the founder of Neoplatonism six hundred years after Plato, in the 3rd century AD, who really wrestled with the problem of whether the Platonist self is sufficiently individual. He was torn between thinking that we should not separate ourselves out from the timeless uni-

---

4. Aristotle *On the Soul* 1.4,408b5–11.

5. Aristotle *EN* 9.1166a32; 1169b7; 1170b6, of one's children 8, 1161b28–29; *EE* 7.12, 1245a30; pseudo-Aristotle *MM* 2.15, 1213a13.

versal Intellect from which we derive, lest we lose our identity as much as those who do not know their father (5.1 [10] 1 (1–17)), and seeking after all to retain some separate individuality when we return to Intellect, as we will see in chapter six. It is only souls that do not attain that identification with Intellect but remain within time that can exercise memory, and Plotinus is anxious to show that they at least could still recognize each other through personality, even if they all received spherical bodies. But what about the individuality of souls that do escape from time and achieve identification with the timeless Intellect? They can be accorded individuality only on the analogy with a theorem in mathematics, which has a certain uniqueness but is intelligible only as part of a whole system.

Plotinus believed we have a number of selves, and can identify ourselves with a higher or a lower one. If we succeed in identifying ourselves with the timeless Intellect, which is one of the selves within, we shall have escaped to a life outside of time in which our obsession with *prolonging* life makes no sense.[6]

Plotinus 1.5 [36] 7 (1–30):[7]

But if we have to consider only the present and not reckon in the past, why do we not do the same in the case of time, and why do we add past time to present time and say that the total is increased? So why should we not claim that happiness is commensurate with the time it lasts? We would then be dividing happiness according to the divisions of time. In fact if we measure it by the present we shall be making it indivisible.

[8] The answer is that there is nothing absurd in counting time which no longer exists, since we would tot up the number of things that have been but are no more, like the dead. But it is absurd to claim that past happiness, which is over and done with, is greater than present happiness. For happiness needs to have persisted, while time over and above present time cannot exist. In general the passage of time scatters to the winds every present moment. That is why it is right to call it 'the image of eternity', since it wishes to banish the permanence of eternity in scattering itself to the winds. So if it removes from eternity its would-be permanence and appropriates it, it destroys it; it does preserve it for a while and in a way because of its eternality, but destroys it if it becomes totally enveloped.

6. Plotinus 1.5 [36] 7 (23–25).

7. Translated by Barrie Fleet, in Richard Sorabji, *The Philosophy of the Commentators, 200–600 AD: A Sourcebook*, vol. 1, London and Ithaca N.Y. 2004.

[20] So if happiness depends on a morally good life, obviously it must depend on the life of real Being, which is the noblest. This is not to be measured by time but by eternity. It is neither more nor less, nor of any length, but is a timeless present, unextended and outside time. So we must not associate Being with non-Being, or time or the everlasting with eternity; nor must we extend what cannot be extended, but it must be taken as a totality (if you 'take' it at all), taking not the indivisibility of time but the life of eternity, which does not consist of many moments of time but is all together beyond the reach of time.

Augustine, who was inspired by Plotinus, was also torn in two directions in his *Confessions*, between on the one hand love of his mother as an individual and hopes that his unnamed dead friend will remember him, and on the other hand aspiration towards a heaven in which there is no genetic relationship and no memory.

5. In the next century, the philosopher-rhetorician Themistius repeats Plotinus' view that it is harder to differentiate intellects than souls (*On Aristotle's On the Soul* 104,14–23). Yet to the relief of Thomas Aquinas in the 13th century, he interprets Aristotle *On the Soul* 3.5 as saying that there is a plurality of distinct human intellects illuminated by the one intellect (103,32–104,6). Thomas Aquinas quotes Themistius' view in his attack on the Islamic philosopher Averroës. Since it is the intellectual soul that Thomas Aquinas takes to be immortal, it is important that human intellect should be not only immortal, but also individually distinct. Philoponus and 'Philoponus' (who may or may not be a student of Philoponus) had said of the human '*active*' intellect that it was immortal and non-intermittent only through the unending succession of mortal thinkers and their thoughts.[8] Averroës went on to apply this to *all* human intellect, which is why the Christian, Thomas, had to oppose him. This famous 'Averroist' controversy, I shall argue in chapter nine, did not arise out of the blue in the 13th century. The seeds were sown in Plato, and the issue was brought to the fore by Plotinus and reflected in the rival interpretations of Themistius and Averroës.

6. A number of the foregoing views about the self offer solace in the face of death either, as in Plotinus, by making the happiest life exempt from time or by offering immortality, as do the Christian talk of resurrection and Plato's talk in the *Phaedo* of 'me' as an immortal rational soul. But an oppo-

---

8. Philoponus *in de Intellectu* 52,23–29, *CLCAG*, Verbeke; 'Philoponus' *On Aristotle's On the Soul 3*, 538,32–539,12.

site solace was offered by Epicurus, who set up his school in Athens at the end of the same century, in 308 BC. The soul is a bunch of material atoms, which will be dispersed at death, so there is no need to fear that we will be punished or otherwise suffer after death.[9]

Epicurus' expositor in Latin, Lucretius, in the 1st century BC, considered the possibility that despite the dispersal of our atoms, they might come together again in the infinity of time, so that we could be punished after all. Lucretius thinks that the interruption of memory solves this, but whether by preventing it being *us* who suffer, or by making it a matter of no concern *despite* its being us, I shall discuss in chapter five.

7. The Stoics believed that I would return each time the universe repeats its history, though only Seneca treated this as a solace.[10] On the standard view, the universe will repeat its history exactly, and its being I who return is guaranteed, despite the difference of time, by the recurrence of my supposedly unique and unshareable characteristic, whatever that may be. Variants on the view were that it would not be the same me, but different mes each time, or that it would not be me, but only someone indistinguishable from me. These views will be discussed in chapter three.

8. A different solace, to which I will return in chapters four, nine, fifteen, and sixteen, is the idea that there is no continuous self anyhow. Your infant self, and even your yesterday's self, are already dead, so why lament the last in a series of deaths, when there have been so many deaths already?

The idea that there is no continuous self was introduced early in the 5th century BC by the playwright Epicharmus, if the text is his, but only as a joke. Philosophers, however, often take jokes seriously. The idea was that just as the number 7 is replaced when it grows to 8, so a person is replaced when he or she grows. This is used by Epicharmus' characters to avoid responsibility for debts incurred and for retaliation against defaulting debtors. It was used later by Platonists against the Stoic school under the name of the Growing Argument and answered with what I shall call a Shrinking Argument, to be described in chapter four, by the Stoic Chrysippus in the 3rd century BC.[11] The controversy will turn out to involve the idea, much discussed in recent philosophy, that the survival of one person cannot depend solely on whether another person survives, because survival and perishing are not merely relational notions. In the meantime, Aristotle had

9. Epicurus *Kuriai Doxai* 2: Lucretius *On the Nature of Things*, 3.31–93; 830–1094.
10. Seneca *Letters* 36,10–11.
11. Epicharmus in Diogenes Laertius *Lives of Eminent Philosophers* 3.12; Chrysippus against Platonist Academics in Plutarch *On Common Conceptions* 1083A–C. See also David Sedley, 'The Stoic criterion of identity', *Phronesis* 27, 1982, 255–75.

raised the problem about persistence through growth in a particular form, and we shall encounter these arguments in chapters three, four, and nine.

A serious use of the idea that everything is in flux was made by Heraclitus in the 5th century BC, when he said that you cannot step into the same river water twice (frag. 12 Diels-Kranz). His follower, Cratylus, is supposed to have said that you cannot do so even once.[12] Heraclitus' view was developed by Plato, who refers to Heraclitus and, for the purpose of his argument, applies the point also to persons. But Plato finishes by reducing the argument to absurdity.[13] Plato further puts into the mouth of Diotima in the *Symposium*[14] the idea that our attributes are forever changing, so that we do not even retain the same knowledge, but have to replace it by repeating it to ourselves, as it slips away.

I have not been convinced by an interesting suggestion that the Cyrenaic philosopher Aristippus, who developed Socrates in a hedonistic direction in the 5th to 4th centuries BC, prefers pleasure over happiness because of uncertainty whether there is a continuing self to enjoy the happiness.[15] His argument that pleasurable motion in the soul gets exhausted over time suggests to me rather that he believes in a continuing self.

The consequences for fear of death are drawn out in a Buddhist text written in Pali in the 2nd century BC, the *Questions of Milinda*,[16] which will be discussed in chapter sixteen. This purports to be a dialogue between a Buddhist monk and a Greek king of Bactria, Menander, and it explains the Buddhist theory that there is no continuous self and the conclusion, among others, that one should not fear death. There may be traces of a similar argument having entered the consciousness of Greek and Roman philosophers in the 1st century AD, because this reason for not fearing death is found in the Stoic Seneca and put in the mouth of an interlocutor or reported as a challenging argument in the Platonist Plutarch. But if they really mean the same, it will be incompatible with the rest of what they say, which suggests that it could be an alien growth.[17] They both treat it as an extension to what Heraclitus had said. But it is incompatible with Seneca's view that we have a

---

12. Aristotle *Metaphysics* 4.5, 1010a10–15.

13. Plato *Theaetetus* 152E–186E.

14. Plato *Symposium* 207C–208B.

15. So Terry Irwin, 'Aristippus against happiness', *Monist* 74,1991, 55–82, with fuller reply by Voula Tsouna-McKirahan, *Cyrenaic Epistemology*, Cambridge 1997.

16. *Milinda's Questions*, trans. I. B. Horner, *Sacred Books of the Buddhists*, vols. 22, 23, London 1964.

17. Seneca, *Letters* 24,19–21; 58,22–23; Plutarch *On the E at Delphi* 392C–E, all translated and discussed in Richard Sorabji, *Emotion and Peace of Mind* 247–48.

life-long self (*ego, me*)[18] and Plutarch's belief that we have genuine memories that we can use to weave our lives into a unity.[19] Seneca may be saying only that one's past *state* and *time of life* have perished, and Plutarch might be expected to say no more than that one acquires a new identity in an everyday sense. The following are the main passages.

Epicharmus in Diogenes Laertius *Lives of Eminent Philosophers* 3.11 = Diels-Kranz frag 2:[20]

> If you like to add a pebble to an odd number — or to an even one if you like — or if you take away one that is there, do you think it is still the same number?
> Of course not.
> And if you like to add some further length to a yard measure, or to cut something off from what's already there, will that measure still remain?
> No.
> Well, consider men in this way too — for one is growing, one declining, and all are changing all the time. And what changes by nature, and never remains in the same state, will be something different from what changed; and by the same argument you and I are different yesterday, and different now, and will be different again — and we are never the same.

Plutarch *On Common Conceptions* 1083B–C, reporting the Platonist version of the Growing Argument used against the Stoics:

> It is wrong that it has become prevalent through custom that these changes are called growth and diminution. It would be appropriate that they should instead be called creation and destruction (*phthorai*), because they oust a thing from its established character into a different one, whereas growth and diminution happen to a body that underlies [the change] and remains throughout it.

Plato *Theaetetus* 152E:

> And on this let all the experts except Parmenides be assembled in succession, Protagoras and Heraclitus and Empedocles and of the poets the leaders in each genre, Epicharmus in comedy and Homer in epic. When he said, 'Ocean the origin of the gods and Tethys their mother' (*Iliad* 14, 201; 302), he meant that all things are offspring of flow and change.

18. Seneca, *Letters* 121,16.
19. Plutarch *On Tranquility* 473B–474B, translated in chapter nine below.
20. Translated by Jonathan Barnes, *The Presocratic Philosophers*, vol. 1, London 1979.

Seneca *Letters* 58,22 – 23:

None of us is the same in old age as he was in youth. None of us is the same to-morrow morning as he was the day before. Our bodies are carried away like rivers. Whatever you see races along with time; nothing that we see stays still. I too, while saying that things change, am changed myself. That is what Her-aclitus says: 'We do, and we do not, step down into the same river twice'. The name of the river stays the same; the water has passed. This is more obvious in a river than in a person, but we too are carried past in a race no less swift. So I am amazed at our madness: we love the most fleeting thing so much, the body, and we fear we are going to die some time, when every moment is the death of our previous state. Will you stop fearing that that will some time happen which happens every day?

Seneca *Letters* 24,19 – 21:

I remember you once treated the commonplace that we do not run into death suddenly, but proceed by degrees: we die every day. Every day some part of our life is taken away. Then too, as we grow, our life shrinks. We have lost our first infancy, then our childhood, then our youth. All past time up to yesterday has perished. The very day we are living we share with death. Just as it is not the last little drop that drains the water-clock, but what has flowed out before, so that last hour at which we cease to be does not on its own produce death; on its own it completes death. That is when we come up against it, but we have come for a long time. When you had described this in your usual voice—you are always powerful, but never sharper than when you are fitting words to the truth—you said: 'It is not a single death that comes; the death that takes us is the last'. I would rather you read yourself than my letter. For it will be evident to you that this death which we fear is the last, but not the only, death.

Plutarch *On the E at Delphi* 392C – E, in the mouth of one interlocutor:

Thus what is coming into being does not even attain to being, because it never desists from, nor halts, its coming into being, and because it rather is forever causing change, making from seed an embryo, then a baby, then a child, next a lad, a youth, then a man, an elder, an old man, destroying the former grow-ings and agings with the ones that supersede them. But we are ridiculous enough to fear one death, when we have already died so many deaths and are still dying. For it is not only, as Heraclitus said, that 'the death of fire is the birth of air, and the death of air is the birth of water', but you can see this still more clearly in our own case. For the man in his prime perishes when the old man comes into being, and the young man perished on turning into the man in his prime. Similarly the child on turning into the young man and the infant on turning into the child. The man of yesterday has died and turned into the man of today, and the man of today is dying in turning into the man of tomorrow. No one stays still, or is a single person (*heis*), but we become many, with matter whirling and sliding round a single image and a shared mold. If we stayed the same persons (*hoi autoi*), how would we enjoy different things now from what we enjoyed before, and love or hate, admire and censure opposite things? How would we use different words and indulge in different emotions without keeping the same appearance or figure or thoughts? It is not plausible that one should receive different characteristics without changing, nor upon changing is one the same person (*ho autos*). And if one is not the same person, one does not even exist, but changes in this respect too, becoming a different person from before. The senses say falsely that what appears to be in existence is so, through ignorance of what being is.

9. Different from this is the denigration of the bodily self by the Stoic emperor of the 2nd century AD, Marcus Aurelius. He uses the phrase that Aristotle sometimes uses for a thing's matter, 'whatever it is that is so-and-so', and speaks as if apart from the governing mind he were just this matter, namely flesh and breath. It is actually completely wrong to suppose that something is just its matter. The form or organization makes all the difference, as Aristotle always insisted, or else we would all write like Shakespeares, since we can all produce the letters of the alphabet. Marcus does not denigrate the governing mind, but he is not offering it immortal release from the body either. He is merely recommending that one imagine and welcome the eventual end of its enslavement to the denigrated body.

Marcus Aurelius *Meditations* 2.2:

> This whatever it is that I am (*ho ti pote eimi*) is bits of flesh and a little pneuma and the governing part. Despise the bits of flesh: gore, bits of bone, and a web, a net of sinews, little veins, arteries. Consider also what sort of thing the pneuma is: an air current, not even always the same, disgorged and gulped in again every hour. Then third is the governing part. Put away your books. Be drawn no longer. It is not granted. But as if already dying, think this: you are old. Do not allow this controlling part to be a slave any longer. Do not allow the sinews to draw it with selfish desires. Do not allow it to be troubled at what has been fated or is present, or to suspect the future.

10. In the 1st centuries BC and AD, I believe there was an explosion of new ideas about the Self. We have already reached Seneca and Plutarch, who belonged to this era, which was particularly fruitful for the subject. As will be explained in chapter nine, Plutarch in the 1st century AD, writing about tranquility, is the first philosopher I know to have made the connection, which has recently been popular,[21] between self and *narrative*, although Seneca had expressed some of Plutarch's idea,[22] and we shall see shortly that the Stoic Panaetius had already connected selves with *personae*, or *roles*. Plutarch's view is that, to secure tranquility, we need to use our memories to weave our life into a unified whole.[23] Otherwise we will be like the man in the painting who is plaiting a rope in Hades. As he plaits it, he throws it over his shoulder, but does not notice that a donkey is eating it up behind him. We shall also be like the people described in the Growing Argument, who have no continuous self. We must weave in the bad parts, as well as the good, for a picture needs dark patches as well as bright, and music needs low notes as well as high. But we must not wallow in the bad parts, like beetles in the place called 'Death to Beetles'.

How we are to understand this argument I shall discuss in chapter nine.

11. Also in the 1st century AD, we find explications of the Stoic theory of justice as based on a naturally felt attachment (*oikeiôsis*). Justice is argued to be *natural*, because it is based on the *natural* attachment that the newborn feel first for their own persons, as will be discussed also in chapter five, and then for their nearest. The Stoics therefore examine the newborn closely, and Seneca argues that, although at any time the attachment is felt towards the current constitution, which will change, it is the life-long self (*me, ego*) that is entrusted to my concern.[24] Around the end of the 1st century, Seneca's Stoic near-contemporary, Hierocles,[25] discussing the same subject, imagines the *mind* (*dianoia*) as being the center point of a set of concentric circles. He thus equates the mind with the self (each of us, *hekastos hêmôn*), which is entirely surrounded by circles. What draws the circles, to express the degrees of attachment it feels, is also a self (a given self, *autos tis*), and this is described not so much as identical with the mind as possessing it (*heautou*).

21. Alasdair MacIntyre, *After Virtue*, London (1982), 1985, 200–201; Charles Taylor, *The Sources of the Self*, Cambridge 1989, 47, 51; Daniel Dennett, *Consciousness Explained*, Boston 1991, ch. 13; Marya Schechtman, *The Constitution of Selves*, Ithaca N.Y., 1996.

22. Seneca *On the Shortness of Life* 10,3–6.

23. Plutarch *On Tranquility* 473B–474B.

24. Seneca *Letters* 121,16.

25. Hierocles *Elements of Ethics* in Stobaeus, eds. Wachsmuth, Hense, vol. 4, *Florilegium*, p. 671, lines 7–16.

Perhaps it is the composite of mind and body. The first circle outside the mind includes one's body, to which a sense of attachment is directed, and circles further out represent other people. If Hierocles thinks, like Chrysippus[26] and Seneca, that the first target of attachment is a self, then one self will feel attachment to the body as self, and altogether three aspects of the person will have been treated as selves.

It has been said that the idea of the body as external to the mind does not come up in epistemological contexts in ancient philosophy,[27] but it is common enough in other contexts, another example being the highly influential 'inner man' of Plato *Republic* book 9. But Hierocles gives us a particularly vivid example. The circles further out represent one's family, friends, fellow citizens, and foreigners. The context is ethical: one should learn to pull the circles inwards, so that one feels as much attachment to family as to one's own body, as much to friends as to family, and so on.

Hierocles, *Elements of Ethics* in Stobaeus, ed. Wachsmuth/Hense, vol. 4, *Florilegium*, ed. Hense, p. 671,lines 7–16:

> Each one of us (*hekastos hêmôn*) is, as it were, entirely surrounded by many circles, some smaller, others larger, the latter enclosing the former on the basis of their different and unequal relations (*skheseis*) to each other. The first and closest circle is the one which a given self (*autos tis*) has drawn as though around a center, namely his own mind (*dianoia*). In this circle is included (*periekhetai*) the body and anything taken (*perieilêmmena*) for the sake of the body. For it is practically the smallest circle and almost touches the center itself.

The Stoic idea reached the Christians, and we find Tertullian, who died c. 220 AD, saying that there is a *natural* progression from giving to one's brothers to giving to everyone.[28]

12. In the same century as Plutarch, Seneca, and Hierocles, the Stoic Epictetus gives us the idea of the inviolable self. Epictetus had had his leg broken when he was a slave. He imagines the following dialogue. 'I will put you in chains'. 'What did you say, man? Put *me* in chains? My leg you will put in chains, but my will (an imperfect paraphrase of *proairesis*) not even God can conquer'.[29]

---

26. *Hautous*, Chrysippus *ap.* Plutarchum *On Stoic Self-Contradictions* 1038B.

27. Myles Burnyeat, 'Idealism and Greek philosophy: what Descartes saw and Berkeley missed', *Philosophical Review* 91, 1982, 3–40 at 29–30.

28. Tertullian *Against Marcion* 4.16.

29. Epictetus *Discourses* 1.1.23.

The implication is that he is his will, although in chapter ten this will be seen to need qualification. The will is something that the tyrant cannot put in chains. Since the will can be molded, the self is also, on Epictetus' view, something that can by effort be fashioned.

In chapter ten I shall ask if there is a conflict between Epictetus' narrowing down the scope of *I* and *mine* in order to achieve invulnerability, and Hierocles' expansion of the idea of *mine,* so as to include other people, for the different purpose of securing justice to others.

13. I shall argue in chapter eight that the source for Cicero's account of personae in the 1st century BC is probably a Stoic from the later part of the preceding century, Panaetius.[30] This is a view about what you must take into account in deciding what it is right to do. You must consider not only the fact that you are a rational being. That is only the first persona, although it is what Kant tells us to consider, when deciding how it is right to act. But Cicero tells us in the passage of much more individual facts that must be taken into account. Among other things, you must be true to your own character, and people with different characters may be called on to act differently in the same circumstances, as Epictetus agrees (*Discourses* 1.2). This is especially true of exceptional or unique characters. In Cicero's star example (*On Duties* 1.112), it was right for Cato to commit suicide when Caesar won the civil war, but it would not have been right for anyone else in the same circumstances (*in eadem causa*). I shall discuss in chapter eight the way in which this goes even further against a Kantian approach. On Kant's view, something cannot be the right thing to do, unless it would be the right thing for anyone to do in the same circumstances. I shall argue that although Kant's view could be made verbally consistent with the Stoic one, there is a real difference of attitude, and that the Stoics of this period have a very important insight. I shall also argue that their attitude shows a special interest in the individual.

14. In chapter seven, we shall encounter in Porphyry's *Isagôgê,* or *Introduction to Philosophy,* yet another view of the individual person. The individual is here defined as a bundle of qualities that cannot be shared by any other individual. On this view, the person *consists* of properties rather than owning them. But one of the points I shall be making, especially in chapter fifteen, is that we need the idea of an owner.

15. I will take a further example from the Platonist tradition. Plato in the *Symposium*[31] suggests that we want to have children, or to leave other

30. Cicero *On Duties* 1.107–15
31. Plato *Symposium* 206E–209E.

works behind, because this is the nearest we can come to immortality. Here the self seems to be invested in offspring. But Plotinus makes the opposite point, already noted, which also contains some truth, when he describes how souls emanated from Intellect, because they wanted to belong to themselves (*heautôn einai*). In fact, however, this search for selfhood got them the opposite result. For in forgetting their origin and their Father, the Intellect, they failed to see themselves (*heautas*) or to value themselves (*heautôn*). Plotinus is making the point that an important part of one's identity is a conception of one's parents or forebears.[32]

16. A final context in which there is relevant talk of *self* is that of self-awareness. A star example is provided by Augustine's Cogito argument, which appears in many of his works starting a little before 400 AD. In the version found in *On the Trinity* (10.10.14 and 16), which is translated in chapter twelve, the argument, as in Descartes 1200 years later, has two parts, and the second part is about the nature of the self, and not only about awareness of it. Augustine's first Cogito argument is that one knows about one's own thinking with certainty. The second is that such knowledge implies one knows one's essence, but since one does not know whether it is bodily, bodily nature cannot belong to one's essence, which must be incorporeal. In Descartes, these arguments are couched in the first-person singular, '*I* think', but in Augustine they are not. The first-person formulation is more dramatic and rhetorically effective. On one view, Descartes' version of the first argument actually requires the first person, because, on this view, 'I think' is to be compared with 'I promise'.[33] By saying 'I promise' in the right circumstances, you actually do promise, whereas saying 'he promises' creates no commitment. In my view, however, the argument that I cannot be mistaken in supposing 'I think' turns on the point that 'I think' claims no more than is presupposed in its being thought. I will come in chapters twelve and seventeen to Lichtenberg's complaint that all I can safely say is 'there is thinking'.

USEFUL AND REAL?

Let me take stock. Are the philosophical conceptions of self or person sketched above useful, and do they correspond to reality? I am not per-

---

32. Plotinus 5.1 [10] 1 (1–17), translated in chapter nine.

33. Jaakko Hintikka, '*Cogito, ergo sum:* inference or performance?' *Philosophical Review* 71, 1962, 3–32.

suaded of all of them, not of the Platonist ones, and not of the denial of a continuous self. But many of the conceptions are useful, and many real or realizable. This would be true of Aristotle's embodied social person, of Hierocles' mind and embodied self, of the four personae. Realizable, rather than already realized, are the woven self and the inviolable self. The creation of the last carries a heavy price in terms of emotional detachment and would not easily recommend itself, except in a very hostile environment. The idea of an immortal self is to many highly attractive, even though fewer consider it a reality.

COULD WE SUBSTITUTE TALK OF PERSON OR HUMAN?

With the background in place, I can now more effectively answer the question of whether all the talk of the self could be replaced by talk of persons, or humans, and aspects of them? Certainly not all. That would completely ruin many of the points being made. The existence of persons, humans, and their aspects is rather a presupposition in these cases. Epictetus is not saying 'you cannot chain the person, or human'. Of course you can. Nor is he saying 'there is an aspect of me you cannot chain, my will'. The tyrant knew that. He is rather saying 'the aspect you cannot chain is *me*'. Similarly, Plutarch is not saying that a person or human can be woven. Those are already there. What he is tempted to say is that the thing that can be woven is *me*. Cato is precisely not to think only about what it would be right for a person to do. He must also ask himself, 'What would be right uniquely for *me?*'. Hierocles wants us to extend our 'me' concerns to other people as well. Augustine's Cogito gives a unique position to my knowledge of myself and your knowledge of yourself, as opposed to anyone's knowledge of others.

It is even more obvious that talk of '*me*' is integral to those contexts where people are considering life of the same individual beyond death. Socrates in the *Phaedo* is not reassuring his friends that some person will continue to exist. He is saying, 'it will be *me*'. Seneca and Plutarch seek to relieve anxiety about death by denying that there is a continuous me. Marcus does so by denigrating the bodily me. To the Epicurean Lucretius, the alarming thought is that it might be *we* who are by chance reassembled after death. And Seneca uses the encouragement that it will be precisely *we* who return when the universe repeats its history. Plotinus was clearly anxious to avoid a total loss of individuality, in his discussion of souls retaining recognizable personality, or at least having the uniqueness of theorems. And this

anxiety derives, of course, from 'I'-thoughts. The story of Heracles pro-
voked the question, 'what is the "he himself" that is eternal and blessed?'.
The Christian resurrection matters because each of us asks, 'what about *my*
survival?'. And this is also why Thomas Aquinas seizes upon Themistius'
recognition in Aristotle of an intellect that is not only human and immortal,
but also individual for each and every one of us.

Not all the examples are best formulated in terms of a self, certainly not
the view of the person as a unique bundle of qualities, which Porphyry ascribes to the Aristotelians, and which I would criticize as like the idea of a
person as a stream of consciousness. For it leaves out the idea of someone
who *owns* the qualities or the consciousness. But even this discussion concerns individuals and how to differentiate them uniquely.

APPARENT DENIALS OF AN
EARLY PHILOSOPHY OF SELF

It will be clear that I think philosophical concepts of self were being formulated very early. But there have been denials or apparent denials. On one
view, a concept of self was developed by philosophers only later, by Plotinus[34] or Augustine.[35]

There are other views that, without naming a *first* invention, nonetheless deny that the idea of selfhood I have been talking about is to be found
as early as I have said. I doubt that Diskin Clay disagrees with me, despite
the title of his article, 'Missing persons, or the selfless Greeks', since I agree
that Plato is not interested in a modern kind of individualism.[36] But Christopher Gill has recently extended to the period of post-Aristotelian Hellenistic and Roman thought down to 200 AD a view he took about Greek thought
as far as Aristotle.[37] On his view, ancient thought down to 200 AD treated
the self in 'objective-participant', not 'subjective-individualist', terms. This
might seem to treat our interest in our own selves as on the subjective side
and therefore as something not considered by the early Greeks. In one of the

---

34. W. Himmerich, 'Platonische Tradition in didaktischer Reflexion: Plotin-Comenius-Scheler', in *Parusia, Festgabe für Johannes Hirschberger*, Frankfurt 1965, 495.

35. Phillip Cary, *Augustine's Invention of the Inner Self*, Oxford 2000.

36. Diskin Clay, 'Missing persons, or the selfless Greeks', in William J. Carroll, J. J.
Furlong, and C. S. Mann, eds., *The Quest of the Individual: Roots of Western Civilization*, New
York 1990.

37. Christopher Gill, *Personality in Greek Epic, Tragedy, and Philosophy: The Self in
Dialogue*, Oxford 1996.

many constructive exchanges we have had over the years, I originally took Gill to intend this. But in the published version of our exchange,[38] he has offered a subtle and nuanced view not open to that interpretation. I am sure this must be right, because I see no incompatibility at all between our interest in our own selves from the first-person perspective and an interest in our social duties and our objective existence as human beings. The first-person interest does not exclude, but rather requires, attitudes that might be called 'objective' or 'participant'. Interest in 'me'-ness and in self-awareness would not arise unless there were such things as persons and higher animals that could be described in more objective terms. As for participation in community, I stress in chapters one and fifteen, in opposition to Descartes, that the infant acquires its idea of 'what *I* am looking at' only in a social exchange and hand in hand with the idea of what *another* is looking at, and I commend analogous insights in the Greeks. Certainly, Epictetus insists on our social character, e.g., at *Discourses* 2.5.24–26, even while in other passages stressing the inviolable *me*.

Both Gill and Pierre Hadot criticize Foucault's description of the Greeks and Romans as concerned with the care of the *self.* Hadot comments that the self that interests the Stoics, no less than the Platonists, is a universal reason, not an individual self.[39] It is true that the Stoics regard our reason as parts of the universal divine reason, and Epictetus emphasizes this, e.g., at *Discourses* 1.14, but he finds that emphasis quite compatible with stressing individuality in the passages I have referred to, and even the Platonists, I shall argue in chapter six, are seriously worried by the tension between the familiar me and the self as universal Intellect.

There are some extreme views that differ more radically from mine. For a time a view was taken of the ancient Israelites by H. Wheeler Robinson, and extended by others to St. Paul, that they saw themselves in terms of 'corporate personality', 'never as single beings, but as irreducibly part of a larger group'.[40] Although this influential view eventually collapsed, it has been replaced by another, that the ancient Mediterranean person, and there-

---

38. Christopher Gill, 'The ancient self: issues and approaches', in Pauliina Remes, ed., *Philosophy of the Self in Ancient Thought*, forthcoming.

39. Pierre Hadot, *Philosophy as a Way of Life: Spiritual Exercises from Socrates to Foucault*, trans. Michael Chase, Oxford 1995, ch. 7, 'Reflections on the idea of the cultivation of the self', 211, referring to M. Foucault, *Le souci de soi*, Paris 1984, translated as *The History of Sexuality*, vol. 3, *The Care of the Self*, New York 1986.

40. H. Wheeler Robinson, 'Corporate personality in ancient Israel', published as an article, Berlin 1936, quoted in Bruce J. Malina and Jerome H. Neyrey, *Portraits of Paul: An Archaeology of Ancient Personality*, Louisville 1996, 12.

fore in particular St. Paul and his contemporaries of the 1st century AD, are group-oriented persons from collectivist cultures. These are contrasted with Western cultures, but 70 percent of the world's population is said to be still socialized to become collectivist selves.[41] The application to Paul and the 1st century AD may seem surprising, given the explosion in that century of the ideas of self I have been discussing, and given that St. Paul tells us so much about inner struggle. But in a 5-page table of views characterizing ancient Mediterranean cultures, it is said that the individual is an artificial or derived construct. Individuals always represent their groups. It is impossible to imagine a self acting independently outside the inherited tradition and the community that upholds it. There is total inattentiveness to one's own contribution to group goals. In a concluding summary, it is explained that such people do not readily distinguish the self from social role. Most social behavior is determined by group goals. I do not recognize any of this as applicable to the 'ancient Mediterranean person'. On the other hand, another claim, that group-oriented selves require another person to know who they are,[42] is one that I have described in chapter one as true of all infants, even in cultures that might be called individualist.

DIFFERENT STARTING DATES
FOR DIFFERENT ISSUES

In contrast to the foregoing interpretations, I have placed the views I have been emphasizing quite early. What I think is true, however, is that there were earlier and later developments in the concept of self. I would assign different starting dates to four different aspects of the subject: the idea of a true self, the interest in personal identity over time, the interest in individual differences in decision making, and the idea that one must look within oneself for the ultimate truths or realities.

The idea of a *true* self goes back as far as Homer and the distinction between Heracles' shade (*eidōlon*) and his true self.

The interest in personal identity over time, however, becomes urgent in the philosophers only in the 3rd century BC or later, when objections are raised to the Pythagorean and Stoic theory that the same people will reappear when the universe repeats its history exactly, and when the Epicu-

---

41. Malina and Neyrey, *Portraits of Paul*, 12, citing a study by Harry C. Triandis.
42. Ibid., 198–201, 227–31.

reans concede that there might in the course of infinite time be a chance reassembly of a person's atoms. Before that, a threat relevant to personal identity had been raised in the 5th century BC, with the idea that all things are discontinuous. But persons had provided only one example of the threatened discontinuity.

A different issue again is the new interest in the individual and in the role of the individual persona in decision-making, which in chapter eight I shall date to a little before the 1st century BC.

Charles Taylor treats another stage of the ancient discussion.[43] When did philosophy first take the inward turn, the radically reflexive stance that is familiar to us from Descartes? What Taylor has in mind is a stance that not only attends to our own experience, but also sees that as the place we have to examine in order to find truth, because truth lies within. Taylor's answer is 'Augustine', who finds God within, but in fact Augustine tells us that he learned his technique of looking inwards from the 'books of the Platonists' (*Confessions* 7.10.16). He had read Latin translations of Plotinus, who repeatedly tells us to look for the chief divinities, the Intellect and the One, *within* ourselves,[44] and who provides a famous autobiographical account of experiencing union with the divine Intellect, an account in which he says that he often withdraws into himself (4.8 [6] 1 (1–11)). Even the phenomenological character of mystical union is taken by Plotinus to indicate how things really are. There is not merely a *sense* of timelessness; the Intellect and oneself as united with it are *really* timeless (3.7 [45] 11). There is not merely a loss of *sense* of where one's own boundary stops and that of Intellect or the One begins (6.5 [23] 7 (14–17)); there is genuine union. Plotinus holds more generally that the source from which something stems is within it, and he applies this to the divine Intellect as our source.

It was a controversial view that the intelligible realities reside within us. Plotinus' pupil, Porphyry, tells us in his *Life of Plotinus* (chs. 18 and 20), that he was made to rewrite his essay three times, with counter-essays by another pupil, before he came to acknowledge that the intelligibles lie within us. This is not a self-evident interpretation of Plato. Despite the interest of Plato's Socrates in the saying of the oracle at Delphi, 'know thyself', the intelligibles on which Plato concentrates, the Forms or Ideas, are not spoken of as lying within. It took the Neoplatonist commentators on Plato to interpret in this spirit the *First Alcibiades*, which they ascribed (rightly, I think)

---

43. Charles Taylor, *Sources of the Self*, Cambridge 1989, ch. 7, London 1970.
44. E.g., Plotinus 1.6 [1] 9 (8), 5.8 [31] 10 (31–43), 6.9 [9] 7 (16–23).

to Plato. They conclude that the starting point for studying Plato and the whole of Philosophy must be the Delphic injunction, 'know thyself'.[45]

Phillip Cary has renewed Augustine's claim as the inventor of the idea of inner self, distinguishing him from Plotinus by Augustine's wanting us to look first within, but subsequently upwards.[46] But quite apart from the fact that Plotinus too recognizes many levels of divinity within, insofar as Cary's point is right, it shows that Plotinus was more thoroughgoing than Augustine in the respect that interests us, in that he locates *everything* divine within. The actual *expression* 'the inner man' was in any case handed down by Plato from *Republic* 589A–B and influenced not only Plotinus and Porphyry but also, according to Theodore Heckel,[47] St. Paul, the Jewish philosopher Philo of Alexandria, and the Nag Hammadi Gospels.

But Plotinus himself was not the first to look for the most important things within. The Stoics looked within not for metaphysical entities, like Plotinus, but for truths. Cicero in the 1st century BC borrows from the Stoics when he says in connection with natural law and justice that one finds them within (*in se*) (*On Laws* 1.22.58; cf. *Republic* 3.22.33). And in the next century, the Stoic Epictetus (*Discourses* 3.22.38–39) says that we find preconceptions about the good within ourselves.

But the Stoics are not necessarily the first either. Among the earliest Presocratic philosophers of the 5th century BC, Heraclitus says, 'I went in search of myself' (frag. 101, Diels-Kranz) and 'You would not by traveling every path find the furthest limits of the soul, so deep is its *logos*' (frag. 45). If this *logos* is the same as the universal truth that he also calls *logos* in fragments 1 and 2, he will have anticipated the view of Plotinus that truth is to be found within. In that case there will not so much have been an inward *turn*. Rather, from the beginning some philosophers, not all, will have been attracted by the idea that truth lies within.

CONTINUITY AND DISCONTINUITY OF INTEREST IN THE SELF

Having located before Augustine the search for truth within in Plotinus, the Stoics, and Heraclitus, I ought to attend to a rival view that stresses the dis-

45. Proclus *in Alc.* 1 5,13–14 Westerink, following Iamblichus *ap.* Proclum *in Alc.* 1 11,11–17, and similarly, *Anonymous Prolegomena to Platonic Philosophy* ch. 26.

46. Cary, *Augustine's Invention of the Inner Self*, ch. 3.

47. Theodor Heckel, *Der innere Mensch*, Tübingen, 1993.

continuity of interest in the self. Michel Foucault has said that there can be no continuous history of the Delphic saying, 'know thyself', because its meaning shifted with different conceptions of how to exercise care of the self.[48] I have learned much from his fascinating *L'Herméneutique du sujet*, published in 2001, which is his lecture course of winter 1982 at the Collège de France, and which contrasts certain views in Plato, in pagan philosophy of the first two centuries AD, in early Christianity, and in Descartes. Certainly the views he selects are often very unlike each other. But taken as a whole, I do not believe that the views of these periods, for all their differences, would show such sharp discontinuities. I think the appearance of such discontinuity is a function of Foucault's selecting particular texts, rather than looking at schools as a whole and their development.

48. Michel Foucault, *L'Herméneutique du sujet*, Paris 2001, 443−44.

PART II

Personal identity over time

CHAPTER 3

Same person in eternal recurrence, resurrection, and teletransportation

One topic concerning the self is this: what makes an individual the same individual over a period of time? Before Plato, the comic playwright Epicharmus (if the text is his) entertained the idea of growth as continuous destruction,[1] and the philosopher Heraclitus considered the flux of things to be so great that one could not step into the same river, nor touch the same mortal substance, twice.[2] Plato developed this idea in his *Theaetetus*[3] in such a way as to represent it as unintelligible, thereby reasserting a certain degree of stability, without, however, offering a criterion of identity over time. In his *Symposium*,[4] by contrast, Plato had earlier made Diotima allow neither people, nor their bodily parts, nor even their knowledge, to remain the same. Knowledge is constantly being replenished by new memories of the same thing. The account that follows will start with Plato's pupil Aristotle. I want to draw attention to two less well-known passages in Aristotle (*On Generation and Corruption* 1.5 and *Physics* 5.4) that I believe to have been key passages.

(i) Biological growth

Although biological growth had been taken since Presocratic times to create a problem for the persistence of the individual, Aristotle's problem in *GC* 1.5 is a special one.[5] He thinks that in some sense every part whatsoever

---

1. Epicharmus frag. 170, Kaibel = Diogenes Laertius *Lives* 3.12. Reconstruction by David Sedley, 'The Stoic criterion of identity', *Phronesis* 27, 1982, 255–75, at 255.
2. Heraclitus frag. 91, Diels-Kranz = Plutarch *On the E at Delphi* 392B–C.
3. Plato *Theaetetus* 152C–153D, 181B–183C.
4. Plato *Symposium* 207C9–208B6.
5. *GC* 321a7–9, 18–22, b10–16.

of the growing thing is increased by the incoming nutriment, but yet that two bodies cannot be in the same place. His solution invokes the form. The nutriment accedes not to every part of the matter, but to every part of the form.[6]

There are various uses of the word 'form'. Intelligible form, to speak very roughly, is the defining characteristics of a type of thing. It is as intelligible form that the soul is elsewhere described by Aristotle as the form of the living body. Perceptible form, by contrast, is a more superficial set of perceptible characteristics. Here Aristotle is talking of a particular kind of perceptible form, the form of the *body*, and indeed of the *individual* body. Moreover, this form is not only a perceptible structure (*skhêma*), but also a dynamic structure that imposes its own shape on the incoming nutriment. He compares the form to a tube (*aulos*) with water flowing through it.[7] The tube both measures the volume of water and has the power (*dunamis*) actively to shape it. It is a self-preserving physical structure, and I take it to be quite unlike the form of the body which Aristotle (*On the Soul* 2.1) identifies with soul, i.e., on Aristotle's conception of soul, with the capacities for life-manifesting activity. Thus when Aristotle says (321b27–8) that the nourishment accedes to the *form*, it can hardly be the *soul* that is said to be receiving the nourishment, for the life-manifesting capacities are not the right sort of thing to receive food, nor can they be compared with a tube. Aristotle is not at this stage depending on his subsequent analysis of soul in *On the Soul*. Rather, form is here equated with structure (*morphê*) and compared with a tube. Moreover, Aristotle will not want to anticipate in this context his analysis of soul. The only echo of soul-talk comes when Aristotle says that the form is a *dunamis*, for the soul is also a *dunamis*. The relevant *dunamis* may in each case be the capacity to maintain a certain shape or structure. But the form here might best be thought of as a perceptible figure or structure that has the capacity to preserve itself. It is this particular figure or structure that is said by Aristotle to persist when matter does not.

Aristotle *GC* 1.5, 321a18–22:

> Of the three things that happen one is that every part whatsoever of the growing extension (e.g., of flesh, if flesh is growing) is bigger, second by the accession of something, and third what is growing is preserved and persists.

6. Ibid. b22–28, 32–34.
7. Ibid. b24–5, 322a28–33.

Aristotle *GC* 1.5, 321b26–28:

The accession is not to every part whatsoever. Rather, some leaves and some arrives, and the accession is to every part whatsoever of the figure (*skhêma*) and form (*eidos*).

Aristotle *GC* 1.5, 322a28–33:

This form, like a tube (*aulos*), is a force (*dunamis*) in matter. If some matter comes in which is potentially tube, with its quantity potential too, these [combined] tubes will be larger. But if the matter can no longer act, but is like water mixed with wine in ever greater amount, which eventually makes the wine watery or water, then it will produce a wasting away. The form, however, persists.

Aristotle is talking about the form of an *individual* body, but he does not further explain what sort of thing that is, apart from giving his analogy of the tube and insisting on its *dunamis*.

Alexander repeats that growth is in form, not in matter[8] and again compares form with a soft tube (*sôlên*).[9] Philoponus calls it a tube made of skin (*dermatinos sôlên*),[10] and adds the comparison of a numerically single shadow falling on running water.[11]

Alexander and Philoponus explain that the tube persists, even though different volumes of water flow through it, expanding or deflating it. Philoponus enters the caveat that form can persist only so long as the replacement of matter occurs bit by bit, not all in one go (*athroon*, 106,8). And this insistence on gradualness is ascribed to Alexander in the Arabic version of *Quaestiones*.[12] This is presented as replacing the excessive suggestion that what the persistence of form requires is the persistence of some of the original matter, and correspondingly Alexander[13] allows form to be preserved by exchange (*diadosis*) of matter. But although persistence of the original matter is not required for the persistence of form, Philoponus comments[14]

---

8. Alexander *Mixt.* ch. 16, 235,23ff; *Quaest.* 1.5.
9. Alexander *Mixt.* 237,26–238,10.
10. Philoponus *in GC* 105,22–26, 107,28, 108,13.
11. Ibid. 106,12–17.
12. Alexander *Quaestiones* 1.5,13,13–16, trans. into German by Ruland, Göttingen 1981.
13. Id. *Mixt.* 235,29–34.
14. Philoponus *in GC* 107,3–7.

that there are independent reasons to think that some of an animal's matter needs to persist. For life-long scars are evidence of some matter persisting unchanged. The 'scars' argument, as Kupreeva has pointed out to me out, is ascribed to Alexander by Averroës.[15] Further, Philoponus seems to treat the persistence of some matter as after all required for some reason or other, citing as evidence that, if our matter could all be safely replaced, we should be immortal. But if this is required, it will be for some extraneous reason, unspecified; it is not required for solving the metaphysical problem of how there can be a persisting subject of nutritional processes.

A distinction is drawn between merely getting larger and genuine growing (*auxêsis,* Latin *augmentari*), and although matter is not allowed to be what grows, it is said to get larger by Alexander, by Philoponus, and by the report on Alexander in Averroës.[16] I take the reference at this point to matter growing, in Kurland's composite translation from Arabic, Hebrew, and Latin manuscripts of the text, to represent a misunderstanding incompatible with Aristotle.

The problem of identity through biological growth had featured not only in commentaries on Aristotle. It had also been intensified and pressed on the Stoics by Platonist skeptics. The Stoic answer is recorded in Stobaeus and 'Simplicius'.[17] There are life-long characteristics in virtue of which a person is distinctively qualified. Moreover, it is not the unqualified matter (here called the substance) of a person that undergoes growth, but the distinctively qualified entity itself, or the qualified part of it that is protected from losing its identity by the life-long qualities. I doubt if it is conceded that the matter *does* lose its identity. But the protection comes from elsewhere—from the life-long quality to which the commentator 'Simplicius' gave the Aristotelian name of 'form', *eidos* (the form, that is, of the person). This life-long characteristic is probably meant to be distinctive in the strong sense that no one else *could* share it. That at any rate would be true of Neoplatonist theory,[18] and unshareability would help the Stoics, if the ability of

15. Averroës *Epitome of GC,* 4.1, trans. Kurland, *Corpus Commentariorum Averrois in Aristotelem,* 117.

16. Alexander *Mixt.* 238,5–7; Philoponus *in GC* 108,10 and 15, 117,32, 118,1–2; cf. 118,19–20; Averroës *Middle Commentary in GC,* text 38; *Corpus Commentariorum Averrois in Aristotelem* 4.1, at least in the Latin translation from Arabic, ed. Fobes (critical apparatus to line 44).

17. Stobaeus vol. 1, pp. 178,10–179,17 Wachsmuth (= LS 28D5–12), 'Simplicius' *in DA* 217,36–218,2 (= *SVF* 2.395, LS 28I).

18. Porphyry *Isag.* 7,16–24; Boethius *in Int*(2) 136,17–138,19.

the Stoic sage to tell any two individuals apart is meant to be infallible. Moreover, unshareability would protect someone from losing their identity through someone else coming to share their previously unique property.

How could there be an unshareable quality? Unfortunately, no Stoic example has been preserved, but one suggestion, made by Eric Lewis,[19] is that each individual person has an unshareable psychological perspective, whose physical basis constitutes the distinctive quality. Although this suggestion is not applicable to inanimate individuals, it is the best suggestion I know for human individuals within a given cycle of the universe. For even if you have an identical twin, you will not be born at exactly the same time and place, and so will not have the same visual perspective. You will also not feed from the same breast at the same time. These differences in perceptual perspective will snowball, creating differences in emotional perspective too. Which twin has got the better breast, or the better grasp of it and position? Within a cycle of the universe, these differences of perspective are unshareable, although we shall later have to consider successive cycles. The physical basis of the unshareable perspective is life-long as regards its original core, although the perspective will be added to throughout life, so that not every aspect of the perspective will have been there from the beginning.

'Simplicius' *in DA 3* 217,36–218,2 (= *SVF* 2.395, LS 28I):

> If in the case of compounds there is an individualized form (*atomôthen eidos*) from which, among the Stoics, the distinctively qualified individual (*idiôs poion*) gets its name, a form that supervenes (*epiginesthai*) and departs all at once (*athroôs*), and remains the same throughout the whole life of the compound, although different parts [of the compound] go in and out of existence at different times, . . .

Posidonius in Stobaeus vol. 1 p. 178,10–21 Wachsmuth (part of Posidonius frag. 96, Edelstein and Kidd, LS 28D5–8):

> [Posidonius says that] the substance neither grows nor shrinks by addition or subtraction, but merely alters (*alloiousthai*), as in the case of numbers and measures. And it results that growth and shrinking occur in the case of distinctively qualified beings like Dion and Theon. And that is actually why the quality of each persists from birth until death, in the case of plants, animals, and suchlike, which admit of death. They [the Stoics] say that in the case of distinctively

19. Eric Lewis, 'The Stoics on identity and individuation', *Phronesis* 40, 1995, 89–108.

qualified beings there are two parts that receive admissions, one at the level of substance, the other at the level of quality. It is the latter, as we often said, that admits of growth and shrinking.

There had been a question, which was seen to be partly parallel, about an inanimate object, the ship of Theseus,[20] of how it can persist when all its parts have been replaced. Ships, according to the Stoics, do not have enough unity to be the bearers of genuine qualities, although in some sense they are qualified.[21] So the Stoics might well have thought that the ship of Theseus did not persist. We can imagine the entirely different answer that Aristotle would have given. The ship of Theseus preserves its form or structure just like the growing plant or animal body in *GC* 1.5, and so will be the same ship. On the other hand, if someone after an interruption built all the rotten planks taken from the old ship into a separate ship, the interruption to the form would prevent this from being the original ship, despite the sameness of matter. Philoponus in *Against Proclus*, however, thinks that the ship will not be numerically the same [22] even if [23] it is the same in a way. Elsewhere Philoponus takes another inanimate example,[24] but one in which form, as well as matter, is changed: the statue whose foot, hand, and head are replaced by differently shaped parts. Here the loss of form destroys the identity.

Plutarch *Life of Theseus* ch. 23:

> The Athenians preserved the thirty-oared ship in which [Theseus] sailed with the youths and maidens and got back safe up to the time of Demetrius of Phaleron, removing the old planks and installing strong ones, fixing them in such a way that the ship became an example even to the philosophers for the controversial Growing Argument. Some of them said the ship remained the same, some not the same.

Simplicius *in Cat.* 214,24–31 (= *SVF* 2.391, LS 28M): [25]

> The Stoics too according to their own assumptions would raise the same difficulty against the argument that states that all qualified things are spoken of in

---

20. Plutarch *Life of Theseus* 23.
21. Simplicius *in Cat.* 214,24–31.
22. Philoponus *Against Proclus* 202,19; 344,6; 502,25.
23. Ibid. 228,6.
24. Philoponus *in GC* 106,18–23.
25. Translated by Barrie Fleet, in Richard Sorabji, *The Philosophy of the Commentators, 200–600 AD: A Sourcebook*, vol. 3, London and Ithaca N.Y. 2004.

terms of a quality. They say that qualities are 'havable' (*hekta*) and restrict 'havables' to things that are unified, while in the case of things that exist in combination (*sunaphê*), like a ship, or in separate parts, like an army, they say there is no one thing that is 'havable', and that no single instance of spirit (*pneumatikon*) is found in their case, or anything possessing a single principle (*logos*) of the sort to achieve the existence of a single state (*hexis*). The qualified, however, can be seen in things that exist in combination and separate parts.

There is a summary of solutions by Simplicius,[26] who reports that what persists may be any of the following: *ousia* in the sense of form, a distinctive quality, the secondary subject (i.e., not prime matter, but matter endowed with further completive properties as explained by Porphyry),[27] or an indivisible but composite essence involving both matter and form.

(ii) Can events, states, or persons return to existence?

Another context for discussing the persistence of individuals over time was the next life. But this involves a new issue: returning to existence after a temporal gap. So we must first consider something whose relevance has been shown in work in preparation by Eric Lewis, Aristotle's discussion (*Phys.* 5.4, 227b27–228b7) of whether events (*kinêseis, alloiôseis, energeiai*) or states (*hexeis, pathê*) can return to existence and be numerically one with the earlier event or state. As emphasized by Simplicius[28] and Themistius,[29] Aristotle does not allow this for events like walking (227b29–32, 228a15– 17, b1–7). Even though, as Simplicius says,[30] the same bed can be disassembled and reassembled, many times from the same material parts, the assemblies and disassemblies are not the same.

W. D. Ross (commentary *ad loc.*) believes that Aristotle does not allow it for states like health either. The question is whether, when somebody regains his health, the later health is numerically one with the former. Aristotle implies at 228a3ff that if events like walking ('changes') cannot return to existence numerically the same, which they cannot, then neither can anything else. For, he says, 'if it is possible for what has gone out of existence to come into existence again numerically one, this change too would be one change'. He further says, apparently confirming that states like health are to

---

26. Simplicius *in Cat.* 140,25–31.
27. Porphyry *ap. Simplicium in Cat.* 48,11–33
28. Simplicius *in Phys.* 886,23–26.
29. Themistius *in Phys.* 175,16–18.
30. Simplicius *in Phys.* 887,7–11.

be treated like walking, 'the principle is the same' (228a12). But although this surely applies to other states, there is a complication with the particular example of health. For Aristotle does not necessarily count the disappearance of health as a non-existence. At any rate, he speaks elsewhere[31] as if recovery of health depends on something or other in the body remaining healthy (*hupomenein hugies*). It is the action of that part that makes recovery seem enjoyable. This fits with Aristotle's insistence in *On Youth and Old Age* that vital heat lasts life-long.

Aristotle regards not only the time but also the subject engaging in an activity as important to its identity. But in *Physics* 3.3, he seems to give a different verdict about the latter. He offers the example of an act of teaching and corresponding act of learning, and in spite of their having two different persons as owners, he decides that they are numerically one activity and extends this to the activities of agents and patients quite generally.

Philoponus is presumably following Aristotle's view that states cannot return to existence after an interruption when he says that the fluidity in steam is a numerically different fluidity from that in the water from which it came; that the heat in a mustard plant is numerically different from the heat in the seed from which it grew, and that the light bouncing off a surface is numerically different from the light that hit that surface, although he allows that intellect lost in drunkenness is remembered and hence numerically the same as the intellect recovered after drunkenness.[32]

Aristotle[33] refers a number of times to the idea in Plato's *Symposium*[34] of things being constantly replaced. Plato applies this idea not only to people, but even to their states like knowledge, which he thinks has to be constantly replaced through rehearsal by new knowledge of the same thing. Aristotle uses the idea in a different way. People return to existence not as numerically the same individuals, but the same only in form. That is, people will come into being, but new ones. Aristotle allows[35] that celestial bodies remain numerically the same (despite Xenophanes' belief in a new sun every day), but recognizes no other exceptions in the physical world.

Aristotle *Phys.* 5.4, 227b29–32:

> For a change (*kinêsis*) to be one without qualification depends on all [three] of these factors: the respect in which [the change takes place], viz. its type, must

31. *EN* 7.14, 1154b17–19; cf. 1152b34–36; 1154b1–2; *Metaph.* 7.9, 1034a12–13, 21.
32. Philoponus *in GC* 65,22–66,9; *in DA* 334,21–25; intellect *in DA* 163,5–7.
33. Aristotle *GC* 2,11, 338b11–19, *On the Soul* 415b6–7, *Meteor.* 2.3,357b26–358a3.
34. Plato *Symposium* 207C9–208B6.
35. Aristotle *GC* 2.11.

be one and indivisible. The when, viz. the time, must be one and not interrupted. And the thing in motion must be one, not accidentally.

Aristotle *Phys.* 5.4, 228a3–19:

If Socrates undergoes a change of quality that is the same in kind, but now at
one time, now at another, then if it is possible for what has gone out of existence to come into existence again numerically one [with what went before],
this change too would be one change. Otherwise it would be the same, but not
one change.

There is a puzzle similar to this, whether health is one in its being, and in
general whether states (*hexeis*) and phases (*pathê*) in bodies are. For the things
that have these qualities are evidently in change and flux. If, then, the health
of this morning and of now are one and the same, why, when somebody loses
and regains his health, would not the later health be numerically one with the
former?

The principle is the same, except that there is this much difference [be-
tween states and changes]. If [the states] are two, by this very fact the activities
[reading: *energeiai* and W. D. Ross's text] have to be two as regards their number, since an activity that is numerically one has to be the activity of something
that is numerically one. But if the state is one, perhaps it would not on that account be thought by anyone that the activity too has to be one, since when
someone stops walking, the walking no longer exists, but will do so when he
walks again. If, then, [the walking] were one and the same, then one and the
same thing would be able to perish and exist many times.

Aristotle *Phys.* 5.4, 228b1–7:

And that is why a change that is without qualification continuous and one must
be the same in type, must belong to one subject and must take place in one
time: in one time, so that immobility shall not intervene. For when the time is
interrupted, the thing has to be at rest, and where rest intervenes, there is not
one change but a plurality. Thus if a change is divided by rest, as it is if there is
an intervening time, it is not one, nor continuous.

(iii) The next life: Stoics

These two texts of Aristotle became relevant to the discussion of the next
life. The Stoics believed in the exact repetition of history after a conflagra-
tion an infinite number of times. Their Aristotelian opponent, Alexander of

Aphrodisias, objected that after an interruption we would not have numerically the same Socrates, even if the same matter was reassembled, for the interruption would prevent it from being the same individual form (*atomon eidos*),[36] the form, presumably, of Socrates. Alexander may here be following out the most natural interpretation of Aristotle's remarks on interrupted health and applying those remarks to the case of form, though not of matter.

Alexander *ap.* Philoponum *in GC* 314,9–22:

> But as Alexander says, one might raise an objection to Aristotle. If matter always remains the same, and the efficient cause is also always the same, what cause would prevent numerically the same things existing again from the same matter, through the same agencies over some enormous cycle of time? Some people say this happens in the rebirth of the world and the Great Year, in which the reinstatement of all the same things occurs. In that case, there would be rebirth and numerically identical return also for particulars whose essence is mortal.
>
> Against this it must be said that, even if it were granted that Socrates is born again, the Socrates who was born later would not be numerically one and the same as the one who was born first. For what is numerically one and the same thing cannot be intermittent. For it attains to being numerically one and the same not by being made of the same things, but by persisting (*diamenein*) as the same thing both earlier and later. That is why the sun is numerically the same, but Socrates, as Aristotle said [*GC* 338b16?] is not numerically the same, since the individual form (*atomon eidos*) does not remain, even if the matter does.

What the Stoics Zeno and Chrysippus are normally thought to have wanted is that in the next cycle of history, there would be numerically the same Socrates,[37] although his actions would be only qualitatively the same, not the same numerically, since events are supposed to be being *repeated*. Ricardo Salles has reinforced this point by highlighting the references to events occurring again (*palin*), and indeed many times (*pollakis*).[38] By con-

36. Alexander *ap.* Philoponum *in GC* 314,9–22.

37. Alexander *in An. Pr.* 180,33–36, 181,25–32; Tatian *To the Greeks* ch. 5.

38. Ricardo Salles, 'The individuation of times in orthodox Stoicism', in his ed., *Metaphysics, Soul, and Ethics: Themes from the Work of Richard Sorabji*, Oxford 2005, 95–115, referring to Alexander *Commentary On Prior Analytics* 180,33–36 ('again') and Nemesius *On the Nature of Man* 111,20–23 ('many times').

trast, Aristotle's discussion in *Physics* 5.4 would seem to make not only the actions, but also the form of Socrates, and hence Socrates himself, numerically distinct, as Alexander says. Is Alexander's objection fair to the Stoics? Tatian *To the Greeks* ch. 5 (= *SVF* 1.109):

> We must deprecate Zeno, who declares that by means of the conflagration the same men arise again engaged in the same [activities], I mean Anytus and Meletus in accusing, Busiris in killing foreigners, and Heracles again in his labors.

Alexander of Aphrodisias *in An. Pr.* 180,33–36, 181,25–31:

> [The Stoics] think that everything in the cosmos comes about again numerically the same after the conflagration, and so too the distinctively qualified individual (*idiôs poion*) exists and comes into existence in that cosmos the same as the earlier individual, as Chrysippus says in *On the Cosmos.* . . .
>
> And [the Stoics] say that differences (*parallagai*) arise between the later distinctively qualified individuals and the earlier ones only in respect of certain external accidents, differences that could arise in Dion without changing him while he is alive and remains the same. For he does not become someone else, if he first has freckles on his face and later has them no more. Such, they say, are the differences that arise as between the distinctively qualified individuals in one cosmos and another.

Alexander reveals (*loc. cit.*) that the Stoics thought in rather different terms, that the numerical identity of Socrates was secured (and secured despite minor accidental differences, for example in respect of freckles,[39] by the recurrence of Socrates' uniquely distinctive quality.

The exception for freckles is a little rash. If Cleopatra had had freckles, the consequences might have been 'amplified', so that Anthony did not fall in love with her, but instead defeated Octavian; the Roman Empire never started, and quite different people were born. Furthermore, if freckles can vary, it sounds as if the determinism in which the Stoics believed, according to which whatever happens has been inevitable all along, holds only within a cycle, not between cycles of the universe. But in that case, it seems an incredible coincidence that different cycles should be as alike as they expect. The concession about freckles might best be cancelled.

39. Alexander *loc. cit.;* Origen *Against Celsus* 5.20.

But would the distinctive quality need itself to be (like Alexander's individual form) numerically the same? Or would it suffice that it should be indistinguishable (*aparallaktos*) from Socrates' distinctive quality in the previous cycle of the universe? The distinctive quality of Socrates, for the Stoics, is something constantly replaced, the *pneuma*, i.e., the air and fire in Socrates, which is also described as a part 'not other' than Socrates, and, on an interpretation mentioned above, is Socrates' soul with its distinctive perspective. It would be reasonable for the Stoics to require that the *pneuma* should be 'disposed', to use their term, in exactly the same way each time. But to require that the distinctive quality can make Socrates numerically the same only by itself being numerically the same seems to threaten either a regress or a circle. A regress will start if it has to be numerically the same by itself possessing a distinctive quality of its own. A circle arises if it has to be numerically the same by belonging to an individual (Socrates) that is numerically the same. It is simpler to suppose that, contrary to Alexander, the Stoics think the mere indistinguishability (*aparallaktos*) of the distinctive quality is enough to secure the numerical sameness of Socrates, whether or not it also secures the numerical sameness of the distinctive quality itself. If it does for independent reasons secure the numerical sameness of the distinctive quality, this may help to confirm the idea that it secures the numerical sameness of Socrates.

For reasons of epistemology, some Stoics held that if A and B were indistinguishable, they were one (otherwise the Stoic sage would fail to tell them apart). But this doctrine is applied to individuals, not to their distinctive qualities. Moreover, some Stoics were pushed, perhaps by Alexander's objection that the individual form would not be the same, into allowing that it would not be Socrates in the next cycle, but only someone indistinguishable from Socrates (*aparallaktos*).[40] Evidently these Stoics did not argue that the indistinguishability of individuals entailed their oneness.

Yet other solutions were offered by some Stoics, probably under pressure from Aristotelians. It would be the same me in the next cycle. But would sameness of essence (*ousia*, in Simplicius' sense) be enough to make it *numerically* the same me? Or would the different location in time imply that there was a numerically different me in each cycle?[41] This variant threatens the kind of reduplication of *me* that philosophers from Locke to Parfit have sought to avoid. The *unshareability* of the distinctive quality pos-

40. Origen *Against Celsus* 4.68.
41. Simplicius *in Phys.* 886,12–16.

tulated by Porpyhry, and probably by the Stoics before him, would have avoided such reduplication *within* a world cycle.

Origen *Against Celsus* 4.68, 5.20:

Those of the Stoics who were embarrassed by the doctrine [of no differences] have said that a small and very restricted difference arises in the cycle as compared with the people in the previous cycle. . . .

But in an attempt somehow to cure the contradictions, the Stoics say—I don't know how—that everyone in the cycle will be indistinguishable (*aparallaktos*) from the people of previous cycles, so that it may be not Socrates who comes into existence again, but someone indistinguishable from Socrates, due to marry someone indistinguishable from Xanthippe, and to be accused by people indistinguishable from Anytus and Meletus. Somehow—I don't know how—the cosmos is always the same, and is not [merely] 'indistinguishable', but the things in it are not the same. They are 'indistinguishable'.

Simplicius *in Phys.* 886,12–16:

The Stoics say that the same I comes into existence in the recurrence. But unsurprisingly they ask whether the present and former I are numerically one through being the same in essence (*ousia*), or whether I differ because of the different location in time of different cosmogonies.

Porphyry gave a verdict like Alexander's, but using Stoic terminology, about soul vehicles. When a new vehicle is recruited at the next incarnation, the same individual one (*auta hekasta*) no longer exists and its distinctive quality does not persist (*diamenein*).[42]

Aristotle's pupil Eudemus[43] raised an objection against the theory of infinite repetition in its Pythagorean version that has to do not with selfhood but with time, so I will mention it only briefly here. On the Aristotelian definition of time as the number (or countable aspect) of events (*kinêseis*), the number, and hence the time, should be the same, so that there would not be a repetition after all. Actually, on the basis of Aristotle *Phys.* 5.4, Eudemus should have recognized that the events would be numerically different after an interruption, but there might be a case for saying that their number would be the same.

---

42. Porphyry *ap.* Proclum *in Tim.* 3.234.23–26.
43. Eudemus *ap.* Simplicium *in Phys.* 732,6–733,1.

One of the merits of the ancient Greek discussion so far is that it makes us consider separately, as we should, the numerical identity of individual persons, events, states, and times.

(iv) The next life: Christians

It was not only discussions with Stoics that were influenced by Aristotle's distinctions. Many Christian discussions focused on the resurrection of the body, rather than on the continuation of the soul, which tended to be taken for granted but not considered sufficient on its own. It was official Christian doctrine that we shall enjoy resurrection, and this was normally (not quite invariably) taken to mean resurrection of the *body*. Controversy among Christians about their belief in resurrection of the body had uncanny parallels with the controversy between Stoics and Aristotelians on eternal repetition, even though most Christians, unlike the pagans, tended to pay attention to matter rather than form. Many Christians thought that a resurrected person needed to have the same flesh, or some of the same flesh, as in this life. But very early on, Christians came to realize that there was a ghastly problem. We are part of a *food chain*, since our bodies will get eaten and our matter will eventually pass indirectly into other humans, so that there will not be enough flesh for all the humans in the chain to be resurrected. The 'food chain' objection was already known to Athenagoras in the late 2nd century.[44] He answers optimistically that human flesh is unnatural food that cannot be assimilated. Augustine in the early 5th century AD has a cannibalistic version of the food chain argument, repeated by Thomas Aquinas in the 13th century:[45] What if a cannibal eats you? Will there be enough matter for you both to be resurrected?

The original version of the food chain argument is found in the 3rd century AD in Origen.[46] I shall be relying on Methodius' reports of Origen. They have been suspected partly because Methodius is so hostile, and partly because he is taken to have misunderstood Origen, e.g., on the nature of *form*. But I shall be arguing that Methodius' representation of Origen, at least on the subject of form, is extremely revealing and sets Origen in the best possible light, much as Methodius would no doubt have preferred to discredit him. Here is Origen's statement of the problem.

44. Athenagoras *On the Resurrection* 4.1–8.5.
45. Augustine *City of God* 22.12 and 20; Thomas Aquinas *Summa Theologiae* suppl. Q2.80.
46. Origen *ap.* Methodium *de Resurrectione*, ed. Bonwetsch in *GCS*, 1.20,4.

Origen in Methodius *On the Resurrection* 1.20.4, in *GCS* ed. Bonwetsch, p. 243 = Epiphanius *Panarion Haer.* 64.12, *GCS* II ed. Holl, Dummer, p. 422:

> As food is assembled in our body, and changes what it is like, so our bodies are changed in carnivorous birds and beasts and become parts of their bodies and again they are eaten by men or other animals and are changed in their turn and become the bodies of men or other animals. When this happens over a long time, necessarily the same body will become part of different humans. Of which human, then, will it be the body in the resurrection?

Augustine[47] offers the solution to his cannibalistic version, that if a cannibal eats you, both can be resurrected, since the cannibal can be reconstituted out of matter that he shed at an earlier date. But would such scattered particles give us the continuity required to constitute the same body as before? I shall argue below that it would not.

Thomas Aquinas discusses the cannibal problem in three works.[48] The most important matter for one's resurrection is the seminal matter that came from one's parent's seeds.[49] So the cannibal problem may seem more serious, if we imagine a cannibal who dines only on embryos and so consumes the seminal matter of his victims. But this first difficulty can be solved by saying that all the seminal matter consumed by the cannibal would revert at the resurrection to the embryo victims, while the seminal matter which the cannibal needs is only that derived from his or her own parents. The bulk can be made up by matter acquired and shed at other times. However, Thomas makes the problem harder. In an ecstasy of conscientiousness, Thomas asks, what about the cannibal's child, whose seminal matter comes from embryo victims consumed by the parent? That too will be alright, because the victim embryos will have been constituted partly by nonseminal matter drawn from their mother's womb, and it is this nonseminal matter that can have turned into the seminal matter of the cannibal's child. Everyone should therefore be able to regain all of their seminal matter, and otherwise will need only to have their stature built up by matter that was at some time or other in their bodies.

47. Augustine *City of God* 22.20, lines 25–39, *CCL* 48.

48. Thomas Aquinas *Commentary on Peter Lombard's Sentences, Book 4*, 44.1.2, Qa4, args. 4 and 5, *Summa contra Gentiles* 4.81, and *Summa Theologiae* Suppl. Q 2.80, article 4, the last compiled by a disciple.

49. I am indebted to Ph. Lyndon Reynolds, *Food and the Body*, Leiden 1999, chs. 13–14.

Defending the requirement of persisting matter has proved difficult. So perhaps we should turn with relief to the very clever alternative solution that is ascribed to Origen himself back in the 3rd century. Resurrection bodies, on his view, will not be of flesh, but will be pneumatic, made of air and fire,[50] the continuity being provided, as in the Aristotelian tradition, by the bodies having the same form (*eidos*) as our earthly bodies.[51] Augustine, while sticking to the orthodox Christian view that the resurrection body will be of flesh, nonetheless reminds us of Origen's talk of *pneuma*, spirit, when he calls the resurrection matter a *spiritual* flesh.[52]

Same bodily form.   Origen in Methodius *On the Resurrection* 1.22.3, in *GCS* ed. Bonwetsch = Epiphanius *Panarion Haer.* 64.14, *GCS* II ed. Holl, Dummer, pp. 423 = Origen *Selecta in Psalmos* XI, pp. 384ff, ed. Lommatzsch:

> Yet Paul or Peter are always the same, and not only in respect of the soul whose substance in us neither flows nor ever receives any accretions. They are the same even if the nature of the body is subject to flow, thanks to the form (*eidos*) that characterizes the body being the same, so that the imprints that provide the bodily quality of Peter and Paul also remain the same. It is because of this quality that scars remain in our bodies from childhood and other uniquely distinctive features (*idiômata*), like freckles and anything further of that sort, [I mean] this bodily form with which Peter and Paul are informed is again draped round the soul in the resurrection, but changed for the better. I do not at all mean this substrate that has been assigned to the soul originally.

Origen in Methodius *On the Resurrection* 3.3.4−5, *GCS* ed. Bonwetsch, p. 391 = Photius *Bibliotheca* 234 (Methodius) 299ab, Budé vol. 5, ed. P. Henry, p. 101:

> Origen, then, wants not that the same flesh should be resurrected for the soul, but that such and such a shape of each, conforming to the form (*eidos*) that now characterizes the flesh, should be imprinted in a different pneumatic body and resurrected, so that each person may again appear the same in shape, and this is the promised resurrection. For he says that the material body is subject to flux and never remains the same in itself, but departs and arrives in connection with the form (*eidos*) that characterizes the shape. It is the form

50. Methodius *Res.* 2.30.8, 3.18.1.
51. Ibid. 1.22.3−5, 3.3.4−5, 3.7.1.
52. Augustine *City of God* 13,22−23.

by which the shape is governed. Thus the resurrection must be in respect of form only.

Pneumatic vehicle.   Origen in Methodius *On the Resurrection* 2.30.8, *GCS* ed. Bonwetsch, p. 388 = Photius *Bibliotheca* 234 (Methodius) 299a, Budé vol. 5, ed. P. Henry, p. 100:

> Any mixture consisting of pure air and pure fire is of the same substance as the angels and cannot have the quality of earth and water since it would then come about that it was earthy. Origen imagined that the human body that is going to be resurrected was of such a kind and of such materials, and he even called it a pneumatic body.

Origen in Methodius *On the Resurrection* 3.18.1, *GCS* ed. Bonwetsch, pp. 414–15 = Photius *Bibliotheca* 234 (Methodius) 300b–301a, Budé vol. 5, ed. P. Henry, p. 105:

> Having expounded the view that, after its departure from here, the soul has a vehicle (*okhêma*) different from but of the same form as (*homoeides*) this perceptible one, he represents the soul as incorporeal by a Platonic rationale. Thus, in the light of his saying that after its departure from the world it needs a vehicle and vestments, as not being able to persist naked, how could it fail to be incorporeal in itself?

Origen speaks of a new body also in *Against Celsus* 7.32, but 4.57 speaks as if it is only the qualities that change. If Origen is taking a leaf from Aristotle, his opponent, the bishop Methodius, is in a way even more Aristotelian. He objects[53] that it cannot be the original (*auto to prôton*) form, given that the original body is replaced by a different one. Aristotle would agree that no state will be the same after a temporal interruption. Alexander, we have seen, says this against the Stoics as regards the person's individual form. Philoponus could be expected to agree as regards the bodily form, at least if the replacement occurs all at once (*athroon, in GC* 106,8), or if he agrees with Aristotle. Yet Philoponus himself takes the same view as Origen that humans are given a new body in the resurrection.[54]

53. Methodius *Res.* 3.6.7.
54. Timotheus of Constantinople *de Receptione Haereticorum* PG 86, 44A; 61C; Nicephorus Callistus *Ecclesia Historia* bk. 18, ch. 47, PG 147, 424D; Paul of Antioch in J.-B. Chabot, 'Documenta ad origines monophysitarum illustrandas', *Corpus Scriptorum Christianorum*

The best answer for Origen and Philoponus might be, in parallel with something said about the Stoics above, that numerical sameness of person does not require numerically the same bodily form, but at most a uniquely similar bodily form. To require numerical sameness of bodily form would be to threaten a regress or circle. We shall next see that even total similarity of form is not required, since accidental blemishes will be removed.

Origen might seem to face some special problems of his own. How can the bodily form be qualitatively the same if the matter is not flesh but *pneuma* and if, as he says,[55] the bodily form is 'changed for the better', so that scars and freckles are removed? The first query is even suggested by Aristotle himself when he says that a soul cannot be inserted in a body of any type.[56] But it can be replied that the pneumatic body will have been designed by God to suit the future life of the human soul. Moreover, the scars and freckles simply echo the freckles that the Stoics allow to be added or subtracted in the next cycle, on the ground that they are accidental, not essential. And Origen knew he had Stoic backing, since he is one of the sources that reports the Stoic view on freckles.[57]

But there is one thing that Origen needs to retract if he is to preserve the idea that the bodily form is, in all essentials, qualitatively the same. He needs to drop his further suggestion[58] that we shall not have the same organs in the resurrection. Methodius points out that the shedding of organs contradicts the sameness of bodily form.[59] Unfortunately for Origen, it is very plausible that the same organs will not be needed, unless the next life is very like this one. But Thomas Aquinas could provide a solution for Origen, since he finds reasons for resurrected bodies to have even genitals, since they belong to the human form and manifest no longer used powers of the soul, and for them to have hair and nails, which are adornments.[60]

Orientalium (*C.S.C.O.*) 17, Paris 1908, 330 (103, Louvain 1933, 230); John of Ephesus, *Historiae Ecclesiasticae* Part III *C.S.C.O.* vol. 106, *Syriac Writers* 55, 2.51, p. 85,26–35; 3.17, p. 106,12–16; cf. 5.5, p. 194,3–14, English translation by Payne Smith; Philoponus frag. 32 in Syriac with French translation in A. van Roey, 'Un traité cononite contre Jean Philopon sur le résurrection', in *Hommage à Maurits Geerard*, Wetteren 1984', where all the fragments are collected.

55. Origen *ap.* Methodium *Res.* 1.22.3–5.

56. Aristotle *On the Soul* 1.3, 407b13–26.

57. Origen *Against Celsus* 5.20, translated above.

58. Origen recorded in Methodius *Res.* 1.7, 1.24; Jerome *Against John of Jerusalem* 25, *PL* 23.375.

59. Methodius *Res.* 3.7.1–7.

60. Thomas Aquinas *Commentary on Peter Lombard's Sentences, Book 4*, 44.1.2, Qa 1, *resp.* 1077a.

Methodius *de Resurrectione* 3.6.7, *GCS* ed. Bonwetsch pp. 397–8 = Photius *Bibliotheca* 234 (Methodius), 300b, Budé vol. 5, ed. P. Henry, p. 104:

But, he [Origen] says, 'yes, for [the soul] will be relocated in a pneumatic body'.

[Methodius]: But then it must be admitted that the original (*auto to prôton*) unique form (*eidos idiôs*) itself will not be resurrected, because its quality is changed (*sunalloiousthai*) together with the flesh and it perishes with (*sumphthinai*) the flesh. For even if it is remolded (*metaplattesthai*) into a pneumatic body, that is not the original unique substrate (*auto idiôs to prôton hupokeimenon*) [of the soul], but a certain likeness of it remolded into a tenuous body. But if neither the form nor the body is resurrected the same, but is different from the preceding one, since what is like is different from what is like it, it cannot be that original one in relation to which it was created.

Report of Origen in Methodius *de Resurrectione* 3.7.1–7 pp. 398.20–399,25, *GCS* ed. Bonwetsch, from German translation of the Old Slavonic ms., with some Greek quotations:

But even here [Origen] is eristical. For after declaring that the form is what is resurrected, when glorification accrues to it, [Origen] took back his words 'as the form (*eidos*) of Jesus, Moses, and Elijah was no different in the Resurrection from what it had been'; he forgot them, and like unreasoning people began to proclaim something else. For not wishing to understand 'Where there is wailing and gnashing of teeth' according to the actual words, he gave instead a formula contradicting the words, as follows. 'What need of teeth is there for those who are being punished? For they will not eat when situated in Gehenna and the Creator fashioned every part of the body for some purpose' and 'it is not possible that we should be resurrected with the same quality, possessed of legs and hands again and suchlike'.

He has said something thoroughly self-contradictory. For how is it not contradictory when he affirms that the persisting form will be resurrected, and further declares that the same imprint ('the same likeness') will not come about, while nevertheless no other form will come about than the identical imprint ('the likeness'), which shows each and every form that is in each and every individual. For he says that it is what shows the quality of the bodily parts in the character (*kharaktêr*) of the shape of each person that is form. Thus, if he hopes that the resurrection happens in the (essential) form one must be resurrected in possession of the form again, which means hands, feet, and other members, even if the body also comes to be changed into something subtle.

Origen says, 'as it is inappropriate to be resurrected in the same form, with feet and teeth and other members'. In that case, if there is absolutely no need there of hands, nor of feet, nor of other (sc. members), then the form is not resurrected. If, however, the form is resurrected, then everything must be resurrected that was in there first. For even if a spiritual body will be the body given to the soul, even so the spiritual body must be assimilated to the first body and must be given its shape, if the resurrection is only in respect of form.

At this point, some philosophers would switch to relying on *psychological* links, rather than bodily links, to secure sameness of person in the next life. But in general Christians preferred a bodily link, and psychological links would be tricky if life beyond death involves a radically different psychology as it does, for example, for Augustine, if his *Confessions* 12–13 intends to describe the saints in the heaven of heaven as shedding all memory and expectation because rapt in contemplation of God. Origen also stressed that in the next life there will be no expectations arising from past marriage.[61]

Origen has been defended by H. Crouzel by saying that the bodily form (*eidos*) that Origen postulates is not, as Methodius takes it, the perceptible form and structure of the body (I have called it a self-preserving structure). Crouzel is right insofar as he recognizes that Origen does not mean by 'form of the body' what Aristotle means when he says that the soul is the (intelligible) form of the body.[62] The soul, for Aristotle, is the set of life-manifesting capacities without which the organic body is not its true self, and since these capacities do not distinguish one member of a species from another, Origen's bodily form must be something different. But Crouzel's difficult suggestion is that Origen's idea of bodily form is based on a strange mixture of Platonic Form, Stoic creative seminal *logos*, and also (though this sounds scarcely compatible) material substance. I feel rather uncertain how such a thing would individuate people. But, more important, Crouzel has overlooked the passage of Aristotle from which we started, *On Generation and Corruption* 1.5, and its extraordinarily close parallel to the account of bodily form supplied by Origen's spokesman in Methodius 1.25.4–7. Just as Aristotle's bodily form is compared to a tube (*aulos*), so Origen's is com-

---

61. Origen *Commentary on Matthew* 22, 23–33, *GCS* ed. Benz and Klostermann, pp. 669–72.

62. Aristotle *On the Soul* 2.1–2. See H. Crouzel, "Les critiques addressées par Méthode et ses contemporains à la doctrine origénienne du corps ressuscité", *Gregorianum* 53, 1972, 679–716. The idea that human bodies are distinguished by their form, in the different sense of soul, though foreign to Origen's discussion, is applied by Thomas Aquinas to the difference between a saint's living body and corpse (*Summa Theologiae* 3. q.25, a.6, ad 3).

pared to a wineskin (*derma, askos*), and both are said to change shape according to the volume of liquid passing through them. Moreover, Origen is represented as repeating the point we found in Aristotle that matter coming in from food avoids collision with what receives it, because what receives it is not matter, but form. It does not seem likely that Methodius invented this ascription to Origen. It revealingly credits Origen with accurate knowledge of a less well-known passage of Aristotle and with putting the passage to use in the most effective possible way, a representation that someone as hostile as Methodius would hardly have chosen to invent, since it does Origen so much credit. Methodius may certainly have failed to realize how revealing he was being.

Origen in Methodius *On the Resurrection* 1.24.5–7:

You must before now have seen how the skin of an animal (*derma zôiou*), or something like it, filled with water, always displays the same form (*eidos*), if it is gradually filled as it gradually empties. For what is inside must take its shape in relation to the state of what surrounds. Thus when the water flows out underneath, if someone adds as much as pours out, and does not allow the skin (*askos*) to be emptied of water all at once, <see> if it is not necessary that what is added looks like the original [water], because the surrounding in relation to which the water flows in and out is the same.

Someone who wants to compare the body to this will not be embarrassed. For it is in the same way that what is introduced from the food in place of the flesh that has been extruded below gets changed into the shape (*skhêma*) of the surrounding form (*eidos*). As much as is distributed to the eyes resembles the eyes, as much as to the face resembles the face, as much as to the other parts resembles them. In this way, each person appears the same, and it is not the flesh, the original substrate, that is in the same place [as what comes from the food]. Rather, the form by which what enters is informed [is in the same place].

So if we are not the same in body even over a few days, but rather in our form, which is in the body, for only form has remained clear of replacement, all the more we shall not be the same in respect of the same flesh at that time [of the resurrection] but in respect of the form that even now is always preserved and stable in us. For the skin in the comparison is the form, and the water is what is added and removed. Just as now the body is not the same, but the character (*kharaktêr*) in respect of the same structure (*morphê*) is preserved the same, so at that time the body will not be the same, but the form will have grown into something more glorious and will be displayed no longer in a perishable, but in an impassible body of pneuma.

So far, we have seen the Aristotelian idea that sameness of (bodily or personal) form is required for persistence used by Aristotle, Alexander, and Origen, and something analogous to form used by the Stoics, while Aristotle, Alexander, and Methodius alike seem to take this as excluding interruptions of matter.

(v) The Platonist soul vehicle

The pagan Neoplatonists had an analogue of Origen's new resurrection body, namely the tenuous material that serves as a vehicle for the soul. A major difference is that their soul vehicle carries the soul in this life as well as after death, being infused through our fleshly bodies. It thereby provides more continuity for the soul than the Christian resurrection body, which is acquired only after an interruption. But some Christians accept the pagan vehicle.[63] Origen himself mentions the vehicle as a Platonist postulate,[64] but as reported by Methodius, he sees the resurrection body in the standard Christian way as acquired, unlike the Platonist vehicle, after an interruption.

(vi) Parfit on survival

We have seen Aristotle's distinctions reflected in discussions with Stoics and among Christians, but the story does not end there. Some of the foregoing ancient disputes are paralleled in modern discussions of individual survival, even though the modern ones are couched not in terms of theological possibilities, but of science or science fiction. Derek Parfit,[65] like Origen, makes us face the implications of surrendering bodily continuity. Origen's belief that he could be resurrected in a numerically different body is analogous[66] to Derek Parfit's belief that he could enjoy something as good as survival if he were 'teletransported'. We would probably make the verbal decision that the survivor was not me,[67] but this, it is said, wouldn't matter. The process of teletransportation, first introduced into the discussion by Robert Nozick,[68] would involve the present body being destroyed, while the informa-

---

63. Boethius *Consolation* 3.9 and Philoponus *in DA* 12 ff.

64. Origen *Against Celsus* 2.60.

65. Derek Parfit, *Reasons and Persons*, Oxford 1984, revised 1987.

66. After writing this, I learned that the next two analogies with Parfit, concerning teletransportation and brain transplant, have already been pointed out by Carolyn Bynum Walker, *Fragmentation and Redemption*, New York 1992, ch. 7.

67. Parfit, *Reasons and Persons*, 285–86.

68. Robert Nozick, *Philosophical Explanations*, Oxford 1981.

tion from it was electronically beamed in the manner of *Star Trek* ('Beam me up, Scottie'), so as to construct an exactly similar body and brain at a distance, say on the planet Mars.[69] This, on a very widespread view, would guarantee that the same psychological attributes would be preserved. Parfit, like Origen, discounts the need for bodily continuity, but for a different reason: he thinks personal identity unimportant, provided the right *psychological* connections are maintained. He also, like Hume,[70] discounts the idea we encountered in Philoponus that it matters whether the original body is replaced gradually or all at once.

Suppose one had to go to Mars, and the only choice allowed was whether to go by rocket, with all the attendant technological risks and loss of time, or whether to go by teletransportation. Suppose that the technology of teletransportation had become at least as reliable as that of rockets. Suppose also that the preservation of brain structure would guarantee the preservation of psychological attributes. Suppose also that we leave out of account, as Origen does in the present discussion, any idea of the same soul continuing. Everyone should consider the question: would it be safer to travel to Mars by rocket than to undergo a teletransportation whose end product, after the sudden replacement of matter, might be a different person? Those who are worried about its being a different person probably ought to transfer this feeling also to Origen's postulate of a 'new body' resurrection. Even though Origen's scenario involves the additional feature of an unfamiliar type of material constitution, this ought not to make his scenario more worrying, because it is intended to supply the positive advantage of a virtually indestructible body.

It might seem that those alarmed at the thought of teletransportation ought to be more comfortable with the different scenario, closer to the orthodox Christian view of resurrection, in which Parfit, following an idea first proposed by Sydney Shoemaker,[71] makes a person enjoy some kind of survival through his brain with his psychological characteristics being transplanted into a numerically different body, so that some of the same matter is preserved. The interest of most Church Fathers in preserving some of the same matter could make it important what burial practices were followed. Christians have often arranged to be buried whole, and Tertullian in the 3rd century AD rejects cremation (*On the Crown* 11). Some ancient Ro-

---

69. Parfit, *Reasons and Persons*, 199–320.

70. Ibid., appendix D, and Parfit, 'The unimportance of identity', in Henry Harris, ed., *Identity*, Oxford 1995, at 38–39; David Hume, *A Treatise of Human Nature* 1.4.6.

71. Sydney Shoemaker, *Self-Knowledge and Self-Identity*, Ithaca N.Y., 1963.

man Christians compromised and had themselves cremated except for the little finger. The preservation of the whole brain, which Parfit discusses, might seem more reassuring.

But the desire for some of the same matter tends to be due to the thought that the resulting bodily continuity would ensure that identically the same person was resurrected, and not an exactly similar replica. This reassurance about its being identically the same person seems to be lost if sameness of matter is secured not by preservation of a significant portion of the original body, but only by reassembling scattered particles from all over the universe. That robs us of the continuity supplied by our matter having traced a single path through space and time. In addition, the scattered particles seem to have little connection with me; they may have acquired as much connection with other people. Moreover, they would be sufficient, if God did not care about my unique identity, to reconstitute several replicas of me. So scattered matter seems to have lost any advantage as regards personal identity over Origen's alternative of a photographically similar body.

But what reason is there to treat Origen's resurrection with a new body as any more reassuring than Parfit's teletransportation? First, God is not going to be subject to technological failure. Second, he will not, if benevolent, and cannot, if he can act only benevolently, multiply us into several different new bodies, in the way that, as Parfit points out,[72] a human teletransporter could. Third, if we could get used to the idea that a very different type of body would be more useful to us in the new circumstances, we could begin to appreciate its invulnerability to damage. Fourth, some people may be afraid that the *physical* replication offered by teletransportation would not guarantee, as God could, the *psychological* replication.[73] Fifth, Origen believes in the same soul, as well as the same body, continuing. But neither he nor the heirs of Locke would consider this sufficient assurance. And in general, I think these points do not supply the chief reason why Origen's proposal has a different feel about it from teletransportation. Rather, the difference is one of emotional context. Teletransportation requires us deliberately to choose to have our healthy body destroyed, and so to risk moving to a worse situation. In the resurrection scenario, by contrast, we are envisaging a time when our body will have been destroyed anyhow, so that the worse situation has already occurred. Suppose we do feel unsure whether an appropriate psychological continuation in a new body would give a form of

---

72. Parfit, *Reasons and Persons*, 267.
73. I thank Pauliina Remes for this point.

'survival' to *us*, or only to someone *like* us. Suppose we also feel unsure whether this is a black-and-white question with a determinate answer. Nonetheless, the only chance of moving to a better situation might be Origen's style of resurrection with a new body. It has therefore become rational to prefer our chance of salvation, even if we are not sure about it, as I am not, in a way that it was not rational to court a risk of annihilation, if we were not sure about it.

Would it make a difference that, if mankind were resurrected, there would be a retrospective consensus about the people having previously lived together on earth? They would not worry about whether God had provided them with the same matter or only with the same bodily form. The trouble is that in the case of teletransportation too there would be a retrospective consensus that it was the original people who had been teletransported back to earth. But we should worry that this consensus might be due to the fact that the original people, with their hesitations and doubts, had been annihilated in the process of teletransportation and replaced by replicas for whom these doubts were no more than (apparent) memories. The retrospective consensus, though hard to resist, would not really settle the issue whether the 'returned' teletransportees were mere replicas. So retrospective consensus should not settle the issue either of whether those who believed themselves to have been resurrected were really the original people. More relevant would be the benevolent and infallible character of God as author of the resurrection, and this would be a matter of faith and trust.

Of course, for Christians who believe that we have a soul that will continue uninterrupted until the resurrection, the situation ought to be more reassuring. The need to preserve the original matter ought to be less, if the original soul is preserved. Origen's alternative of a photographic likeness ought then to be assessed for its compatibility with Scripture, rather than as something needed to preserve personal identity.

There is one more twist, which I shall explain in chapters four and fifteen. Parfit offers a series of reasons why after all we should be content with teletransportation as offering us something just about as good as, though different from, personal identity. If that argument is sound—though I shall argue it is not—we should be equally content with Origen's resurrection by form, not matter.

We have seen the same question recurring in three very different contexts: those of eternal recurrence, of resurrection, and of science fiction. In each case, we have had to ask whether the important thing is the same matter or the same form. Derek Parfit has argued that religion has been an impediment to progress at least in ethical theory, and his examples in the present metaphysical discussion have been carefully drawn from science fiction, not religion. But in this case at least, it seems to make no difference whether the context is physics, religion, or science fiction: the question of same matter or same form recurs equally in all three contexts. Ideas seem easier to resurrect than persons.

CHAPTER 4

Stoic fusion and modern fission: survival cannot depend on what happens to someone else

I shall next examine the principle that survival cannot depend merely on what happens to someone else, and how it was applied in Antiquity to imaginary cases of fusion and in modern times to imaginary cases of fission.

In the 3rd century BC, the Stoic Chrysippus discussed the individuation of persons and denied that two individuals with distinctive qualities, like the persons Dion and Theon, could occupy the same substance (*ousia*), i.e., matter. He did so in a treatise replying to 'the Growing Argument'. That argument maintains that a new person replaces the old every time growth occurs, just as the number 7 is replaced, if it grows to 8. I follow in important respects the very ingenious interpretation of David Sedley, but I suggest two variations, each of which serves a purpose. First, let us see the version of the Growing Argument pressed against the Stoics by the Platonists.

Plutarch *On Common Conceptions* 1083B–C:

> (i) All individual substances are in flux and motion, letting go parts of themselves and receiving others coming from elsewhere.

> (ii) The numbers and quantities to which they come or from which they go do not remain the same but become different, as the substance accepts a transformation with the said comings and goings.

> (iii) It is wrong that it has become prevalent through custom that these changes are called growth and diminution. It would be appropriate that they should instead be called creation and destruction (*phthorai*), because they oust a thing from its established character into a different one, whereas growth and diminution happen to a body that underlies [the change] and remains throughout it.

What Chrysippus offered in reply, I suggest, might be called the 'Shrinking Argument'. Suppose Theon was born with one foot missing. Suppose he then grows a foot. According to the Growing Argument, just translated, which insists on his destruction (*phthora;* Plutarch *On Common Conceptions* 1083B–C), he will perish and be replaced by a two-footed person — call him Dion. But then what if Dion's foot is amputated? The Growing Argument would expect that Theon would now come back into existence, just as 7 would return to existence, if 1 was subtracted from 8. But Chrysippus insists that Dion is still in existence. Sedley conjectures that this is because it is Dion who is hopping around saying, 'I have lost my foot'. Theon cannot be saying this, since he never had a foot. Now, we are told, Chrysippus uses the principle he established in advance, that there cannot be two people occupying the same substance, i.e., matter (*ousia*). So the Growing Argument is wrong, since it is Dion who is alive and Theon who is dead. Of course, according to the propounders of the Growing Argument, Theon had died already, when the leg grew, so it may sound confusing to say that he is dead (*diephtharthai,* perfect tense) when the leg is amputated. But what is meant, I suggest, is that after the amputation he cannot come back to life, as they supposed, but *remains* dead. This neatly matches Chrysippus' wording according to which Dion *remains* alive (*menein*). We should not translate the perfect tense as 'has died', as if Theon had hitherto remained alive. The Growing Argument treats 7 as having perished (*phthora*), not as remaining existent within 8. This is the first of my two variations on Sedley's classic interpretation, because I do not keep Theon alive within Dion, making them like a set of nested Russian dolls. Admittedly, Philo complains that Theon has been 'snatched away', but this reflects not Chrysippus' real position, but the perspective of the Growing Argument. For since the Growing Argument expected Theon to return to life, his remaining dead looks to them like a second death.

The advantage of this first variation is that Chrysippus' opponents would not have needed to agree with Chrysippus, if he had argued in the way suggested, accusing them of being committed from the start to the absurdity of Dion and Theon sharing the same matter simultaneously. On my interpretation, Chrysippus' opponents will only commit themselves to that absurdity if at the end of the argument they try to wriggle out of the conclusion that Theon remains dead by denying Chrysippus' ban on sharing matter, and trying to make Theon come back to life as a part of Dion. But then they will have been forced to bring this bizarre outcome on themselves as the final consequence of the argument in the text, and will not implausibly have made Theon a part of Dion from the beginning.

My second suggestion is relevant to persistence over time. It concerns the complaint made in the text against Chrysippus: how can Theon remain deprived of life (from the Growing Argument perspective, die a second death) solely because of the survival of someone *else*, Dion? Philo asks this in support of the Platonists who want it to be Theon who comes back to life. His point is that being dead cannot be a merely *relational* matter.

I conjecture, but this is *only* a conjecture, that the question may first have been raised by Chrysippus, who never wanted Theon to go out of existence in the first place. Chrysippus may have been complaining that it is the Academic defenders of the Growing Argument who, by making identity depend on size, make Theon a candidate for coming back to life. But an operation on Dion should never have been thought to make Theon a candidate, since coming to life is not a *relational* matter. Moreover, if Theon is a candidate, he will be a loser. There might, as remarked in chapter three, be a parallel criticism against the Stoics' own criterion of identity, the unique quality. The criticism would be that identity could be lost through someone else coming to share the previously unique quality, and the Stoics may have deliberately tried to avoid this by making their unique quality *unshareable*.

Chrysippus' argument is expounded as follows.

Philo *On the Eternity of the World* 48 (= *SVF* 2.397):

Chrysippus, the most distinguished among the Stoics, produces a portent of the following sort in his *On the Growing Argument*. First he establishes in advance (*prokataskeuazein*) that two distinctively qualified individuals cannot co-exist in the same substance (*ousia*, i.e., matter). Then he says, 'For the sake of argument, let one of them be conceived as having limbs intact, and the other as being without one foot. Let the intact one be called Dion and the maimed one Theon. Then let one of Dion's feet be cut off.'

When it is asked which of the two is dead, he says that Theon is the more appropriate one. This is the verdict of a paradox-monger rather than of someone speaking the truth. For how can Theon have been snatched away when he has had no part amputated, while Dion, who has had his foot cut off, is not dead (*oukhi diephthartai*)?

'It is inevitable', Chrysippus replies, 'for Dion, who has had his foot cut off, has retreated into the maimed matter (*ousia*) of Theon and two distinctively qualified individuals cannot exist in the same substrate (*hupokeimenon*). Therefore Dion must remain alive (*menein*) and Theon be dead (*diephtharthai*)'.

WILLIAMS ON NONRELATIVITY
AS A CRITERION OF IDENTITY

Philo's idea that one person's survival is not merely relative to the survival of another was raised by him, and perhaps by Chrysippus before him, in connection with a thought experiment about the *fusion* of two persons. It has been raised in modern times in connection with thought experiments about the *fission* of one person. The principle that survival is non-relative was revived by Bernard Williams. One of his requirements for identity is that whether a future person will be identical with me cannot depend on what happens to *other* people.[1] Nor, he adds, can it depend on something trivial. This principle has since been discussed by others in the context of imaginary examples in which one person, myself, is surgically split into two persons both exactly like my original self. My survival in the first resulting body ought not, if the principle is right, to depend on the success or failure of the subsequent operation performed on the *other* body, a success or failure that may depend on trivial accidents. Yet, as I shall explain more fully below, if the second operation does succeed in producing someone equally like my original self, the two resulting people could not both be identical with my original self, since they are not identical with each other. Because of this, on Williams' principle, I would not survive even the first operation, since if I did, my identity with my former self would depend on what happened to the *other* surgical patient.

This principle of not depending on what happens to the *other* has been questioned by Robert Nozick.[2] Taking a case of group identity, Nozick pointed out that whether a group of 3 refugees, meeting in Istanbul after the Vienna circle was disbanded, should be identified with the Vienna Circle could depend on what *others* were doing, e.g., on whether there were nine members of the original circle still meeting clandestinely in Vienna, after surviving attempts at extermination. If the splitting of persons became common, we might have to treat the identity of persons more like the identity of groups.

---

1. Bernard Williams, 'The self and the future', *Philosophical Review* 79, 1970, 161–80, repr. in his *Problems of the Self,* Cambridge 1973, 46–63, which uses the principle at 57. Parfit, *Reasons and Persons*, cites Williams' use at p. 267.

2. Robert Nozick, *Philosophical Explanations*, Oxford 1981, 32–33.

PARFIT ON SPLIT PERSONS AS SHOWING
THAT IDENTITY DOES NOT MATTER

Parfit does not accept Williams' principle as a criterion of identity,[3] but we shall see shortly that he uses it instead as a criterion of what matters. He points out that we may have opposing intuitions about what matters when we think about different imaginary examples. We tend to think it matters whether I, the very same person, continues to exist. But Parfit wants to argue that what matters is not sameness of person, but a certain psychological connectedness and continuity, which can be enjoyed in the absence of personal identity. Our prejudice that personal identity is what matters may seem to be reinforced by the thought experiment of teletransportation, mentioned in chapter three, which Parfit adapts from Nozick and discusses in a version called 'branch line'.[4] If a mere replica of me were created by electronic copying of my physical structure somewhere else in some different matter, while I, the very same person, continued to exist here, I would not feel for the replica the sort of special concern I feel for myself, even if the replica had the closest psychological connections with me, seeming to remember doing what I did, and seeking to carry out actions I planned. A sincere impostor would be just a serious nuisance. This might make it seem that identity, not mere psychological continuity, is what matters.

But in reply Parfit asks us to consider a person who splits into two.[5] Physical splitting was introduced earlier in one version by C. B. Martin and Graham Nerlich, and in the version involving a split brain by David Wiggins. Some of the main issues to emerge were already raised by Elizabeth Anscombe in connection with the real life case of a single human zygote splitting into two identical twins.[6]

Imagine (regardless of whether this will ever be technically possible, which I doubt) that, as I grow old, my brain is surgically removed and one half, carrying enough of my psychological characteristics, is rehoused in a young body. If the transplant takes, it might seem that I had survived with a

---

3. Parfit, *Reasons and Persons*, 266–67, 270.

4. Ibid., 200–201.

5. Ibid., 254–73.

6. C. B. Martin, 'Identity and exact similarity', and Graham Nerlich, 'Sameness, difference, and continuity', in *Analysis* 18, 1958, 83–87 and 144–49; David Wiggins, *Identity and Spatio-temporal Continuity*, Oxford 1967, 52 ff.; Elizabeth Anscombe, 'Were you a zygote?', *Royal Institute of Philosophy*, supp. vol. 1984, 111–15.

new lease of life. But now suppose that the other half of my brain is transplanted with equal success. The two resulting persons will not be identical with each other, and it is part of the logic of identity that they therefore cannot both be identical with my former self. Let us suppose too that neither is a better candidate for identity than the other. Suddenly, the second transplant appears to have brought it about that there is no one left identical with my former self, even though it appeared that there was such a person after the first transplant.

Parfit uses this thought experiment as one of two main arguments for the conclusion that personal identity is not what *matters*. For the reduplication would have robbed me of identity,[7] but, although there would be dismaying changes to my life resulting from there now being rival claimants to my rights[8], the loss of identity would not be felt in the same way as annihilation. In fact, Parfit urges, the split into two persons would be just about as good as ordinary survival,[9] i.e., identity,[10] thanks to the preservation of psychological links.

Is this right? As regards horror at the thought of annihilation, the pre-operative person would not be likely to feel it very strongly at the prospect of the first death of the two survivors, so is less closely involved with that death. But he or she might feel it just about as strongly as ever at the prospect of the second death.[11] So from this point of view, the person before the operation might think of the operation as if it postponed annihilation, despite the loss of identity. After the operation, either survivor would have vivid memories of, and feel loyalty to, the pre-operative person. But each would need to reflect that, because of the other survivor, he or she is not the same person as the pre-operative person, though he or she would have been, and so would have had a different and earlier origin, but for the existence of that other. So far the story does seem to retain, both prospectively and retrospectively, something, though not everything, of what we have in ordinary survival with personal identity. What about the preoperative person's interest in, concern for, and empathy with the two products of the split? This might be great for the two products in their earlier stages, though it would be harder to maintain in relation to them insofar as they were envis-

7. Parfit, *Reasons and Persons*, 255, 260–62.
8. Ibid., 264. The importance of this concession is strongly argued by Susan Wolf, 'Self-interest and interest in selves', *Ethics* 96, 1986, 704–20.
9. Parfit, *Reasons and Persons*, 261.
10. Ibid., 271.
11. I thank Ray Martin for the point.

aged as diverging from each other over time. And Nozick has pointed out that, if the split were to be into a hundred people, the problem of how to empathize would be exacerbated.[12] For empathy in many different directions would become increasingly impossible.

Parfit's claim that we have something just about as good as ordinary survival, i.e., identity, is so far, with qualifications, holding up moderately well for the case of a split into two. For we must admit that the person about to be split will attach much value to the two products of the split despite the absence of identity. But although this certainly shows something, I believe it shows less than Parfit maintains.

What it shows is that there is one element within the concept of identity to which we attach less importance, namely, that identity is a one-to-one relation between entities, and not a relation that can hold between one entity and many. That aspect of identity, despite its undoubted utility, is not an aspect whose prospective loss fills us with the horror associated with annihilation. That means that we can be resigned at the prospective loss of anyone identical with our former selves, provided that that loss is brought about only for this reason. But it does not follow that we ought to be equally resigned at the prospect of losing other aspects of identity. The original example of teletransportation is alarming in a way that the branch-line version is not, because it requires that my body shall be utterly destroyed at the moment when a psychological replica of me is created elsewhere. This removes, all at one go, any bodily continuity with the psychological replica and means that the mental states of the replica lack their normal causal basis in my brain, further severing their connection with me. The case of splitting is quite different, and so our different reaction to it is perfectly reasonable. If the splitting is brought about by transplanting the two halves of my brain, with attendant consciousness of my life, into different healthy bodies, after my body has become diseased, then at least as much physical continuity as possible is being preserved, and the two products of the split will each owe their consciousness to the usual cause: my brain, or half of it. If splitting took place naturally in a more amoeba-like way after a certain age, with the whole body as well as the brain gradually forming into two bodies and becoming detached, then there would be still more preservation of physical continuity and of normal causation of consciousness. Our greater readiness to accept splitting and branch-line teletransportation than ordinary teletransportation is thus entirely explicable. For the former allow us to retain

12. Robert Nozick, *Philosophical Explanations*, Oxford 1981, 64.

some of the reassuring features that we get from ordinary identity, even though identity itself has been lost through the loss of one aspect, the one-to-one relationship.

I do not intend by this argument to bestow on bodily continuity the indispensability I denied to one-one relationships. We would not mind bodily discontinuity, if it turned out that we all moved discontinuously like figures on a cinema screen, disappearing from one spot and reappearing a moment later at another microscopically further on. Rather, we would easily re-identify the same body and person. I have not objected either to the view that we can afford to have very limited bodily continuity, as would happen if it became possible to transplant the brain, with all psychological characteristics into a healthy body that was sufficiently similar to the ageing original body. A more poetic version of this idea is to be found in Thomas Mann's short story, *Transposed Heads*. I have further said in chapter three that once we had lost bodily continuity after the death of our bodies, the second best hope might be provided by Origen's style of resurrection, in which a discontinuous replica of myself is created by God. But it does not follow that I ought happily to accept for purposes of travel the gratuitous and permanent destruction of any body that could be called mine.

PARFIT ON NONRELATIVITY AS A CRITERION OF WHAT MATTERS

I turn now to Parfit's second attempt to question the value of personal *identity*, as against psychological linkage. He uses Bernard Williams' criterion of not depending on *another* as a criterion, not of identity, but of what *matters*. He argues that the psychological links that he favors, unlike personal identity, satisfy the criterion, taken as a criterion of what *matters*, thereby discrediting the importance of personal *identity* further.[13]

Ernest Sosa has replied[14] that exclusivity is often considered important, not trivial. We value exclusive rights to job, partner, and inheritance. Originality in academic discoveries would be another example. If we apply this to psychological continuity with a person at another time, it could very well matter, we can now see, whether it was exclusive. Furthermore, Sosa points

13. Parfit, *Reasons and Persons*, 266–71.
14. Ernest Sosa, 'Surviving matters', *Nous* 24, 1990, 297–322.

out, what seems trivial in isolation may cease to seem trivial in light of its consequences. How your parents spent a particular evening may seem trivial until it is realized that your conception depended on exactly how the evening was conducted. It will not be trivial to the pre-operative person whether he or she foresees two transplants or one, nor to the post-operative person whether his or her origin must be post-dated because of a second transplant.[15] This seems to me to answer Parfit's second argument for the unimportance of identity.

PARFIT'S OTHER REASONS FOR IDENTITY NOT MATTERING

Parfit has several further reasons for holding that identity does not matter. First, it will emerge in chapter fifteen that he cannot think the *identity* of the owner of psychological activities matters, since he thinks that talk of *ownership itself* is only a *façon de parler*.

Second, the difference between psychological continuity and identity seems minor if it is merely the ban on continuity holding between many persons and one.

Third, identity is not, as is often supposed, a determinate relation. Witness how the question of whether the same *club* still exists can fail to have a determinate answer.

Finally, in a later paper of 1995,[16] Parfit offers a further reason for denying the importance of identity, although the reason is, I believe, invalidated by the still later paper of 1999. Once the other facts are known, the question of whether personal identity holds is said to be 'in the belittling sense, merely verbal',[17] and it is so whether the correct answer to the question of identity is 'yes', 'no', or 'indeterminate'. Parfit infers[18] that being merely a

---

15. An initial impression of triviality is in any case retained by Parfit's account, Sosa points out, because it may be a trivial question just where he sets the threshold at which there is insufficient psychological connection between the pre-operative and the post-operative person, although this too could come to seem important, rather than trivial, in the light of its consequences.

16. Derek Parfit, 'The unimportance of identity', in Henry Harris, ed., *Identity*, Oxford 1995, 13–45.

17. Ibid., 24–25.

18. Ibid., 30–33.

question of what language to use, it cannot be important. But in his 1999 paper,[19] he acknowledges that the idea of there being an *owner* of acts and experiences goes beyond the other facts he was referring to (facts about a psychologically continuous embodied stream of consciousness). He still thinks the idea of ownership an unimportant addition, but he does not claim it is merely verbal.

TWO PEOPLE ALL ALONG?

I shall finish by mentioning, but only to set it to one side, an entirely different type of response to the split brain cases, which attempts to deny that the brain split would cause a loss of identity at all. On this view, championed in different ways by John Perry and David Lewis,[20] persons should be regarded as four-dimensional beings. They are thus never present as a whole. No more than a temporal part of them is present at a time, a feature that Aristotle ascribes only to processes such as the Olympic games, in which now the hurdles are present, now the javelin throwing.[21] In the thought experiment of a person splitting into two, the earlier temporal parts of the two persons will have overlapped, and it is claimed that there is a sense in which there are two people present over the whole period, even though their earlier temporal parts overlap. As to how there are two people over the period even before the transplants, there are different suggestions, and I shall not go into details. Lewis suggests a weak kind of identity holding between the two original persons. Perry appeals, among other things, to the ancient point that what can be said may vary according to the time of utterance. In the example offered just after Aristotle's time by Diodorus Cronus, if Helen of Troy had three husbands in succession, there is a time when we can say, 'she has had three husbands', but no time at which anyone can say, 'she now has three husbands'.[22] To translate Perry's proposal into these terms, after the split, it would be true to say, 'there were two persons all along', but before the split it would not be true to say, 'there are two persons now'.

19. Derek Parfit, 'Experiences, subjects, and conceptual schemes', *Philosophical Topics* 26, 1999, 217–70.

20. David Lewis, 'Survival and identity', expanded in his *Philosophical Papers*, vol. 1, from the earlier version in A. Rorty, ed., *The Identities of Persons*, Berkeley 1976, 17–40; John Perry, 'Can the self divide?' *Journal of Philosophy* 69, 1972, 463–88.

21. Aristotle *Phys.* 3.5.

22. Diodorus Cronus, reported by Sextus *Adversus Mathematicos* 10.91–92; 97–101.

I believe these elaborate revisions of our way of thinking are not needed, because a simple description for the split brain case is possible. I would prefer to substitute for identity in such a case not Parfit's something 'just about as good as identity or survival',[23] but an idea closer to the one that he offered in a preview article, which appeared in *Philosophical Review* in 1971. Parfit there speaks of a *survival* that admits of degrees and suggests that in a certain sense the thing that survives to a degree is *me*. Unlike the suggestions that Parfit considers and rejects[24], this proposal does not take it that either of the persons who exists after the split originally was, or was the same as, me. Rather, I (my present self) would survive to a degree *in* two people who are *not* identical with my present self. Parfit's formulation in the 1971 article is close to this,[25] when he talks of surviving *as*, rather than surviving *in*, the two later people.

I am less happy, for reasons to be given in chapter fifteen, with Parfit's talk of me surviving as two later *selves*. This no longer seems appropriate once we take on board his further wish, which I will discuss there, to be able to speak only of embodied streams of psycho-physical events. For I agree with the modification he offers in his article of 1999, that talk of streams does not after all, as he argued in the book, capture the idea of *selves*, since one cannot deduce from it the idea of experiences, acts, and bodies being *owned*.

Does bodily reduplication threaten the Christian belief in resurrection? Although in principle more than one body could be constituted with the same form as mine, or with some of my shed matter or seminal matter, God's goodness is commonly thought of as necessary in such a way that it is not possible that he would take the less benevolent course of creating several replicas.

23. Parfit, *Reasons and Persons*, 261, 271.

24. Ibid., 257–58.

25. Derek Parfit, 'Personal identity', *Philosophical Review* 80, 1971, 3–27, speaks of me surviving *as* two *later selves*, but since neither of them is considered to be me, I hope my formulation emphasizes this more.

CHAPTER 5

Memory: Locke's return to Epicureans and Stoics

John Locke has been called the father of the modern theory of personal identity, thanks to the second edition (1694) of *An Essay Concerning Human Understanding*, with its new chapter on identity. At that time, the Christian view prevailed, that personal identity depended partly on the persistence of an undetectable immaterial substance, the soul. In addition, in the resurrection, our bodies would be restored to us, although Locke drew attention to the view we have found in Origen, that we might then be given *new* bodies. Indeed, as Philoponus argues, St. Paul speaks of a new heaven and a new earth.[1]

Locke did not deny the Christian belief in an immaterial soul, but treated it as irrelevant to personal identity and the self. Instead, he focused on something more detectable than the soul, namely on psychological links as a criterion of personal identity. Certainly, from the point of view of modern English-speaking philosophers, this is an improvement, because sameness of soul is not an idea that many such philosophers find intelligible nowadays, unless at least it is reinterpreted in terms of a completely different sort. Among the psychological links stressed by Locke, the one most emphasized by him and most attended to nowadays was *memory*, a link he would have found playing an important role in his copies of the Epicurean, Lucretius. But I shall draw attention to two other links that are important to him and that give his ideas a connection with other ancient views and a different slant from many modern discussions of personal identity. One of these links was *appropriation,* which was an interest of the Stoics, and *con-*

---

1. Locke in the *Essay* of 1694, 2.27.15; and in *Letters to Stillingfleet*, 1696–98.

cern, which he could have found in both Lucretius and the Stoics. Locke's choice of these links went along with an interest in personal identity from moment to moment within life, as well as in personal identity after death. In a revealing book, Raymond Martin and John Barresi[2] have argued that Locke made possible a whole range of new inquiries about personal identity, which flourished in the 18th century, disappeared in the 19th, and were then revived or reinvented in a new wave late in the 20th century. Among the many inquiries made possible, Martin and Barresi give particular emphasis to thought experiments about one person undergoing 'fission' into two or more people, which have increasingly been a feature of modern discussions. It is true that these are entirely different from the reduplication questions recorded in chapter three about different mes in different cycles of the Stoic universe. But we saw in chapter four that an ancient thought experiment about *fusion* raised some of the same issues.

This picture of ideas disappearing and reappearing, in a modified form, in waves seems to me valuable, and I only want to add that the waves did not start with Locke. Rather, Martin and Barresi have given us a survey of the two most recent waves, taken from the last three centuries. Before asking more generally how far the Lockean revolution was re-opening the gates to the consideration of ancient issues, I should like to introduce some relevant ancient texts. The first three connect the self with memory in various ways. They are from the Epicurean philosopher Lucretius, the Platonist Plutarch of Chaeroneia, and the Christian Augustine. The first text is the one most likely to have influenced Locke, and it is discussed by Martin and Barresi. A final pair of texts introduces the Stoic idea of attachment to one's body.

EPICUREANS: MEMORY, CONCERN, AND PERSONAL IDENTITY

A major Epicurean is Lucretius, who expounded Epicureanism in Latin verse in the 1st century BC, 200 years after Epicurus. Lucretius tells us not to worry about punishment or suffering after death, because our atoms (also called seeds) will have been scattered, so that we will not be there to feel anything. Some people, Plutarch[3] at any rate, complained that that was just

---

2. Raymond Martin and John Barresi, *Naturalization of the Soul*, London 2000.
3. Plutarch *Epicurus Makes a Pleasant Life Impossible*, chs. 25–28, 1104A–1105C.

what he was afraid of, but Epicurus is usually seen as not addressing the fear of annihilation, only the fear of punishment after death.[4] About that Lucretius entertains a doubt: would not our atoms in the infinity of space and time eventually be reassembled in the same arrangement? For simplicity, let us assume that he is thinking of reassembly in full-grown adult form, although chance might produce other results too. Presumably, soul atoms are included in the reassembly, since it would be arbitrary to exclude them, as some interpreters do, and the inclusion of soul atoms in the reassembly is also what makes it plausible that the light of life would be restored.

On the face of it, Lucretius seems to endorse, not merely to raise, the idea that if by chance our atoms were reassembled in the same arrangement, it would be *us* (*nobis*) to whom the light of life would again be given (*On the Nature of Things* bk. 3, line 849). He repeats the reference to *us* when he says in the following lines (852–53) that we (*nobis qui ante fuimus*) could also have been so assembled in the past, although he seems to lose the thread at 861–63 by speaking as if in the future case it would not after all be the same person (*ipse quoque esse*). Nonetheless, he is clear at first about the future case, and his point about it is that any pain felt then would be of no concern to us, since the memory of what was ours would have been interrupted (*interrupta, vitai pausa*). It is the future painful *life*, not the preceding death, that Lucretius is here saying would be of no concern.[5] In other words, the suffering, though ours, would not be a suitable basis for concern. The idea that concern may come apart from identity in the opposite direction (concern without identity) has been argued in recent times by Derek Parfit.[6]

Although our atoms would be reassembled in the same arrangement, Lucretius envisages that we might have different experiences and might undergo punishment such as we did not endure in the present life. This would be possible even if as most interpreters think, but not all,[7] physical conditions determine fully for Epicureans what experiences will be felt. For there could be different atoms impinging from outside on the reassembly of our atoms, and within that same arrangement of atoms our soul atoms could be making different movements, less regular ones, for example.

4. As to whether he does address it, see chapter seventeen note 2 below.

5. James Warren suggests he is saying both: 'Lucretian palingenesis recycled', *Classical Quarterly* 51, 2001, 499–508.

6. Parfit, *Reasons and Persons*, Oxford 1984, corrected edition 1987.

7. David Sedley, 'Epicurus' refutation of determinism', in *Suzetesis, Studi sull' epicureismo greco e romano offerti a Marcello Gigante*, Naples 1983, 11–51.

What does Lucretius mean by saying that memory would have been 'interrupted'? He is not appealing to Aristotle's idea, encountered in chapter three, that any interruption prevents us from having numerically the same thing. He is talking about interruptions of memory in particular. But mere interruptions of memory are common, e.g., in sleep. Moreover, Lucretius can hardly deny that chance might supply us with apparent memories of our previous life, even though that would not follow from the arrangement of atoms being the same. What form, then, does the interruption take?

One point is that the apparent memories, though accurately fitting our past lives, would not be genuine memories, because,[8] first, they would not have been *caused* by our past experiences and, second, they would not have been *retained* ever since our past experiences in the way they are in sleep, so that our memory would be a *new* one, not the *original* one.[9] Third, such apparent memories would not be recognized by us as being of the previous life, but would seem, illusorily, to be of the recent past. On all three counts, they would not be genuine memories of our past lives, and, fourth, we would have no memory of the intervening gap since then either. But that leaves a problem, for why should the interruption of memory, in any of these ways, remove concern?

When Lucretius turns to the possibility of past assemblies of our atoms, the situation begins to look different. He does, at 859 (and earlier at 672–3), seem to acknowledge, as one has to, that we have *no* memory, not even an apparent one, of *past* assemblies of our atoms. Moreover, he seeks to explain this absence of memory by the lack of retention or causation in the interim, since he appeals at 860–1 to the atomic motions having been scattered. So perhaps he is assuming that the interruption of memory makes apparent memories unlikely in the future reassembly as well. Certainly, if there are not even apparent memories of the past assemblies, no concern is to be expected for those past assemblies, even if we are convinced on grounds of probability that there will have been such past assemblies, and are further convinced that they were us. For we do not feel concern about the pain or illness that we suffered during the unremembered part of our infancy. But why should the future case be the same? For if we foresee that future re-

8. For the next four points about memory I thank Peter Lautner, Alan Code, Nick Waghorn, and Bob Sharples.

9. Compare the point made in Plato's *Symposium* that, even within life, we are constantly having to refresh our knowledge, which is alleged to be a matter of replacing it, 207C–208B.

assemblies are probable, and if we are convinced that those future assemblies will be us (*nobis*), surely we should feel concern. The foreseen is typically an object of concern in a way that the forgotten is not.

This is a serious objection that makes a different solution necessary. And Lucretius may be offering one, for he makes another shift, when he considers past assemblies, as I have said. For at 861–63, he moves to the idea that, with memory interrupted and indeed missing, it will not be the very person (*ipse*) after all. In that case, he will move to a view closer to that of John Locke. He appears to take the same view earlier at 677–78, where he infers from our not remembering an earlier life that any past soul has perished and our present soul only now been created.[10] On this *alternative* view, the retention of memory is necessary for personal identity, which is not to say that memory must be actually exercised. Rather, the basis for its exercise must be retained. I think it is plausible that an assembly of the same atoms will not give us the same person, but to me it is plausible not because the memory has been interrupted, but because there has been an interruption in the continuity of the body far more extreme than the interruptions that in chapter four I argued can be accommodated without loss of personal identity.

Lucretius *On the Nature of Things* 3.843–64:

(843) And if the nature of the mind and power of the soul has sensation after it has been dragged away from our body, still this is nothing to us who are constructed and fitted together in a union from the joining and conjunction of body and soul.

(847) Again, if time reassembled our matter after our death and again restored it as it is arranged now, and the light of life was again given to us (*nobis*), even if that was done, it would still not be of any concern to us, when once the memory of what was ours (*repetentia nostri*) was interrupted (*interrupta*).

(852) Even now we are not at all concerned for our former selves (*nobis qui ante fuimus*). Already in this case distress does <not> afflict us at all about them. For when you look back at the whole past space of immeasurable time and at how diverse are the movements of matter, you could easily believe that these same seeds of which we are now composed have often before been placed in the same arrangement as now. But we cannot recapture that in our mind's

10. James Warren contests this interpretation, but I do not know how he takes the lines I have just referred to, 677–78, 861–63, since his quotations on pp. 505–6 stop just short of them. David Sedley has suggested to me that there might be a way of reinterpreting *ipse*, but I must leave this to him.

memory, for in between is cast a gap (*vitai pausa*) in life, and all the movements have wandered astray everywhere away from our senses.

(861) For if by chance it is going to be wretched and sad, the very person (*ipse*) must exist then at that time, in order that evil can befall him.

PLUTARCH ON MEMORY AND THE SELF

We have seen that Lucretius finishes up after all making personal identity depend on memory. There is another attempt in Antiquity to connect the self with personal memory that is more thoroughgoing than that of Lucretius, namely the attempt of Plutarch. I devote chapter nine to that attempt. The role of personal memory in accounts of the self was otherwise sparser than one might have expected. In Stoic eternal return, the people who come back in the next cycle of the universe have no memory of their lives in the previous cycle. Let us see what other connections with personal memory were made.

AUGUSTINE AND MEMORY

One philosopher who connects the self with personal memory is Augustine. But his *Confessions* offers two different views. On the one hand, he feels that the infancy he does not remember has nothing to do with him and is not part of his life.[11] On the other hand, in his account of the heaven of heavens, the community which includes angels and probably saints, in books 12 and 13 of the *Confessions*, the occupants have no memory of their previous life on earth because they are rapt in contemplation of God. The first of the two passages runs as follows:

> This [infancy] is a stage of my life, Lord, that I do not remember having lived, concerning which I rely on the testimony of others, and which I have conjectured that I lived on the basis of other infants. Although that is a very safe conjecture, it goes against the grain to count it as part of this present life of mine, which I am living in the present generation. For so far as concerns the shadows of my forgetting, it is on a par with the time I lived in my mother's womb. But if I was even conceived in iniquity and my mother nourished me in her womb

11. Augustine *Confessions* 1.7.12. I thank Gerard O'Daly for the reference.

in sins, where, I ask you, my God, where, Lord, where or when have I, your servant, been innocent? But, see, I am omitting that time. What do I now have to do with it, when I recall no traces of it?

PLATO AND MEMORY

It may seem that Plato should be added to the list of those who connect the self with memory. Does not Plato's Socrates in the *Phaedo* cite recollections from before birth as evidence that the true self is the soul that existed before the present body, and does he not in Plato's *Phaedrus* suggest that the type of person you are depends on the god you followed last time your soul was given a chance to view the Platonic Forms? [12] He does, but I believe that what is recollected is the Forms and the god and truths about them, not the experience of viewing or following them. Plato does not share the belief of his pupil Aristotle,[13] that when one remembers something, one also remembers that one experienced it before, or even remembers the experience. The slave who remembers geometrical truths in Plato's *Meno* is quite unaware of having encountered them before. Plato's *Meno* and *Phaedo* make it an *inference* that we must have encountered things before birth. Plato's *Phaedrus* (250A) is explicit that lovers fail to realize that they are attracted to the beloved because of their past experience of the Form of Beauty. So I think the self is not being connected with memory of one's own experience.

PLOTINUS AND THEMISTIUS: THE BEST SELF HAS TIMELESS THOUGHTS, NOT MEMORIES

Some thinkers actually resisted a connection between personal memory and the self. I have already referred to the lack of personal memory in Augustine's heaven of heavens and in Stoic eternal return. But in addition, according to the Neoplatonist Plotinus and to Themistius as an interpreter of Aristotle, our highest self would rise to the intelligible world and, for Plotinus, the soul that has come to be in the intelligible world will not remember that it engaged in philosophy or that it is Socrates. Indeed, since the intelligible world is timeless, memory is impossible there.[14] After Plotinus, Themistius

---

12. I thank Bana Bashour and Nick Pappas for putting the question.
13. Aristotle *On Memory* 1, 449b22–23.
14. Plotinus 4.4 [28] 1 (1–14); 4.4 [28] 2 (1–3); 4.4 [28] 5 (11–13).

commented on Aristotle's *On the Soul*, and, as is emphasized by Bob Todd in translating Themistius' commentary, he thinks that for Aristotle the true self is the intellect and that Aristotle denies memory to the imperishable part of our intellect, when he says in *On the Soul* 3.5, 430a23, 'we do not remember'.

It is in the intermediate realm of the heavens below the intelligible world that memory plays a role. Souls there can remember either the intelligible world,[15] or the earthly world.[16] The latter is how souls recognize each other.[17] Heracles is cited as an example of someone whose soul remembers earthly life, but who has no memory insofar as he is in the intelligible world. The reference to Heracles comes from Homer (*Odyssey* 11, 601–2), where Heracles' shade (*eidōlon*) turns out to be in Hades, while he himself (*autos*) is with the gods. Plutarch of Chaeroneia[18] and Plotinus both identify Heracles' shade with his soul. Heracles himself they identify respectively with intellect and with the more divine soul. Plotinus says it is the latter that makes us what we are (*kath' hēn hēmeis*), but the shade is us (*hēmas*).[19] It may sound odd to have the hero of so many physical labors elevated to the intelligible world, but Proclus says that this is because he had been purified,[20] and Plotinus explains that his practical life is what accounts for Homer ascribing to him a shade in Hades as well as locating him with the immortal gods.

Plotinus 4.3 [27] 32 (1–2); (11–18); (24–27); 4.4 [28] 1 (1–14):[21]

Q: What about memories of our friends, our children and our spouses? What about those of our country and all the things that it would not be absurd for a refined (*asteios*) citizen to remember? . . .

[11] For it could be the case that the superior soul is morally good, but that the other soul is by nature inferior and only kept under forcible control by the superior. The more urgently the soul rises, the more it will forget—unless of course its whole life on earth has been such that its memories are only of what is nobler. For on earth 'it is noble to detach oneself from human concerns' [Plato, *Phaedrus* 249C–D]; this must also be the case with its memories. So in this sense it would be right to call the good soul forgetful. . . .

15. Plotinus 4.4 [28] 3 (1–7); 4.4 [28] 5 (22–25).

16. Plotinus 4.4 [28] 5 (12–31); 4.4 [28] 3 (1–7); 4.3 [27] 32 (1–27).

17. Plotinus 4.4 [28] 5 (11–22); Proclus *Commentary on Plato's Republic* 2,165,22–26.

18. Plutarch *On the Face Appearing on the Orb of the Moon*, Moralia 944E–945B.

19. Plotinus 4.3 [27] 27 (1–8).

20. Proclus *Commentary on Plato's Republic* 1,119,23–120,15.

21. Translated by Barrie Fleet, in Richard Sorabji, *The Philosophy of the Commentators, 200–600 AD: A Sourcebook*, vol. 1, London and Ithaca N.Y. 2004.

[24] Heracles might tell of his brave deeds while in the heavens; but when he is taken to a holier place and arrives in the intelligible world he will consider them insignificant, triumphing over the other Heracles in the contests in which the wise compete. . . .

[4.4 [28] 1 (1)] Q: What then will it say? What will the soul remember when it arrives in the intelligible and transcendent world?

A: Well, it is consistent to say that it contemplates the contents of the world it is now in, and that its activity is concerning them; otherwise it could not be there.

Q: So will it remember nothing of the things on earth, for example that it thought philosophically, or even that when on earth it contemplated the upper world?

A: If it is not possible, when one apprehends anything in thought, to do anything other than think and contemplate it (the awareness of having thought is not included; one would say that this awareness, if it occurs, occurs later on and is part of a development), then it would not be possible for anyone who is purely in the intelligible world to have memories of what he had done on earth. And if all thought is timeless, as it seems to be, since the Beings of that world are in eternity, not time, then it would be impossible to have memories in that world, not only of events on earth but of anything at all.

Plotinus 4.4 [28] 5 (11–16); (22–26): [22]

So according to this account (*ek tou logou*) memory [sc. on the downward journey] seems to have its beginnings in the heavens, when the soul has already abandoned the *intelligible* world. So [sc. on the upward journey] when it has left the *sensible* world and come to rest in the heavens it would not be surprising if, assuming that it had memory of many of the things in this world as described, it also recognized many of the souls it knew. . . . [22] Q: But what is the situation when they descend from the intelligible world?

A: The answer is that they arouse their memory of the same things, but less powerfully than those other souls; they have other things to call to mind, and the passage of time causes them to forget much completely.

Q: But if they turn to the sensible world and here fall into the process of becoming, what will be the quality of their memories?

A: Well, they do not need to fall to the uttermost depths. For even if their movement has proceeded quite far, it is possible for it to halt; and nothing pre-

22. Translated by Barrie Fleet, ibid.

vents them, before they reach the furthermost regions of becoming, from beginning to shed their garments again.

Plotinus 4.4 [28] 3 (1–6): [23]

When the soul leaves the upper world, unable to tolerate this unity, it falls in love with itself, and seeking a new identity it leans forward, so to speak; it is at this point that it apparently begins to remember. One part of its memory, which is of the upper world, still prevents it from falling; its memories of the lower world carry it downwards, while its memories of the heaven keep it there. In general it is and becomes what it remembers.

Plotinus 4.4 [28] 2 (1–3): [24]

Q: How will [the person in the intelligible world] have memory of himself?

A: Well, he will not have any memory of himself, either that it is he (for example Socrates) that is contemplating, or that he is soul or Intellect.

Plotinus 4.3 [27] 27 (1–25): [25]

But to which soul [does memory belong?] The one we call the diviner soul, which makes us what we are (*kath' hên hêmeis*), or the other soul that is derived from the whole? Well, it must be stated that both have memories, individual in the one and shared in the other. When the two souls are united, all the memories are united; but when the souls are separated—provided they both survive—each remembers its own concerns longer and those of the other soul for a shorter time.

[7] At least the shade (*eidôlon*) of Heracles in Hades—and in my opinion this is the shade that we should consider to be us (*hêmas*)—remembers all that was achieved during his life, since it was first and foremost his life. But the other souls, even when they became composite souls, still had no more to talk about than the events of life on earth (and they themselves knew these) unless perhaps [they could talk about] something pertaining to justice. But it was not stated [by Homer] what Heracles—the one without the shade—said. So what would the other soul, isolated and alone, say? For the soul that tows anything at all [of this world] along with it in its wake could recount anything that the man did or experienced; but as time progresses after his death, other memories from former

23. Translated by Barrie Fleet, ibid.
24. Translated by Barrie Fleet, ibid.
25. Translated by Barrie Fleet, ibid.

lives will appear, so that the soul will disregard and reject some of its more recent memories. Becoming purer than body, it will recall even things that it does not remember from this life. If it emerges into another body it will recount the events of its past life—the memories that it has just rejected—as well as many from former lives. But with the passage of time it will forget forever many of the things that happened to it. But when it is alone, what will it remember?

Well, we should first consider to which power of the soul memory belongs.

So far it appears that there were not many antecedents in Antiquity for Locke's connection between personal memory and personal identity, apart from Lucretius, who will turn out to be closely relevant. But there is one other set of ideas, different from memory, that I think may have been relevant to Locke's account. For Locke's discussion of personal identity is not only about memory, but also about concern and appropriation.

STOIC ATTACHMENT TO ONE'S BODY

Lucretius discusses whether we should be concerned about the sufferings of a reassembled self. But also relevant to concern is the Stoic idea, explained in chapter two, that each person is attached (Latin in Seneca: *conciliari*) to his or her bodily parts, and to his or her current constitution. A common English paraphrase is that each person *appropriates* his or her body, and this is fitting because the Greek word *oikeiôsis* is connected with *oikos*, the household, and the verb *oikeioun* would literally mean accepting into the household, accepting as one's own. Locke, we shall see, talks both of appropriating and of reconciling. In the following texts, two Stoics, Chrysippus and Seneca, explain the idea of attachment. A further text on the subject by the Stoic Hierocles was translated in chapter two.

Plutarch *On Stoic Self-Contradictions* 1038B (= *SVF* 3.179):

How, then, does he [the Stoic Chrysippus] wear us out, by writing again in every book of physics and, by God, of ethics, that immediately from birth we are attached (*oikeiousthai*) to ourselves and our parts, and to our own offspring?

Seneca *Letters* 121, 15 and 16:

Each age has its own constitution (*constitutio*), different for the infant, boy, and old man. Everyone is attached (*conciliari*) to the constitution in which they find themselves. . . .

Different are the age of the infant, the boy, the adolescent, and the old man, but I (*ego*) am the same. Thus although each person's constitution (*constitutio*) is forever different, the attachment (*conciliatio*) to their own constitution is the same. For nature does not entrust (*commendare*) to me the boy, or the youth, or old man; it entrusts me (*me*). Therefore the infant is attached (*conciliari*) to that constitution of his that then belongs to the infant, not to the one that will belong to the youth.

JOHN LOCKE

I started the chapter with John Locke's discussion of when we have the same *self* and the same *person* at different times. I drew attention to his reluctance to allow these questions to turn on the presence or absence of something as undetectable as the same soul. Instead, he made it turn on ownership of various psychological links and above all on owning what he calls *consciousness.* He does not omit the idea of ownership, as we shall later see Parfit doing, but he does, like Parfit, stress the links. In 2.27.9 of his *Essay,* he tells us that a person is

> a thinking intelligent being that has reason and reflection and can consider itself as itself, the same thinking thing in different times and places.

This presumably covers future as well as past, but there is a stress on memory of the past, as when he adds that

> as far as this consciousness can be extended backwards to any past action or thought, so far reaches the identity of that *person:* it is the same *self* now as it was then.

Locke speaks of how far the consciousness *can* be extended into the past; he does not require that it should actually be extended. Perhaps the focus on memory of the past is connected with the fact that in 2.27.26 Locke regards 'person', though not 'self', as a forensic term, connected with reward and punishment to be meted out in the law courts for *past* actions. Locke's library included three copies of Lucretius, as James Warren has reminded us,[26] and he would have read the passage of Lucretius discussed

---

26. James Warren, 'Lucretian palingenesis recycled', *Classical Quarterly* 51, 2001, 499–508.

above in this chapter in which Lucretius considers whether the same people could exist as candidates for punishment after death, connecting the question in some way, as we saw, with memory. I shall come below to yet another source that has been suggested to me as a likely influence on Locke's interest in memory.

But Locke's focus cannot be exclusively on the past. In 2.27.26, he connects the interest in reward and punishment with a concern for happiness. Moreover, in 2.27.17–18, he speaks of the self as having concern for the body and its parts.

In 2.27.14, Locke says that if someone had the same soul as was once in Nestor or Thersites at the time of the Trojan War, he would not be the same person as either of them if he had no consciousness of their actions, but he would be the same person as Nestor if he had consciousness of any of Nestor's actions, whether or not he had the same soul. The unimportance of the soul to Locke's question may have been startling to his Christian contemporaries, but it would not have been startling to Lucretius or the ancient Stoics. Lucretius started the passage cited earlier in this chapter by saying at 3, 843–46 that sufferings after death, if any were possible for our soul, would have nothing to do with us, because we are not soul, but a compound of soul and body. Admittedly, if we are reassembled, we will need a soul, but Lucretius' stress is not on its being the same soul after the interruption, but on its being the same atoms in the same arrangement. The Stoic theory of eternal recurrence discussed in chapter three justified talk of the same people returning in the next cycle, even though they did not believe that their souls had been in continuous existence. Nor did they base the return of the same person on the return of the same soul. The same soul would indeed return along with the same person, but this would be guaranteed by the appearance in the next cycle of the universe of something different, namely, the person's unique quality. Locke's dismissal of the importance of soul for personal identity is a return to what the Epicureans and Stoics took for granted.

In the next paragraph (2.27.15), Locke moves to the alleged unimportance of same body. He considers the possibility that the same consciousness might be found in a new body, either in the resurrection, which he here envisages in the same way as in chapter three we found in Origen, or even in this world, if something fantastic happened, such as the consciousness of a prince entering the body of a cobbler. Presumably, the prince does not, as in the modern teletransportation sequel, have to have his body deliberately destroyed. According to Locke, the difference of body would only prevent it from being the same *man*, but the sameness of consciousness would make it the same *person*. That a difference of body would prevent one from having the same man is not the important point, although it is a point that Locke had already made in paragraph 6 in connection with the pagan theory of reincarnation in different bodies.

The point had already been made by Plotinus (*Enneads* 5. 7 [18] 1) that thanks to the fact of reincarnation, an individual soul will be no more the soul of Socrates than of Pythagoras. But Plotinus had made no attempt to introduce Locke's distinction of Socrates possibly being the same person, even though not the same man.

In 2.27.17–18, Locke moves on to the point that the self has concern for itself, and that includes concern for the body and its parts. Consciousness is still important, because the concern extends only as far as consciousness can be extended. Indeed, Locke makes a very startling claim about consciousness, that if a little finger was cut off, and consciousness then went along with the little finger rather than with the rest of the body, the little finger would be the same person and self. Yesterday the concern would have been for the rest of the body, but today, we may infer, it would be only for the little finger.

A connection between memory and concern was made in our passage from Lucretius, with which Locke was undoubtedly familiar. But his talk of concern for the body is also reminiscent of the Stoic theory of attachment to our bodies. Moreover, the reminiscences of Stoicism continue further, as we shall see.

Locke discusses not only concern *for* the body, but also in paragraphs 14 and 26 concern *in* past actions. And in treating the little finger in 17–18, he says that the finger that lacked consciousness of the former body would not attribute to itself, own, admit as its own, or have imputed to it, any of the actions of that body. The subject is resumed in 2.27.26, where the acknowledgment of past actions is again connected with consciousness, since it is said to be brought about *by* consciousness.[27] But here something new happens, for Locke uses some distinctively Stoic terms in describing the acknowledgment of past actions as one's own. His talk of our *reconciling* and *appropriating* certain past actions reminds us of the Stoic talk of *oikeiôsis*, which is often translated as 'appropriation' and of the Latin equivalent, *conciliatio*, which is used in Seneca's account of the theory of appropriation.[28] Where I spoke of attachment, the alternative translation 'appropriation' is

---

27. I thank Michael Sevel for the observation.
28. Seneca *Letters* 121, 15–16, translated above.

apt, because of the point made above that the etymological root of the Greek word *oikeiôsis* suggests belonging to the household, and *oikeioun* is to treat as belonging or to claim ownership. There is the difference that the Stoics were talking of appropriating bodily parts, not actions. In other words, they were discussing the subject of Locke's paragraphs 17–18, concern for the body. But Locke in those paragraphs combined the two subjects in one, concern for the body and acknowledgment of past actions.

Locke *Essay* 2.27.26:

> This personality extends itself beyond present existence to what is past only by consciousness, whereby it becomes concerned and accountable; owns and imputes to itself past actions. . . . Whatever past actions it cannot reconcile or appropriate to that present self by consciousness, it can be no more concerned in than if they had never been done.

The net result of Locke's theory seems to me to be that, like many of the Stoics, he seems to be allowing, whether he wants to or not, that one has a hand in creating one's self.[29] The idea that one partly creates one's own identity is endorsed also by Parfit.[30] For Locke, it is not a deliberate self-creation, as it is in the passage of Plutarch discussed below in chapter nine. It is more like the involuntary and natural appropriation of bodily parts that we find in Stoic theory, and Locke himself appeals to appropriation. For Locke the appropriation of bodily parts and of actions depends on how far our consciousness can extend. But this too, we would now think, allows an element of involuntary self-creation.

Self-creation through memory involves dangers that do not beset self-creation through conscious choice such as we shall see Epictetus advocating in chapter ten. For what past actions people can bring to consciousness may depend on how comfortable or uncomfortable it would be to bring to consciousness, as if one were remembering them, various past actions. No doubt, Locke did not intend to allow this. Rather it is a criticism of his theory that it does not seem to exclude a self-serving inability to remember discreditable actions, and ability to bring to consciousness creditable actions as if one were remembering them. This is a danger that also beset the ideas of Plutarch on creating an identity by memory. Locke cannot reply that he

29. I am grateful to Jim Hankinson for improving my formulation by opposing this interpretation.

30. Parfit, *Reasons and Persons*, 446.

means to be speaking only of remembering actions that really were mine. For on his theory, for them really to be mine is for them to be able to be brought to consciousness as if remembered. Nor can he say that for them to be really mine is for them to be genuinely remembered. For genuine memory *presupposes* the idea that the previous experience of them was really mine, and so cannot be used to explicate the idea of being really mine. Locke is rightly careful to avoid appealing to genuine memory and speaks of consciousness instead.

LEIBNIZ AND KANT

There will have been other influences on Locke, and Leibniz had already accepted Locke's view of memory as necessary for personal identity and concern and had given the famous example that it would not benefit you to be made king of China if it was on condition of losing your memory. This was in his *Discourse on Metaphysics* (34), which, as Bana Bashour has pointed out to me,[31] was published in 1686, before the first edition of Locke's *Essay* in 1689. But both here and later, in his reply to Locke in the *New Essays Concerning Human Understanding* bk. 2, sec. 12, 114–15, Leibniz held onto and defended the need for a continuing substance or soul.

Kant, however, was to support Locke against Leibniz on the dispensability of a continuing soul, although he drew a very different conclusion of his own. An outside observer of me can indeed not be sure whether I contain one continuing inner substance enjoying consciousness, or a series of substances, each communicating the previous consciousness to the next, as elastic balls communicate motion to each other. Of course my first-person experience, Kant says, does postulate a continuing substance, but this only shows that the idea of a continuing inner substance is a necessary condition of my thought, not that it is a reality. The conditions of thought are all that Kant attempts to specify.

Immanuel Kant *Critique of Pure Reason,* trans. Norman Kemp Smith, London 1929, A362–64, *Transcendental Dialectic* bk. 2, ch. 1, critique of third paralogism:

> Consequently, I refer each and all of my successive determinations to the numerically identical self. . . .

31. I thank her for the references.

In my own consciousness, therefore, identity of person is unfailingly met with. But if I view myself from the standpoint of another person (as object of his outer intuition), it is this outer observer who first represents *me in time*, for in the apperception *time* is represented, strictly speaking, only *in me*. Although he admits, therefore, the 'I', which accompanies, and indeed with complete identity, all representations at all times [A363] in *my* consciousness, he will draw no inference from this to the objective permanence of myself. For just as the time in which the observer sees me is not the time of my own but of his sensibility, so the identity which is necessarily bound up with my consciousness is not therefore bound up with his, that is, with the consciousness which contains the outer intuition of my subject.

The identity of the consciousness of myself at different times is therefore only a formal condition of my thoughts and their coherence, and in no way proves the numerical identity of my subject. Despite the logical identity of the 'I', such a change may have occurred in it as does not allow of the retention of its identity, and yet we may ascribe to it the same-sounding 'I', which in every different state, even in one involving change of the [thinking] subject, might still retain the thought of the preceding subject and so hand it over to the subsequent subject.

[Note] An elastic ball which impinges on another similar ball in a straight line communicates to the latter its whole motion, and therefore its whole state (that is, if we take account only of the positions in space). If, then, in analogy with such bodies, we postulate substances such that the one communicates to the other representations together with the consciousness of them, we can conceive a whole [A364] series of substances of which the first transmits its state together with its consciousness to the second, the second its own state with that of the preceding substance to the third, and this in turn the states of all the preceding substances together with its own consciousness and with their consciousness to another. The last substance would then be conscious of all the states of the previously changed substances, as being its own states, because they would have been transferred to it together with the consciousness of them. And yet it would not have been one and the same person in all these states. [End of note.]

[A364] Although the dictum of certain ancient schools, that everything in the world is *in a flux* and nothing is *permanent* and abiding, cannot be reconciled with the admission of substances, it is not refuted by the unity of self-consciousness. For we are unable from our own consciousness to determine, as souls, whether we are permanent or not. Since we reckon as belonging to our identical self only that of which we are conscious, we must necessarily judge that we are one and the same throughout the whole time of which we are conscious. We cannot, however, claim that this judgment would be valid from the standpoint of an outside observer. For since the only permanent appearance which we encounter in the soul is the representation 'I' that accompanies and connects them all, we are unable to prove that this 'I', a mere thought, may not be in the same state of flux as the other thoughts which, by means of it, are linked up with one another.

Kant's strictures against belief in a continuing soul are not directed against belief in the kind of continuing embodied self that I advocated in chapter one. My argument there even shared something with Kant's, in that it presented a continuing individual owner of consciousness only as something in terms of which we need to think, and did not present this as a proof of such a thing's existence. But it did, unlike Kant's argument, present it as shifting the onus of proof onto those who would deny such a continuing owner

I have been saying that Locke's treatment of the soul as not a central issue in personal identity constituted a radical break from the ideas of Christianity, but was partly a return to ideas more like those of the Stoics and Epicureans and that Leibniz denied, but Kant accepted, Locke's attitude.

PART III

Platonism: impersonal selves, bundles, and differentiation

CHAPTER 6

Is the true self individual
in the Platonist tradition from
Plato to Averroës?

For the Platonist tradition there is a problem, as briefly mentioned in chapter two, of whether the true self is individual. The problem starts with Plato's belief that the true self is the rational soul or the *intellect*. Many people tend to think of intellect as a less distinctively individual part of their psychology, although it may seem more distinctive to philosophers, whose profession is intellectual discussion. As regards soul, Plato himself speaks as if all soul is one, indivisible except amongst bodies (*Timaeus* 35A 1–6). And we shall see that Plotinus and Themistius think it even clearer that all intellect is one and indivisible.

PLATO

The problem about the intellect and its comparative lack of individuality already emerges, perhaps, in the *First Alcibiades,* if that is by Plato. At 133C 4–6, he makes the true self to be the intellect. But at 130B 3–5, if *auto to auto* means the true self, he contrasts the true self with the individual (*auto hekaston*). Admittedly, on another interpretation, *auto to auto* is taken to mean what it is for a thing to be itself.[1]

Plato *First Alcibiades* 130D3–5:

> [We passed over] what was said just now in some such way as this, that we should have first to consider the thing itself (*auto to auto*). As it is, instead of the 'itself', we have considered what each individual (*auto hekaston*) is.

1. Nicholas Denyer, ed., *Plato Alcibiades,* Cambridge 2001.

Plato *First Alcibiades* 133C4–6:

[Speaking of the place in the soul where its excellence, wisdom (*sophia*), comes to be, and around which there is knowing (*eidenai*) and understanding (*phronein*)] So this [part] of the soul looks like god, and whoever looks at this and recognizes all that is divine would recognize god and understanding (*phronêsis*) and thus also himself (*heauton*) most of all.

There are many passages in Plato that encourage the idea that the true self is reason. In the *Phaedo*, Plato treats the soul as rational and insists that this rational soul is the self, first by using the first person at 63B–C, but then more dramatically at the conclusion of the dialogue in 115C. There, when asked, 'how are we to bury you?', he replies, 'however you wish, provided you can catch me and I do not escape you'. He is reminding them of the whole purport of the dialogue, that he is the rational soul, not the body. After the *Phaedo*, from the *Republic* onward, Plato has a more complex view that there are irrational parts of the soul, which were sometimes called emotional, and then his view is that the true self is the rational *part* of the soul.[2] But the most influential passage is that in which he discusses the 'inner man' at *Republic* bk. 9, 589A6–B6. Plato here says that each human contains an inner human, a lion, and a many-headed beast. These correspond to reason or intellect, the aggressive part of the soul, and the appetitive part of the soul. It is because the reason is described as the man or human that Plato is taken to mean that reason is the true man or the true self. The influence of this passage has been found in St. Paul, Philo, and the Nag Hammadi Gnostics. It also influenced Plotinus and Porphyry.[3]

Plato *Republic* 9, 589A6–B6:

So one who says that justice pays would claim that we must do and say what results in the man within (*ho entos anthrôpos*) being the strongest [part] of the man, and in his taking care, like a farmer, of the many-headed creature, nurturing what is tame and domesticating it, preventing what is wild from growing, turning the lion's nature into an ally, and nurturing by caring for all the [parts] in common and making them friendly to each other and to himself.

2. Passages suggesting this include Plato *Republic* 4, 439E6–440A3; 10, 611B–612A; and *Timaeus* 69C.
3. See Theodor Heckel, *Der innere Mensch*, Tübingen 1993; Plotinus 1.1 [53] 7 (14–24); 1.1 [53] 10 (15); Porphyry *On Know Thyself ap.* Stobaeum 3,582,13–26 Hense, Fr. 275F Smith.

The introduction of emotional parts of the soul makes the soul more individualistic, but these parts are not found in disembodied souls except in the *Phaedrus*, which takes a more positive view of emotion. By contrast, the emotional parts are called 'mortal' in *Timaeus* 69C, and at *Republic* 10, 611B–612A the soul has parts only in the imperfect condition in which we see it now. Some of the problem of dividing the soul into parts is that the parts are represented as acting independently of each other, as if they were three selves. But Plato thinks that this is indeed a true danger, to be cured only by allowing the rational part to dominate.

ARISTOTLE

It is commonly thought that Plato's pupil, Aristotle, accepts his view, which he cites four times, that the true self is the intellect.[4] But, as mentioned in chapter two, he cites it always with qualifications. He presents the idea as received opinion (*endoxon*), and he qualifies it by saying that the true self is *especially* intellect. In fact, Aristotle cannot afford to agree entirely with Plato's view for a very simple reason. Unlike Plato he believes the soul perishes at death. Or at least I believe that his *On the Soul* 3.5 would have to have been much more explicit if it intended to say otherwise. So there will never come a time when humans can engage in a life of pure intellectual thinking. They will always need food, as he emphasizes in *Nicomachean Ethics* 10.8, 1178b33–35, and so must engage in social life, where the moral virtues have to be exercised and one cannot spend the whole time in intellectual thought.

Aristotle *EN* 10.8, 1178b33–35:

> But, being human, one will need provisions. For human nature is not self-sufficient for philosophizing, but there is need of bodily health, food, and other support.

It is interesting that in his earlier work, the *Protrepticus*, Aristotle refers to the myth that some humans after death may go to the Isles of the Blessed, as Socrates conjectures he will at *Phaedo* 115B–C. If this happened, Aristotle says, such humans would pass their time in pure intellectual thought. Even in this early work, Aristotle does not endorse the myth as a possibility.

---

4. Aristotle *Protrepticus* Frag. 12; *EN* 9.4, 1166a16–17; *EN* 9.8, 1168b34–1169a3; *EN* 10.7, 1178a2 and 7.

By the time he comes to write the *Nicomachean Ethics,* he has replaced the humans in the Isles of the Blessed with the gods. It is only the gods who in 10.8 could live the life of pure intellectual thought. The life of pure thought is not a possible life for humans. I take it that the preceding chapter, 10.7, re-hearses both sides of the case by way of a dialectical debate, but does not yet endorse either side. Aristotle reports as something that is '*thought*' (*doxeie*) Plato's view that the true self is the intellect, and adds an 'if' (*eiper*), 1178a2 and 7. He pits this against the rival view that such a life is suited only to the gods. Neither view is endorsed in 10.8, but rather the compromise that the closer the human approaches this life, the happier he or she will be.

In 10.8, 1178b8–23, it is only the gods of whom Aristotle denies that they can exercise the familiar virtues, since they don't have money, face death, have people to give to, or appetites to restrain. But he does not do what Plotinus and Porphyry were later to do, that is, to suggest that some humans too can rise to more and more spiritual levels of virtue. This view is found in Plotinus 1.2 [19], and Porphyry *Sentences* 32, which is virtually a commentary on the former, and is reflected in Porphyry's *Letter to* (his wife) *Marcella,* which reminds her that he did not marry her as a woman.

PLOTINUS

Plotinus, whom we regard as the founder of Neoplatonism, taught nearly 600 years after Aristotle. He is very sensitive to the problem that Plato had created. Although he is drawn to Plato's idea of reason or intellect as the true self, he fully appreciates the fear that in becoming one's true self one might thereby lose one's individuality.

Plotinus' view of the self might be summarized by saying that there are *multiple* selves, two or three, or an indefinite number. In explaining this mul-tiplicity, he sometimes speaks of the '*true man*' as against '*we*' as being the other of two.[5] Once he says that '*we*' is ambiguous. It may refer to just the rational element of the soul, Plato's 'man within' or to that plus Plato's 'beast within'.[6] Sometimes Plotinus says that there are three men in us, the higher ones illuminating the lower ones.[7] Again, he speaks of there being three el-ements of soul or powers of soul in us.[8] Moreover, '*we*' should be seen as the middle of three, that is as the rational element of the soul that engages in

5. Plotinus 1.1 [53] 7 (14–24); 1.1 [53] 11 (1–8).
6. Id. 1.1 [53] 10.
7. Id. 6.7 [38] 6 (10–19).
8. Id. 2.9 [33] 2 (4–12).

step-by-step reasoning.[9] And '*we*', whoever that is, can direct this middle downwards to our bodily interests or upwards towards our intellect,[10] where the intellect is higher than reason, since it no longer needs to engage in step-by-step reasoning but has already achieved understanding and so can rest in static contemplation of what it understands. Plotinus further says that we *are* the one of these three according to which we act.[11] Sometimes Plotinus speaks as if there is an indefinite number of higher and higher parts of oneself, and we should always follow the next highest daemon or guardian spirit above the level we have so far reached, because each soul contains many levels.[12] So far it is the step-by-step reasoning faculty that has been presented as the true self, perhaps because it is the most characteristically human. But Plotinus also says that one can see oneself as intellect, though he adds that one then sees oneself not as human but as other.[13]

E. R. Dodds has described Plotinus' conception of self in a vivid phrase as a 'fluctuating spotlight of consciousness'.[14] I would only qualify this fine description by saying that the self seems to be what is spotlit, rather than the spotlight. I do not, however, accept the further claim that has sometimes been made, that Plotinus invented the concept of a self for the first time.[15] He does not even invent the idea that the self is something that you yourself can shape rather than something that has just been given you by nature. Such an idea is already to be found before Plotinus in the Stoic Epictetus and the Middle-Platonist Plutarch. Moreover, it has recently been pointed out by David Sedley that the idea of having your personal *daemon* well ordered, by choosing the pursuit of truth instead of the appetites, is already said by Plato (*Timaeus* 90B–C) to give you a kind of immortality.[16]

Plotinus is torn also in an opposite direction, because in one way he thinks beings are better off if they are not individuated and separated from their source. Those who seek their own identity by forgetting their father finish up by losing their identity.

9. Id. 5.3 [49] 3 (34–39).
10. Id. 1.1 [53] 11 (1–8).
11. Id. 6.7 [38]6 (10–19); 6.4 [22] 15 (37).
12. Id. 3.4 [15] 3 (1–10; 18–22).
13. Id. 5.3 [49] 4 (8–13).
14. E. R. Dodds, comment on H. R. Schwyzer, in *Les Sources de Plotin*, Fondation Hardt, *Entretiens* 5, Geneva 1960, 385–86, and 'Tradition and personal achievement in the philosophy of Plotinus', *Journal of Roman Studies* 50, 1960, 1–7, at 6.
15. W. Himmerich, 'Platonische Tradition in didaktischer Reflexion: Plotin-Comenius-Scheler', *Parusia*, Festgabe für Johannes Hirschberger, Frankfurt 1965, 495.
16. David Sedley, 'Becoming like God in the *Timaeus* and Aristotle', in Tomas Calvo and Luc Brisson, eds., *Interpreting the Timaeus-Critias*, Sankt Augustin, 1997, 327–39.

Plotinus 5.1 [10] 1 (1–17):[17]

What is it, then, that has made souls forget their father, God, and be ignorant of themselves and him, even though they are apportioned (*moirai*) from there and wholly belong to him? The starting point of their evil was their arrogance (*tolma*), their birth, the beginning of their differentiation (*heterotês*), and their willing (*boulesthai*) to belong to themselves (*heautôn einai*). When they made their appearance here, reveling in this self-determination (*autexousion*) and en-joying this self-movement (*kineisthai par'hautôn*), going against the flow and having greatly distanced (*apostasis*) themselves, they lost sight of the fact that they came from that world. They are just like people snatched in childhood from their parents, who are unaware of themselves and their parents because of their lengthy upbringing away from them. So our souls no longer see either their father God or themselves (*heautas*); they disregard (*atiman*) themselves and regard everything else more highly than themselves through ignorance of their origin; they show admiration (*thaumazein*) and experience shock (*ekpla-gênai*), delight, addiction, so that they have divorced themselves as far as they are able, disregarding what they have abandoned (*apostrephesthai*). As a result their regard for all this and their disregard for themselves (*heautôn*) has be-come the cause of their utter ignorance of him [God].

Despite this preference for remaining merged with one's source, Ploti-nus also feels the attraction of retaining distinct identity. He is, for a start, very interested in the question what makes us distinct from each other. He says that our souls are distinct from each other independently of being housed in distinct bodies.[18] When we are embodied it is very easy to distin-guish our souls first by the fact that they are in different bodies. But even within a single body, Plotinus says, one of my hands can be unaware of the experience of another, so that the soul is not uniform even there.[19] Further-more you and I may be in different mental states, one of us enjoying mys-tical union, another engaging in discursive reasoning, while someone else is exercising desire.[20] One soul may be active and another inactive at the same time.[21] Again there are differences of function and of character be-

---

17. Translated partly by Barrie Fleet, partly by Richard Sorabji, in Sorabji, *The Philosophy of the Commentators, 200–600 AD: A Sourcebook*, vol. 3, London and Ithaca N.Y. 2004.

18. Plotinus 6.4 [22] 4 (37–39); cf. Porphyry *Sentences* 37, *init.*

19. Plotinus 4.9 [8] 1 (15); 4.9 [8] 2 (10, 29–34).

20. Id. 4.3 [27] 8 (11–18).

21. Id. 6.7 [38] 6 (23).

tween souls.[22] These differences in our souls may be due to different principles (*logoi*) that were ready and dominant in our parents when we were
conceived.[23]

It is harder to say what distinguishes us after death when some of us will
rise from the sensible world, not as far as the intelligible world, but as far as
the heavens, having shed our fleshy bodies. Others will descend down to the
heavens after visiting the intelligible world, and Plotinus speaks of arrival in
the heavens from both directions.

In the heavens, our souls will have tenuous bodies that are called vehicles, and these vehicles will have shapes. We shall be able to recognize
each other as distinctive individuals especially if the vehicles have distinctive shapes. But even if the vehicles are spherical, like the stars that served
as vehicles for our rational souls in Plato's *Timaeus* (41D–E), Plotinus says
we could still display our characters (*êthê*) and distinctive behavior (*idiotês
tôn tropôn*) through our vehicles. It would be even easier to recognize each
other as distinct individuals if we retained speech. Plotinus adds[24] that
vehicles are so much purer than earthly bodies that they do not conceal
thoughts, but souls can understand each other, as even on earth one can understand by the look in someone's eyes. Proclus agrees in his *Commentary on
Republic*[25] that souls can hear, see and converse through vehicles, but adds[26]
that they might also know each other incorporeally. Plotinus' discussion in
4.4 [28] 5 (11–22), already cited in chapter five, shows how interested he is
in our retaining our individuality.

Plotinus 4.4 [28] 5 (11–31):[27]

So according to this account, memory [sc. on the downward journey] seems to
have its beginnings in the heavens, when the soul has already abandoned the
intelligible world. So [sc. on the upward journey] when it has left the *sensible*
world and come to rest in the heavens it would not be surprising if, assuming
that it had memory of many of the things in this world as described, it also recognized many of the souls it knew; for they must clothe themselves in bodies
of similar configuration. Even if they changed the shapes of their bodies to
spheres, would they not recognize each other by their characters and the par-

22. Id. 4.9 [8] 1 (15–23); 4.9 [8] 2 (22–29).
23. Id. 5.7 [18] 2 (6, 11).
24. Id. 4.3 [27] 18 (13–22).
25. Proclus *Commentary on Republic* 2,166,16–21.
26. Ibid. 2,165,16–19.
27. Translated by Barrie Fleet, in Richard Sorabji, *The Philosophy of the Commentators,
200–600 AD: A Sourcebook*, vol. 1, London and Ithaca N.Y. 2004.

ticular nature of their behavior? This is not absurd. Although they may have put aside their accidental properties, there is nothing to prevent their characters from persisting. Also if they were able to converse (*dialegesthai*) they would recognize each other.

Q: [22] But what is the situation when they descend from the intelligible world?

A: The answer is that they arouse their memory of the same things, but less powerfully than those other souls; they have other things to call to mind, and the longer time causes them to forget much completely.

Q: [26] But if they turn to the sensible world and here fall into the process of becoming, what will be the quality of their memories?

A: Well, they do not need to fall to the uttermost depths. For even if their movement has proceeded quite far, it is possible for it to halt; and nothing prevents them, before they reach the furthermost regions of becoming, from beginning to shed their garments again.

But there is a harder problem as to what differentiates us if we rise, disembodied, as far as the intelligible world of Platonic Forms. Plotinus tells us in the passages cited above that there is no memory in the intelligible world, but one may remember it after leaving it. The point is repeated elsewhere that there is no memory within it and indeed there cannot be, because it is a world outside of time.[28] Nor is there in the intelligible world any speech.[29] Yet Plotinus is still very interested in saying that by shedding your lower concerns you do not lose yourself but even increase yourself (*seauton*).[30] The idea that it will be your self contrasts with the idea debated by Aristotle that you would become a god, not a human, if you engaged in a life of pure intellect.

How do we remain distinct from each other in the intelligible world? It does not help, I believe, that Plotinus seems to have accepted Forms of individual human souls. Although this seems recently to have become the consensus, it does not help, because Plotinus also believes in reincarnation. Socrates may be the reincarnation of Pythagoras. The form is the form of the individual soul that was once the soul of Pythagoras and later the soul of Socrates. Hence it does not distinguish Socrates from Pythagoras, as Plotinus himself is aware (5.7 [18] 1).

28. Plotinus 4.4 [28] 1 (1–14); 4.4 [28] 2 (1–3); 4.4 [28] 5 (11–13, 22–23).
29. Id. 4.3 [27] 18 (13–22).
30. Id. 6.5 [23] 12 (19–25).

This last point seems to me to raise a wider problem. We have seen that the reasoning soul is the most characteristic human self. We shall also see Plotinus anxious to say that some individuality is retained by souls, even when they shed everything bodily and contemplate the same world of intelligible Forms. So far, so good. But how does it fit with this that, as Plotinus says at 5.7 [18] 1 (1–11), Socrates might be the reincarnation of Pythagoras? Is Pythagoras in that case still a different individual from Socrates? If so, it is unclear how Pythagoras can be envisaged as continuing if the soul that was his own self has been borrowed by another individual. And if he does somehow continue, he might well complain that, after he has taken great trouble to elevate his soul to the intelligible world, the soul has been borrowed by a different individual, Socrates, and dragged in a different direction from the one he intended. Perhaps, however, consistency requires that Pythagoras should be the same individual as Socrates. After all, he must at any rate be the same soul, because that soul was once his very self and is now the self of Socrates. This view would be consistent, but I am not sure that Plotinus takes it, because he seems to say in the passage to be quoted that the soul of each individual contains the principles of all the individuals it will go through during its incarnations, as if there were many such individuals, not just the one individual corresponding to the one soul. In any case, if Plotinus wished to present Pythagoras as being the same individual as Socrates, more would need to be done to make it plausible that Pythagoras and Socrates even *could* be the same individual. I shall suggest in chapter seventeen that the Indian systems may have done more to show how this could be possible, but Plotinus has not.

Plotinus 5.7 [18] 1 (1–11):

Is there an Idea also of the individual (*kathekaston*)? If I and each one has an ascent to the intelligible [world], the principle of each one is there. If Socrates and the soul of Socrates exist always, there will be a Socrates-himself, according as the soul is individual there too, insofar as it is said to be there. But if it does not exist always, but what was Socrates becomes different souls at different times, for example Pythagoras or someone else, this individual is no longer there.

But if the soul of each one contains the rational principles of all the [individuals] that it will go through, they will all be there, since we say that every soul contains as many rational principles as the cosmos contains. If, then, the cosmos contains the rational principles not only of human, but also of the individual animals, so also will the soul.

The last suggestion, that every soul contains the principles of every individual, raises fresh problems about how souls are differentiated from each
other. But I shall confine myself to the initial problem created by the belief
in reincarnation.

A quite different method might be used in order to show how Plotinus
could preserve individuality for souls in the intelligible world. Thus although we have no memory when we are in the timeless intelligible world,
we can nonetheless, as already mentioned, remember intelligibles when we
descend again from that world.[31] If we can remember the intelligibles that
we have contemplated, would that not show that we must have been distinct
individuals in the intelligible world? No, it would not. For it would remain
to be shown that the intelligibles that we remember had been presented to us
as distinct individuals rather than having been presented to a merged unitary intellect. It might be said that if we remember different aspects of the intelligible world, we could infer, by using what modern philosophers call inference to the best explanation, that we must have been apprehending the
intelligible world as distinct individuals, since the best explanation would be
that we attended to different aspects of it. That would explain our different
memories. A principle of this kind is found in the later Neoplatonist Proclus
in his commentary on the *Timaeus*.[32] Proclus says that incorporeal and immaterial entities can be distinguished not directly but only by their effects.
The distinctive memories of the intelligible world might be viewed as effects
and so serve to distinguish our souls as they were in the intelligible world.

Plotinus' favorite and best-known solution, however, is a different one.
In two passages he suggests that our souls and in a third passage that our intellects might retain their distinctness in the way that theorems remain distinct in a mathematical science.[33] In 4.3 [27] 2, Plotinus insists that our souls
should not be viewed as part of a larger whole in any ordinary sense of
'part'. But our souls might be parts of the divine hypostasis soul, in the sense
of 'part' in which the theorem is part of a larger science. This is a special
sense of 'part', a sense that is compatible with saying that our souls also
derive from (*apo, ek*) the hypostasis soul (4.3 [27] 5 (16–19); 4.3 [27] 8 (2)).
Normally one does not think of a part as also deriving from the whole. But
this makes sense in the case of a theorem. A theorem derives from the mathematical system as a whole and yet is also part of that system. We should, I
suppose, not understand that there are literally any theorems in the intelli-

31. Id. 4.4 [28] 3 (1–6); 4.4 [28] 5 (22–26).
32. Proclus *in Tim.* 1.431, lines 1–7; vol. 2, p. 253, 23–244, 8, Diehl.
33. Plotinus 4.3 [27] 2 (49–58); 4.9 [8] 5 (7–26); 6.2 [43] 20 (5–23).

gible world, because I have been convinced, contrary to a former suggestion of mine, that there are no propositions in the intelligible world and therefore nothing as complex as a theorem. What interests Plotinus about a theorem is that each theorem presupposes the rest of the mathematical system. In 4.9 [8] 5, Plotinus speaks of the geometer 'analyzing' a theorem. To analyze a proposition in Greek geometry was to unfold it so as to reveal the premisses from which it derives. These premisses were thought of as being included in the theorem. In that sense, a theorem contains all the higher premisses in the mathematical system. But it also contains theorems that come below it and all other propositions in the system, in that to understand a theorem fully as a theorem one would need to see its place in the entire system.

Plotinus makes another important point in 4.9 [8] 5. One theorem can be prominent (*protetaktai*) while others escape attention (*lanthanein*). This of course is only an analogy. The idea is that our souls could be united with universal soul and yet also be parts of it in the way that a theorem pre-supposes the whole of the science and yet can sometimes be given more prominence than the other theorems, which shows its distinctness.

Plotinus 4.3 [27] 2 (49–58):[34]

> Is it not then a part in the way that a scientific theorem is said to be a part of a particular science? The science is in no way diminished, and each division is a sort of expression (*prophora*) and actualization (*energeia*). In such a case each part potentially contains the whole science, which is thereby nonetheless a whole. To apply this analogy to the soul as whole and parts: the whole whose parts are of this kind would not be the soul of something, but soul pure and simple; so it would not be the soul of the universe, but that too will be one of the partial souls. Therefore all souls are parts of a single soul and are uniform.

Plotinus 4.9 [8] 5 (7–26):

> Knowledge is a whole, and its parts are such that the whole persists and the parts are derived from it. The seed too is a whole and the parts into which it naturally divides are derived from it; each part is a whole, and the whole per-sists as an undiminished whole which the matter divides—all the parts com-prise a unity.

---

34. The three Plotinus passages comparing a theorem are translated by Barrie Fleet, in Richard Sorabji, *The Philosophy of the Commentators, 200–600 AD: A Sourcebook*, vol. 3, London and Ithaca N.Y. 2004. I owe the point about "analyzing" to Michael Frede and Paul Kalligas.

[12] But you might claim that in the case of knowledge the part is not a whole.

The answer is that in this case the part needed is being dealt with in actuality and is given prominence (*protetaktai*), but the other parts are in attendance, lurking (*lanthanein*) in potentiality; all are present in the one. Perhaps it is in this sense that 'whole' and 'part' are being used here. In the former case all the parts are together in actuality, so to speak, so that each part that you wish to deal with is accessible; the accessibility is in the part but it is given its potency by its sort of closeness to the whole. But we should not think that it is separate from the other propositions; if it were, it would no longer be to do with art or knowledge, but mere childish prattle. So if it is to do with knowlege, it will contain all the parts in potentiality. The scientist understands one part of his field and infers the rest by a sort of deduction. In his analysis (*analusis*) the geometrician demonstrates that the one proposition contains all the prior ones which he uses to conduct his analysis as well as the subsequent ones generated from it.

Plotinus 6.2 [43] 20 (4–23):

Each [science] is the potentiality of all of its parts, although it is itself none of them. But each part is itself in actuality and all the other parts in potentiality. This is true of science in general. The specific sciences lie within the whole in potentiality; they take in what is specific, and are the whole science in potentiality, since the whole, and not just part of the whole, is predicated of them. Yet the science itself must remain pure within itself. In just this way Intellect as a whole—the Intellect which is prior to the individual actualized intellects— is spoken of in one sense, and the individual intellects—the intellects that are partial and are brought to completion by the totality of things—in another; the Intellect which lies above all things supplies the individual intellects; it is their potentiality and embraces them in its universality, while they in turn, being partial within themselves, embrace (*ekhein*) the universal Intellect, just as a particular science embraces Science in general. Furthermore, the great Intellect exists *per se*, as do the partial intellects, which exist within themselves; and the partial intellects are included (*emperiekhesthai*) within the whole, and the whole within the partial; the partial intellects exist on their own and in another, and universal Intellect exists on its own and in them; all intellects exist within that one, which exists on its own in potentiality and is 'all things together' in actuality and each thing separately in potentiality; the partial intellects are what they are in actuality, and are the whole in potentiality.

AUGUSTINE

We have seen Plotinus wrestling with the problem that Plato bequeathed to him of how to combine the idea that our souls are all one with the idea that we remain distinct individuals. This problem was already created by Plato and was endemic in Platonism. We can see another famous Platonist, the Christian Augustine, just before 400 AD wrestling with the very same problem. It has been pointed out[35] that at first Augustine shared Plotinus' uncertainty, based on Plato (*Timaeus* 35A), whether there is just one soul or many souls. As regards our prospects after death, it was mentioned in chapter two that Augustine is torn in two directions. On the one hand, he thinks the best prospect might be a life rapt in contemplation of God without memory or expectation (*Confessions* bk. 9, ch. 10, and bks. 12–13) and without genetic ties (*On the True Religion* 46.88–89; *Confessions* 9.13). On the other hand, almost in the same breath, he expresses the close tie with his mother (*Confessions* 9.10) and hopes a dead friend will remember him (*Confessions* 9.3).

Augustine's repeated remark that 'we are all Adam' may sound as if it belongs on the impersonal side of this tension. But even if it was Plotinus who originally encouraged Augustine to think in this way, the saying is eventually cashed, as Rombs stresses (see note in previous paragraph) merely in terms of our being genetically related to Adam.

I want to show now how doubts in Platonism about permanent individuality continued until we reach the great 13th-century debate between Thomas Aquinas and Averroës. Thomas rejected the view of Averroës that there is only one intellect. Such a view was a threat to the Christian belief in individual immortality for the rational part of the human soul. But this debate did not spring out of nowhere in the 13th century.

COMMENTATORS ON ARISTOTLE

To understand the debate, we need to bring in Aristotle as well as Plato, because it was a question in the interpretation of Aristotle too whether there is a part of the human soul that is both immortal and individual. For Themistius, we shall see, the debate on whether Aristotle's intellect is individual is continuous with Plotinus' debate on whether the Platonist intellect

35. Ronnie Rombs, 'St. Augustine's inner self: the soul as "private" and "individuated"', in *Studia Patristica* forthcoming, referring to Augustine *On the Greatness of Soul* 32.69.

is individual. And after Themistius, many of the Neoplatonist interpreters wanted the views of Plato and Aristotle to be aligned. The crucial passage in Aristotle is his account of different types of intellect in *On the Soul* 3.5. From his talk there first of *poiêtikon* and *energeia*, second of *hulê, dunamei,* and *pathêtikos*, and third of *hexis*, the Aristotelian commentator, Alexander, whom Plotinus read, had introduced three intellects: first, material or potential, second, dispositional or acquired, and third, active or productive. The productive intellect is God, for Alexander,[36] and is not part of the human soul.[37] The dispositional intellect, on his view, contains stored concepts (*apokeimena noêmata*).[38] I shall italicize the words in Aristotle from which Alexander draws his distinction of three kinds of intellect.

Aristotle *On the Soul* 3.5, 430a10−25:[39]

Since, as in every [branch of] nature, there is something [which is] the *matter* (*hulê*) for each kind [of object] (and this is what is *potentially* (*dunamei*) each of these objects), and something else that is the cause and the *producer* (*poiêtikon*), by *producing* all things [of that kind], as, e.g., happens with the [relevant] art in relation to its *matter*, these distinctions must necessarily obtain too [in the soul]. And one [type of] intellect (*nous*) is such by becoming all things, and one by *producing* all things, as [being] a certain *dispositional state* (*hexis*), like light; for in a way light too makes *potentially* existing colors into *actually* (*energeiai*) [existing] colors. And this intellect is separable and not passively affectable (*apathês*) and unmixed, being *actuality* (*energeia*) in [its] essence (*ousia*). For that which *produces* is always more valuable than that which is *passively affected*, and the source (*arkhê*) [is more valuable than] the *matter*. And *actual* (*kat' energeian*) knowledge is identical with [its] object, while *potential* knowledge is prior [in time] in the individual, though in general it is not even [prior] in time. But [the active intellect] does not think (*noein*) at one time and not at another. And when it is separated, it is only what it really is, and this alone is immortal and eternal. But we do not remember, because this is not passively affectable, whereas the *passively affectable* intellect (*pathêtikos nous*) is perishable—and without this nothing thinks.

36. Alexander *On the Soul* 89,9−19.
37. Alexander? *Mantissa* 108, 22−23.
38. Alexander *On the Soul* 86,4−6.
39. Translation adapted from Alan Lacey, in Richard Sorabji, *The Philosophy of the Commentators, 200−600 AD: A Sourcebook*, vol. 1, *Psychology*, London and Ithaca N.Y. 2004, 3g1.

Alexander *On the Soul* 89,9–19:[40]

Moreover, if the intellect that is of this sort is the first cause, which is the cause and principle of being for all the rest, in this way too it will be productive (*poiētikos*), in that it is the cause of being for all the objects of thought. And intellect of this sort is separate and unaffected and unmixed with anything else; all these [properties] it has because it is separate from matter. For it is separate and exists on its own for this reason. None of the forms that are in matter is separable, or only in thought, because separation from matter is their destruction. It is also free from being affected, because what is affected in all things is the matter and what underlies. Being free from being affected and not mixed with any matter it is also imperishable, being actuality and form apart from potentiality and matter. Aristotle has shown that this is what the first cause is like, [the first cause] which is also intellect in the strict sense.

Alexander *On the Soul* 85,20–86,6:

The disposition (*hexis*) of this sort is produced in the intellect initially by a transition from the continuous activity over sense objects, with the intellect taking from the sense objects a sort of theoretical vision, as it were, of the universal. At first, the universal is called a thought (*noēma*) or concept (*ennoia*), but once it has grown and become complex and versatile, so that it can do this even without a leg up from perception, it is by that time intellect. For when through continuous activity it has acquired such a disposition as to be able thereafter to act through itself, then the intellect spoken of as a disposition comes into being. It is analogous to the knower who is between the so-called potential knower and the one who is active as regards knowledge, and who overtakes the potential knower as much as he is thought to fall short of the one who is active as regards knowledge. But when this disposition is active, it becomes the intellect in actuality (*kat' energeian*). For the dispositional intellect is in a way the thoughts (*noēmata*) that are stored (*apokeimena*), assembled and at rest.

Alexander *On the Soul* 84,19–21:

For intellect makes even sense objects thinkable for itself by separating them from matter and contemplating what constitutes their being.

40. Translated by R. W. Sharples, in ibid., 3g3.

The next extant commentary on Aristotle's discussion is that of Themistius, who knew the writings of both Alexander and Plotinus and was
later read by both Averroës and Thomas Aquinas. There is a Greek text of
Themistius and the 13th-century Latin translation made by Thomas Aquinas' collaborator William of Moerbeke. In IV 1 (= Armstrong IV 2, lines 7–
9), Plotinus had stressed that intellect is more indivisible than soul. We find
Themistius agreeing. In the Greek at 104, 14–23, Themistius says that the
debate as to whether all souls are one would be better conducted into whether
all intellects are one because that is a more compelling suggestion.

Themistius, like Alexander, takes Aristotle *On the Soul* 3.5 to distinguish at least three intellects as belonging to humans, if we ignore his anom-
alous addition of the 'common intellect'. The three are the potential (*dunamei*), actual (*energeiai*), and productive (*poiêtikos*) intellects. Confusingly,
the last is also called actual (*energeiai*), and the Latin text of Themistius used
by Thomas Aquinas uses cognate Latin words for the actual and productive
intellects (*actu, activus*), while Thomas speaks of the agent intellect (*agens*).

Themistius denies Alexander's view that the immortal productive intellect is God.[41] On the contrary, it is human. But this does not settle the
question of human immortality, because there remain further questions,
whether there are different productive intellects for each individual human,
or just one for the human race. And if there is only one, are the lower material and dispositional intellects immortal and different for each individual
human?

For Aristotle the productive intellect is said by Themistius to be *me*,[42]
while for Themistius the actual intellect (= productive *in DA* 103,36–38)
provides the *essence* of me, whereas the combination of potential and actual
intellect is what he considers to be me.[43] It is the productive intellect (103,36)
that is argued by Themistius, despite its immortality and humanness, to be
unitary and therefore not a source of *individual* immortality. Themistius'
grounds for its unitariness are the fact of human mutual understanding.[44] He
appeals to Plato *Gorgias* 481C5–D1 on the similarity of human experience
and reminds us of Plotinus' case above for the unity of soul, which is based
on the facts of sympathy, love, and magic spells.[45]

For Themistius, however, we have seen, this unitary intellect is not me,

41. Themistius *in DA* 102,36–103,19.
42. Ibid. 101,9–15, cf. 100,37–101,1.
43. Ibid. 100,16–22.
44. Ibid. 103,32–104,6; 104,14–23.
45. Plotinus 4.9 [8] 3 (1–16).

but only my essence. He allows, at 103,30–104,6, that besides the unitary il-luminating intellect, there is a plurality of illuminating and illuminated in-tellects. Themistius' talk of the intellects illuminating each other reminds us of Plotinus 6.7 [38] 6 (10–19), where the three men he mentions are spoken of as illuminating each other, the higher illuminating the lower. It is the plu-rality of illuminating and illuminated intellects on which Thomas Aquinas seized when he received the Latin translation of Themistius from William of Moerbeke. These plural intellects are indeed individual, although it is less clear that they are also immortal, as Thomas would wish.

'Philoponus', who may or may not be a pupil of the real Philoponus, canvasses the idea that the actual intellect of humans is immortal only through the *succession* of individual thinkers and is not itself an instance of *individual* human immortality.[46] Philoponus himself says the same about the non-intermittence of the active intellect's thinking.[47] Philoponus is not here giving his own view, since, as a Christian, he believed in individual im-mortality, but is commenting on Aristotle. In talking of immortality and non-intermittence through *succession*, these texts are only bringing out what was implicit in Themistius. The idea of immortality not of an individual, but through the succession of mortal individuals, is what Averroës was to pos-tulate not just for active intellect, but for all human intellect.

Themistius *in DA* 103,30–104,6:[48]

From what source will the potential also come to think all objects, if the intel-lect that advances it to activity does not think all objects prior to it? Now [the solution is that] the intellect that illuminates (*ellampôn*) in a primary sense is one, while those that are illuminated (*ellampomenoi*) and illuminate (*ellampon-tes*) are, just like light, more than one. For while the sun is one, you could speak of light as in a sense divided among the organs of sight. That is why Aristotle introduced as a comparison not the sun but [its derivative] light, whereas Plato [introduced] the sun [itself], in that he makes it analogous to the good [*Repub-lic* 502C–509C]. There is no need to be puzzled if we who are combined from the potential and the actual (*energeiai*) [intellects] are referred back to one pro-ductive (*poiêtikos*) intellect, and that what it is to be each of us is derived from that single [intellect]. Where otherwise do the notions that are shared (*koinai ennoiai*) come from? Where is the untaught and identical understanding of the

---

46. 'Philoponus' *in DA* 538,32–539,7.

47. Philoponus *in de Intellectu* 49,48–54; 91,40–49.

48. Themistius passages translated by Robert Todd, from *Themistius on Aristotle on the Soul*, London and Ithaca N.Y. 1996.

primary definitions and primary axioms derived from? For we would not understand one another unless there were a single intellect that we all shared. And Plato's [statement at *Gorgias* 481C5–D1] is true: 'If there was not <experience (*pathos*)> that was identical, although individually different for different human beings, but instead any one of us was uniquely affected in comparison with other people, it would not be easy for that person to indicate to another how he was personally affected'.

Themistius *in DA* 100,16–20; 100,37–101,1; 101,9–15:

We, then, are either the potential intellect or the actual (*energeiai*) [intellect]. So if, in the case of everything that is combined from what is potential and actual, this something (*to tode*) and what it is to be this something (*to tôide einai*) are distinct, then I (*to egô*) and what it is to be me (*to emoi einai*) will also be distinct, and while I am the intellect combined from the potential and the actual [intellects], what it is to be me comes from the actual [intellect]. . . .

So we are the productive (*poiêtikos*) intellect. . . .

But for now we can more confidently affirm that he [Aristotle] believes that we are the productive (*poiêtikos*) intellect when he raises a problem, and solves it, by saying 'But we do not remember because this [productive intellect] is unaffected, while the passive intellect is perishable' [*On the Soul* 3.5]. For the problem implied here is also common to everyone who posits the intellect as immortal: 'Why after death do we not remember the content of our lives (*ta en biôi*), and exchange neither friendship nor hostility, nor appear to the family to whom we are most attached?'

'Philoponus' *in DA3*, 538,32–539,12: [49]

[538,32] And the third thing fits it, that intellect always thinks. Not, as Plotinus believes, because the same intellect thinks always throughout everything, for we are not saying that the intellect which thinks always is one in number; but because in the whole cosmos there is always a human intellect thinking. Even if I am not thinking, still, someone else is, and 'always' applies by succession, so that God's irradiation may never cease to shine on us. For if we did not think always, but at times we did not think, it would cease. If this is how we say it always thinks, this belongs to human intellect. That it thinks always we apply not

49. Translated by William Charlton, in *'Philoponus' on Aristotle on the Soul* 3.1–8, London and Ithaca N.Y. 2000.

to one intellect in number but to all, just as we say that man lives always, not because of Socrates but because there is some man always living. Or else [we may say] that it is said always to think because it is always capable of thinking. The person who has intellect thinks at whatever hour he wishes. So this belongs to human intellect. For Intellect from outside is the one intellect in number that thinks all things. So much is said to outline the doctrine (*theôria*). But it is our task to indicate the ten points in the text and fill them out. That is the doctrine.

Philoponus *in de Intellectu* 52,23–29, ed. Verbeke, *CLCAG:*[50]

It is, then, because in the universe as a whole that which is in potentiality does not have to precede in time that which is in actuality that he [Aristotle *On the Soul* 3.5, 430a22] says it does not sometimes understand and sometimes not—as happens in the individual—but always understands; for in the universe as a whole there are always intellects in actuality. Hence the words 'it understands always' are applied to all and to the pool of souls in the whole universe, not because each person on his own understands always.

AVICENNA, AVERROËS, THOMAS AQUINAS

Themistius is important because Thomas Aquinas in the 13th century uses him against Averroës' view that even the material intellect, though immortal, is unitary, so that there is no *individual* immortality for human intellects. Thomas says (*On the Unity of Intellect* § 120, Keeler) that Catholics interpret Themistius' productive intellect as God. This is a misinterpretation of Themistius, but at the same time Thomas seizes on Themistius' allowing a plurality of illuminated intellects and uses it in support of the Christian belief in individual immortality for the human intellect. But first how did we get to the view of Averroës' followers, who are opposed first by Thomas' teacher, Albert the Great, and then by Thomas?

The Arabic world of the 9th century AD had Themistius' commentary and also had[51] a paraphrase of the second half of Plotinus' works, *Enneads*

---

50. Translated by William Charlton, in *Philoponus on Aristotle on the Intellect*, London and Ithaca N.Y. 1991.

51. See Fritz Zimmermann, 'The origins of the so-called *Theology of Aristotle*', in J. Kraye, W. F. Bryan, and C. Schmitt, eds., *Pseudo-Aristotle in the Middle Ages*, London 1986; Peter Adamson, *The Arabic Plotinus*, London 2002.

4–6. In the early 11th century, Avicenna distinguished even more levels of the human intellect than Alexander and Themistius. Whereas Alexander had called the actual intellect 'acquired' (*On the Soul* 82, 1), the acquired intellect is in Avicenna an extra level of intellect. But Avicenna shared with Themistius the view that there is a single agent intellect that we all need to contact.[52] This intellect is, as with Themistius, well below the level of the divine Intellect, but it is not within the human. Avicenna held that to access the forms which we think, we must contact the agent intellect which thinks them uninterruptedly.

Avicenna treats the human soul as well as human intellect. It is this soul whose incorporeality he maintains in the Flying Man argument reported in chapter twelve below. As he explains in his *Al-Shifā (The Healing)*, in the part translated into Latin in 12th-century Toledo as *On the Soul (De Anima)* and edited in Avicenna Latinus by S. Van Riet, he considers the human soul, unlike Aristotle's 'form of the body', to be independent of the body (Avicenna Latinus V.2), individualized (V.3), and immortal (V.4). It is therefore unlike Aristotle's soul as 'form of the body'. *De Anima* V.3 discusses what makes this soul individual.[53]

The soul did not exist, as it does for Neoplatonists, before its embodiment, and it is initially individuated by its body and its attachment to its body, V.3,[54] although it turns out in V.4 that the body is at most an accidental cause of the multiplicity of soul, which is essentially multiple anyhow.[55] But what about the individuation of soul after it is detached from the body? Here Avicenna confesses he is unsure and we see him trying out no fewer than six alternatives. Did his uncertainty influence Averroës' later denial of individual immortality?

Avicenna Latinus, *De Anima* V.3, pp. 111–13, lines 20–43, S. Van Riet:

> But doubtless there is something by which the soul is made individual, but it is not the impression of soul on matter, because we have already destroyed that. Rather, it is some of the affects, and some of the virtues, and something from the accidental spiritual attributes, or a composite from those things, although

52. E.g., Avicenna Latinus *De Anima* V.5, pp. 126–27, ed. Van Riet.
53. Thérèse-Anne Druart, 'The human soul's individuation and its survival after the body's death: Avicenna on the causal relation between body and soul', *Arabic Sciences and Philosophy* 10, 2000, 259–73.
54. Avicenna Latinus *De Anima* pp. 108–9.
55. Avicenna Latinus *De Anima* pp. 124–25. Cf. Plotinus 6.4 [22] 4 (37–39), cited above, where the soul exists before the body and is already both multiple and unitary.

we do not know it. But after it comes to be individual on its own, it is impossible that it should be a numerically different soul, and that the two souls should be one essence. We have said much to deny that elsewhere. But we will demonstrate that since the soul is created with a creation involving some combination, it is possible (1) that after it there should be created some affect in rational actions and in rational passions by the combination of which its action differs from similar action in another soul, and (2) that the acquired affect that is called intellect in actuality should be so defined in one soul that that soul differs from another through that affect, and (3) that because it falls to it to perceive its own individual essence, it has some affect from what it perceives that is unique to itself and possessed by no other. It is also possible (4) that there arise in the soul from its bodily virtues a unique affect that depends on moral affects, or the moral affects themselves, or (5) that there are yet other properties there hidden from us that accompany souls when they are created and after they have been created, and differentiate them, like the individual traits of bodily forms that accompany them, and (6) that souls exist in such and such a way, but are differentiated in their properties on account of which bodies have or have not been created, whether we know those dispositions or some of them, or not.

In the 12th century, late in his career, Averroës wrote his large commentary on Aristotle's *De Anima*, which survives in Michael Scot's 13th-century Latin translation, not in Arabic. He denies individuality to the material intellect and in general to theoretical intellect (*speculativus*), presumably as opposed to the practical intellect that we shall see Aristotle and Epictetus making so central. He seems to connect his claim of the intellect's being one and the same for all people with the idea that the object of the intellect's understanding is one and the same for all. Like Themistius, he speaks of common notions, which in this case are primary propositions, but, unlike Themistius, he makes them objects of the lowest intellect, the material intellect. Insofar as they are intentional objects of an individual's thought, they are fleeting and multiple. But in relation to the material intellect, they are common to all humans, and so, perhaps because of the identity supposed between intellect and object, is the material intellect that receives them. M. Geoffroy and Carlos Steel have found the idea of the material intellect as non-individual already a little earlier in Averroës' *Letter 1 On the Natural Perfection of the Intellect.*[56]

56. *Letter 1 On the Natural Perfection of the Intellect,* in French translation, §20 from the Hebrew = §10 from the Latin, in M. Geoffroy and C. Steel, eds., Averroès *La béatitude de l'âme,* Paris 2001, 210–11.

Averroës *Commentarium Magnum in DA3*, pp. 406–7, lines 575–96, Crawford, trans. from the Latin:[57]

Therefore because we have decided from this discussion that the material intellect is one and the same (*unica*) for all humans, and have also decided from this that the human race is eternal, as has been made clear elsewhere, it is necessary that the material intellect should not be stripped of natural principles common to the whole human race, that is of the primary propositions and of the simple concepts (*formationes singulares*) common to all [humans]; for these objects of understanding are unique (*unica*) as regards the receiver, and multiple as regards the intention (*intentio*) received.

So as regards the manner in which they are unique, they are necessarily eternal. For being does not abandon the subject (*subiectum*) received, that is the mover which is the intention (*intentio*) of the imagined forms, and there is no impediment there on the part of the receiver. So they have no beginning and ending resulting from the mode in connection with which they are unique, but only if beginning and ending result from the multiplicity that falls to them. Hence, when some true object of understanding from among the primary objects of understanding has come to an end in respect of some individual through the ending of its subject (*subiectum*) insofar as it was joined to us, necessarily that object of understanding is not terminable without qualification, but is terminable in respect of each individual. And in this way we can say that theoretical (*speculativus*) [as opposed to practical] intellect is one and the same in all [humans].

57. I am grateful to Richard Taylor for showing me a preview of his translation from the Arabic, and to Martin Stone for commenting on my translation of the medieval Latin.

CHAPTER 7

Bundles and differentiation of individuals

The differentiation of disembodied intellects has proved in chapter six to be very difficult. I want to go back down now to the more mundane differentiation of persons and things in the physical world.

FORMS OF INDIVIDUALS IN ARISTOTLE

Plato already had much to say on individuals,[1] and I shall come back to him shortly, but I shall start with his pupil Aristotle. That Aristotle believed in forms of individuals, especially of persons, has been convincingly argued by others.[2] Aristotle even speaks of 'what it is to be you' and 'what it is to be Socrates' (*to soi einai, Sôkratei einai*).[3] Normally these forms are not thought of as bestowing individuality, but rather as deriving it from the individuals. But David Balme has drawn attention to another conception of form where Aristotle discusses individual resemblances in offspring to the father's or mother's side, in *Generation of Animals* 4.3.[4] Balme's suggestion that these individual resemblances constitute individual form (767b30−33 speaks of es-

---

1. See M. M. McCabe, *Plato's Individuals*, Princeton 1994.

2. Rogers Albritton, 'Forms of particular substances in Aristotle's *Metaphysics*', *Journal of Philosophy* 54, 1957, 699−708; Robert Heinaman, 'Aristotle's tenth aporia', *Archiv für Geschichte der Philosophie* 61, 1979, 249−70; A. C. Lloyd, *Form and Universal in Aristotle*, Liverpool 1981.

3. Aristotle *Metaphysics* 7.4, 1029b14−15; 7.6, 1032a8.

4. D. M. Balme, 'Aristotle's biology was not essentialist', *Archiv für Geschichte der Philosophie* 62, 1980, 1−12, repr. in Allan Gotthelf and James Lennox, eds., *Philosophical Issues in Aristotle's Biology*, Cambridge 1987.

sence, *ousia*) has been doubted,[5] but on the other side attention has been drawn[6] to *Generation of Animals* 4.1, 766a20, which may mean that the male parent produces a female when he does not bring the matter over into his own distinctive form (*to idion eidos to hautou*). On Balme's view, the individual form contains *non-essential* characteristics like color of eye or hair and snubness of nose, which are discussed in *Generation of Animals* 4.3.

Yet it is matter, not form, that bestows individuality and differentiates Socrates from Callias, according to Aristotle (*Metaphysics* 7.8, 1034a5–8). This would mean that the non-essential characteristics constituting Balme's individual form would need to be thought of as due to *matter*.

An alternative to Balme's view is that individual form is merely the form of the species, human, individuated by matter. Another is the view that is taken at least most of the time by Alexander, according to which forms like mortal, rational animal, though not *intrinsically* particular or universal, have more reality qua particulars. For universals are mere mental constructs, which we make when we see particular forms as having the very unimportant and accidental property of being actually shared (and not merely as in Aristotle shareable) by at least two particulars. Any such sharedness is merely accidental and no part of their nature.[7]

THE INDIVIDUAL AS A UNIQUE BUNDLE OF CHARACTERISTICS

If Aristotle postulated such a collection of distinctive characteristics in the individual as Balme suggests, they would still have to be embedded in *matter*. So the individual would not simply *consist* of such a collection, but of such a collection embedded in matter. When, therefore, the Neoplatonist Porphyry expresses the idea of the individual as a mere bundle of characteristics in his *Introduction* or *Isagôgê* 7,19–8,3, calling the distinctive characteristics *idiotêtes* (Latin *proprietates*), I believe he is drawing not on Aristotle,

5. Charlotte Witt, 'Form, reproduction, and inherited characteristics in Aristotle's *Generation of Animals*', *Phronesis* 30, 1985, 46–57.

6. Andrew Coles, *Matter, Life, and Organisation: Biological Themes in Philosophy and Medicine in Ancient Greece*, Ph.D. diss., University of London 1992.

7. I have given this interpretation of Alexander's view of universals in *The Philosophy of the Commentators, 200–600 AD: A Sourcebook*, vol. 3, *Logic and Metaphysics*, 5(e), London and Ithaca N.Y. 2004. Mental constructs: *DA* 90,2–11; *Quaestio* 2.28, 79,16–18; 78,18–20; 1.3, 17, 8–23. Actually shared: *Quaestio* 1.11, 23,25–31; *in Top.* 355,18–24. A more robust view of the reality of universals is suggested by *Quaestio* 1.11, 24,22, which A. C. Lloyd has, however, regarded as inauthentic in his *Form and Universal in Aristotle*, 51.

but on Plato. Plato in (*Theaetetus* 209C) speaks of an individual (*atomon*), such as Socrates, consisting of (*ex hôn ei*) uniquely distinctive characteristics (the word *idios* is used earlier at 154A, 166C), such as his distinctive snubness of nose. Plato has the idea that one cannot think of Theaetetus at all without having his distinctive characteristic in mind. In Porphyry what is unique may be a bundle (*athroisma*, a word used at Plato *Theaetetus* 157B–C, or *sundromê*) of characteristics, rather than a single one, and for Porphyry it is unique in the strong sense that it *would* (*ouk an*) not belong to another individual. Boethius (*Commentary on Isagôgê*[2]), was inaccurate when he translated this merely as 'will not' (*erit*).

The idea that honey should be considered a bundle, *athroisma*, of qualities is picked up from the *Theaetetus* by the Middle Platonist Alcinous (*Didaskalikos*, ch. 4, 156,1–14).

The Stoics borrowed from Plato the idea of uniquely distinctive characteristics (*idiotêtes*, Latin *proprietates*) for each individual. But they are not so relevant because, like Aristotle, they kept the idea of matter, which they called substance (*ousia*), as the subject of qualities, and did not follow Plato in making the individual consist of a bundle of qualities only. So Porphyry was Platonizing, unless he was able to find these ideas in the Aristotelian Alexander.

I doubt if the Neoplatonist Simplicius can be trusted when he says[8] that the Aristotelian Alexander did think of individuals as constituted (*huphestanai ek*) out of characteristics. It is true that in *Quaestiones* 7,32–8,5, Alexander postulates distinctive characteristics (*idia*) for individuals. But it is a further question whether he also spoke of constitution out of characteristics, or whether Simplicius read this into him. Simplicius, I believe, could have been misled by Porphyry.

Because Porphyry's work was presented as an introduction to many of Aristotle's ideas, the notion of the individual as a unique bundle of characteristics was taken by subsequent Neoplatonists, by Simplicius here, by Proclus,[9] and possibly by 'Philoponus'[10] as representing the Aristotelian view, despite the lack of any reference to matter or to a subject for the characteristics to inhere in.

But why should Porphyry have offered the *Theaetetus* and Alcinous' view of individuals in an introduction to Aristotle? I suspect because he is speaking to beginning students who are about to read Aristotle's *Categories*,

8. Simplicius *Commentary on Categories* 83,16–20.
9. Proclus *ap.* Olympiodorum *Commentary on Alcibiades i* Westerink 204,8–12.
10. 'Philoponus' *in An. Post.* 2 437,21–438,2.

which does not even mention matter and form, so Porphyry does not want to go into those complications. Alcinous' treatise is also an introduction, albeit an introduction to Plato, not like Porphyry's to Aristotle, so Porphyry has a precedent. If, moreover, Porphyry read Aristotle in the same way as Balme, then the idea of distinctive character still would have seemed Aristotelian to him, even if not the idea of the individual as bundle. Porphyry was not to know that Proclus and Simplicius would wrongly infer that the view was Aristotelian. Different explanations have been offered by others.[11] But one interpretation, that the treatment of individuals by the Stoic Seneca, in *Letter* 58,12, is ascribed to Aristotle, rather than being Stoic, incurs the difficulty that the other ideas in that passage are clearly un-Aristotelian.

There is a further question, as Avicenna pointed out,[12] how it can be that the bundle of characteristics unique to Socrates *would* never be (so Porphyry and Proclus), rather than merely happening not to be, shared. It would not be satisfactory to reply that the characteristics are themselves individuated as belonging to Socrates, if they are needed for the opposite role of showing how Socrates is individuated. But the unshareability is nonetheless important, if one is to avoid the possibility of Socrates being reduplicated, which is the threat to personal identity posed in modern discussions.

Two further ideas should be distinguished from the idea that the individual is a unique bundle of characteristics. First, the Neoplatonist Plotinus thought of Aristotelian substance as a conglomeration (*sumphorêsis*) but one including matter as well as qualities (6.3 [44] 8 (19–37)). Second, when the bishop Gregory of Nyssa maintained in three works that bodies are bundles (*sundromai*) of God's ideas, he was giving an idealized version of Porphyry's idea.

Boethius left a complete Latin translation of Porphyry's *Isagôgê*, which is used also, but only incompletely, in his second commentary on that work.

Plato *Theaetetus* 209C:

> But I think there will not be in me an opinion about you, Theaetetus, until this snub-nosedness of yours has stamped and deposited in me a reminder that is different from the other snub-nosednesses that I have seen, and the same with the other [characteristics] of which you consist (*t' alla ex hôn ei su*).

11. Riccardo Chiaradonna, 'La teoria dell' individuo in Porfirio e l'*idiôs poion* stoico', *Elenchos* 20, 2000, 303–31; Jaap Mansfeld, *Heresiography in Context*, Leiden 1992, 92–98.

12. See Avicenna *al-Madkhal* 15,1–6, translated by Bäck, with Latin version from *Logica* 2r, col. 2; Allan Bäck, 'The Islamic Background: Avicenna (b. 980; d. 1037) and Averroës (b. 1126; d. 1198)', in Jorge J. E. Gracia, ed., *Individuation in Scholasticism*, Albany N.Y., 1994, ch. 3.

Alexander *ap*. Simplicium *Commentary on Categories* 83,16–20:[13]

Perhaps Alexander has this in mind when he thinks that [the common feature] is posterior to individuals. Nevertheless, he does not preserve consistency with his own account when he says that the individuals are constituted (*huphestanai ek*) out of the common feature (*to koinon*) and the differences, unless perhaps he considers their constitution (*hupostasis*), too, in the conceptual mode (*kata tên ennoian*) which yields the definition and exposes the common feature.

Porphyry *Isagôgê* 7,16–24 from the Greek:

What is most generic is said of all the genera, species, and individuals under it, while the genus prior to the most specific species is said of all the most specific species and the individuals, the mere species is said of all the individuals, and the individual (*atomon*) is said of only one of the particulars (*ta kata meros*).

Socrates is called an individual, and so is this white thing and this son of Sophroniscus, who is approaching (if Socrates is Sophroniscus' only son). So things like this are called individuals because each is composed of distinctive qualities (*ex idiotêtôn sunestêken hekaston*), the conglomeration (*athroisma*) of which would never (*ouk an pote*) come into being identically in anything else. For the distinctive qualities of Socrates would not come into being identically in another particular.

Porphyry *Isagôgê*, last two sentences above in Latin translation by Boethius, at Busse, *CAG* 4.1, p. 33,4–7 (also used in Boethius *Commentary on Isagôgê*[2], *CSEL* 48 p. 235, Brandt):

Things of this kind are called individuals because each of them consists of (*consistit*) distinctive characteristics (*proprietates*) the collection (*collectio*) of which will (*erit*) never be the same in any other. For the distinctive characteristics of Socrates will never be the same ones in any other of the particulars whatever.

Proclus *ap*. Olympiodorum *Commentary on Alcibiades 1* Westerink 204,8–12:

The Peripatos was wrong about the individual (*atomon*), for it thought that the individual came into being out of (*ginesthai ek*) the concurrence (*sundromê*) of

---

13. Translated by Frans de Haas, in *Simplicius on Aristotle Categories 5*, London and Ithaca N.Y. 2001.

accidental properties (*sumbebêkota*). This is why it defined the individual as: that whose conglomeration (*athroisma*) would never come into being in anything else. Thus they tried to put together the better things out of (*epoioun apo*) the worse, that is, out of accidental properties.

'Philoponus' *Commentary on Posterior Analytics* 2, 437,21–438,2:

Sense perception sees Socrates and Alcibiades, and takes an impression not only of the particular distinctive qualities (*merika idiômata*) in them (the particular distinctive qualities are one man's being long-haired and pale, the other not), but also of something of the shared characteristics that it finds in them, that is, their being animals, or rational, or something of that sort. It then sends this along in the first instance to the imagination . . . For sense perception grasps not only particulars (*merika*), that is, the accidental (*sumbebêkota*) and distinctive qualities (*idiotês*) of which the particulars consist (*ex hôn sunestêkasin*), but also the universal man, that is, some of the things of which the universal man consists (*sunistatai*).

The idea of an individual as a bundle of properties leaves out the idea of ownership on which I have been insisting since the opening chapter, and for which I shall argue more fully in chapter fifteen. An individual owns properties rather than consisting in them. I have objected elsewhere to bundle theory insofar as physical things have been called bundles of properties.[14] Whether universal or particular properties are meant is one problematic question for decision. The theory also shares many of the difficulties of the idea of a stream of consciousness, which I shall discuss in chapter fifteen. Having rejected the familiar relationship of a thing *having* properties, the bundle theorist needs to specify alternative relationships that hold the bundle together at one time, while keeping it distinct from other bundles, and to specify further relationships that unite the bundle at different times. The theorist must recognize too that most properties are found only at some locations and at some times within the bundle, and so must be ready to give an account of this fact as well. What relationships might be postulated as holding together at one time the bundle that supposedly constitutes a person? Not contiguity or location in the same place, for the color of the tea I have drunk may be located with my tongue without being part of the bundle, while my thoughts may be part of the bundle without being co-located.

14. Richard Sorabji, *Matter, Space, and Motion*, Ithaca N.Y. 1988, 58–59.

INDIVIDUALS TREATED LIKE SPECIES

The Stoic idea of an individual's distinctive characteristic (*idiotês*) enables Porphyry to take the further view, which is also Stoic, that an individual can be treated like a species. Just as a species is defined by genus and differentia, so Socrates falls under human, which thus acts like a genus, and is differentiated by his distinctive characteristic. Again just as a species is said of individuals, so an individual (*atomon*) is said of one particular (*to kata meros*), as we have just seen in Porphyry *Isagôgê* 7,16–19. The scheme that treats individuals like that came to be known as the 'tree of Porphyry' and was very influential. But the idea that the individual is the most specific kind of species had already been made explicit by the Stoics themselves, according to Diogenes Laertius *Lives* 7.61. As Mansfeld points out,[15] a similar view may also be expressed in the Stoic Seneca,[16] and with names favored by the Stoics (Dion, Theon) in Sextus.[17]

Diogenes Laertius *Lives* 7.61:

The species is what is embraced by the genus, as human is embraced by animal. Most generic is that which, while being a genus, does not have a genus, e.g., the existent. Most specific is that which, while being a species (*eidos*), does not have a species, e.g., Socrates.

Porphyry *Isagôgê* 7,16–19:

What is most generic is said of all the genera, species, and individuals under it, while the genus prior to the most specific species is said of all the most specific species and the individuals, the mere species is said of all the individuals, and the individual (*atomon*) is said of only one of the particulars (*ta kata meros*).

Because Porphyry put this idea of individuals as species in his introduction to Aristotle, it too, like the idea of the individual as a bundle, came to be accepted as Aristotelian. But in fact the idea that an individual can be '*said of*', or predicated of, anything appears to contradict Aristotle. The *species* man is 'said of' Socrates (Aristotle *Categories* 2a11–b6) in the technical sense that not only the name 'man', but also the definition (mortal, rational animal) can be predicated of Socrates. But the individual Socrates has no

---

15. Jaap Mansfeld, *Heresiography in Context*, Leiden 1992, 92–98.
16. Seneca *Letters* 58,12.
17. Sextus *Adversus Mathematicos* 8.41 and 338.

definition, according to Aristotle, and so cannot be 'said of' anything in the technical sense. Can Socrates be in some looser sense predicated of anything? Aristotle discounts as either no predication at all or as a merely accidental predication such cases as 'the approaching thing is Socrates' (*Posterior Analytics* 1.22, 83a1–23).

WHAT DIFFERENTIATES INDIVIDUALS?

What differentiates individuals? The three answers—distinctive qualities, place, and matter—sound very different from each other. I shall suggest that they are closely interrelated, and that it should be no surprise to find the same philosopher or school backing more than one candidate.

(i) Distinctive qualities

Porphyry is evidently committed to saying that individuals are distinguished from each other by a distinctive bundle of characteristics. Boethius agrees, saying that these are accidental characteristics not communicable to another individual. He maintains (*On the Trinity* 1,24–31) that if other accidents could be removed, there would still be the difference of place, which is an accident. He coins the rather unhelpful word 'Platonicity' to describe the distinctive characteristic.

Whereas Boethius *Commentary on Isagôgê*[2] records Porphyry as saying, and itself says, merely that the distinctive characteristics are not, or will not be shared, Boethius *Commentary on de Interpretatione*[2] says that the distinctive characteristic (now singular, but perhaps still a bundle) is *not shareable* (*incommunicabilis*). And this fits with Porphyry's original claim in *Isagôgê* 7,16–24 that the *athroisma would* never come into being identically in anything else. The Stoics are likely to have agreed that the distinctive characteristics *cannot* be shared, if their distinctive qualities afforded the sage *infallible* powers of discriminating individuals, and if one was not to be at risk of losing one's identity through someone else coming to share one's previously unique quality. One suggestion,[18] as noted in chapter three, has been that each individual person has an unshareable psychological perspective whose physical basis is the distinctive quality.

Porphyry *Commentary on Categories* 129,8–10:[19]

---

18. Eric Lewis, 'The Stoics on identity and individuation', *Phronesis* 40, 1995, 89–108.

19. Translated by Steven Strange, in *Porphyry on Aristotle's Categories*, London and Ithaca N.Y. 1992.

[Nor] are they [state and condition (*hexis, diathesis*)] differentiated from one another in number, as Socrates differs from Plato: for Socrates does not differ from Plato in virtue of specific differentiae, but in virtue of a distinctive combination of qualities (*idiotêti sundromês poiotêtôn*), in virtue of which Plato differs from Socrates.

Boethius *Commentary on Isagôgê*[2] 235,5–236,6, *CSEL* ed. Brandt:[20]

Since above he used the expression 'individual' (*individuum*), he tries to give an account of this word. Those things only are divided that are common to more things than one: for each is divided among those things to which it is common and the nature and likeness of which it contains. Those things into which something common is divided share in a common nature and what is distinctive of (*proprietas*) the common thing belongs to these things to which it is common. But what is distinctive of an individual is not common to anything. What is distinctive of Socrates, if he was bald and snub-nosed and had a pot belly, other lineaments of body, cast of character or sound of voice, did not belong to anyone else. For these distinctive characteristics (*proprietates*), which came to him from accidents and joined to make up his form and figure, belonged to no one else. And since a thing's distinctive characteristics belong to nothing else, they cannot be common to anything; and if a thing's distinctive characteristic is not common to anything, there is nothing that shares it. If a thing is such that nothing shares its property, it cannot be divided into those things that do not share. Rightly, then, the things whose distinctive characteristic does not belong to anything else are called 'individuals' (*individua*). But what is distinctive of human, that is, the species, belongs to Socrates and Plato and the rest, whereas their distinctive characteristics, since they come from accidents, in no way belong to any other single thing whatever.

Boethius *Commentary on de Interpretatione*[2], 136,17–137,26, ed. Meiser:[21]

For we see that there are some qualities in things of this kind that cannot belong to anything other than some one single and particular substance; for one kind of quality is particular (*singularis*), e.g., to Plato or Socrates; there is another that is shared with more than one and gives its entire self to individuals and to all, e.g., humanity itself. For there is a quality of this kind that is both

20. Translated by William Charlton, in Richard Sorabji, *Philosophy of the Commentators 200–600 AD*, vol. 3, *Logic and Metaphysics*, London and Ithaca N.Y. 2004, 6d2.
21. Translated by Andrew Smith, work in progress.

whole in individuals and whole in all. For whenever we think of something like this in our mind, in our mental processes we are not led by this name to any single person, but to all who share in the definition of humanity. Hence it comes about that this is common to all, but the former cannot be shared (*incommunicabilis*) with all, but is distinctive (*propria*) of one. For if I may coin a new word, I would call the single particular quality that cannot be shared with any other substance by an invented name to make clearer exactly what I mean. Let us call that distinctive characteristic (*proprietas*) of Plato that cannot be shared 'Platonicity'. By inventing a word, we can call this quality Platonicity in the way in which we call the quality of a man humanity. And so this Platonicity belongs to only one man and that not to anyone you like but only to Plato, whereas humanity belongs to Plato and to all the rest who are embraced by this word. And so it happens that because Platonicity belongs only to Plato, the listener's mind refers the word 'Plato' to one person and one particular substance, but when he hears 'man' he refers the concept to as many as he knows are embraced by humanity. And so since humanity is both common to all men and is whole in the individuals (for all men have humanity to the same extent as one man; for if this were not so, the definition of the species man would never belong to the substance of a particular man), man is said to be something universal, whereas Platonicity and Plato are particular.

Boethius *Commentary on de Interpretatione*[2], 139,18–19, ed. Meiser:

Therefore Platonicity itself is a quality that, as they put it (*ut dictum est*), is unshareable (*incommunicabilis*).

Boethius *On the Trinity* 1, lines 24–31:

But it is the diversity of accidents that produces numerical difference. For three men are distinct (*distare*) neither in genus nor in species, but by their accidents. For even if we should in our mind remove all accidents from them, nonetheless each would have a different place. We cannot in any way imagine that to be one and the same, since two bodies will not occupy one place, and place is an accident. They are plural in number because they are made plural by their accidents.

Simplicius *Commentary on Categories* 229,17–18:

No distinguishing set (*idiaȝon plêthos*) bundles together (*sundramein*) to produce a numerical distinction (*diastasis*).

(ii) Place

The Neoplatonist Dexippus, though often drawing on Porphyry, rejects the distinctive characteristics answer and suggests instead that in order to be distinct, individual things need to be countable and that means being separated (*diestêkota*). This agrees with the stress on place as differentiating found just above in Boethius (*On the Trinity* 1.24–31) and shortly below in the Stoic Posidonius. Unfortunately, the Neoplatonists allow a number of things to be in the same place after all: soul vehicles, celestial spheres, certain lights, space viewed as a kind of light, and certain daemons.

Dexippus *Commentary on Categories* 30,20–34:[22]

> Seleucus: But if a species is that which is predicated of a multiplicity of numerically different entities in the mode of essence (*ti esti*), in what way does one thing that is individual and one differ from another thing that is individual and one? For both the one and the other are numerically one.
>
> Dexippus: Those who seek to solve this problem by reference to the concept of 'distinctively qualified object' (*idiôs poion*), i.e., by claiming that one person, for instance, is definable as 'hook-nosed', 'fair-haired', or by some other conjunction of qualities, another as 'snub-nosed' or 'bald' or 'gray-eyed', and another again by other qualities, do not seem to me to solve it properly. For it is not the conjunction (*sundromê*) of qualities that makes them differ numerically, but, if anything, quality as such. We should rather reply to the problem as follows: that things that are numerically distinct (*hetera*) do not differ (*diapherein*) from each other in nature and essence, but their distinctness resides in their countability. They are different, then, in being countable; for it is in the process of each being counted one by one that number arises. So, it seems to me that to say that things are numerically different implies 'separate (*diestê-kota*) so as to be countable', so that what is being said about the species is somewhat as follows: that the species is what is predicated of a multiplicity of entities separate so as to be countable, so that we may take 'different' in the sense of 'separate'.

(iii) Matter

Aristotle (*Metaphysics* 7.8) says that Callias and Socrates are distinguished from each other by matter, by having *this* flesh and *these* bones. It is not de-

22. Translated by John Dillon, in *Dexippus on Aristotle's Categories*, London and Ithaca N.Y. 1990.

nied that they are alike in being made of flesh and bone. So the commentators on Aristotle sometimes take matter to be relevant as being the seat of other distinguishing characteristics. We can thus now see that the three criteria for differentiation are interrelated. Differentiation by matter (iii) is the same as differentiation by distinctive qualities (i). Moreover, Boethius sees place (ii) as just an instance of distinctive accidents (i). In addition, if Balme's account of Aristotle's individual form is right, this form is merely a set of accidents due to matter, and so again is not a distinct alternative.

The answer of Alexander on behalf of the Aristotelian school was that it is matter (*hulê*) or material circumstances (*hulikai peristaseis*) that individuate individuals like Socrates, and the matter presumably houses the distinctive characteristics (*idia*) to which he also refers (*Quaestiones* 7,32 – 8,5; see below). The appeal to matter is still upheld in late Neoplatonism by Ammonius.

Aristotle *Metaphysics* 7.8, 1034a5 – 8:

Once we have the whole, such and such a form in this flesh and bones, this is Callias or Socrates. They are different because of the matter, for this is different, but are the same in form, for the form is indivisible.

Alexander(?) *Quaestiones* 1.3, 7,32 – 8,5:[23]

For mortal rational animal, if it is taken along with (*lambanein meta*) the material circumstances and differences that the existence (*hupostasis*) of [particulars] goes with (*meta*) and that are different in different cases, produces (*poiein*) Socrates and Callias and particular human beings; but if it is taken apart from (*lambanein khôris*) these, it comes to be common, [and common] *not* because it is not in each of the particular human beings (for the distinctive features of particulars go with these [particulars]), but because it is the same in all.

Alexander *On the Soul* 85,15 – 20:

For the person who takes (*lambanein*) the form of human being apart from the material accompaniments has the common human being; for the difference between particular (*kath' hekasta*) human beings derives from their matter, since their forms, in virtue of which they are human beings, have no difference. The

23.   The next two passages are translated by R. W. Sharples, in *Alexander of Aphrodisias Quaestiones* 1.1 – 2.15, London and Ithaca N.Y. 1992; and in Richard Sorabji, *Philosophy of the Commentators 200 – 600 AD*, vol. 3, *Logic and Metaphysics*, London and Ithaca N.Y. 2004, 5e4.

person who observes (*sunidein*) what is common to particulars, in turn, takes (*lambanein*) the form apart from the matter. For this [the form] is what is common and the same in them.

Alexander *Commentary on Metaphysics* 216,2 – 3: [24]

For the differences between particular men are material.

Ammonius *Commentary on Isagôgê* 60,16 – 21: [25]

Of those [spoken sounds, *phônai*] predicated substantially some are said of things differing in species, viz. genera and differentiae, and some of things that differ numerically, viz. the [ultimate] species of individuals that differ from each other not in species but in matter — for instance I say 'horse' of Xanthus ['Chestnut'] and Balias ['Dapple'].

THE STOICS

The philosophers on whom I have been concentrating date from the Aristotelian Alexander around 200 AD through the following four centuries of Neoplatonists. But it needs to be said that even before these philosophers, the Stoics had accepted all three modes of differentiation — distinctive qualities, place, and matter — and probably influenced Alexander and the Neoplatonists in this.

(i) Stoics: distinctive qualities

The Stoics believed, following Plato (*Theaetetus* 209C), that each individual had a distinctive quality to distinguish it from other individuals. In debate on the sage's infallibility, the Stoics insisted against Platonist skeptics that the Stoic sage had a way of distinguishing individuals, because the distinctive quality meant that no two individuals were ever exactly alike. [26] Compare the Stoic view that a proper name indicates a distinctive quality

24. Translated by Arthur Madigan, in *Alexander of Aphrodisias on Aristotle Metaphyics 3*, London and Ithaca N.Y. 1992.

25. Translated by William Charlton, in Richard Sorabji, *Philosophy of the Commentators 200 – 600 AD*, vol. 3, *Logic and Metaphysics*, London and Ithaca N.Y. 2004, 6d12.

26. Plutarch *On Common Conceptions* 1077C (= LS 28O); Cicero *Academica* 2.85 (= LS 40J).

(*dêloun idian poiotêta*).[27] Ships and armies, we are told, do not have sufficient unity to be the bearers of qualities, although they are 'qualified', and so presumably can be distinguished.[28]

Plutarch *On Common Conceptions* 1077C:

> So one can hear [the Stoics] and encounter them in many writings disagreeing with the Academics shouting that they confuse all things with their 'indistinguishabilities' (*aparallaxiai*), and force a single qualified individual to inhere in two substances. And yet there is no human being who does not think this and hold it on the contrary to be amazing and paradoxical, if in the whole of time there has not come to be one dove indistinguishable from another, nor one bee from another bee, nor one grain of wheat from another, nor one proverbial fig from another.

It is not clear that the Stoic distinctive quality was, like the Neoplatonist one, a *bundle* of commonly shared qualities. As Eric Lewis points out,[29] that would make it hard for the Stoic sage to be sure he or she had correctly identified an individual. What bundle would distinguish this individual? Would no other individual ever possess just this bundle, and why not? Would this individual continue to possess it and why? The Neoplatonist Dexippus, in a passage translated above,[30] is taken by some to be referring to the Stoics (though his source may merely be Porphyry's *Isagôgê*) when he rejects the view of 'some people' that the individually qualified object (*idiôs poion*) is distinguished by a concurrence (*sundromê*) of properties, none of which is *on its own* unique. But this leaves Lewis' questions unanswered.

(ii) Stoics: place

It is a further feature of the Stoic view in Posidonius, and this time Dexippus agrees, that two different (*hetera*) individuals must be separate in place, even though in chemical mixtures, according to the Stoics, the ingredients can be in the same place. Nor can one be *part* of the other, and 'part' here includes co-extensive parts like the matter (*ousia*) of a thing.

Posidonius in Stobaeus vol. 1, 178,21–179,8 Wachsmuth (= Arius Didymus frag. 27, *Dox. Gr.* 462,25 ff. = part of Posidonius frag. 96, Edelstein/Kidd = LS 28D9 ff.):

27. Diogenes Laertius *Lives* 7.58.
28. Simplicius *Commentary on Categories* 214,24–37.
29. Lewis, 'The Stoics on identity and individuation'.
30. Dexippus *Commentary on Categories* 30,20–26.

[Posidonius] says that the distinctively qualified thing (*to poion idiôs*) and the substance (*ousia*) out of which it is [constituted] are not the same, but are not different either, merely not the same, because the substance [reading *ousian*] is part of the distinctively qualified thing and occupies the same place, whereas things that are said to be different from others must also be separate from them in place and not seen as part of them. Mnesarchus says it is clear that a thing viewed as distinctively qualified and a thing viewed as substance are not the same, because things that are the same must have the same attributes.

(iii) Stoics: matter

The Stoics accepted differentiation also by matter. Chrysippus, the Stoic, is said to have replied to the Growing Argument, which makes growth tantamount to death, with a scintillating puzzle, studied in chapter four above, about the effects that that would imply for shrinking. What is relevant here is that his reply starts from the premiss that two distinctively qualified individuals cannot co-exist in the same substance (*ousia* = matter).

Philo *On the Eternity of the World* 48 (= *SVF* 2.397):

> First he [Chrysippus] establishes in advance (*prokataskeuazein*) that two distinctively qualified individuals cannot co-exist in the same substance (*ousia* = matter).

PLOTINUS ON THE DIFFERENTIATION OF PERSONS

Let us now return to Plotinus on differentiation of persons during life on earth. I have said in chapter six that Plotinus did not find it hard to differentiate embodied souls, but he considered even disembodied souls distinct. He has a major discussion in 5.7 [18] 1–3. He seems convinced at 5.7 [18] 3 (4–13) that in nature, whether or not among artifacts, no two specimens are completely alike. It is in 5.7 [18] 1 that he appears to introduce a distinct form for each soul, but he sees that this will not differentiate persons if different people share the same soul in different incarnations. So he turns to discussing different rational forming principles (*logoi*) at work in the parents of each newly incarnated person. The principles are not identical with form (*eidos*), but are closely related to it.[31] But a new problem now arises: since

31. Plotinus 5.9 [5] 12 (7); 5.7 [18] 2 (15); 5.7 [18] 3 (11).

each soul contains all the *logoi* of all individuals,[32] this might seem to obliterate all distinctions among souls. But despite this, he suggests that embodied persons may come out different because in parents different *logoi* will be to hand (*prokheiroi*) at different times (5.7 [18] 2 (6)), and different ones may dominate (*kratein*) the embryonic matter (5.7 [18] 2 (11)).

Plotinus is in effect here differentiating individuals by their distinctive characteristics. So far, these characteristics arise from the chance selection of parental *logoi*. It is said that differences in beauty, shape of nose, or color can be due to form,[33] evidently again thanks to the *logoi*. He adds that it is not matter that causes the differences, except in the case of deformation (*aiskhos;* 5.7 [18] 2 (15−16)). But elsewhere he allows that character can be affected by the kind of body the soul has entered; the blend (*krasis;* 4.3 [27] (23−26); 4.4 [28] 31 (42)) of hot, cold, fluid, and dry in the body, the climate (airs, waters, places), nurture, and fortune (4.3 [27] 15 (7−11)), and matter can impede the development of a soul (1.8 [51] 14 (40−50). So the characteristics that differentiate embodied persons can be caused in some cases by matter as well as by *logoi*.

There is a difficulty with Plotinus' genetic account. Although it has the merit of recognizing that it is not the male alone or chiefly who provides the *logoi*,[34] the role for genetics is hard to square with other things he says. There is a tradition stemming from the myth of Er in Plato's *Republic* (10, 617D−620D), in which souls *choose* their next lives, including lives of animals, in order that God may not be responsible. This is the tradition that Plotinus favors especially when he is thinking of humans being reincarnated as animals,[35] and it leaves little role for parents. Moreover, in two passages Plotinus describes how a soul may help to create the body for its next incarnation,[36] and in the first passage imaginatively compares the soul to a dancer dancing a part. Here too there is no mention of the genetic story of parental *logoi*. These latter ideas make the soul responsible for the form its reincarnation takes. On the other hand, it fits with the genetic story, not with the responsible choice story, when he says at 4.3 [27] 12 (37−9), that there is a body similar (*kath' homoiôsin*) to the soul awaiting its arrival.

Plotinus 5.7 [18] 1 (1−11), which introduces the idea of an individual form for each soul and of rational forming principles in each soul, was

32. Plotinus 5.7 [18] 2 (6); 5.7 [18] 1 (9−11).
33. Plotinus 5.7 [18] 2 (15); 5.7 [18] 3 (11); 5.9 [5] 12 (7).
34. Plotinus 5.7 [18] 2 (8−12); cf. Simplicius *Commentary on Physics* 313,5−27.
35. Plotinus 3.4 [15] 2 (16−30); 4.3 [27] 8 (6−10); 4.3 [27] 15 (10−11).
36. Plotinus 6.7 [38] 7 (8−16); 1.1 [53] 11 (8−15).

translated in chapter six. The following extracts come from the succeeding chapters.

Plotinus 5.7 [18] 2 (1–8):[37]

> But if it is the admixture of the rational forming principles of the male and female that gives the offspring their differing characteristics, then there will not be a particular forming principle of each child, and it will be one of the parents, for example the male, who produces the child not in accordance with differing rational forming principles but in accordance with one of his own or his father's.
>
> The answer is that nothing prevents parents from producing children with differing characteristics, since they contain all the rational forming principles, of which some are to hand (*prokheiroi*) at any one time.
>
> What about differences in children from the same parents?
>
> Well, they are due to unequal predominance (*epikratēsis*).

Plotinus 5.7 [18] 3 (4–13):

> If this is so [that there is only one rational forming principle in the case of indistinguishable (*aparallaktoi*) twins] then there will not be as many rational forming principles as there are individuals.
>
> In fact there are as many different rational forming principles as there are individuals where the difference is not due to a failure in the form. Why shouldn't there be [different rational forming principles] even when the individuals are without difference (*adiaphora*), if in general some things are entirely without difference? For even if the craftsman is producing artifacts without difference, he must still make a mental distinction that will allow him to produce another one, applying difference (*diaphora*) to its sameness. In nature, where one thing comes into being after another not by calculation but only because of rational forming principles (*logoi*), the different characteristics must be linked to the form (*eidos*), even if we cannot perceive the differences.

37. The next two passages are translated by Barrie Fleet, in Richard Sorabji, *The Philosophy of the Commentators, 200–600 AD: A Sourcebook*, vol. 3, London and Ithaca N.Y. 2004.

PART IV

Identity and persona in ethics

CHAPTER 8

Individual persona
vs. universalizability

We saw earlier that the question of what constitutes personal identity over time can sometimes have an ethical dimension. Plato's true self in chapter six was an ideal self to be separated out from bodily concerns, and Locke in chapter five saw personal identity as a forensic concept concerned with reward and punishment. I now move from the sort of subject discussed by Derek Parfit to the sort treated in Charles Taylor's *Sources of the Self*, from the question of what constitutes personal identity and difference to the rather different idea of possessing an identity in ethical contexts. An example of the latter idea was mentioned in chapter two, namely, the individual persona. This idea presupposes that we have one and the same continuing person, but there is a further question about the identity of that person, which is relevant to a number of ethical issues. The idea of an individual persona, which became prominent in Stoicism in the late 2nd century BC, manifests an increased interest in the individual. It could even be said to constitute a form of individualism entirely unlike modern individualism.

In one way, the Stoics continue to play down the individual in the context of ethics. Seneca is still saying in the 1st century AD that we should think of ourselves merely as parts of a larger whole, like stones in an arch (*Letters* 95, 53). But Seneca's context is different. It is not the question how to make decisions in general, but the undesirability of privileging one's own interests. His preference for whole over part fits with the fact that the suffering of the individual had long been regarded by the Stoics as a matter of 'indifference'. What was important was virtuous character. Admittedly, the Stoic stress on character gives some importance to the individual, because the individual's virtuous endeavor is treated as more important than its effects in society at large. Admittedly too, the thesis of the 'indifference' of individual suffering had called for a lot of attention to individuals to help them absorb the thesis.[1] But what is new is the concern with the varied peculiarities of individuals.

In the 1st century BC, Cicero provides a theory of personae, which I, like others, take to go back to the Stoic philosopher Panaetius in the later part of the previous century.[2] This is a view about what you must take into account in deciding what it is right to do. You must consider not only the fact that you are a rational being. That is only the first persona, although it is what Kant tells us to consider, when deciding how it is right to act. Complaints have been made about how thin a conception that of rational being is for the purpose of moral decision making.[3] It is not that of being a rational Indian or American, nor that of being a rational male or female. Panaetius does not abandon this first requirement, which as we shall see imposes a very important restriction on his other requirement. But he does want a thicker requirement in place as well. You need to make decisions in the light also of your individual persona, that is, of the position you have been born into, the choices you have made, and what fortune has brought you. Personae are constituted partly by our roles in life, and many of these roles, like fatherhood, are common to many people. But in some cases of special interest, there is a unique persona, as also in Indian thought.[4]

Thus it is said that when Julius Caesar won the civil war, it was right for Cato to commit suicide in those circumstances, even though it would not have been right for others 'in the same circumstances (*in eadem causa*)'. This again sounds like the opposite of Kant's view, for Kant tells us that something cannot be the right thing to do unless it would be the right thing for anyone to do in the same circumstances. Such a view is already suggested by Aristotle's account of *natural,* as opposed to legal, justice, as conceived by Empedocles. What is just for one is just for all (*Rhetoric* 1.13, 1373b14–17). In one way, I presume that Cicero or Panaetius would agree that *if* there

---

1. I further compare Stoic philosophy of the individual and philosophy of society in the introduction to the volume on Stoics and Epicureans, one of two volumes edited by Richard Sorabji and R. W. Sharples, *Greek and Roman Philosophy 100 BC–200 AD, Bulletin of the Institute of Classical Studies*, supp. vols. 2006.

2. Cicero *On Duties* 1.107–15.

3. Bernard Williams, *Ethics and the Limits of Philosophy*, London 1985; Alasdair MacIntyre, *After Virtue*, London 1981, 2nd ed. 1985.

4. See on Karna's choice in the *Mahâbhârata*, 5.139–44, not to be king, Aditya Adankar, 'Karna's choice: courage and character in the face of an ethical dilemma', in T. S. Rukmani, ed., *The Mahabharata: Whatever Is Not Here Is Nowhere Else*, New Delhi 2005, ch. 9. But Karna resists considerations of rationality—the Stoic first persona. On Confucianism see below.

were anyone exactly like Cato (and a Kantian could make that one of the relevant circumstances), then it would be right for that person in those circumstances to commit suicide. But that is not the interesting point about people. The interesting point is that there *was* no one else like Cato. He had always stood for a kind of austerity that no one else began to match. One could say that he is presented as an example of authenticity. And that is why it would be right for him to commit suicide, but not for the others in the circumstances that prevailed. That this is the interesting point has been brought out in modern times by Peter Winch.[5] Cicero would admittedly have had an extra reason for insisting that the need for suicide applied to none of the others in those circumstances, given that he too was among the losers in the civil war, though not defeated in battle like Cato.

There is a difference between the subjects addressed by Kant and by Cicero and the Stoics. For Cicero and the Stoics, we shall see, are concerned not only with making the right *moral* decisions (e.g., whether to defy injustice), but also with making the right practical decisions in general (choosing the right career), whereas Kant is concerned only with the right *moral* decisions. But that difference does not account for Kant's silence on being true to yourself as a second requirement. For, we shall see, the Stoics expect you to consider your individual persona also in deciding whether to defy an injustice.

Cicero tells us only in general terms that his model in the first two books of his *On Duties* is the book of the Stoic Panaetius on the subject.[6] But if the insistence on the unique individual is Cicero's own, he is a much greater philosopher than I had previously realized. It would also be a mystery how the ideas in Cicero's Latin would have reached the Greek-speaking Epictetus in the next century. I have not seen this insistence on the individual in Stoicism earlier than Panaetius, so my inclination is to ascribe it to him, even though the *example* of Cato must, because of the date, be Cicero's.

Cicero may be making amends to Cato, whom he had earlier in *On Ends* 4.79 urged to adopt the more moderate Stoicism of Panaetius.[7] In that case, the way he does so is by showing that Cato's austerity fits the philosophy of Panaetius after all.

Cicero distinguishes some personae as being due to our own choice (*iudicium*) and will (*voluntas; On Duties* 1.115). We must decide who (*quos*) we wish to be and what kind of people (*quales*) and in what walk of life (*in quo*

---

5. Peter Winch, 'The universalisability of moral judgement', *Monist* 49, 1965, 196–214.

6. Cicero *On Duties* 2.60; 3.7.

7. Jonathan Powell, introduction to his, ed., *Cicero the Philosopher*, Oxford 1995, 23.

genere vitae). But we are young when we make this choice (1.117) and likely to follow our parents or popular choice (1.118). It is only people of exceptional ability who deliberate and make a choice on the basis of their own individual nature (*ad suam cuiusque naturam;* 1.118−20). Chance and even more nature influence the decision, and we should take account of both. But if we choose the wrong walk of life, we must change it (1.120). We do not have to follow our parents and our nature may not allow it (1.121).

In this discussion, we have seen reference to one's own *nature*, and this is a theme from the beginning, not only where the subject is choosing a walk of life, but where he or she is acting in accordance with natural character. It is nature that has given a persona to each individually (*proprie singulis;* 1,107). Cicero then illustrates the great variety of characters and concludes that natures and habits (*naturae, mores*) have innumerable differences, but (a point that will turn out to be significant) none of those he mentions are to be criticized (*vituperari;* 1.109). Even if other pursuits are better, we must measure our pursuits by the rule of our own nature, for it is no use fighting against our nature (1.110). You cannot imitate the nature of others and leave out your own (1.111). It is the difference in natures (*differentia naturarum*) that made Cato's suicide uniquely right, because nature had endowed Cato with an exceptional gravity, which he had strengthened by practice (1.112). It is because of different natures that the same conduct is not right for all.

This variability is illustrated in the next example, where Ulysses, as Odysseus is called in Latin, puts up with all sorts of indignities to achieve his objective of getting home, whereas Ajax (who killed himself because of shame on finding that he had in a fit of madness been slaughtering cattle instead of Trojans) would have died a thousand times rather than put up with them. As at 1.109, neither is criticized. Rather, each person must weigh what he has as his own peculiarity (*quid quisque habeat sui*) and must not want to try how he would be suited by another's (1.113). We should know our peculiar talent (*ingenium*) and what we are good and bad at, and behave in life like an actor choosing a part that suits his peculiar talent, even though necessity may sometimes drive us to parts that do not belong to that talent (1.114).

The first persona, our common human rationality, still plays an important role. It rules out acting on vicious character. The variability allowed is variability within the limits set by rationality and acceptable character.

As Francesca Alesse has shown particularly fully,[8] much of this is re-

---

8. Francesca Alesse, *Panezio di Rodi e la tradizione stoica*, Naples 1994, 267−78.

peated by Epictetus in the next century. It emerges what a commitment Epictetus took it to be to adopt the persona (Greek: *prosôpon*) of philosopher. It was then a badge of being a philosopher to wear a beard, and Epictetus says it is better for a philosopher to have his head cut off than his beard.[9] Henry Chadwick has described the philosopher's beard as exercising the same attraction and repulsion as the modern priest's dog collar.[10] Its origin is said to have lain in a misconception that arose when the clean-shaven Romans were smitten by a delegation from Athens in 155 BC of three bearded Greeks who were the leading philosophers of the day. The Romans assumed that the beard was the mark of a philosopher.[11] Similarly, the athlete who refused a life-saving excision of his genitals did so as a male and as a male who had been proclaimed at the Olympic games, not merely as one who had been to Bato's wrestling school (1.2.25−29).

Epictetus recognizes the same mixture of choice and nature, and uses the same metaphor of an actor's roles (*Discourses* 1.29.41−47; 4.7.13; *Handbook* 17), but with the complication that he sees our roles, character, ability, occupation, and status, as to some extent assigned by God [*Discourses* 3.22.4−8 (character, ability); 1.29.41−47; 4.7.13; *Handbook* 17 (occupation, status, physical disability)]. Nonetheless, we have choice. We must tell ourselves who we want to be (*tis einai theleis*) and then act accordingly, like an athlete choosing his speciality. There are, as in Cicero, a general reference point (*koinê anaphora*), viz. acting like a human being, not a sheep or a wild beast, and an individual reference point (*idia*), concerning our occupation (*epitêdeuma*) and will (*proairesis*), e.g., being a lyre-player, carpenter, philosopher, orator, cobbler, or geometer (3.23.1−8).

Epictetus *Discourses* 1.2 is devoted to the subject, and nature and choice are combined when we are urged to perceive what corresponds to (*kata*) our persona. What is reasonable or unreasonable differs for different people, so we have to fit our preconception of reasonableness to particular agents according to their nature. To make that decision, each person has to consider values that conform to (*kata*) his own persona (1.2.5−7). One slave is willing to hold a chamber pot for his master, another is not (1.2.8−11). As in Cicero, neither is criticized, although Epictetus makes clear that he admires

9. Epictetus 1.2.29. In modern times, Robert Nozick recognizes both the possibility of contributing to self-formation and of doing so in the light of persona or profession. Nozick, *Philosophical Explanations*, Oxford 1981, 106.

10. Henry Chadwick, *The Early Church*, Harmondsworth 1967.

11. Nicely told by John Sellars, *The Art of Living: The Stoics on the Nature and Function of Philosophy*, Aldershot 2003, introduction.

the defiant. But the main point is that the most admired conduct is not right for everyone, because each must act according to individual persona. Epictetus cites the examples of people who defied emperors, while others calculated external utilities. Again neither is criticized, although Epictetus is not so even-handed as Cicero, who gives Ulysses as his example of one who puts up with indignities. Indeed, Epictetus says that the calculator can come close to one who has forgotten his own persona (1.2.14). Nonetheless, the unusual and significant feature that is found also in Cicero is present, namely that this is not considered the right conduct for everyone. It is right only for those very exceptional people who have the corresponding persona. The purple thread depends on most threads being gray (1.2.18).

Next come the philosopher and the Olympic champion who prefer death to losing their beard or genitals, because that conforms to (*kata*) their persona (1.2.25–29). How does each person perceive what conforms to his persona? The bull knows this right away and charges the attacker without waiting, and the same will be true of those who are all ready to be philosophers (1.2.30; 4.8.41–42). But it can require reflection (*epilogismos*). Each persona as family member, as young or old, or as city councillor, when reflected on, sketches out the actions that are appropriate to it (2.10.11).

You cannot combine different roles. If you choose to be a philosopher, then you must change your whole way of life and cannot live like a tax gatherer, an orator, or a procurator of Caesar (3.15.10–13). This passage insists that different people are fitted by nature (*pephuke*) for different things (3.15.10), and Epictetus also insists on the different nature and constitution (*phusis, kataskeuê*) given to different types of animal as opposed to human, and compares the differences between wrestler, runner, and pancratist. Each must act according its own nature (1.6.15–16; 3.1.3–4).

Seneca[12] also takes up the point that whether you engage in public life should depend on your nature (*natura tua*).

Epictetus comes close to repeating the idea of a unique persona like Cato's. Only Agamemnon could command the Greek army, only Achilles fight Hector. If Thersites claimed command of the Greek armies at Troy, instead of Agamemnon, he would either not get it or would disgrace himself if he did (3.22.4–8). Speaking of Helvidius Priscus, who defied the emperor, he says that had the emperor Vespasian told another man in such circumstances to avoid confrontation by not attending the Senate, he would gladly have accepted. The Greek for 'in such circumstances' is *en toiautêi*

---

12. Seneca *On Tranquility* 6–7.2.

peristasei, which was presumably the Greek original for Cicero's Latin *in eadem causa*. In Cicero, the expression was used to make the point, with which Epictetus agrees, that others *should* not act like Cato. Here it tells us that others *would* not act like Priscus. This comes close to presenting the defiant Helvidius Priscus as unique (1.2.23–24).

In 3.1.19–42, Epictetus returns to the subject and talks at 23 and 30 about *my* nature, which has made me different from the rest, and *your* nature. Kronenberg was wrong to delete the reference to *my*. You must know who you are, as the Delphic oracle says (23), not merely what it is to be human in general. Rather (27–35), a male must act like a male, not like a woman, and the exceptional person is again compared at 23 with the purple stripe.

It is striking how often Cicero and Epictetus use proper names to make their point that different action is called for in the same circumstances when character differs. At least they use proper names when character is exceptional or unique: Cato, Ulysses, Ajax, Agamemnon, Achilles, Agrippinus, Helvidius Priscus. The proper name conjures up the entire biography of Cato, or an entire epic, the twenty-four books of the *Odyssey* for Ulysses, the twenty-four books of the *Iliad* for Ulysses, Ajax, Agamemnon, and Achilles. It would not be possible to formulate a rule about who should put up with what indignities by mentioning a couple of characteristics of Ulysses. It is the entire epic that shows why it was right for him.

The Stoics had a special interest in exceptional circumstances, and their word for circumstances was the one we have just met in Epictetus, *peristaseis*. What is new since Panaetius is treating the individual persona as something else that may be exceptional. But there are plenty of other exceptions. Not only is suicide sometimes permissible,[13] but also a vow like Agamemnon's to slay his daughter should not be kept.[14] Lies may be allowed.[15] A borrowed sword, as Plato said, should not be returned to a madman.[16] Parents are not always to be obeyed, if they forbid you to study philosophy.[17] A Stoic need not always engage in public life.[18] Sometimes it is better to mutilate

13. Besides the texts already discussed, see Cicero, *On Ends* 3.60–61; Olympiodorus, *Commentary on Plato's Phaedo* 1.8, ed. and trans. L. G. Westerink, *The Greek Commentaries on Plato's Phaedo*, vol. 1, Amsterdam 1976.

14. Cicero *On Duties* 3.92–95.

15. Stobaeus 2.111.13–17, Wachsmuth; Philo, *On the Cherubim* 14–15, LS 59H.

16. Plato's example from *Republic* bk. 1, borrowed by the Stoics; Philo *On the Cherubim* 14–15.

17. Musonius Rufus frag. 16 in Teubner edition, trans. Cora Lutz, *Yale Classical Studies* 10, 1947.

18. Cicero *On Duties* 1.70–71; Seneca, *Letter* 68.

oneself, or to give away one's property.[19] Sometimes it is better for your foot to get muddy, or for you to be ill.[20] It all depends on circumstances. Circumstances qualify doctrines about what is to be preferred or dispreferred[21] and about what your duty is.[22] Only sometimes can the exceptions be brought under rules of any useful sort. One cannot say in general when and how things are to be done, nor whether to commit suicide.[23] In general, I believe the Stoics did not think that ethics could be covered by a system of rules.[24] In this they were like Aristotle, who insists, especially in *Nicomachean Ethics* bk. 6, that perceptivity is needed that can bend rules, and that if one lacks that perceptivity oneself, one must follow someone who has it.[25] As with Aristotle, the wise person is the only interpreter of and standard of what is lawful.[26] One is advised to have a mentor, or, if none is available, to select a person one knows of and ask oneself what he would do (e.g., Epictetus *Handbook* 33.12, Seneca *Letters* 6.5–6).

Although some Stoics find precepts, or general rules of thumb, and also syllogisms useful, the precepts cannot tell you exactly what to do.[27] And Seneca comments that the syllogisms available on virtue are as yet very few.[28] The so-called 'doctrines' that Seneca contrasts with precepts in *Letters* 94 and 95 should not be thought of as moral rules or principles particularly, but as any of the Stoic theories that he mentions in his letters and treatises and especially in these two letters, only some of which are ethical. The ethical ones are not all presented as rules of behavior, but will include, for example, statements about what matters and what is indifferent, or what the goal of life should be. But the non-ethical ones may be equally relevant. A good example would be the theory of the nature of emotions, which has practical implications concerning the right approach for calming them. Epictetus calls it a rule (*kanôn*) to treat as indifferent whatever is not under the control of your will, in a passage translated in chapter ten (*Discourses* 3.3.14–19), but this does not cover the whole of ethics. Cicero is drawing on

19. Diogenes Laertius *Lives* 7.108–9, trans. LS 59E.

20. Epictetus *Discourses* 2.6.9, trans. LS 58J.

21. Epictetus *Discourses* 2.6.9, approving Chrysippus.

22. Diogenes Laertius *Lives* 7.109.

23. Seneca *Letters* 22.1–2, 95.4–5, 70.11.

24. In this I agree with Brad Inwood, 'Rules and reasoning in Stoic ethics', in Katerina Ierodiakonou, ed., *Some Topics in Stoicism*, Oxford 1999, ch. 4.

25. Richard Sorabji, *Necessity, Cause, and Blame*, London and Ithaca N.Y. 1980, ch. 16.

26. Stobaeus 2.102, lines 8–9 Wachsmuth.

27. Seneca *Letters* 95.4–5 and 51.

28. Seneca *Letters* 87.11.

other Stoics, Diogenes of Babylon and Antipater, when in *On Duties* 3 he speaks both of a rule (*regula*) and more broadly of a *formula* for dealing with ethical dilemmas,[29] but neither tells you whether you should confess that your house has rot when you are selling it.

I have said this in order to suggest that the Stoics differ from Kantians in the restrictions on their reliance on rules and in their interest in exceptions that do not always fall under rules. But the particular need to be true to your self, and in cases where that self is unique, is a special case of this attitude. I take the doctrine of individual persona and nature to give Stoicism a new interest in the individual in the period from Panaetius (who died in 109 BC) through the 1st century AD. I agree with Alesse and others that Epictetus derives the ideas of individual persona and nature from his Stoic predecessor Panaetius. This provides a further example, to add to those in chapter ten, of Epictetus not merely conforming to the early Stoics. But why should Stoicism have developed this new interest in the individual? I am impressed by David Sedley's suggestion[30] that earlier Stoic ethics had typically set up the ideal sage as model. Panaetius is credited (see Cicero *On Duties* 1.46) with having a new interest in the imperfect person who is merely progressing towards sagehood. Seneca reports that Panaetius set aside the question of whether the sage would fall in love and said that you and I, who are a great distance from the sage, should avoid it (*Letters* 116,5).

I shall return to Epictetus in chapter ten below and to his idea of the self being inviolable, provided that I am my *proairesis*, very roughly, my will. I shall argue there that Epictetus does not go back in this doctrine to the early Stoics of the 3rd century BC, but is developing something new, though something clearly Stoic in character. On the present issue too, that of the acting according to individual persona and nature, I believe he is not going back to the early Stoics, but rather is deploying, with his own rather austere slant, the ideas of the much later Stoic Panaetius.

Kant's lectures on ethics, as recorded by a student, display knowledge of the uniqeness of the case for Cato's suicide,[31] but only as a point about the legitimacy of suicide, not as a general point about decisions, and only as something put forward by the defenders of suicide rather than as something

29. See especially Cicero *On Duties* 3.19–22.

30. In conversation and in 'The Stoic-Platonist debate on *kathêkonta*', in Katerina Ierodiakonou, ed., *Topics in Stoic Philosophy*, Oxford 1999, 151.

31. Kant, *Lectures on Ethics*, translated by Louis Infield, London 1930, 149; also translated by Peter Heath in Kant, *Lectures on Ethics*, in the series *Cambridge Texts in the History of Political Thought*, Cambridge 1997. I owe the reference to Dan Robinson.

read at first hand. The defenders' case is that Cato's life, if continued, would have been deprived of value, of prudence and virtue, and he could not go on living as Cato. But this is mentioned only at the very end and what they put first is a consequentialist consideration that is foreign to Cicero, namely that Cato's falling into Caesar's hands would have put an end to the struggle for freedom. In putting this first, they bring the apparent exception under a general rule, in a different spirit from Cicero's. The only faint analogue in Cicero's text to this consequentialist consideration is the point that suicide in the case of people other than Cato might have been attributed (*datum*) to cowardice.[32]

The notes of Kant's lectures suggest that Cato's case is unique in the history of the world, and, like Augustine (*City of God* 1.19), they reject the case for Lucretia committing suicide when she had been raped. Let us see the texts where the Stoic development occurs. Cicero's words come from that part of his *On Duties* which draws extensively from Panaetius.

Cicero *On Duties* 1.46:

> But since life is lived not in company with perfect people who are truly sages, but with those who are doing very well if there are likenesses of virtue in them, I think this too must be understood, that no one should be entirely neglected in whom any hint of virtue appears.

Once the Stoics are concerned with the imperfect, the differences between individuals gain a new importance. The interest in imperfect progressives is prominent in Seneca, in Epictetus, and in Epictetus' teacher, Musonius Rufus, whose fragments[33] discuss such questions as the education of girls, when to obey your parents, what clothes to wear, and when to get your hair cut. In favor of earlier Stoic interest, attention has been drawn to the qualified support that Seneca says was already given as early as Cleanthes, the second head of the Stoic school in the 3rd century BC, to precepts (*Letter* 94,4).[34] Precepts are there described as rules of thumb directed to each persona—to husband, father, or master of slaves—rather than to human beings taken generally (94,1). But Cleanthes is here said to have con-

---

32. I thank Deborah Modrak for pointing out the analogy.

33. Musonius Rufus fragments ed. Hense, trans. Cora Lutz, *Yale Classical Studies* 10, 1947, 3–147.

34. Teun Tieleman, 'Panaetius' place in the history of Stoicism', forthcoming in Proceedings of the Symposium Hellenisticum held in Rome, July 2004: Between Greece and Rome: Hellenistic Philosophy and Roman Culture from 150 to 88 BC.

sidered the use of precepts feeble unless it flowed from the universal and recognized the theoretical doctrines of Stoic philosophy. So there is as yet little sign of comparable interest in making the individual central.

It would be wrong to say that there were no antecedents at all outside the Stoic school. For one thing, Alex Cohen has pointed out to me that Socrates is represented in Plato's *Crito* as appealing to his particular attachment to Athens and his never having left it except on military service to show why it is right for him not to escape his execution by leaving now. This provides an example of appealing to what Cicero will call a persona. But what Panaetius has done is to generalize the need to take the individual persona into account.

Christopher Gill[35] has most valuably drawn attention to another set of antecedents. Among the atomist philosophers, already in the 5th century BC, the Presocratic Democritus urged people not to undertake activities beyond their own capacity and nature (*huper te dunamin . . . tên eâutou kai phusin*), and the talk of not forcing oneself beyond one's ability is repeated by the atomist Epicurus at the end of the next century.[36] Epicurus is also reported critically by Plutarch as saying that those who can't bear inactivity should indulge their nature (*têi phusei khrêsthai*) by engaging in public life. Evidently, however, Panaetius' theory of personae goes far beyond this.

The idea of being true to yourself which we have found in the late Stoics has been described by Charles Taylor as a relatively new ethic peculiar to modern culture and a child of the Romantic period.[37] He finds it articulated by Rousseau and Herder and he sees merit in it, not the Stoic merit of Cato's high morality, or of a wiser choice of conventional career, but the potentiality for a fuller and more differentiated life. But his version of the idea is not constrained like the Stoic one by the requirements of the first persona—being rational—nor by the constraints of acting according to such inherited roles as being a prince or a slave. That is what makes it something new in the Romantic period. Other forms of individualism have also been assigned to later periods.[38] Possibly closer to the Stoics is the Confucian

35. Christopher Gill, 'Peace of mind and being yourself: Panaetius to Plutarch', in *Aufstieg und Niedergang der römischen Welt* 2.36.7, 4599–4640.

36. Democritus frag. 3, Diels-Kranz; Epicurus frag. given by Diogenes of Oenoanda, cited in Diels-Kranz vol. 2, p. 132, n. 1.

37. Charles Taylor, *The Malaise of Modernity*, Concord, Ontario 1991, 15, 24–28, 74. I thank Vasanthi Srinivasam for the reference.

38. One form is denied to the Greeks by Diskin Clay, 'Missing persons, or the selfless Greeks', in William J. Carroll, J. J. Furlong, and C. S. Mann, eds., *The Quest for the Individ-*

view of the individual as organizing a unique place in the center of a social network,[39] but that must wait for another occassion.

I finish with quotations of the main passages discussed.

Cicero *De officiis* 1.107, 109, 110, 112, 113, drawing on Panaetius:

(107) It must also be understood that we are endowed by nature with, as it were, two personae, of which the communal one derives from the fact that we all participate in reason and in that superiority by which we excel over animals and from which is drawn all good and proper conduct and from which is found the method for ascertaining our duty. The other persona is that attributed to individuals as special to them (*proprie*). . . .

(109) There are innumerable other dissimilarities among natures (*natura*) and habits (*mores*) that are still in no way to be criticized (*vituperandi*).

(110) But everyone must hold firmly onto what is his own, so long as it is not vicious but special (*propria*) to him, so that that proper conduct that we are seeking may more easily be secured. For we must act in such a way that we in no way oppose universal nature, but, with that safeguarded, we follow our own special (*propria*) nature. . . .

(112) And this difference of natures has so much force that sometimes one man ought to commit suicide, while another in the same situation (*in eadem causa*, not in all mss.) ought not. For was Marcus Cato in a different situation from the others who surrendered to Caesar in Africa? But perhaps with the others it would have been attributed to moral failure if they had killed themselves, because their lives had been less austere and their habits more easygoing. Since nature had conferred on Cato an incredible gravity, and he had strengthened it by unceasing consistency, and had always persisted in his resolved purpose, it was right for him to die (*moriendum*) rather than to look on the face of a tyrant.

(113) How much Ulysses endured in his long wanderings, when he submitted even to women, if Circe and Calypso are to be called women, and de-

---

ual Roots of Western Civilization, New York 1990. Another is ascribed to the twelfth century by Colin Morris, *The Discovery of the Individual 1050–1200*, London 1972; another to the thirteenth to sixteenth centuries by Robert Rehder, *Wordsworth and the Beginnings of Modern Poetry*, London and Totowa N.J. 1981, 17–43, 74–80; and another to the fourteenth to sixteenth centuries by Thomas Greene, 'The flexibility of the self in Renaissance literature', in Peter Demetz, Thomas Greene, and Lowry Nelson Jr., eds., *The Disciplines of Criticism*, New Haven 1968, 241–64. Morris appeals inter alia to the idea of first movements of temptation, which I have elsewhere traced back from the eleventh century to the fourth.

39. Roger T. Ames, 'The focus-field in classical Confucianism', in his (ed.) *Self as Person in Asian Theory and Practice*, Albany N.Y. 1994, 187–212.

cided to be affable and pleasant to everyone. Indeed, back home, he put up even with the insults of male and female servants, in order that he might eventually reach the object of his desire. But Ajax, given the cast of mind that is reported of him, would have met death a thousand times rather than endure that. As we contemplate this, each person must weigh what he has as his own peculiarity (*quid quisque habeat sui*) and must regulate that and not want to try how he would be suited by another's. For what suits each person best is what is most peculiar to him.

(120) Since the greatest influence on this calculation is possessed by nature, the next greatest by fortune, it is quite essential to take account of each in choosing a way of life, but more account of nature. For it is much stronger and more stable, so that fortune sometimes seems to be fighting like a mortal with an immortal nature. Whenever, therefore, someone has conformed his whole plan of life to his kind of nature, assuming it is not vicious, let him exercise perseverance, for that is the most fitting thing, unless by chance he realizes he has made a mistake in choosing a way of life. If this should happen—and it can happen—a change must be made in his manner of life and occupations. . . .

(121) But since it was said a little earlier that we must imitate our elders, the first exception should be that vices are not to be imitated, and then [the second arises] if one's nature will not allow certain things to be imitated (as the son of the older Africanus, the one who adopted this son of Paulus, could not, because of ill health, resemble his father as much as the father had resembled his). If, then, one cannot defend court cases, or hold the people with orations, or wage war, nonetheless one will have to maintain what is in one's power, justice, fidelity, generosity, moderation, temperance, so that what one lacks may be the less missed in one.

Epictetus *Discourses* 1.2.8–24:

(8) For one person it is reasonable to hold someone's chamber pot, looking only at the fact that if he does not, he will get a beating and will not get food, whereas if he does hold it, he will suffer no rough or painful treatment. (9) For another not only does it seem intolerable that he should hold it, but even that he should put up with another's holding it. (10) If, then, you ask me, 'shall I hold the pot or not?', I will say to you that there is more value in getting food than in not getting food and more disvalue in being flayed than in not being flayed. So if you measure what belongs to you by this, go off and hold the pot. (11) 'Yes, but that would not be like (*kata*) me'. That is for you to bring into consideration, not for me. For you are the one who knows yourself, how

much you are worth to yourself, and for how much you sell yourself. Different people sell themselves for different amounts.

(12) For this reason, when Florus was considering whether he should go in for Nero's spectacle, so as to make a contribution to it himself, Agrippinus said to him, 'Go in for it'. (13) But when Florus asked, 'Why are you not going in?', (14) Agrippinus replied, 'I would not even think about it'. For once someone has stooped to the consideration of such things and to the evaluation of externals and calculates them, he is close to those who have forgotten their own persona. (15) What are you asking me? 'Is death or life preferable?' I say life. (16) 'Pain or pleasure?' I say pleasure. 'But if I don't take part in the tragedy, I shall have my head cut off'. Go off, then, and take part in the tragedy, but I will not take part in it. (17) 'Why?' Because you consider yourself one thread among those that make up the cloak. 'What, then?' You had to think how you might be like the other people, just as a thread too does not want to have something distinguishing it from the other threads. (18) But I want to be the purple thread, that small shining part that makes the others appear handsome and beautiful. 'Why then do you say to me, "Be like the majority"? How else will I still be the purple?'

(19) Helvidius Priscus saw this too—he saw and acted. When Vespasian sent him a message not to go to the Senate, he replied, 'It is up to you not to allow me to be a Senator, but so long as I am, I have to go'. (20) 'Very well', says Vespasian, 'but when you go, stay silent'. 'Don't ask my opinion and I will stay silent'. 'But I have to ask your opinion'. 'And I have to say what appears to me just'. (21) 'But if you speak, I shall kill you'. 'When did I say to you, then, that I am immortal? You will do what it is yours to do, and I what is mine. It is yours to kill, mine to die without trembling. Yours to banish, mine to leave without grieving'. (22) What good did Priscus, then, do, being just one person on his own? What good does the purple do to the cloak? What more than that it stands out in it as purple and is presented as a beautiful model for the other threads? (23) If Caesar had told another in such circumstances (*en toiautêi peristasei*) not to go to the Senate, he would have said, 'I thank you for sparing me'. (24) Such a person Caesar would not even have tried to prevent from going, but would have known that either he would sit like a pot, or, if he spoke, would say what he knew Caesar wanted and would heap still more on top of that.

Epictetus *Discourses* 1.2.29:

'Come then, Epictetus, shave off your beard'. If I am a philosopher, I say, 'I will not shave it off'. 'But I will take off your head'. 'If that is better for you, take it off'.

Epictetus *Discourses* 3.22.4, 3.22.7–8:

(4) The same also happens in this great city [the world]. For here too there is a master of the house who arranges everything. . . . (7) 'You are able to lead the army against Troy. Be Agamemnon. You are able to fight in single combat with Hector. Be Achilles.' (8) But if Thersites came along and claimed command, either he would not have got it, or if he got it, he would have disgraced himself in front of many witnesses.

Epictetus *Discourses* 3.23.4–5:

It remains that there is one reference common to all, and one individual (*idia*) reference point. First, that I am human. What is included in this? First, not to act well in the manner of cattle, nor harmfully in the manner of a wild beast. The individual reference looks to the occupation and will (*proairesis*) of each person. The lyre player is to act like a lyre player, the carpenter as a carpenter, the philosopher as a philosopher, the orator as an orator.

Kant *Lectures on Ethics: Suicide,* trans. Louis Infield, London 1930, p. 149:

There is another set of considerations which make suicide seem plausible. A man might find himself so placed that he can continue living only under circumstances which deprive life of all value; in which he can no longer live conformably to virtue and prudence, so that he must from noble motives put an end to his life. The advocates of this view quote in support of it the example of Cato. Cato knew that the entire Roman nation relied upon him in their resistance to Caesar, but he found that he could not prevent himself from falling into Caesar's hands. What was he to do? If he, the champion of freedom, submitted, everyone would say, "If Cato himself submits, what else can we do?" If, on the other hand, he killed himself, his death might spur on the Romans to fight to the bitter end in defence of their freedom. So he killed himself. He thought that it was necessary for him to die. He thought that if he could not go on living as Cato, he could not go on living at all.

It must certainly be admitted that in a case such as this, where suicide is a virtue, appearances are in its favor. But this is the only example which has given the world the opportunity of defending suicide. It is the only example of its kind and there has been no similar case since. Lucretia also killed herself, but on grounds of modesty and in a fury of vengeance.

CHAPTER 9

Plutarch: narrative and a whole life

Another ancient philosopher made memory constitute the self, Plutarch of Chaeroneia, the Middle Platonist of the 1st century AD. This is in the text that I described in chapter two as making the earliest connection I knew between self and narrative, and I there considered two different interpretations. Writing about tranquility, Plutarch says that in order to attain it we need to use our memories to weave our life into a unified whole. If we do not, we will be like the man in the painting who is plaiting a rope in Hades and who throws it over his shoulder as he plaits it, but does not notice that a donkey is eating it up behind him. Seneca has a version of the same advice and uses the metaphor of allowing one's life to fall into an abyss and the time one is granted to escape through the holes in the mind like water through a leaky vessel.[1] He is criticizing those who are too engrossed in their current strivings. For such people it would not even be pleasant if they did look back. Among the Stoics' rivals, Epicurus also claimed to gain tranquility on his painful deathbed by recalling, not indeed his life as a whole, but his past philosophical discoveries[2] and enjoyable philosophical conversations from the past.[3] Seneca seems to have modeled his remarks on an Epicurean account in Lucretius 3.933–62, which describes people who are forever seeking something new, instead of savoring what they have, as having poured everything into a leaky vessel.

Plutarch, but not Seneca, adds that we shall also be like the people described in the Growing Argument, translated above in chapter four, who have no continuous self. We must, as mentioned in chapter two, weave in

1. Seneca *On the Shortness of Life* 10, 2–6.
2. Cicero *On Ends* 2.96; *Tusculan Disputations* 5.88.
3. Diogenes Laertius *Lives* 10.22.

the bad parts, as well as the good, for a picture needs dark patches as well as bright, and music needs low notes as well as high. But we must not *wallow* in the bad parts, like beetles in the place called 'Death to Beetles', where beetles struggle until they die. Tranquility results not merely from the use of memory, but from the skilful weaving in of good and bad.

Plutarch is committed, like Epictetus as described in chapters two and ten, and like Locke as interpreted in chapter five, to the idea that to some extent we create ourselves, and like Locke to the idea that memory plays a role in this. Epictetus, by contrast, recommends self-creation through training our choices, not, like Plutarch, our memory.

On one of the two interpretations of Plutarch, there is no continuous self, until the weaving has been done. On the other, there is already a human being, but until that human being weaves the story of their life, they will not have adopted an identity of their own. This kind of identity is very well described by Marya Schechtman in her book, *The Constitution of Selves*,[4] where she uses, without referring to Plutarch, the very same idea of weaving the story or narrative of one's life. This kind of identity is also recognized by Parfit, who speaks of major changes of value as producing a different self.[5] It is rather like the creation of a persona by memory, rather than by nature and choice, although that is not the way Plutarch puts it. The appeal to the Growing Argument suggests the more radical view that there is no continuous self unless it is woven.

It might be thought that this more radical interpretation must be ruled out, because who would there be to do the weaving if the self needs first to be woven? But this is not decisive, as shown by Daniel Dennett, who confronts a similar problem when he treats life stories as fictions.[6] Who, in that case, he asks himself, does the story telling? It is enough, he replies, that one of the uncoordinated elements in our brain should produce one fragment of story and another another. The illusion will arise of a continuous life story. So if Plutarch, like Dennett, takes a more fragmented view of persons, he might equally reply that each of the momentary selves can contribute a fragment of the story, only on his view, the process will produce a true story, not a Dennettian fiction, because the story telling will weave the momentary selves into one, at least if the last momentary self can 'remember' earlier contributions to the story.

4. Marya Schechtman, *The Constitution of Selves*, Ithaca N.Y. 1996.

5. Derek Parfit, *Reasons and Persons*, Oxford 1984, revised 1987, 327–29.

6. Daniel Dennett, 'Why everyone is a novelist', *Times Literary Supplement*, 16–22 September 1988, 1016; *Consciousness Explained*, Boston 1991.

But there is evidence that Plutarch backs away from the idea of there being no self until woven, despite this being suggested by his appeal to the Growing Argument. For one thing, Plutarch relies on the idea that the memories woven in are genuine memories, in other words, memories of the very same human who originally had the experiences remembered. This suggests that he may be taking the Schechtman view rather than the more fragmented one. And this is further confirmed when he goes on to suggest that it is not the self that lacks unification, as reference to the Growing Argument would have suggested, but only the life led.

The resulting view might be put by saying that, without the process of weaving, one will have no persona. But that way of putting it, which is not Plutarch's, brings out the view's weakness. For the Stoics, it was seen in the last chapter, held that one gained a persona partly from nature, partly from one's chance position in society, and partly from choices. It would be more plausible if Plutarch had said that, without the further weaving through memory, one will not sufficiently develop one's persona.

Plutarch *On Tranquility* 473B–474B:

> That everyone has within himself the store-rooms of good and bad cheer (*eu-thumia, dusthumia*) and that the jars of goods and evils are laid down not on the threshold of Zeus, but in the soul, is clear from the differences in people's emotions (*pathē*). For foolish people overlook and neglect even present goods because they are always intent in their thoughts on the future. But wise people make even what no longer exists to exist vividly for themselves by the use of memory. The present, which allows contact with only the smallest portion of time and then escapes observation, no longer seems to the foolish to be anything to us or to be ours. But just as the man pictured in Hades plaiting a rope allows a grazing donkey to consume what he is plaiting, so forgetfulness, unaware of most things and ungrateful, snatches and overruns things, obliterating every action and right act, every pleasant discussion, meeting, or enjoyment, and does not allow our life to be unified, through the past being woven together with the future. Whatever happens, it immediately consigns it to what has not happened by forgetfulness, and divides yesterday's life from today's as something different, and tomorrow's similarly as not the same as today's. Those in the schools who refute the fact of growth on the grounds that substance is perpetually flowing make each of us in theory ever different from himself. But those who do not preserve or retrieve the past in memory, but allow it to flow away from under them, make themselves needy every day in

actual fact, and empty and dependent on tomorrow, as if last year and yesterday and the day before were nothing to them and had not actually happened
to them.

This is one thing that disturbs good cheer. Another does so more, when
people drift away from cheerful and soothing things and get enmeshed in recollections of the disagreeable. It is as when flies slip off the smooth patches on
mirrors and catch hold of the rough and scratched ones, or rather as they say
that beetles in Olynthus, falling into a place called 'Death to Beetles', are unable to get out, but twist and turn there until they die. That is how people who
slide into the memory of ills do not want to recover or revive. What we should
do is make the bright and shining events prominent in the mind, like the colors in a picture, and hide and suppress the gloomy ones, since we cannot rub
them out or get rid of them altogether. For the harmony of the cosmos, like
that of a lyre or bow, involves bending in two directions, and nothing in human affairs is pure or unmixed. But as in music there are high and low notes,
and in language consonants and vowels, and a musician or language specialist
is not one who dislikes either of these, but one who knows how to use them all
and mix (*mignunai*) them appropriately, so . . . we too should make the mixture (*migma*) of our life harmonious and appropriate for ourselves.

When a self is created, whether by memory like Plutarch's, or by nature, by chance acquisition of roles, and by choices as in Cato and Epictetus,
it will not necessarily be present from the moment of birth. The same applies
not only to the woven life and to the individual persona insofar as it is based
on choice rather than nature, but also to Epictetus' self as rightly directed
will. And we have noticed in chapter five that Augustine does not count his
unremembered infancy as part of his life. But none of this means that the interest is in short-term selves. That is what Plutarch is warning against. It is
the exception, we saw in chapter two, when short-term selves are invoked
to counteract worry about the death of the long-term self.

Is Plutarch's advice on achieving tranquility through using our memory sound? One problem that Plutarch recognizes is that those who wallow
in bad memories will not gain tranquility. But more serious may be the case
of those who have traumatic memories and may need to do something more
complicated than weaving in the dark patches.

Second, it is perhaps even more important to weave in future projects.
The late Russian neuropsychologist, A. R. Luria, wrote a book about a man
who had lost his memory of who he was through being shot in the brain in

the Second World War. His life's project was trying to discover who he was and writing a diary at the rate of about a word a day describing his efforts. Luria comments that those of his patients who lost the ability to plan future projects disintegrated far more than those who had lost their memories.[7] For tranquility, no doubt, this man would have had to succeed in remembering his past. But to have a firm identity, the continuing project was enough. Admittedly the project involved certain kinds of memory, memory that he had lost something, memory of the plan to regain it, the motor memories required for writing, and so on, but not memory of episodes in his past.

Third, there is the danger of self-serving falsification, if identity is allowed to depend on memory. In fact, in its earliest version with Epicharmus in the 5th century BC, the Growing Argument's fragmentation of the self was designed to disclaim responsibility for what was done by selves falsely deemed to be other. If the fragmentation is to be repaired by weaving a narrative, the weaver must not be allowed to weave a narrative that equally falsifies by wrong inclusion and exclusion of data. Some such problem was later to attend Locke's account of the self as constituted by memory. Self-creation by use of memory is more liable to falsification than self-creation through the choices that one makes. Cato's austerity, bestowed by nature but strengthened by consistent choices, was cited from Cicero (*On Duties* 1.112) in chapter eight. Epictetus' narrowing of his self down to a rightly directed will, so that his body is not an object of concern, will be described below in chapter ten. Such self-creation through choice does indeed create an identity without particularly inviting self-deception about one's identity. But even in the case of self-creation through choice, falsification can come in, as it does in the case of the waiter described by Sartre in his account of bad faith. The role of a waiter, which in Sartre's opinion is freely chosen, can be deliberately over-acted so as to distance oneself from the role in an act of bad faith.[8] Cicero warns of another sort of falsification, in the text discussed in chapter eight above, arising from choosing the profession of your parents against your own nature (*On Duties* 1.118–20). It was a commonplace that it is very hard to go against one's nature, and some said that only philosophy could enable you to do so,[9] although Aristotle put a lot of trust in early habits as providing second nature.[10] Another source of falsifying choices

7. A. R. Luria, *Man with a Shattered World*, London 1973.
8. Sartre, *Being and Nothingness*, trans. Hazel Barnes, London 1969, ch. 2, II, pp. 59–60.
9. Cicero *On Fate* 10; *Tusculan Disputations* 4.80; Philoponus *in DA* 51,13–52,1.
10. Aristotle *EN* 1152a31–33; *On Memory* 452a30; ps-Aristotle *MM* 1203b30–32.

arises when you find yourself at odds with the choices of your former self, as in George Elliot's *Middlemarch,* with Dorothea's life commitment to foster the late husband's work now seen to be valueless.[11]

I am not persuaded by a fourth anxiety, though it is related, that acting according to a life story or a role would restrict our freedom.[12] In the example discussed in chapter eight above, Cato could do no other when he decided on suicide, but given his life history, that did not remove his freedom. Sartre's waiter acting in bad faith is freely choosing to distance himself from his role by overacting it, according to Sartre.

But finally, is it so disastrous as Plutarch claims if someone does not weave the story of his or her life? Christopher Pelling argued, in his inaugural lecture as professor of Greek at Oxford in 2004, that biographies up to Plutarch's time did not narrate the whole of a life, but only the striking parts. He reminded his audience that curricula vitae in the U.S.A. were often written backwards, so that the latest achievements would be read first.

IS A LIFE NARRATIVE NEEDED FOR MORAL DEVELOPMENT?

Galen Strawson has made a powerful and interesting case for the dispensability of life-pictures in an article, 'Against narrativity',[13] of which he has been kind enough to show me a longer version. I am indeed agnostic whether a life-view is needed to make people tranquil. It is rather for the kinds of moral development widely favored in ancient philosophy, whether or not that involves the development of tranquility, that a picture of much of one's life seems to be needed. I would make only two qualifications. First, the picture often, as we shall see, looks to the future as much as to the past. Second, in certain cases one's past life may work unconsciously, without having to be recognized as a narrative. But I doubt whether one can count on reflection not being required on one's past or future life, and certainly most ancient theories would deny this. Let us look at some examples.

Socrates is represented by Plato in the *Crito* as choosing not to es-

11. Discussed by Peter Winch, 'Text and context', in his *Trying to Make Sense,* Oxford 1987.

12. The anxiety about freedom is expressed by Samantha Vice, 'Literature and the narrative self', *Philosophy* 78, 2003, 93–108.

13. Galen Strawson, 'Against narrativity', *Times Literary Supplement,* 13 Oct. 2004.

cape from prison in order to remain consistent with the rest of his life. Aristotle's students in his *Nicomachean Ethics* are supposed to work out policies (*proaireseis*) for achieving the most important goals in life, as I shall describe in chapter ten. Cato was presented by Cicero as committing suicide to maintain consistency with his whole life. Epictetus' wish to narrow the self down to exclude the body and anything except a rightly directed will requires constant attention to how one is doing. So does the self-interrogation practiced every night by another Stoic, Seneca, as described in chapter two, a practice borrowed from the Pythagoreans and bequeathed to the Christian Basil of Caesarea.[14] The very idea, encouraged by the Stoic Panaetius and followed by Seneca, that we can at least *progress* (*prokoptein* is the Stoic term) in the direction of being sages requires us to look at much of our lives. The Platonist Plutarch wrote a treatise on how to judge one's moral progress.

Aristotle further approves, in *Nicomachean Ethics* 1.10, Solon's saying, 'Call no man happy until he is dead', and adds 'if then', meaning that one cannot evaluate a life except as a whole and in the light of its outcome and whether its projects finally come to fruition.[15] This represents a different context, not decision-making, but evaluating a life. In the story told by Herodotus, Croesus, king of Lydia, was prematurely considered happy for his wealth. But when conquered by Cyrus, king of Persia, and placed on top of a bonfire for burning, he cried out, 'Oh, Solon! Solon!' Cyrus asked the meaning and on being told that Solon had said 'Call no man happy until he is dead', he was so impressed that he brought Croesus down from the bonfire.

The idea of progress appealed in religious as well as secular contexts. Ascetic Church Fathers like Evagrius founded a whole Christian tradition, using the Stoic word for progress, which was conceived as being towards the Stoic ideal of freedom from emotion.[16] Evagrius believed in the perfectability of man, a belief with a long history, secular as well as religious, which John Passmore has traced from Homer to the present day.[17] The Christian Augustine disagreed, charging that Evagrius overlooked original sin and the need for God's Grace, but he still sees himself in his *Confessions* as trying to make progress through his life towards God. The idea of the human as a wayfarer (*viator*) in this life returning to his heavenly home is borrowed

14. Basil *Ascetic Sermons* 1, col. 882, *PG* 31.
15. My thanks to Jan Opsomer for the reminder.
16. See Richard Sorabji, *Emotion and Peace of Mind*, Oxford 2000, ch. 23.
17. John Passmore, *The Perfectability of Man*, London 1970.

from Neoplatonism by medieval Christianity.[18] John Bunyan's *Pilgrim's Progress* presupposes this kind of survey of one's life, but it is influenced in this case not by Stoicism, but by a Pythagorean work of the 1st century BC or AD, very popular up to the 19th century, *The Table of Cebes*, which tells of the choices between good and evil to be made at many crossroads on the way to a Pythagorean heaven. Among Neoplatonists, Plotinus recommends, as we saw in chapter six, that you identify with higher and higher selves, as you follow higher and higher daemons through your life (3.4 [15] 3 (1–22)). His pupil, Porphyry, describes a series of types of virtue through which you can ascend (*Sentences* 32). The whole Neoplatonist teaching curriculum after Iamblichus was designed to lead the student in an ascent towards God.[19]

Are there examples on the other side among ancient moral theories? The Stoic emperor, Marcus Aurelius, famously tells himself in his *Meditations* that we should live only in the present. But this is one of the exercises in a book of exercises designed to shape his whole life. He seeks to free himself from the fear of assassination by the exercise of placing value only on the present. The exercises, to be renewed every day, are directed to the future, to maintain him in Stoic attitudes as long as he lives. Are hedonists confined to the present in a more relevant way? But according to Plato's *Protagoras* (356C–D), they may require a calculus to avoid misestimating the size of future pleasures. This may be true of Epicurus too, and we have already seen him drawing on past pleasures to gain tranquility on his deathbed. Aristippus was the only ancient hedonist to say that we should merely seek the pleasure of the present moment.[20]

Moral development, as I have acknowledged, can occur unconsciously without any conscious survey of much of one's life. But I am not sure that ancient moral theories left it to chance in this way. And I am not sure that one can count on reflection not being required on one's past or future life. Certainly most of the ancient theories cited would deny this.

If the moral theories most discussed at present do not ask one to consider much of one's life, I do not think there was any necessity that this should be so. The interest in life as a whole did not originally depend on re-

18. See Gerhart B. Ladner, 'Homo viator: mediaeval ideas on alienation and order', *Speculum* 42, 1967, 233–59.

19. Texts translated in Richard Sorabji, *The Philosophy of the Commentators 200–600 AD: A Sourcebook*, vol. 1, *Psychology*, London and Ithaca N.Y. 2004, ch. 15.

20. Diogenes Laertius *Lives* 2.89–90.

ligious belief. The philosophy of Kant may have encouraged people to think about moral rules, but these could have included rules about one's whole life, so it is an accident if these have been overlooked. Among the utilitarians, Mill and Rawls did expect one to organize one's life. Modern intuitionism has a precursor in Aristotle, who stresses in *Nicomachean Ethics*, bk. 6, that moral judgment requires *nous*, which is treated as an eye for spotting what the particular situation requires. Yet this intuition is to be used in seeing how to apply long-term policies for life, or *proaireseis*.[21] I do not know if there is a feeling that the interest in one's whole life is too self-absorbed. But insofar as it has been dropped, I think this has happened without any rationale being given, and I wonder if it is an unjustified peculiarity in modern ethics.

21. Richard Sorabji, 'Aristotle on the role of intellect in virtue', *Proceedings of the Aristotelian Society*, 74, 1973–74, 107–29, repr. in Amelie Rorty, ed., *Essays on Aristotle's Ethics*, Berkeley 1980, 201–19.

CHAPTER 10

Self as practical reason: Epictetus' inviolable self and Aristotle's deliberate choice

I want now to discuss the Stoic Epictetus, who borrows from Aristotle the idea of *proairesis*, a precursor of the idea of will, and says that he *is* his *proairesis*.

PROAIRESIS IS SELF

Epictetus' aim is to create an inviolable self. He had had his leg broken when he was a slave. He imagines the following dialogue.

Epictetus *Discourses* 1.1.23:

> 'I will put you in chains'. 'What did you say, man? Put *me* in chains? My leg you will put in chains, but my will (my imperfect translation of *proairesis*) not even God can conquer.'

The implication is that he is his *proairesis*, or as I shall say for short until the concept is clearer, his will.

This seems not to be straightforwardly the case for everyone, for elsewhere he says[1] that you can locate 'I' in the flesh, or in external possessions, or in your will. If so, there is good will and bad will. Those who locate 'I' in the flesh or external possessions, instead of in a good will, can be said to be expressing a bad will, but have not located their 'I' in a *good* will. In Epictetus' case, the will is a good one and is set only on those very few things that are under the control of the will, namely good character and rationality.

---

1. Epictetus *Discourses* 2.22.19–20.

That is why the tyrant cannot touch him. Once again this is a self he has molded, not found waiting for inspection. And if we ask, 'What is the self that has done the molding?', the answer is clear. It is the whole embodied person, as we can see from his description of how he molds his students.

He sends the students out along the streets at dawn and asks them to report what they saw.[2] One saw a man grieving over his child. 'Is death under the control of the will?', Epictetus asks. 'No'. 'Away with it then'. Another student reports with pleasure that he saw a consul. 'Is the consulship under the control of the will?' 'No'. 'Away with it'. By this process, the student is to be narrowed down to his will, and his will to what is under its control. And the agent who does the narrowing is the embodied person who walks the streets at dawn.

Epictetus might be seen, like Plutarch, as creating a persona, although that is not how he puts the point any more than Plutarch does. But what he says must be squared with his views on personae, and he does not think it right for everyone to exclude his body from his conception of himself. When the prize athlete was told he could avoid death by having his diseased genitals surgically removed, he was right, not perverted, in refusing. In his persona a perfect manly body was a crucial element (*Discourses* 1.2, 25–26).

I have described elsewhere (*Emotion and Peace of Mind* 225–27) how Admiral Stockdale, who had his leg broken when his plane was shot down over Vietnam, endured four years of solitary confinement and nineteen occasions of physical torture exerted partly on his leg, by following the precepts of Epictetus. And a central precept was to decide what is and what is not under the control of the will. Stockdale learned his Epictetus from a lecture course at Stanford University. But Epictetus describes the training he gave his own students in the following passage.

Epictetus *Discourses* 3.3.14–19:

> It is especially for this kind of thing that you must perform exercises (*gumnasteon*). Go out at first light, examine whomever you see or hear, and answer as if you had been asked a question. What did you see? A good-looking man or woman? Apply the rule (*kanôn*). Is this subject to your will (*proairetikon*) or not (*aproaireton*)? No: remove it. What did you see? A man grieving at the death of his child? Apply the rule. Death is not subject to your will. Move it out of the way. Did a consul meet you? Apply the rule. What sort of thing is consulship, subject to your will or not? No: remove that too; it is not approved

2. Epictetus *Discourses* 3.3.14–19; cf. 3.8.1–5.

(*dokimon*). Throw it away; it means nothing to you. If we did this and took exercise for this every day from dawn to dusk, I swear we'd get results. But as it is, we are caught right away gaping by every appearance and only wake up a little, if at all, in the classroom. If we then go out and see someone grieving, we say, 'He is ruined', if a consul, 'He is happy', if an exile, 'He is wretched', if a pauper, 'The poor fellow has no source of food'. These, then, are the bad opinions that we must knock out, and pull ourselves together on the subject. For what is wailing and lamenting? A belief. What is misfortune? A belief. What are quarreling, dissension, reproach, accusation, impiety, foolery? They are all beliefs, nothing else, and beliefs that things not subject to our will are good or bad. Let someone transfer these beliefs to things that are subject to his will, and I guarantee that he will be steady, whatever his surrounding circumstances.

The stress here is on what is subject to the control of your will (*proairesis*). This is because Epictetus is seeking to cultivate not any kind of will but a will that is directed to what is under its control. And what is under the control of your will? Not death, not the consulship, but only your character. This does not mean that character is the only thing that matters, because good character requires you in normal circumstances to be energetic in pursuing for yourself and others such natural objectives as life, health, and prosperity. But these objectives have only a secondary value deriving from the primary value of exercising just character. And if through no fault of your own you fail to secure them despite your very best efforts, you will have accomplished the only thing that matters in the end, the exercise of good character. The tyrant cannot constrain a will dedicated in this way to good character. But that inviolability comes at a price that I would regard as too high, the price of giving other things only secondary importance.

The lesson that Stockdale taught his fellow captives was that they need not be ashamed of having given away more than their name and number, because that is something that it was not in their power to avoid under torture. But they had overlooked what was in their power, namely to court torture again by minor disobediences towards their captors. This a number of them agreed to do and they again gave away more than their name and number. But it no longer mattered bcause they had regained their pride, and this robbed the captors of what they really wanted: the captives' agreement to join their propaganda effort. They had become inviolable by switching their aim to what was in their power.

There are many further passages that declare inviolable the self as *proairesis*.

Epictetus *Discourses* 1.18.17:

But the tyrant will put in chains . . . —What? Your leg. But he will cut off . . . —What? Your head. What then will he neither put in chains nor cut off? Your will. That is why the ancients proclaimed, 'Know thyself'.

Epictetus *Discourses* 1.19.8:

But it is one's judgments that disturb one. For when the tyrant says to some-one, 'I shall put your leg in chains', the one who has valued his leg says, 'No, have pity', but the one who has valued his will says, 'If it seems to you more advantageous, put it in chains'.

Epictetus *Discourses* 3.18.3:

What, then, is that to you? That your father is making certain preparations. Against what? Surely nothing against your will? How could he? But merely against your body and your possessions. You are safe. It is not against you.

Epictetus *Discourses* 4.5.23:

But they will get hold of me all the more. What are you saying?—'me'? Can anyone harm your will, or prevent your treating appearances as nature re-quires? Why then are you still feeling disturbed or wanting to show yourself intimidated?

Epictetus *Discourses* 4.5.12:

But my utensils are broken. Are you a utensil, then? No, rather your will.

Epictetus *Discourses* 3.1.39–40:

[The gods tell you] not to undo what is satisfactory, nor to try to fix it, but to let a man be a man, a woman a woman, the good-looking a good-looking per-son, the ugly an ugly person. Because you are not flesh or hair, but will. If you keep your will good-looking, you will be good-looking.

Epictetus *Handbook* 9:

Illness is an impediment to the body, but not to the will if that does not wish it. Lameness is an impediment to the leg, not to the will. And say this at each thing that befalls you. For you will find it an impediment to something else, but not to you.

This is Epictetus' basic message: that you are inviolable, so long as you are your will. But there are many passages that call for qualifications of the kind we have already noticed, namely that there is more than one you, and more than one type of will. It is a good will with which you must identify, not a bad one. And you must not be like those who have identified themselves with their body, possessions, or family. As we try to get clearer about this, we shall also acquire a better sense of what *proairesis* is and of how Epictetus differs from Aristotle and from earlier Stoics.

FIRST PROBLEM: MORE THAN ONE *PROAIRESIS*

The first problem about consistency is this. If in the passages quoted Epictetus says that you *are* your *proairesis*, how can he go on to say that you can locate 'I' *outside* your *proairesis* in the flesh or in externals (2.22.19–20)?

Epictetus *Discourses* 2.22.19–20:

> A living thing must incline to where I and mine are. If they are in the flesh, there must be the controlling force (*to kurieuon*), if in *proairesis*, there, if in externals, there. So if I am where my *proairesis* is, it is only so that I shall be a friend, a son, and a father of the kind I should be.

Again, how can he say at 4.4.23 that by valuing office or freedom from office, business or leisure, you can destroy your *proairesis?* And how can he warn against selling your *proairesis* at 1.2.33?

These passages raise two sorts of question. First, what is the 'I' that is outside my *proairesis*, or the 'you' that destroys its *proairesis* and survives its destruction, or the 'you' that sells its *proairesis?* This will become clearer when we have taken in how Epictetus recognizes more than one you. But there is also the question why valuing flesh, externals, office, freedom from office, or selling something is not itself described as an act of *proairesis*, rather than as an act of bypassing, destroying, or selling *proairesis*. If my concern is with the flesh or externals, why is that represented as bypassing my *proairesis?* Why is it not a case of my *proairesis* being a choice of the flesh, or of externals? After all, Aristotle, who first made *proairesis* a concept central to ethics, recognized bad *proairesis*, and so does Epictetus in passages several of which will be discussed below.[3] For that reason, one may need to purify (*ekkatharai;* 2.23.40) or correct (*epanorthein;* 3.5.2) one's *proairesis*.

3. Epictetus *Discourses* 1.29.1; 2.1.6; 2.23.19; 4.5.32; and 1.17.26.

This is where we must appeal to the solution that there is more than one kind of *proairesis*, just as there is more than one self. Epictetus does indeed say that in cases of duress, your *proairesis* is free and not compelled by anything else; rather, your *proairesis* compels (*anankazein*) your *proairesis* (1.17.23–26). Here we have more than one *proairesis* in play. Similarly, at 3.19.2, nothing can impede (*kôluein*) or harm (*blaptein*) your *proairesis*, except your *proairesis*. Epictetus explains (2.23.19) that it is a perverted (*diastrapheisa*) *proairesis* that impedes (*empodizein*) your *proairesis*. The idea that a bad will must have been *perverted* reflects the early Stoic view of Chrysippus that children are naturally attracted (*oikeiousthai*) to virtue, although the Stoic Posidonius complained against him that in that case moral perversion is hard to explain.[4]

Epictetus *Discourses* 2.23.19:

But what is of a nature to impede will (*proairesis*)? Nothing unwilled, but it, when perverted, impedes itself.

This gives us our clue for explaining 2.22.19–20. When you locate 'I' outside your *proairesis* in flesh or externals, I suggest, you locate it outside the *unperverted proairesis*. You cannot, presumably, escape locating it in *proairesis* in some way, because the choice of flesh or externals represents a *proairesis*, though a perverted one. The perverted *proairesis* might be a single decision, as it would probably be in a case of giving in to duress, or it might be a tendency contrary to the correct tendency in *proairesis*.

This can now be used to explain the case of destroying or selling your *proairesis* (4.4.23; 1.2.33), e.g., by valuing office or freedom from office. These bad choices are not described as *proaireseis*, but perhaps we can now assume that they are not so called because they could only represent the perverted kind of *proairesis*, or a *proairesis* that is, in the terms of 2.23.40 and 3.5.2, uncorrected and unpurified. That sort of *proairesis* they could represent.

SECOND PROBLEM: MORE THAN ONE SELF

The second problem is that Epictetus seems to recognize more than one self, in which case the idea that *proairesis* is the self is going to need qualification. At least he talks of you relating to yourself and of me relating to myself in

4. Posidonius *ap.* Galen *PHP* 5.5.3–14, pp. 316–20 De Lacy.

various contexts in which it is not clear that he can be talking of the same self.[5] Two of the passages that seem to recognize more than one self equate one of the two selves with *proairesis*. Thus at 4.12.12, Epictetus, again stressing the freedom of *proairesis*, says that God has entrusted (*sunistanai*) me to myself and subjected (*hupotassein*) my *proairesis* to me alone. And 1.2.11 and 33 in almost the same breath warn you to watch at what price you sell your *proairesis* and tell you that you are the one who knows what you are worth to yourself and at what price you sell *yourself*.

Epictetus *Discourses* 4.12.12:

> God has entrusted (*sunistanai*) me to myself and subjected (*hupotassein*) my will (*proairesis*) to me alone.

Epictetus *Discourses* 1.2.11 and 33:

> For you are the one who knows yourself, how much you are worth to yourself, and for how much you sell yourself. . . . Only watch at what price you sell your will (*proairesis*). If nothing else, man, do not sell it cheap.

The double reference to selves occurs also at 2.8.21–23, where we are told that God entrusted (*pisteuein*), committed (*parakatatithenai*), and handed over (*paradidonai*) you to yourself alone. At 2.18.19, we find the exhortation, that you are to be pleasing to yourself (*aresai autos seautôi*) and that you should become pure in the company of your pure self (*meta katharou sautou*). At 4.6.7, we are told that you have not convinced (*peithein*) yourself about what is good and evil, even though you keep company with (*suneinai*) yourself, and are the one most persuasive (*pithanos*), well-disposed (*eunous*), and akin (*oikeios*) to yourself. At 4.9.13, we hear that you are not willing to rescue yourself (*boêthein*) by talking (*lalêsai*) to yourself, even though you are most likely to persuade, and be persuaded by, yourself (*peisthênai, pithanos*).

I think we need not feel that there is anything very extraordinary about this. It is just common sense that a person is an entity with many aspects. For some purposes, one wants to pick out the total entity with a pronoun like 'you'; for other purposes one wants to pick out an aspect, for example the *proairesis*. Where there is interaction between the totality and an aspect or between two aspects, one may use the pronoun in the same sentence or para-

---

5. See A. Bonhöffer, *Epiktet und die Stoa*, Stuttgart 1890, 83–86.

graph to pick out different things. Often, but not in Epictetus' examples, one of the things picked out is merely the bodily aspect, as when we speak of having cut ourselves, i.e., cut a part of our body.

EPICTETUS' *PROAIRESIS*: DIVERGENCE FROM ARISTOTLE

I find plausible the view of R. Dobbin[6] that in speaking of *proairesis*, Epictetus is deliberately reviving a term of Aristotle's that had been neglected by earlier Stoics. But, as Dobbin would agree, Epictetus' use of the term is very different. For one thing, his *attitude* is in some ways very different from Aristotle's. I argued in chapter six that Aristotle believes humans must compromise with their needs. Because they need to eat, they must engage in social virtues and cannot ever become, as Socrates hoped, full-time philosophizers. Epictetus, while not denying this, provides the opposite emphasis: humans need not compromise with their needs, since starvation and death is a route open to them that robs the oppressor of his power.

We can also now see that Epictetus' concept of *proairesis* is itself bound to be different in many ways from that of Aristotle, even though Aristotle's statement about *proairesis*, 'such an origin [of action] is a human being' (*Nicomachean Ethics* 6.2,1139b4−5) may remind us superficially of Epictetus' equation of *proairesis* with the self. I have given an account of Aristotle's concept of *proairesis* elsewhere.[7] I think that for Aristotle *proairesis* is a policy decision, e.g., a dietary policy decision such as having a diet of fowl, that is based on prior deliberation about achieving what matters in life, e.g., health. The deliberation stops before action when it reaches a course of action that might be brought about through ourselves (*di' hêmôn; Nicomachean Ethics* 3.3, 1112b15−27). And we deliberate only about things that are up to us to do or not to do (*Nicomachean Ethics* 3.3, 1112a30−31; *Eudemian Ethics* 2.10, 1226a20−30). It is not up to us to become healthy just like that or to eat light food without more deliberation about what food is light. But adopting a diet of fowl is up to us. At that point, deliberation stops and we refer the source of action (*arkhê*) to the leading part (*hêgoumenon*) of ourselves (*Nicomachean Ethics* 3.3, 1113a5−7.) Here Aristotle's word already puts us in mind of the later Stoic term for what takes decisions, *hêgemonikon*, the command

---

6. R. Dobbin, 'Prohairesis in Epictetus', *Ancient Philosophy* 11, 1991, 111−35.

7. Richard Sorabji, 'Aristotle on the role of intellect in virtue', *Proceedings of the Aristotelian Society* n.s. 74, 1973−74, 107−29.

center. That the policy decision is made in advance of action comes out further when Aristotle points out that some people do not stick by (*ouk emmenetikos; Nicomachean Ethics* 7.10, 1152a17–19) their deliberation, and he is referring to the deliberation involved in *proairesis*. This, I think, is why the prefix *pro* is appropriate for Aristotle's *proairesis:* the policy decision is taken *in advance of* action.

At first sight, Epictetus' concept may appear to have a lot in common with Aristotle's. Aristotle's point that *proairesis* is *about* what is up to us may seem close to, although it is not in fact the same as, Epictetus' point that *proairesis* is *itself* up to us[8] and free.[9] But Epictetus' point is different in more than one way. He wants you to confine your choices, *proaireseis*, to what is up to you, in a much stronger sense than that envisaged by Aristotle. Epictetus would not have considered a diet of fowl to be up to you. The butcher might have none, or the tyrant might deny you any food at all. In his exercises, he tells his students to disregard death, the grandeur of consulship, other people's conduct, the threat of disinheritance, or condemnation by Caesar. These things all depend on other people. The examples here of what is up to you and hence a proper object of choice, *proairetikon*, are only whether you are distressed or bear things nobly. So the approved subject matter of Epictetus' *proairesis* is narrower than that of Aristotle's. Aristotle's diet of fowl is not a proper object of choice, *proairetikon*, because its availability is not up to you alone. On the other hand, the choice of a diet of fowl does not look like a perverted choice either.

Epictetus' claim that *proairesis* is up to us is different in another way too from Aristotle's point that it is about what is up to us. Epictetus is saying that no one else can force you to make a choice (*proairesis*, 1.17.25– 26). Aristotle is less decided, about action (not choice) due to compulsion. In *Eudemian Ethics* 2.8 and *Nicomachean Ethics* 5.8, I have argued elsewhere,[10] he thinks, in contrast with Epictetus' view about choice, that such action is *not* voluntary. In *Nicomachean Ethics* (3.1, 1109b35–1110a26), he decides that it is voluntary, but may deserve pardon (*sungnômê*). This contrasts with Epictetus' view that only your *proairesis* can constrain your *proairesis* (1.17.23–26).

As regards the freedom of *proairesis*, Epictetus speaks of freedom in two different senses. On the one hand, *proairesis* is by nature free, 1.17.21 and 23;

---

8. Epictetus *Discourses* 2.5.4–5; 1.22.10.

9. Epictetus *Discourses* 1.17.21 and 23; 2.2.3; 2.15.1.

10. Richard Sorabji, *Necessity, Cause, and Blame*, London and Ithaca N.Y. 1980, ch. 17, 272–75.

2.2.3; 2.15.1, and the context of the first two passages suggests that this is true for everyone, because only their *proairesis* can constrain their *proairesis*. On the other hand, as Michael Frede has pointed out to me, he adds that you may need to *make* your *proairesis* (genuinely) free 1.4.18; 3.5.7. In this sense, the only *proairesis* that is free is that of the wise person, who can, for example, tell the tyrant that he cannot be chained, because he is his *proairesis*. If one gives in to duress, one is in the first sense free, but in the second sense not free.

In the case of duress, it looks as if Epictetus' concept of *proairesis*, which we found to be in one context narrower than Aristotle's, is in this context wider, for it covers cases which Aristotle's does not. Aristotle does not suggest that giving in to duress is a *proairesis* in his sense of deliberate policy. Epictetus is calling it a *proairesis*, even if an unsatisfactory *proairesis*.

Epictetus *Discourses* 1.17.25−26:

Someone says, 'If someone imposes the fear of death on me, he compels me'. It is not what is imposed that compels, but the fact that you believe it better to do one of these things than to die. So once again it is your belief (*dogma*) that compelled you, that is, will (*proairesis*) compelled will.

Epictetus *Discourses* 3.5.7:

May it befall me to be snatched away concerned with nothing other than my will (*proairesis*), to make it unaffected, unfrustrated, uncompelled, free.

Further features of Epictetus' concept have already emerged that constitute differences from Aristotle's. Aristotle recognizes cases in which one *proairesis*, e.g., the policy of having a light diet, is opposed by a rival opinion, e.g., that everything sweet is pleasant. But he does not, as Epictetus does, mention cases in which one *proairesis* conflicts with another *proairesis*. This is probably because a *proairesis* is for Aristotle always a thought-out policy decision in which the best means have already been worked out. For Epictetus, by contrast, although the ideal *proairesis* is indeed a well-thought-out dedication to what is under the will's control, perverted *proaireseis* can conflict with each other and with it. Epictetus allows, we have seen, that one *proairesis* can compel, impede, or harm (*anankazein, empodizein, blaptein*) another (1.17.23−26; 2.23.19; 3.19.12). It can do so when it is (2.23.19) perverted.

Aristotle, by contrast, does not even allow that the opinion that everything sweet is pleasant conflicts *directly* with the *proairesis* for a light diet.

Admittedly, following the commonest (but not the only) interpretation,[11] I have taken Aristotle to mean at *Nicomachean Ethics* 7.3, 1147a31–34, that an opinion to the effect that everything sweet is pleasant may be in potential conflict with a *proairesis*, according to which, e.g., heavy food is not to be tasted. Even here, however, Aristotle wants to insert a qualification in defense of Socrates' view that that right opinion, in this case the one forbidding such food, cannot be directly overruled. The opinion about how pleasant the food would be is only *accidentally* opposed (1147a5–b3) to the dietary *proairesis*. Moreover (1147b9–17), what is overpowered (reading *periginetai* at 1147b16) by the desire for pleasure is not the dietary *proairesis* itself, but only full attention to the fact that this food is, e.g., heavy. This plea for imperfect attention is not made, I have argued (*Necessity, Cause, and Blame*, 259–62), in book 5 of the same work.

The fact that *proaireseis* are for Epictetus, unlike Aristotle, not always thought-out policy decisions has a further consequence, concerning the sense of the prefix *pro-* in *proairesis*. We have a Stoic definition of *proairesis* preserved at Stobaeus 2.87, Wachsmuth, according to which *proairesis* is a choice (*hairesis*) *before* a choice (*hairesis*). This is not too far from the Aristotelian concept of *proairesis*, which is a (policy) choice made *before* the time for action. But the idea of two choices with a chronological priority for the proairetic one makes no sense for Epictetus' concept, at least if we take perverted *proaireseis*. Epictetus' concept seems to have evolved at this point beyond both Aristotle and the Stoics who tried to define the term. And this is not perhaps surprising, given the well-known point that the term, though perfectly well known to earlier Stoics, played no important role in their systems at all. Nor did it later in that of Marcus Aurelius.

EPICTETUS' DIVERGENCE
FROM EARLIER STOICS

This last point illustrates the fact that Epictetus differs also from earlier Stoics, or so I believe, and R. Dobbin has drawn atttention to a still more important divergence from them.[12] In the very first quotation cited in this chapter, Epictetus says: 'My *proairesis* not even God can conquer' (1.1.23). But in his Stoic predecessors everything was supposed to be subject to God and, equivalently, to fate. What has happened? It would not make the view-

---

11. Ibid., 275–78; Sorabji, *Emotion and Peace of Mind*, Oxford 2000, 310–13.
12. Dobbin, 'Prohairesis in Epictetus', 121–22.

points compatible to say that God made Epictetus' will to be as it is, for Epictetus seems to suggest that God cannot un-make his will. In any case, Epictetus does not seem to seek any such reconciliation. He says in another passage cited above (4.12.12) that God has subjected my *proairesis* to me alone, as if God chose to leave it not subject to himself.

There is another idea of the earlier Stoics to which Epictetus pays little attention. They had made a distinction different from his. A choice that is directed to the good, to what really matters, that is, to good character and rationality, is a *hairesis*. But most things, according to the Stoics, things like health or wealth, are not really good or bad, but indifferent (*adiaphora*). Correspondingly, our choices of such things are called not *haireseis*, but selections, *eklogai*.[13] Similarly, choices to avoid dispreferred indifferents, like sickness and poverty, are called disselections, *apeklogai*. As so often, Epictetus is perfectly well aware of older Stoic terminology and ready to use both terms (e.g., at 4.7.40), and he must have expected his students to know them. But if we ask what is central for him, in such of his thought as has been preserved, I think that more often than normally recognized, the old Stoic distinctions, though acknowledged, are not central. What is central for Epictetus is what is up to you in his strong sense, according to which nothing else could possibly interfere, and he does not make a point of using the word *eklogê* for choices of other things, even though he has the word available. Interestingly, at 4.10.30, Epictetus uses the word *eklogê* in order to *deny* that he can select among things that are not up to him. Thus at the point where his Stoic predecessors would have counseled careful selection, Epictetus denies that selection is available at all.

Much the same is true of the Stoic idea that such things as health and wealth are indifferent (*adiaphora*). Epictetus sometimes uses the Stoic term, but it is not only, as Francesca Alesse has well pointed out,[14] that he prefers his own terms 'not subject to will (*aproaireton*)', or 'not belonging to us (*allotrion*)'. It is that he wants to put in the forefront his point that health and wealth are not subject to our will and so do not belong to us. It is merely a consequence of this that they are indifferent.

Once again, Epictetus' Stoic predecessors would have made a distinction that Epictetus uses only very occasionally: for them it is alright to select a diet of fowl with the reservation, 'if God wills', so that you will not have set your heart on it. This talk of reservation appears briefly at *Hand-*

---

13. Diogenes Laertius *Lives* 7.104–5; Stobaeus 2.84.24–85.1, 2.79.12–17, Wachsmuth.

14. Francesca Alesse, *Panezio di Rodi e la tradizione stoica*, Naples 1994, 268–69.

book 2.2, and in a passage to be discussed below, frag. 177, but Epictetus has explained by other means how to avoid depending on your dietary choices.

There are further contrasts with the early Stoics. Chrysippus had identified the self with reason as a whole, locating it in the chest, as Galen tells us in *PHP*, bks. 2 and 3), with far-fetched pieces of evidence about where one's finger or chin points, when one says '*ego*'. Epictetus, at least in the surviving ethical lectures, identifies the self with only one aspect of reason, its practical judgments and tendencies for practical judgment, *proaireseis*.

I found in Epictetus a narrow conception of the idea that only certain mental things are in one's power (*eph' hautôi*). It might be thought that this idea is already in the Stoic Antipater, who preceded Panaetius and died around 129 BC. But Antipater at least did not make it clear that he intended so narrow a conception, if and when he said that the archer must do everything in his power (*kath' hauton*) to aim aright, although it is not always in his power to hit the target.[15]

Epictetus diverges on other central subjects, besides that of self, from earlier Stoic views, for example from their celebration of family love as the evidence that shows it natural to extend justice to all mankind. As pointed out by Brad Inwood,[16] ordinary family love is said (*Discourses* 2.22) not to be true and steadfast, because, having failed to appreciate that everything except character and rationality is 'indifferent', it is easily turned by jealousy from love into hate. Only the detached Stoic version of family love is exempt from failure. And that is why the Stoic notoriously reminds himself when kissing his wife and child, 'I am kissing a mortal'.[17] Admittedly, that position needs squaring with Epictetus' insistence that your personae will include your roles as father, mother, brother, or son, and that these duties must be carried out. This side of things has been well brought out by A. A. Long and Gretchen Reydams-Schils.[18] Many of the family cases that Epictetus considers involve fathers and brothers who are difficult, and his point is that that in no way reduces your obligations as a brother or son. But when

---

15. Antipater, in Stobaeus 2.76.13–15, Wachsmuth, with Cicero *On Ends* 3.22; Plutarch *On Common Conceptions* 1071B–C, discussed in Sorabji, *Emotion and Peace of Mind* 332.

16. Brad Inwood, 'L'oikeiôsis sociale chez Epictète' in K. Algra, P. van der Horst, and D. Runia, eds., *Polyhistor: Studies in the History and Historiography of Ancient Philosophy*, Leiden 1996, 243–64.

17. Epictetus 3.24.84–88; 4.1.111; *Handbook* 3.

18. A. A. Long, *Epictetus*, Oxford 2002, 77–78 and ch. 9; Gretchen Reydams-Schils, *The Roman Stoics: Self, Responsibility, and Affection*, Chicago 2005, ch. 4. They cite Epictetus *Discourses* 1.11; 1.23; 2.10.7–12; 2.22.18–21; 3.2.4; 3.3.5–10; 3.21.71–74; 3.24.60.

he says that Socrates, despite choosing not to escape death, loved the children he was leaving (3.24.60), he adds that he loved them as a man who was free and remembered that first one must be a friend of the gods. The remark is part of a passage on family affection (*philostorgia*) from 58 to 66 that repeats that one must not depend on family members staying alive, nor be miserable about them, nor plead that dependent family members preclude the fulfillment of other duties.

Epictetus' narrowing of the self contrasts with the view of a Stoic probably his contemporary, Hierocles, who was mentioned in chapter two.[19] Hierocles sees one self, the mind, as the center of a set of concentric circles. It feels attachment to another self, the body, in the first circle around it. But one should try in the process of *oikeiôsis,* which Locke was to call 'appropriation', to pull the next circle, which represents one's family, inwards so that one feels the same attachment to it as one felt to one's bodily self. And the next circles, representing friends, fellow citizens, and foreigners, should be pulled inwards too. Hierocles is not necessarily enlarging the scope of *me,* but he is enlarging the scope of *mine* so that it includes family and ideally all mankind. The distinction of *me* and *mine* is made not by Hierocles but by Epictetus in the passage quoted above in this chapter (2.22.19). But Epictetus is there saying that *I* and *mine* should be narrowed down and located not in the flesh nor in externals, but only in one's *proairesis.* Is Hierocles instead expanding *mine* when he locates it in a more traditional Stoic way not only in one's own body, but also, by analogy with that, in other people? That depends. If he were only making concern for other people a matter of deliberate choice, he would not so far be placing *mine* outside his *proairesis.* But insofar as he is also extending his feeling of attachment to his own body, in the traditional Stoic way, to other people, there is at the very least a tension with Epictetus. Hierocles' extension of *mine* to include other people is designed for the different purpose of securing justice to others. It inevitably involves a tension with Epictetus' purpose of securing invulnerability.

Occasionally, Epictetus reveals another conception of the self that widens it, though not in Hierocles' way. For he sometimes (e.g., in *Discourses* 1.14) treats our reason as part of universal reason. From this point of view, self or *proairesis,* being a kind of rationality, can be seen as a specific form of universal rationality.

I am now in a better position to correct the loose paraphrase of Epictetus' *proairesis* as 'will'. There is no element of will *power* in the notion; it is

19. Hierocles *Elements of Ethics,* in Stobaeus, eds. Wachsmuth, Hense, vol. 4, *Florilegium,* p. 671, lines 7–16.

more intellectual than that, being a kind of reason. Admittedly, it may, as in Aristotle, involve desire, but desire itself for the Stoics is also an intellectual judgment about how it is appropriate to act.[20] The term is used for decisions about how it is appropriate to act, and not only for policy decisions as in Aristotle, but for particular decisions as well as for overall policy, and for tendencies towards good or bad decisions

I have presented Epictetus' view as verbally close to Aristotle's, but as in fact different both from that of Aristotle and from that of other Stoics. I will finish by comparing him with the Platonist schools that succeeded him.

EPICTETUS AND NEOPLATONIST SELF-AWARENESS

Learning to attach importance only to the *proairetikon* involves a lot of self-interrogation. You have to question appearances: is what *appears* important really good or bad, as it appears? This is one reason why self-awareness was vital for Epictetus and other Stoics. Another reason for the relevance of self-awareness came from the Stoic theory of a natural sense of attachment (*oikeiôsis*). The attachment that new-born animals and infants feel towards their own physical persons is naturally extended to others, and in the case of humans underpins a sense of justice to other humans. The attachment to their own persons depends on an awareness of them, which is a kind of self-awareness. The newborn animal is aware of just how to use the parts of its own body.

Seneca tells us of a particular technique of self-interrogation that he practiced every night, having learned it from the Pythagorean Sextius. He went over in his mind everything he had done in the day, and admonished or congratulated himself. It was a procedure that he found pleasant and calming.

Seneca *On Anger* 3.36:

> The mind should be called to give account every day. Sextius [Pythagorean] used to do this, so that when the day was over and he had taken himself to rest for the night, he would interrogate his mind. 'What fault of yours have you cured today? What vice have you opposed? In what part are you better?' Anger will decline and be more moderate if it is conscious that it must go before

20. Stobaeus 2.86,17–18, 2.88.1, Wachsmuth; Plutarch *On the Self-Contradictions of the Stoics* 1037F (= *SVF* 3.169,171,175).

the judge each day. Is there, then, anything more beautiful than this habit of sifting the whole day? What sort of sleep it is that follows the self-recognition, how tranquil, how deep and free, when the mind is either congratulated, or admonished, and the secret self-examiner and critic has recognized its own habits.

I use this facility and every day I plead my case before myself. When the light has been removed from sight and my wife has fallen silent, now aware of my habit, I scrutinize my whole day and measure again my deeds and words. I myself hide nothing from myself and pass over nothing. For why should I fear any of my errors, when I can say: 'See that you do not do that any more. For now I pardon you. In that dispute you spoke too aggressively. Do not again associate with inexperienced people. Those who have never learned do not want to learn. You admonished him more freely than you ought and so did not improve him, but offended him. In future consider not only whether what you say is true, but also whether the man you are talking to can stand the truth. A good man is pleased by admonition; the worse a man is the more harshly he views his corrector.'

Although the Neoplatonists, as will be seen in chapter fourteen, developed thinking about self-awareness in new directions, it is perhaps unsurprising, in view of the Stoics' interest, that six of the Neoplatonist terms for self-awareness were borrowed from the Stoics and especially from Epictetus. Three of the terms, *epistrophê*, *prosokhê*, and *paratêrêsis*, appear in the following single paragraph of Epictetus.
Epictetus *Discourses* 3.16.15:

You have no fine habit, you offer neither attention (*prosokhê*) nor reflection (*epistrophê*) on yourself and watchfulness (*paratêrêsis*), [which asks] 'How am I treating (*khrêsthai*) the appearances that fall on me—as nature requires, or contrary to nature? How am I answering them—as one should, or not as one should? Am I saying (*epilegein*) to what is not a proper object of *proairesis* (*aproaireta*), "You are nothing to me"?'.

The other three terms borrowed were *sunaisthêsis* (with *sunaisthanesthai*), *parakolouthein*, and *suneidenai*. I have discussed them elsewhere.[21]

In chapter two, I asked whether it was only the terminology that the Neoplatonists borrowed, or whether they borrowed the Stoics' ideas about

---

21. Richard Sorabji, *The Philosophy of the Commentators 200–600 AD*, vol. 1, *Psychology*, London and Ithaca N.Y. 2004, ch. 4, Self-awareness, section (d).

self-awareness too. I said that there is at least one passage in Epictetus that expresses the idea not that metaphysical entities, but that truths are to be found waiting within. Thus at 3.22.38–39, Epictetus uses the verb *epistrephein* and recommends you to turn to yourself, in order to discover your true innate preconceptions about the good:

> Turn (*epistrephein*) to yourselves and discover what preconceptions (*prolêpseis*) you have. What sort of thing do you imagine the good to be?

This search for truth within would exactly suit the Neoplatonists. I have further pointed out in chapter two that Cicero borrows some of the Stoic idea when he says that the divine laws of justice are to be found within (*in se; On Laws* 1.22.58; cf. *Republic* 3.22.33).

SELF AS PRACTICAL REASON

There is a contrast between Platonist theories that connect the self to theoretical reason and theories that connect it to practical reason. One example of the latter that appeared in chapter eight was the Stoic notion of the self as persona to be used in practical reasoning. Another example, I argued in chapter six, was supplied by Aristotle, who modified Plato's view that the true self is intellect, on the grounds that we have to eat, and so must be partly social beings. It fits with this that, when he talks about *practical* reason and the deliberate choice of policies in one's life, which is what I take his *proairesis* to be, he says about *proairesis* 'such an origin [of action] is a human being' (*Nicomachean Ethics* 6.2, 1139b4–5). This is not to deny his further view belief in 10.8 that the more a human can engage in the life of *theoretical* reason and philosophy, the happier that life will be.

Epictetus' view that I am my *proairesis* is another view that makes practical reason central to self, but it was not the standard Stoic view, since Chrysippus identified self with a rational command center that gave its assent not merely to practical proposals, but to propositions quite generally, including mere data of sense. The same had been true of Plato's view that the true self is reason or intellect. This reason too was not confined to *practical* reason. The same is true of the Neoplatonists, even though they borrowed Epictetus' terminology. Plotinus, we saw in chapter six, distinguishes many levels of self, but focuses on self as the understanding of intelligibles, rather than as practical reason.

PART V

Self-awareness

CHAPTER 11

Impossibility of self-knowledge

IMPORTANCE AND PROBLEMS

Self-awareness is a subject not entirely distinct from selfhood. For the kind of identity I discussed in chapters eight through ten depends partly on a person's *conception* of his or her self.

Self-awareness in other forms was already an important subject for Plato, especially if he was the author of the *First Alcibiades*, and for Aristotle, especially in his treatment of friendship. But the Stoics, given their interest in self-interrogation, in basing decisions on the individual persona, in finding some truths within and in the newborn's consciousness of its own person, made it more important still. I have quoted Seneca's account of his self-interrogation techniques in chapter ten. For the Neoplatonists, it was still more important again, because, from Iamblichus on, they regarded the Delphic saying 'Know thyself' as the gateway to knowledge of Plato and of the whole of philosophy and accordingly made the *First Alcibiades* the first work for students to study in the curriculum of treatises ascribed to Plato.[1] Plotinus repeatedly stresses that the search for the highest divinities, the Intellect and the One, and mystical experience of them, are to be found *within*.[2] And this influenced the Christian tradition, because Augustine tells us that it was from the books of the Platonists that he too learned to look for the truth within himself,[3] a tradition familiar to modern readers from Descartes.

---

1. Proclus *in Alc* ı 4,19–21; 5,13–14 Westerink; *Anonymous Prolegomena to Platonic Philosophy* ch. 26, lines 13–44 Westerink.

2. Plotinus 5.1 [10] 12 (12–20), 4.8 [6] 1 (1–3), 1.6 [1] 9 (6–7), 5.8 [31] 10 (31–43), 6.9 [9] 7 (2–5, 16–23).

3. Augustine *Confessions* 7.10.16; cf. 7.17.23, 10.7.11; *On Free Choice of the Will* 2.14–16; *On the Trinity* 9–11.

Self-awareness can take a variety of different objects, and I shall explain this more fully in chapter thirteen, by which time we shall have encountered a range of examples. It can be awareness of one's current activity, of one's motivation, of one's character, or of one's essence or true nature as a human.

Self-awareness has been thought problematic in modern Continental philosophy, on the ground that the subject and object of awareness ought to be distinct from each other.[4] Among analytic philosophers too, David Armstrong, for example, has argued that a state of mind cannot be conscious of itself, any more than a man can eat himself up.[5] But on the face of it, a man can maintain himself or destroy himself by eating or not eating, can encourage himself, question himself, or teach himself, so more discussion of which case self-awareness would resemble is needed. I say, 'on the face of it', because someone might attempt to do for all cases what Aristotle tries to do for self-movement,[6] and claim that really one part moves *another*, so that nothing moves itself. But it would need *showing* that nothing is aware of itself.

Two paradoxes of self-awareness discussed in Antiquity concerned the questions of whether it would be contentless or infinitely regressive.

SELF-AWARENESS AS CONTENTLESS

Plato in *Charmides* 167A–169C raises doubts about the idea that temperance is knowledge of what one knows and does not know. He remains uncertain whether there can be knowledge of knowledge (*epistêmê epistêmês*) because of doubts about the analogous case of vision. Vision cannot be vision of itself and not of color.

On the most obvious interpretation, this point about vision requiring color as its object would have no analogue in the case of knowledge, which can be directed to *any* fact, and so presumably to the fact that one has knowledge. Ought we, then, to look for another interpretation? One would be that vision of vision would have no content, if it was vision of a seeing that was viewed separately from any connection with color. Such a complaint about the contentlessness of vision of vision may arise also in Indian philosophy, as I shall explain in chapter nineteen. Certainly contentlessness features in a

---

4. F. Brentano, *Psychologie vom empirischen Standpunkt,* Leipzig 1874, 179–83, trans. A. C. Rancurello, D. B. Terrell, and L. L. McAlister as *Psychology from an Empirical Standpoint,* London 1973, 127 ff.; Dan Zahavi, *Self-Awareness and Alterity,* Evanston Ill. 1999, 6–8, 15–19, 28–30.

5. D. Armstrong, *A Materialist Theory of Mind,* London 1993, 385.

6. Aristotle *Physics* 8.5.

different way as an objection to self-knowledge in one of the paradoxes in Sextus, to be described below.

One answer, Aristotelian in spirit, to the problem so conceived would be that, when we are aware of seeing, we perceive that we perceive *color*. So color is not excluded after all in the way supposed. This is, as we shall see, one of several answers indicated by Aristotle (*On the Soul* 3.2, 425b13−14).

SELF-THINKING IMMUNE BECAUSE OF IDENTITY OF ACT WITH OBJECT

Aristotle treats *self-thinking* as a special case different from self-perceiving, so we need to consider separately whether that is subject to the threat of being contentless. He believes that a disembodied intellect thinks itself. But on one interpretation of what he means,[7] he would avoid the difficulty of contentless thought. Self-thinking is postulated in *On the Soul* 3.4, 430a2−4; *Metaph.* 12.7, 1072b19−21 (see also *On the Soul* 3.4, 429b9; *Metaph.* 12.9, 1074b38−1075a5). In the first two passages a reason is given (as the word 'for' indicates) why the self-thinking occurs, and the reason is Aristotle's idea that a *disembodied* intellect is identical with what it thinks. In what way is it identical?

The identity that Aristotle postulates between *intellect* and what it thinks is the restricted kind of identity that he puts forward as a general causal principle in *Physics* 3.3. There he says that the act of teaching and the act of learning, though not having all properties in common, are to be counted, if one is counting, as one activity, not two, even though 'teaching' and 'learning' do not mean the same thing. This identity is sometimes called *numerical* identity and it is applied to the acts of agent and patient quite generally, to the acts of perceptible and perceiver in *On the Soul* 3.2, and to the acts of intelligible and intellect in *On the Soul* 3.4; 3.7; 3.8. When the patient is a thinker, he will not, if embodied, be identical with the object of thought; only his act of thinking will be so identical. But in the case of disembodied intellects, the divine ones, and the human intellect if it can be considered separately from the body, the identity applies to thinker, as well as to activity of thinking, since a disembodied intellect consists of nothing but its activity of thinking.

7. Anscombe is the only modern philosopher I know who has liked this identity theory of Aristotle's, but she gives her own reasons, different from Aristotle's, to support it in her chapter on Aristotle in Elizabeth Anscombe and Peter Geach, *3 Philosophers*, Oxford 1961, 60.

This, then, though not the only explanation, is one explanation of Aristotle's divine Intellect being a self-thinker: what he thinks is identical with himself. The 'identity' explanation for self-thinking in the case of a disembodied intellect is given by Aristotle, by Alexander, by pseudo-Alexander *in Metaph.*, and by Philoponus, and is endorsed as true of divine Intellect by Plotinus.[8] The point is put in terms of Intellect thinking itself incidentally (*kata sumbebêkos, secundum accidens*) by Alexander and Philoponus.[9] Aristotle himself says it appears that scientific understanding, perception, opinion, and discursive thought are directed to themselves only as a side effect (*en parergôi*).[10]

We can now see how this kind of self-thinking would be immune to the charge of being contentless. Its thought may have a rich intellectual content. The divine Intellect postulated by Aristotle may be thinking philosophical propositions. But in doing so, it thinks itself, because the propositions it thinks are in a certain way *identical* with itself.

I have just mentioned thinking propositions, not thinking *of* propositions. This illustrates an ambiguity in the notion of *objects* of intellect. Aristotle says in *DA* 3.8, 431b28−432a1, that the object with which thought is identical is not, e.g., stone but the form of stone. On the other hand, it is presumably stone, not the form of stone, *of* which I think a proposition, e.g., that it is hard. That is one reason why in many translations we find talk of thinking forms, or objects, or intelligibles, rather than *of* forms, objects, or intelligibles.

There are several reasons besides the one mentioned for the divine Intellect to think itself. First, it thinks only the best, but it itself is best (Aristotle *Metaph.* 12.9, 1074b29−35; Alcinous *Didaskalikos* ch. 10, 164,27−31). Second, it is simple and so must think what is simple, and that is itself (Alexander(?) *Mantissa* 109,4−110,3). Saul Rosenthal has pointed out to me a further reason for self-thinking, namely that the divine intellect thinks first principles and is itself a first principle.

Alexander(?) *Mantissa* 109,4−110,3, which may or may not be by Alexander, offers several reasons for intellect to think itself. First, it (i) repeats the identity argument for intellect thinking itself in connection with the human dispositional intellect (*nous en hexei*), and then it adds an extra reason, (ii) that this intellect thinks all intelligibles, and it is one of the intelligibles. In both ways it thinks itself incidentally. But it further adds (iii) that the pri-

8. Aristotle as above; Alexander *On the Soul* 86,14−23; ps-Alexander *in Metaph.* 698,1−15; Philoponus *On Aristotle on Intellect* 20,90−21,93; 21,7−16; Plotinus 5.3 [49] 5 (42−8).
9. Alexander *On the Soul* 86,14−23; Philoponus *On Aristotle On Intellect* 21,7−11
10. Aristotle *Metaph.* 12.9, 1074b35−6.

mary Intellect in actuality is different. Although the same reason for self-thinking (*dia tên autên aitian*) —which reason? —applies to the primary Intellect (109,24), the primary Intellect needs to be simple and so thinks *only* itself and presumably no other intelligibles.

Does the thought of Alexander(?)'s primary Intellect escape being contentless? The problem is that if its thinking is to be simple (a requirement that Plotinus avoids), it does indeed run the risk of being contentless.

Alexander(?) *Mantissa* 109,4–110,3:[11]

(i) The intellect which [possesses] the disposition [for intellection] and is active is able to think itself. For it [does] not [do so] in that it is an intellect for [in that case] it will possess thinking and being thought at the same time and in the same respect—but, first, in the way in which intellect in actuality is the same as things that are thought in actuality. Thinking these it thinks itself, if the things which it thinks, in being thought of come to be intellect. For if the things that are thought are intellect in actuality, and it thinks these, it comes to think itself. For in thinking it comes to be the same as the things that are thought, but when not thinking it is other than they. In this way sensation too may be said to sense itself, since it senses the things which in actuality become the same as it. For as we said, sensation in actuality, too, *is* the thing that can be sensed. For both sensation and intellect apprehend their proper [objects] by grasping the forms separately from the matter.

(ii) [109,14] Moreover, intellect may be said to think itself not in that it is intellect, but in that is itself intelligible. For it is as intelligible that it apprehends [itself], just as [it does] each of the other intelligibles too, [and] not as intellect. For it is an attribute of intellect that it is also intelligible; for since it too is one of the extant things, and it is not perceptible by the senses, the remaining [possibility] is that it be intelligible. For if it was as intellect and in that it is intellect that it was thought by itself, it would not think anything else that is not intellect, and so it would think only itself. But [as it is], in thinking the intelligibles which are not intellect before they are thought, it also thinks itself as [being] of this sort, as one among the intelligibles. So this intellect incidentally comes to think itself, advancing from the material intellect.

(iii) [109,23] And the primary intellect, intellect in actuality, also thinks itself in a similar way and for the same reason. But it has something more than this [human intellect]; for it does not think anything other than itself. For by being intelligible it is thought by itself; and, by being intelligible in actuality

11. Translated by R. W. Sharples, *Alexander of Aphrodisias, Supplement to On the Soul*, London and Ithaca N.Y. 2004.

and in its own nature, it will always be thought; and clearly [it will be thought] by what is <always> thinking in actuality. But it is itself the only intellect that is always thinking in actuality; so it will always think itself. [It will think itself] alone, inasmuch as it is simple. For intellect that is simple thinks what is simple, and nothing else is a simple intelligible except itself. For it is unmixed and immaterial and having nothing in potentiality in itself. So it will think itself alone. Thus in that it is intellect, it will think itself as intelligible; in that it is in actuality both intellect and intelligible, it will always think itself; in that it alone is simple, it will think itself alone. For itself alone being simple it is able to think something simple, and it itself alone among the intelligibles is simple.

SELF-AWARENESS AS INFINITELY REGRESSIVE

Aristotle at *On the Soul* 3.2, 425b12−28 raises the second problem, whether there might be an infinite regress of *types* of faculty for being aware that we see, and being aware of being aware that we see. More plausible would be the threat that there is an infinite regress of *individual* acts of such awareness, but Aristotle, we shall see, may have addressed this worry too. Worries about infinite regress in self-awareness are also a modern anxiety.[12]

The simplest answer is well explained, for example, by Colin Radford for the parallel case of a regress of knowing that we know.[13] As in the song 'I thought you thought I was thinking', Radford shows that it is too complicated for the human mind to indulge in many iterations of knowing that one knows, by telling a story whose twists and turns would facilitate a number, but only a small number, of iterations. Any regress will be finite, and it is a mistake to think that we are aware of every act of awareness.

But does this mean that inevitably there will be in each case some act of which we are not aware? Yes, for if I think of all my acts of thinking, and additionally think that I am thinking of them, I will still not yet be thinking that I am thinking of the last act. But there is nothing objectionable about admitting that one act will be overlooked. There is no level at which my latest act of awareness of awareness is in principle immune to inspection. It is merely fatigue that makes me leave one such act uninspected. A divine mind, if infinite, might be able to inspect infinitely many, but we cannot.

Alexander(?) (*Quaest.* 3.7, at 92,31) takes it that Aristotle's aim in our passage is precisely to stop a regress of acts of awareness when he says at *On*

12. For one treatment, see Sartre, *Being and Nothingness*, introduction.
13. Colin Radford, 'Knowing and telling', *Philosophical Review* 78, 1969, 326−36.

the Soul 3.2, 425b26 ff. that there is a sense in which an act of perceiving is numerically identical with what it perceives. In that case, a regress of acts of awareness will not even begin, and this is the view that Franz Brentano endorses,[14] drawing on Aristotle. There would still, however, be a regress of *descriptions* of the one act, with the last description being overlooked, if the regress is finite.

Aristotle (*On the Soul* 3.2, 425b12–28), follows Plato's *Charmides* in taking vision as his central example for discussing self-awareness. His verdict is that we do not see the fact that we are seeing, but perceive it by using our sight. The difference between seeing and perceiving by sight is illustrated by reference to the case of darkness, which is similar in the relevant respect,[15] since we do not see, but perceive indirectly (*en parergôi*) by trying to use our sight (and in this particular case failing). This solves all the problems that Aristotle raises.

First, perceiving by sight does not introduce a second type of faculty, but only the generic perceptual faculty under which sight falls, and this stops the threatened regress of faculties (425b15–17).

Second, perceiving by sight escapes the problem (13–15) that, to avoid the *Charmides* threat of being contentless, it would have, like seeing, to include color as one of its objects, but then cannot be a second faculty altogether distinct from sight ('*two* faculties for the same thing'), since faculties are identified by their objects (*On the Soul* 2.4, 415a20–22, following Plato *Republic* 477C–D). This is unproblematic because, as already said, the ability to perceive by sight does not introduce an altogether distinct faculty from sight, but merely the generic faculty of perception under which sight falls.

Third, perceiving by sight provides one of two answers to the objection (17–20) that if we *see* that we see, then (since sight by definition apprehends color; *On the Soul* 2.6) that which reveals that we see would need to be colored.[16] The main answer is that perceiving by sight is not the same as seeing. But additionally, even if it had been, that which sees (the eye) does in a way, on Aristotle's theory, take on colors when it sees. I have elsewhere taken this to mean that the eye jelly takes on color patches.

This account has the further advantage of harmonizing *On the Soul*

14. F. Brentano, *Psychologie vom empirischen Standpunkt*, Leipzig 1874, 179–83, trans. A. C. Rancurello, D. B. Terrell, and L. L. McAlister as *Psychology from an Empirical Standpoint*, London 1973, 127 ff.

15. I accept Victor Caston's point that it is not similar in other respects: 'More on Aristotle on consciousness: reply to Sisko', *Mind* 113, 2004, 523–33, at 526.

16. I say 'that which *reveals* that we see' in order to meet Victor Caston's objection that Aristotle can hardly want to argue that the *fact* of seeing is colored; ibid., 525.

with *On Sleep* ch. 2, 455a12–22, where we hear more about the kind of perception involved in perceiving that we see. The perceiving, when we use our
sight, is not an act of one of the five senses as opposed to another, but an act
of perception in its generic capacity. He speaks of the common capacity
(*koinê dunamis*), which elsewhere he three times calls the common sense
koinê aisthêsis).[17] His wording, when he says that one does not see that one
sees (*On Sleep* 455a17) is slightly distorted by the fact that he is trying to
make another point at the same time, namely that it is not by sight that one
distinguishes sweet from white. Running the two points together, he says
that it is not the case that by sight one sees that one sees or distinguishes
sweet from white. The 'not by sight' gives the wrong emphasis to the first
point. He would have done better to say, 'one does not see, but merely perceives by sight'. I think this is what he intends, especially as the immediately
following lines refer back to *On the Soul*.

Alexander in his non-commentary treatise *On the Soul* 65,2–10, repeats
Aristotle's view from *On Sleep* 2 that it is by the common sense that we perceive ourselves seeing, and he, rightly, evinces no feeling of inconsistency
when in *Quaestiones* 3.7, 92,13–93,2, he reports Aristotle's discussion of
perceiving by sight that we see from Aristotle *On the Soul* 3.2, 425b12–28.

Aristotle *On the Soul* 3.2, 425b12–28:

> [Perceiving that we see] Since we perceive that we see and hear, one must
> perceive that one sees either by sight or by something else.
>
> [By sight: reasons for] (i) But the same faculty will be a faculty both of
> sight and of the underlying color [to avoid the contentlessness threat of Plato
> *Charmides*]. So that either there will be two faculties [contrary to the practice
> of distinguishing faculties by objects, 415a20–22] for the same thing [color], or
> sight will be sight of itself.
>
> (ii) Again, if indeed the perception of sight were a faculty different from
> sight, either the faculties will go to infinity, or some faculty will be a faculty of
> itself, so that this ought to be brought about in the case of the first faculty.
>
> [Difficulty] But there is a puzzle: if perceiving by sight is seeing, and what
> is seen is color, or what has color, if anyone is to see that which sees (*to horôn*),
> the first thing that sees will have color.
>
> [Solution (1): perceiving by sight is not seeing] It is evident, then, that
> perceiving by sight is not a single thing. For even when we are not seeing, we
> by sight discriminate darkness from light, but not in the same way.

17. Aristotle *On Memory* 450a10–11, *On the Soul* 425a27, *Parts of Animals* 686a27.

[Solution (2): anyhow the organ is in a way colored] Again, what sees is besides in a way colored, since each sense organ is receptive of the sensible [quality] without matter. And that is why even when the sensibles have gone away, there are sensations and appearances (*phantasiai*) in the organs.

[No regress arises of *acts* of awareness] The activity of the sensed object and of the sense is one and the same activity, but the being of each is different. I mean, for example, active sound and active hearing.

Aristotle *On Sleep* 2, 455a15–22:

But there is also a certain common capacity (*koinê dunamis*) that accompanies all the senses by which one perceives that one sees and hears. For it is not the case that by sight one sees that one sees and indeed discerns and is able to discern that sweet is different from white, nor is it by taste, nor sight, nor both, but by a certain part common to all the sense organs. For there is a unitary (*mia*) sense faculty, and the controlling sense organ is single (*hen*), although what it is to be a sense varies for each class such as sound or color.

CONTENTLESS SELF-COGNITION RE-OPENED

The problem of contentless self-cognition is re-opened by the Pyrrhonian skeptic Sextus Empiricus, a contemporary of Alexander, at *Math.* 7.284–6; 310–12. The reference to sight suggests he, or his source, is drawing on Plato's *Charmides*. Man cannot apprehend (*katalambanein*) himself, nor can his intellect, any more than sight can see itself. For if part is supposed to apprehend part, how will the apprehending part in its turn be apprehended? A regress threatens. This first difficulty is analogous to one already mentioned, that when I am aware of my experiences, fatigue ensures that at some level or other, I shall not be aware of my awareness, so that I cannot be aware of the whole of my experience. Sextus' next move does indeed concern the whole. He says that if, on the other hand, whole apprehends whole, will the whole be the apprehender? If so, that leaves no content to be apprehended. Or will the whole be the apprehended? But that leaves no apprehender. Sextus' reasoning appears to involve a fallacy, although this is not the point that Plotinus picks up when he answers Sextus. Sextus moves (7.311) from 'intellect as a whole apprehends itself' to 'intellect will be as a whole [i.e., wholly] apprehension and apprehending'—as if it would be nothing else, and so could have no content. Sextus makes the same invalid move in 7.286

from 'as a whole he is investigating' to 'he is conceived as a whole [i.e., wholly] with the investigating'—as if he does nothing else, so has nothing to investigate.

I am not sure why someone should not apprehend themselves as apprehending an item, and as apprehending themselves, and as being apprehended by themselves. The problem seems rather to lie at a different point, that at some level the higher acts of apprehension will, in a finite mind, remain unapprehended so that one does not apprehend the whole of oneself. But this should just be accepted.

IDENTITY OF INTELLECT
WITH OBJECT AS A REPLY

Plotinus[18] considers and rejects Sextus' part-part option at 5.3 [49] 1, and in 5.3 [49] 5 prefers the whole-whole option. He need not fear that the divine Intellect's self-thinking will be contentless, because at 5.3 [49] 5 (42–48) he bases the self-thinking on the Aristotelian identity of thinker with object thought, whose content may be rich. As regards Sextus' question of whether the whole is apprehender or apprehended, he stresses at lines (21–28) this same identity between thinker and object, which he compares with interpenetrating lights (5.6 [24] 1 (16–23)). Presumably, his idea is that Sextus is offering a false dichotomy in asking his question, for the whole is both apprehender and apprehended, these being identical. Consequently Sextus is wrong to ask us to choose between apprehender and apprehended as if they were different. This does not stop Plotinus from reminding us a little later, at 5.3 [49] 10 (24–26), that the sameness is always accompanied by difference, and he makes explicit at 6.7 [38] 40 (16–19) that the sameness of which Aristotle speaks is not one of definition.

Plotinus 5.3 [49] 5 (21–28):[19]

> If this is the case, the act of contemplation must be identical with what it contemplates, and Intellect must be identical with the intelligible; otherwise there

18. Plotinus' reply to Sextus is discussed by Ian Crystal, 'Plotinus on the structure of self-intellection', *Phronesis* 43, 1998, 264–86, and in his *Self-intellection and Its Epistemological Origins in Ancient Greek Thought*, Burlington Vt. 2002.

19. Translated by Barrie Fleet, in Richard Sorabji, *The Philosophy of the Commentators, 200–600 AD: A Sourcebook*, vol. 1, London and Ithaca N.Y. 2004.

can be no truth. For that which contains real Beings will contain an image that is other than them—which is not the truth, for the truth cannot be the truth of anything but itself; it is just what it affirms. So Intellect, the Intelligible, and Being, this primary being are a unity, a primary Intellect containing real Beings—or rather an Intellect that is identical to real Beings.

CHAPTER 12

Infallibility of self-knowledge: Cogito and Flying Man

AUGUSTINE: SOUL PRESENT TO ITSELF, NOT SOUGHT THROUGH IMAGES

Augustine stands the puzzle tackled by Plotinus on its head, when he argues in *On the Trinity* that the soul knows itself by being present (*praesens*) to itself,[1] not absent.[2] That is how the Delphic command, 'Know thyself', can be obeyed. So the soul does not need to seek itself.[3] If it did have to seek itself, it would fail, for then it would find only images and traces.[4] That is how Plato suggested that we know ourselves best, by seeing ourselves reflected in the eyes of another (*First Alcibiades*, 132E–133C, translated in chapter thirteen below). But in fact the soul is present to itself, and so the problem becomes (and this is a decisive turn in Descartes' direction) how the soul ever makes a mistake about its own nature. This privileging of self-knowledge fits with Augustine's later *On the Trinity* 15.10.9–20, making soliloquy causally prior to communication rather than the other way round.

The discussion of self-knowledge seems closely related to the first fifteen lines of a chapter in Plotinus whose following lines, I shall be arguing, may have had an even more important influence on Augustine (5.5 [32] 2 (1–15)), even though it is about a somewhat different subject: intellect and its knowledge of intelligibles and of itself. Intellect does not *seek* intelligibles, nor have mere *images* or *traces* of them, but rather is blended with the intelligibles themselves and is evident (*enargês*) to itself.

Mistakes about self, on Augustine's view in *On the Trinity*, result from

1. Augustine *On the Trinity* 10.3.5, 10.7.10, 10.9.12, 10.10.16 (72–85).
2. Ibid. 10.8.11.
3. Ibid. 10.3.5, 10.8.11; cf. *Confessions* 10.8.15, 10.16.25.
4. Augustine *On the Trinity* 10.3.5, 10.8.11.

relying on images of bodily things.[5] The soul thrusts its love onto these images, but it should realize that it is actually more internal to itself than these images are, and it should shed the corporeal accretions that mislead it (10.8.11). We may again compare Plotinus, who says that the corporeal is an accretion to the soul,[6] and that images do not reveal it.[7] Admittedly, we shall in this chapter and the next find Plotinus ascribing self-awareness of the soul's *activities* to the mirror of imagination, and Proclus criticizing this at least as a method for self-awareness of the soul's *essence*. But we shall also find "Simplicius" (= Priscian?) sharply distinguishing self-awareness of activities and of essence, even if he thinks that the soul's essence can be *inferred* from its activities.

Augustine *On the Trinity* 10.3.5, Mountain *CCL* 50:

> But if the mind makes an image of itself as like what it is, then when it loves this image, it loves itself before it knows itself, because it gazes at something like itself. So it knows other minds from which it makes an image of itself, and is known to itself by the generic [likeness].
>
> Why, then, when it knows other minds, does it not know itself, since nothing can be more present to the mind than itself? But if it is as with eyes of the body, which know other eyes better than they know themselves, let the mind then not seek, since it will not find. For eyes will never see themselves, except by mirrors. But let it not in any way be thought that anything like that can be applied to the contemplation of incorporeal things, in such a way that the mind knows itself as if in a mirror.

Augustine *On the Trinity* 10.8.11, Mountain *CCL* 50:

> What is so much in the mind (*mens*) as the mind itself? But because the mind is in those things that it thinks with love, and is habituated with love to perceptible, that is to corporeal, things, it is not able to be in itself without images of those things. It is hence that there arises for it the blemish of error, so long as it cannot separate from itself the images of things perceived so as to see itself on its own. The perceived things are amazingly stuck to it by the glue of love. And this is the mind's (*eius*) uncleanness, since when it tries to think (*cogitare*) itself on its own, it believes that it is the thing without which it cannot think. So when it is ordered to know (*cognoscere*) itself, let it not seek itself as though withdrawn (*detracta*) from itself, but let it withdraw what it has added

5. Ibid. 10.3.5, 10.5.7–10.6.8, 10.8.11, 10.10.16 (72–85).
6. Plotinus 1.6 [1] 5 (43), 1.6 [1] 9 (11), 4.7 [2] 10(11).
7. Id. 5.3 [49] 5 (21–28).

to itself. For the mind is more internal not only than those perceptibles that are obviously outside, but also than the images of them that are in a certain part of the soul (*anima*) that beasts also possess in spite of lacking intelligence, which is restricted to the mind. Since, therefore, the mind is more internal, it in a way departs from itself when it has exerted (*egerit*) the emotion of love upon these traces, so to speak, of many acts of attention. These traces are, as it were, imprinted on the memory when those corporeal things that are outside are perceived in such a way that, even when they are absent, images of them are at hand for thinking. So let the mind know (*cognoscere*) itself not as if it were seeking an absent self, but let it set the attention of its will, by which it was wandering among other things, upon itself and let it think itself. Thus it will see that it never failed to love itself, never failed to know itself, but by loving something else along with itself, it confused that thing with itself and in a way grew it onto itself.

Augustine *On the Trinity* 10.10.16, lines 72 – 85, Mountain *CCL* 50:

It cannot in any way be brought about that the mind thinks that which it is in the same way as it thinks that which it is not. It thinks all the latter things by an image of the imagination, whether it be fire or air, or this or that body, or any part or combination and blend [cf. Plato *Phaedo* 86B7–C3; Galen *Quod animi mores* 44,6–20 (*scripta minora* 2)] of bodies. Nor is it said to be all those things indiscriminately, but some one of them. But if it were any one of these things, it would think that thing differently from the others, not indeed by a feigned image, the way one thinks absent things that have been touched or are of the kind that are touched by bodily sense. It would think it by some internal, not simulated but true presence (for nothing is more present to it than itself), just as it thinks that it lives, remembers, understands, and wills. For these things it knows within itself and does not imagine them as if it had touched them outside itself by sense in the way that all corporeal things are touched.

Augustine *On the Trinity* 10.9.12, Mountain *CCL* 50:

When the mind is told, 'Know (*cognoscere*) thyself', at the instant it understands what is said, 'thyself', it knows (*cognoscere*) itself, for no other reason than that it is present to (*praesens sibi*) itself.

Plotinus 5.5 [32] 2 (1–15):

We must therefore neither seek the intelligibles outside, nor say that there are imprints of real beings in the intellect, nor rob intellect of truth by making intelligibles unknown and unreal and also destroying intellect itself. Rather, all [realities] must be given to intellect, if we must introduce knowledge and truth, and safeguard real beings and knowledge of what each thing is, not merely of what it is like, as if we had an image (*eidôlon*) and trace (*ikhnos*) of each thing, not the things themselves with which we keep company and are blended. In that way, intellect would know and truly know, and not overlook things and go around seeking, and truth will be in it and it will be the seat of real beings and will live and think. All this must belong to the most blessed nature. For indeed in this way it will need no proof or convincing argument that it is so, for [intellect] is so and is evident (*enargês*) to itself.

Plotinus 5.3 [49] 5 (21–28):[8]

So if the objects of contemplation are present in the act of contemplation, if they are mere images, then he does not contain them; but if he does contain them he does not contain them by seeing them as a result of self-division. Rather he contemplated and contained them before any self-division took place. If this is the case, the act of contemplation must be identical with what it contemplates, and Intellect must be identical with the intelligible; otherwise there can be no truth. For that which contains real Beings will contain an image which is other than them—which is not the truth, for the truth cannot be the truth of anything but itself; it is just what it affirms. So Intellect, the Intelligible, and Being, this primary being are a unity, a primary Intellect containing real Beings—or rather an Intellect that is identical to real Beings.

WHOLE KNOWS WHOLE

Augustine knows of Sextus' puzzle to which Plotinus replied, but he has a different answer. It would indeed be intolerable if only part of the soul could be known by part. But in fact the soul as a whole (*tota*) has knowledge. So, since it knows itself as knowing, it knows itself as a whole (*totam*). *On the Trinity* 14.6.8 repeats the denial that the soul knows itself by a part–part relation, or by becoming twinned with itself.

Augustine *On the Trinity* 10.4.6, Mountain *CCL* 50:

What, then shall we say? That the soul knows (*nosse*) itself partly and partly not? But it is absurd to say that it as a whole (*tota*) does not know (*scire*) that

8. Translated by Barrie Fleet, in Richard Sorabji, *The Philosophy of the Commentators, 200–600 AD: A Sourcebook*, vol. 1, London and Ithaca N.Y. 2004.

which it knows. I am not saying 'it knows the whole (*totum*)', but 'it as a whole knows that which it knows'. So when it knows something about itself, which except as a whole (*tota*) it cannot do, it knows (*scire*) itself as a whole (*totam*). But it knows that it knows something, and it cannot except as a whole (*tota*) know anything. So it knows itself as a whole (*totam*).

TWO LEVELS OF SELF-AWARENESS, ONLY THE LOWER ONE CONTINUOUS

For Augustine there are two levels of self-awareness. Only the lower one of them belongs to infants and is possessed continuously, the knowledge that he calls *nosse*, *notitia*, cf. *nota*. Thinking, *cogitare*, is more intellectual and happens only from time to time. The soul never ceases to know itself, at least in the way we retain things in the memory even when not attending to them.[9] Even infants have an implicit self-knowledge (*nosse*, cf. *notitia*) of themselves,[10] but not yet, the last passage adds, self-thought (*cogitare*), because they are too intent on sensibles. Of this intentness Augustine gives evidence from his own experience, reporting cases where a wrongly placed candle gave infants a permanent squint. Presumably, the infant's *nosse* is due to the soul being present to itself, whereas the *cogitare*, which is impeded by the bodily senses, would require the kind of turning back on itself that the Neoplatonists also describe as impeded by the bodily senses. The soul knows itself as soon as it understands the command,[11] although it may then look in the wrong direction[12] when it starts thinking (*cogitare*) instead of knowing (*nosse*).[13] All the soul has to do in order to know itself is to revert to itself (*revocari conversione*, cf. the Neoplatonist *epistrephesthai*, a term discussed in chapter eleven; 14.6.8 (lines 29–34)).

Augustine *On the Trinity*, 14.5.7, Mountain *CCL* 50:

> Should we believe that [the infant's mind] knows (*nosse*) itself, but, being too intent on the things that it has begun to sense with the bodily senses, with pleasure all the greater for being new, while it cannot fail to know (*ignorare*) itself, is yet not able to think (*cogitare*) itself?

9. Augustine *On the Trinity* 10.8.11, translated above; 14.6.8–9.
10. Ibid. 10.3.5, translated above; 14.5.7.
11. Ibid. 10.9.12, translated above; 10.9.16.
12. Ibid 10.9.12.
13. Ibid. 10.5.7, 14.5.7–14.8.11.

[A sign of the infant's soul being intent on sensibles]

If someone thoughtlessly, or in ignorance of the possible effect, places a nightlight where the infant is lying in a part [of the room] where its eyes can turn, as it lies, but its neck cannot bend, its gaze is so inseparable from [the light] that we have known several who have even become cross-eyed from this.

Augustine *On the Trinity* 14.6.8–9, lines 29–34, 45–50, 55–61, Mountain *CCL* 50:

(29) It remains, then, that it is something belonging to the nature of the mind that it should view (*conspectus*) itself, and that it should be called back (*revocari*) to the mind when it thinks (*cogitare*) itself, not as across a space, but by an incorporeal conversion (*conversio*). But when it is not thinking itself, it is admittedly not in its own view, nor is its gaze concerned with the mind, and yet it nonetheless knows (*nosse*) itself as if it were to itself a memory of itself.

(45) When by thinking (*cogitare*) the mind views itself as understood (*intellecta*), it does not generate that knowledge (*notitia*) it has as if it had previously been unknown (*incognita*) to itself. Rather, it was customarily known (*nota*) to itself in the way that things are known (*notae*) that are contained by memory even if they are not thought (*cogitare*), since we say that a person knows (*nosse*) letters even when they are thinking (*cogitare*) of other things, not of letters.

(55) But since we have said around the end of the same tenth book that the mind always remembers itself and always understands and loves itself although it does not always think (*cogitare*) itself as separate from the things that are not what it is, it must be asked in what way understanding (*intellectus*) belongs to thinking (*cogitatio*), whereas knowledge (*notitia*) of each thing that is in the mind when it is not thinking about itself is said to belong only to memory.

AUGUSTINE'S COGITO AND
PLOTINUS ON IRREFUTABILITY
OF INTELLECT'S SELF-KNOWLEDGE

In *On the Trinity* 10.10.14, Augustine produces some of his many versions of the Cogito argument that Descartes was much later to offer in his *Second Meditation*. First, doubt is impossible, because if you doubt, then you are alive, think, understand, judge, want to resolve the doubt, know your ignorance, are cautious, and so you cannot rightly doubt the existence of these mental operations (10.10.14). Augustine makes the basis of the argument even clearer than Descartes does, and in more than one way. He is not appealing to the supposed infallibility of introspection, of which we are all the more suspicious in the wake of Freud. Instead, he is looking for those conditions that have to be fulfilled if any doubt is to be entertained at all. If there is doubt, there is thought, life, understanding, desire, and, he adds, judgment, self-awareness, and caution. Augustine's list is like Descartes' in his *Second Meditation,* but Augustine explains the list rather more clearly than Descartes: desire, for example, comes in because doubt, in his view, creates a desire for resolution. One might add that if there is thought, there is time, unless one accepts Plotinus' belief in timeless thought. The point is that if these are the very conditions of doubt, one cannot rightly doubt them, because that very doubt guarantees their fulfillment. Augustine puts this particularly clearly by saying, 'Whoever acquires a doubt from any source ought not to doubt any of these things whose non-existence would mean that he could not entertain doubt about anything'.

Lichtenberg's reply to Descartes' formulation was that Descartes should have asserted an impersonal 'it thinks', instead of 'I think', presumably because the momentary thinker without a history, which is all that Descartes could be certain of, is an empty notion. Descartes certainly means to refer to a continuous thinker with a history, since he speaks more than once of his thought being indubitable *whenever* he entertains it, as if it were the same *he* doing the entertaining. Augustine shares the assumption of continuous thinkers with histories, but he continues to guard himself, as Descartes does some of the time, with a dialectical 'if'. *If* anybody opposes Augustine with doubt, then that continuing person with a history must be thinking.

Dominic O'Meara has pointed out[14] that even before Augustine, Plotinus (5.5 [32] 2 (13–21)) argues for the irrefutability of the intellect's self-knowledge. He uses the identity of intellect with its object not merely as we have seen him doing above, to repel skeptical attack, but to go on the offensive and claim irrefutability. It strengthens O'Meara's case that, as I have already said, the opening of Plotinus' chapter is a likely influence on Augustine, because it starts by saying that the objects of intellect are inside it, so that we do not merely have an image (*eidôlon*) or trace (*ikhnos*) of the realities, but are blended (*sunkrathênai*) with them, and the intellect is evident to itself and cannot overlook them or go seeking them. In lines 18–21, Plotinus concludes that intellect is irrefutable because of the identity: what it says it

---

14. D. J. O'Meara, 'Scepticism and ineffability in Plotinus', *Phronesis* 45, 2000, 240–51.

is, and what it is it says. The structure of this argument matches that of versions of the Cogito argument of Augustine and Descartes. A thought like 'I think' confines itself to asserting nothing outside the preconditions that are presupposed by its occurrence. It cannot therefore be wrong if someone thinks it. Confining itself to asserting its own preconditions is not unlike confining itself to what it is identical with, except that for Plotinus intellect is identical with a whole network of intelligible entities, not just with a few preconditions. Here is his argument for irrefutability.

Plotinus 5.5 [32] 2 (13–21):

> For indeed in this way it will need no proof or convincing argument that it is so, for [intellect] is so and is evident (*enargês*) to itself, and [it is evident] that if there is anything prior to it, it derives from that, and that if there is anything subsequent, that is itself, and no one is more convincing to it about itself, and [it is evident] that this is reality in that [intelligible] world. So that the real truth, conforming with itself and not with something else, says nothing other besides itself, and what it says it also is, and what it is it also says. Who then could refute it? From where would he bring the refutation?

Augustine *On the Trinity* 10.10.14, Mountain *CCL* 50:

> But who will doubt that he lives, remembers, understands, wills, thinks, knows, and judges? For even if he doubts, he lives. If he doubts where his doubt comes from, he remembers. If he doubts, he understands that he doubts. If he doubts, he wants to be certain. If he doubts, he thinks. If he doubts, he knows that he does not know. If he doubts, he judges that he ought not rashly to give assent. So whoever acquires a doubt from any source ought not to doubt any of these things whose non-existence would mean that he could not entertain doubt about anything.

I do not think it a significant difference from Descartes that Augustine uses the third person, not the first person, 'I doubt'. In his most quoted version, '*Si fallor, sum*', he does use the first person, 'If I am deceived, I exist'. But here he offers the argument in a generalized form, leaving each reader free to apply it in the first person to himself or herself. There are a good many other versions in Augustine of the Cogito argument (*On the Happy Life* 2.7–8; *Against the Academics* 3.9.19; *Soliloquies* 2.1; *On the Trinity* 15.11–12; *On Free Choice of the Will* 2.3; *City of God* 11.26). The context in *Against the Academics* is, as in Descartes, that of answering the Skeptics.

AUGUSTINE'S SECOND USE OF THE COGITO:
KNOWING SELF AS NON-BODILY

But now Augustine puts the Cogito to a *second* use. The incorrect, but crucial, principle is offered that a thing can only rightly be said to be known if its essence is known. So the soul knows with certainty not only the operations listed in the Cogito argument above, but also its own essence. But it has no certainty whether it is air, fire, or any other body, or bodily thing. So it is none of these (10.10.16). The conclusion follows, if it means that it is not *essentially* any of these. But the premiss is exposed as ambiguous, for example by Aristotle in his *Posterior Analytics* bk. 2 ch. 8. Aristotle shows there that there are different ways of knowing (*eidenai*) something, e.g., lunar eclipse, namely by knowing the whole essence, a little of the essence, or a merely inessential feature. Typically, his contemporaries would know that a lunar eclipse was a certain distinctive loss of light by the moon, the most accessible part of the essence, and they would not confuse lunar eclipse with cloud cover, or waxing and waning, so in a good sense, they knew lunar eclipse. But only a few intellectuals in Aristotle's time would have known Anaxagoras' discovery that lunar eclipse, unlike solar, was due to the earth's shadow, which completes its essence. It is only as a prerequisite for scientific understanding (*epistêmê*), not for ordinary knowing (*eidenai*), that knowledge of the full essence is required. Augustine then needs to show that the soul knows itself in the strong sense in which knowing does involve knowing the whole essence. But for all he has shown, it may know itself only in a weaker sense.

The idea that the essence (*ousia*) of the soul can be known by its activities would be closer to what Augustine needs, and this idea is used by Porphyry in his *Against Boethus on the Soul*, frag. 244F, Smith). At lines 6–12, Porphyry bases himself on Plato *Phaedo* 64A8–65A2 and says that the soul shows its divine *ousia* by engaging in activities similar to God's. If *ousia* may be taken to mean essence, then he is claiming the authority of Plato's *Phaedo* for the view that the essence of soul can be known from its activities. That principle would have been enough for Augustine's purposes, had he used it. The same principle is also ascribed to Plato and Aristotle on one interpretation of the later Neoplatonists Damascius and Priscian and generalized to other essences.[14]

---

14. See Carlos Steel, *The Changing Self*, Brussels 1978, 16, on Damascius, *Commentary on Plato's Phaedo* Series 1.72, Westerink, and pseudo-Simplicius (Priscian?), *On Aristotle on*

Augustine *On the Trinity* 10.10.16, Mountain *CCL* 50:

> In no way is anything rightly said to be known (*sciri*) so long as its essence (*substantia*) is not known (*ignorari*). Hence so long as the mind knows (*nosse*) itself, it knows (*nosse*) its essence, and when it is certain (*certus*) about itself, it is certain about its essence. But it is certain about itself, as the points made above establish. It is not at all certain whether it is air or fire or any body, or anything bodily. So it is none of those things.

DESCARTES' SECOND USE OF THE COGITO TO SHOW THAT HE IS NOT ESSENTIALLY BODILY

Descartes' own use of the Cogito to show that he is not essentially bodily uses extra premises: that he has a clear and distinct idea of himself as an unextended thinking thing and of body as an extended non-thinking thing (this contrast is already in Augustine),[15] and that what he can thus separately understand clearly and distinctly God at least can make to exist separately.

Descartes *Sixth Meditation:*

> And first because I know that everything that I understand (*intelligo*) clearly and distinctly can be made by God to be the way I understand them, it is enough that I am able to understand one thing clearly and distinctly without the other for me to be certain that one is different from the other, because by God at least they can be positioned separately. The question by what power that is done does not affect their being considered different. Therefore from the very fact that I know that I exist, and that meanwhile I notice nothing plainly different as belonging to my nature or essence except this alone, that I am a thinking thing, I rightly conclude that my essence consists in this one thing, that I am a thinking thing. And although perhaps, or rather, as I shall later say certainly, I have a body that is very closely conjoined to me, nonetheless because on the one hand I have a clear and distinct idea of myself insofar as I am only an unextended thinking thing, and on the other hand a distinct idea of body insofar as it is only an extended non-thinking thing, it is certain that I am really distinct from my body, and can exist without it.

---

the Soul 41,31; 146,22. Westerink takes the references to be to Plato *Phaedo* 64E8–65A2 and Aristotle *On the Soul* 403a10–11.

15. Augustine *On the Greatness of Soul* 3.4; *On the Soul and Its Origin* 4.21.35; *Letters* 166, 2.4.

KNOWLEDGE OF SELF AS NON-BODILY: AVICENNA'S FLYING MAN

Long after Augustine but long before Descartes, the Islamic philosopher Avicenna (Ibn Sina, c. 980–1038) offers an argument, 'the Flying Man', that is surprisingly close to Augustine's second use of the Cogito. He could not have known Augustine's Latin, since the texts available to him in translation were Greek. But the Flying Man has a similar purport to Augustine's second use of the Cogito, being designed to show that the soul is not bodily (*De Anima* (= *Shifâ, Healing,* bk. 6, pt. 2) pt. 1, ch. 1, and pt. 5, ch. 7, ed. S. Van Riet, Avicenna Latinus). Avicenna considers the argument no more than a pointer.

Avicenna imagines a man who comes into existence moving through air or vacuum without perceiving anything, not even the sensation of touching limbs. Once again, the argument turns on a claim about essence. The man would know directly that his essence[16] existed, but he would not know that body exists. Avicenna concludes that his essence, which he takes to be soul, is independent of body. There are further references to the Flying Man in Avicenna's *Ishârât* (*Remarks and Admonitions*),[17] in his *Masriqiyn* (*Easterners*), which exists only in manuscript, and in his *Almahad* (*The Return* [sc. of the soul after death], surviving in Latin only. The last was translated by Alpago (died 1522) and became available to Latin readers a hundred years before Descartes in the Venice edition of 1546, repr. Farnborough 1969. Avicenna further explains what he meant in *Reply to Bahmanyâr and al Kirmânî*.[18] In this valuable set of notes, he urges a former pupil not to be misled by the misinterpretations of his doctrine propounded by a tiresome sheikh.

Avicenna gives his reason why the Flying Man must grasp his essence only in this recently translated text (*Reply to Bahmanyâr,* paras. 58–59, Michot). It is that nothing grasps a thing without grasping its *own* essence as grasping. Augustine argues, admittedly differently (*On the Trinity* 10.10.16), that nothing knows a thing without knowing *that thing's* essence. Avicenna's principle seems to me at least as dubious as Augustine's, although we shall find a precedent in Priscian that may derive from Porphyry. But the value of the new text is that it supplies the principle that was left unstated elsewhere.

16. Dag Hasse argues for the translation 'his essence' rather than 'he' in his *Avicenna in the Latin West,* London 2000, 80–92.

17. = *Livre des Directives et Remarques,* French trans. A. M. Goichon, Beirut, 1951.

18. French trans. Jean (= Yahya) Michot in *Le Muséon,* 2000.

FURTHER COINCIDENCES BETWEEN
AVICENNA AND AUGUSTINE

In fact, Avicenna's discussion has so much in common with Augustine's *second* application of the Cogito in *Trin.* 10.10.16, to prove incorporeality that I am inclined to wonder, given that Avicenna could not have known Augustine, whether there was not a common Greek source for at least some of their ideas. (1) First, in *Al-Shifâ* (*The Healing*): *Soul* (= *De Anima*, 1.1),[19] Avicenna has the same insistence on bodily things that are imagined (*yatakhayyalu*, Latin *imaginari*) not being part of one's essence (*dhâtihi*, Latin *essentia*). (2) Second, in the same treatise,[20] he insists that the soul is 'present to itself' (*mawjûd*) and not absent (*ghayb*) from its own essence. The reference to the soul being present to itself (*mawjûd*) is further explained in a reply to a student's questions about it, in the *Book of Discussions*, Bidarfar p. 226, no. 675, where true intellectual perception of essence through the *presence* of the essence is paraphrased by a different expression, *yakûnu lahu*. (3) Third, the same passage of *The Healing* points out that, because a thing cannot be absent from its own essence, it also cannot revert to it. This reminds us of Augustine saying in *On the Trinity* 14.6.8, translated above, that reversion does not happen all the time, although Augustine, unlike Avicenna, allows that it can happen.

The parallels with Augustine continue. (4) In the *Book of Discussions*, Bidarfar pp. 185–86, no. 550, Avicenna allows, fourth, that the intellect does not continuously intelligize (*'aqala*) its essence (*dhât-ahu*), but insists that the soul has continuous consciousness (*shu'ûr*) of its existence (*wujûd*), and that when it [soul] intelligizes, it has continuous consciousness of its intelligizing. This continuous consciousness of existence reminds us of the *nosse* that Augustine allows to the infant because of the soul being present to itself. The Flying Man was allowed in the letter, which uses a term cognate to *shu'ûr*, a certain consciousness also of his essence.[21] Elsewhere in *Taliqat* (*Glosses*) by Avicenna or a student, pp. 79–80 Badawi, the point is put in terms of the soul forgetting its essence and needing to be awakened to itself. (5) Avicenna stresses, fifth, even more than Augustine, that one knows oneself as engaging in activities and knows one's essence even when dream-

---

19. Trans. Rahman *Soul* 15,18–16,17 = Avicenna *De Anima* 1.1, from the Latin of Avicenna Latinus, ed. S. Van Riet.

20. Trans. Rahman 259,6–9 = Van Riet 5.7.

21. I thank Saul Rosenthal and Markus Glodek for these last two observations.

ing (*Reply to Bahmanyâr*, Michot para. 68). Elsewhere he says that one's essence is not distant from oneself even when asleep or drunk, even though the representation of it is not then present to memory (*Ishârât*, ed. Dunyâ, vol. 4, p. 319, translated by Goichon as *Livre des directives et remarques*, group 3, p. 303).

Avicenna, *Al-Shifâ (the Healing): Soul*, I.1 (Rahman 15.18–16.17) from the Arabic (= *De Anima* 1.1, from Latin of Avicenna Latinus, ed. S. Van Riet):[22]

> The inquiry leads us to concern ourselves with grasping the quiddity (*mâhiyya*) of this thing that is called 'soul'. We must here indicate a way to affirm the existence (*wujûd*, Latin, *esse*) of our soul with an affirmation that may serve as an admonition and reminder. This will be a pertinent indication for one who has the ability to observe the truth by himself, without needing to be instructed or rebuked, or averted from errors.
>
> We say that one of us must imagine (*yatawahhamu*, Latin, *putare*) himself as if he were created all at once and as a whole, but with his sight covered so that he cannot see anything external, and created falling through the air or a vacuum, but falling in such a way that he encounters no air resistance nor anything else that would allow him to have any sensations, and with his limbs separated from one another so that they do not meet or touch. Then consider whether he will affirm the existence of his essence [or: of himself, *dhâtihi*, Latin *essentia*]. For he will not have any doubt in affirming existence for his essence, yet he will not along with this affirm [the existence of] the extremities of his limbs, nor his innards, his heart, his brain, or anything external to him. Instead, he will affirm [the existence of] his essence, without affirming that it has length, breadth, or depth. Nor, if in that state he were able to imagine (*yatakhayyalu*, Latin *imaginari*) there to be a hand or other body part, would he imagine (*yatakhayyalu*, Latin, *imaginari*) that it was a part of himself (*dhâtihi*) or a condition for his essence (*dhâtihi*, Latin, *essentia*).
>
> You know that what is affirmed is different from what is not affirmed, and that what is grasped immediately [literally: 'what is near at hand'] is different from what is not so grasped. Therefore the essence (*dhât*, Latin *essentia*) whose existence is affirmed [by the Flying Man] is proper to him, insofar as it is his self (ʿayn), not his body or his limbs, which he does not affirm. Thus he is admonished and has a way of being awake to the existence of his soul as something distinct from the body and immaterial, and he knows and is aware of it [sc. his soul]. But if he is oblivious of it, he will need to be rebuked.

22. Translated from Arabic by Peter Adamson.

Avicenna *Reply to Bahmanyâr and al-Kirmânî*, paras. 58–59, Michot:[23]

What [the Flying Man] will then have grasped (*adraka*) is his essence (*dhât-uhu*), which he will then perceive (*sh'ara bi;* same root as *shu'ûr*). Indeed there is nothing which grasps a thing without grasping its [own] essence (*dhât-ahu*) as grasping.

Avicenna, *Al-Shifâ (the Healing): Soul*, V.7 (Rahman 259.6–9) from the Arabic (= *De Anima* 5.7, from Latin of Avicenna Latinus, ed. S. Van Riet:[24]

One cannot say of the activities of the soul that the soul is absent (*ghayb*), because what is absent is present (*mawjûd*) to itself, but not to something else. But these activities are not existent (*mawjûda*) at all except when the soul is present to them. So it is not absent from them. A thing cannot be absent (*ghayb*) from its own essence (*dhât*), nor revert upon it.

Avicenna *Book of Discussions*, no. 550, pp. 185–86 Bidarfar:[25]

Our intellect does not intelligize ('*aqala*) its essence (*dhât-ahu*) continuously (*dâ'iman*). However, our soul has a continuous (*dâ'im*) consciousness (*shu'ûr*) of its existence (*wujûd*). If it [soul] intelligizes in actuality something other than its essence, it has a continuous (*dâ'im*) consciousness (*shu'ûr*) that it intelligizes as long as it intelligizes.

Avicenna, *Book of Discussions*, Bidarfar p. 226, no. 675:

Student: 'The fact, for a thing, of perceiving its essence is for it to be existent (or 'findable', or 'found', *mawjûd*) [+ in some mss., 'to its essence'], not that its true nature (*kunh*) would be present to it (*ḥâsil la-hu*)'. This answer that he (= Avicenna) wrote is not in line with what I had heard from him. So may he do me the favor of offering me what he had promised.

Avicenna: 'The fact that a thing is perceiving its essence (*li-dhâti-hi*) in an intellectual perception consists in this: the reality (*ḥaqîqa*) of its essence is present to it (or 'belongs' to it, *yakûnu la-hu*) whereas the fact, for a thing, of perceiving its essence (*li-dhâti-hi*) in an unrestricted (*muṭlaq*) way is something

---

23. Translated by Jean (Yahya) Michot, in *Le Muséon*, 2000.
24. Translated from Arabic by Peter Adamson.
25. The next three passages are translated by Jean (Yahya) Michot, the third one orally.

else. What we were saying was related to the fact of the separate (beings) being intellects. He should remember this!'

Avicenna(?) *Taliqat* (*Glosses*), Badawi pp. 79–80:

The Soul can forget its essence exactly as it can forget the first principles and then it needs to be awakened to itself.

PORPHYRY AS POSSIBLE SOURCE

What we seem to have in Augustine and Avicenna is discussions of the same topic, an argument that the soul is not bodily, with divergent proposals about them. But Avicenna could not have read Augustine, since he wrote in Latin, a language not considered worth translating for philosophical purposes. Do they instead have a common source? Gilson noticed the general similarity between Augustine's use of the Cogito here and Avicenna's Flying Man, and appears to suggest as common sources Plotinus and Proclus,[26] but this cannot have been his intention, since Proclus is too late to influence Augustine. If there is a common source, I think it is likely to be Porphyry. If O'Meara is right that it is Plotinus (5.5 [32] 2) who suggests to Augustine the infallibility argument, it may be his pupil Porphyry who suggests the second use of the Cogito to prove that soul is not bodily. For one thing, it may well be Porphyry who gives to Augustine and Avicenna the idea of soul being present to itself. At any rate, Courcelle has compared with Augustine's phrase 'present to itself' Porphyry *Sentences* 40, where Porphyry says that you are by nature present to a self that is present to you, *parôn paronti*, although you can absent yourself, rather as Augustine thinks that the soul ignores its presence to itself when it searches for itself through images.[27] Plotinus has something less close than the idea of presence to itself when he says that intellect is evident (*enargês*) to itself at 5.5 [32] 2 (13–21), translated above.

In his very next chapter (*Sentences* 41, pp. 52,7–53,5, Lamberz), Porphyry distinguishes intellect from the senses as not owing its essence (*ousiôsthai*) to body. The argument appeals, like Augustine's and Avicenna's, to self-awareness. The point is that in turning to itself, intellect both knows it-

---

26. Étienne Gilson, 'Les sources gréco-arabes de l'augustinisme avicennisant', *Archives d'histoire doctrinal et littéraire du Moyen Âge* 4, 1929, 1–149, at 41.

27. P. Courcelle, *Connais-toi toi-même*, Paris 1974, vol. 1, 113–64.

self and exists intact, in separation from body. Perception, by contrast, cannot withdraw from the body and still know itself or even remain intact. In fact, on Porphyry's view, perception does not know itself directly at all, but only through an image. Intellect, by contrast, knows itself when it withdraws from body, and that is when it exercises its intellective function best.

In what sense does intellect withdraw from body and perception not? Points that Porphyry could make about perception are that perceivers have to use a bodily organ to grasp bodies. Further, they grasp them as spatially related to their own bodies, which in turn means that perceivers have to be aware of bodies. None of this is true of intellect, and indeed Plato's *Phaedo* makes the point at 64D–65A that the philosopher withdraws (*aphestanai*) from the concerns of the body.

Porphyry has here drawn a conclusion about the nature of reality, that intellect does not owe its essence to body, from a premiss about the nature of knowledge, that intellect knows itself and remains intact, when withdrawn from body. In this Porphyry is like Augustine.[28] He draws a conclusion about the essence of intellect, and his premiss about intellect's ability to withdraw from body may be at least partly about its ability not to consider body at all. This is admittedly no more than analogous to Augustine's point in *On the Trinity* 10.10.16 that the soul does not know whether it is body. Moreover, Augustine there introduces an incorrect but further principle, which is not used in Porphyry's passage, that a thing can only rightly be said to be known if its essence is known.

Porphyry *Sentences* 41 does not offer Avicenna's premiss either, a premiss that is slightly different from Augustine's, and that says that nothing grasps a thing without grasping its *own* essence as grasping. But like Porphyry, Avicenna draws a conclusion about the incorporeality of a certain essence from the fact of knowledge of essence persisting despite a withdrawal from body. In Avicenna's case, the withdrawal takes the form of not knowing that body exists. In Porphyry, the withdrawal admittedly does not take this form. But if the analogies are close enough to require an explanation in terms of a common source of inspiration, rather than being a matter of great minds thinking alike, then Porphyry is the most plausible common source that I know.

Porphyry *Sentences* 40, pp. 49,9–51,2, Lamberz:

One distances oneself from oneself at the same time as one distances oneself from being. And if one takes a stand in oneself, present to a self that is present

28. I thank Ariela Tubert, who first drew my attention to this.

to itself, (*parôn paronti*), then one is present also to being which is everywhere. But when one abandons oneself <and distances oneself from oneself>, one distances oneself also from being. Such is the value that attaches to being present to what is present to itself and being absent from what has departed from itself. And if, <when we are present to ourselves,> being is present to us, and non-being absent, whereas when we are with other things, being is not present, being did not come in order to be present, but rather when it is not present, it is we who have gone away. And is that surprising? For when you are present to yourself, you are not absent from yourself. And when you look at other things, giving up looking at yourself, you are not present to yourself, despite being present and despite its being yourself who is present and absent. If, when present in this way to yourself, you are not present, and for this reason are ignorant of yourself, and you find everything that is far from you rather than finding yourself, even though you are naturally present to yourself (*sautôi phusei parôn*), why are you surprised if [being] which is not present is far from you, through your having come to be far from yourself? For it is to the extent that you are present to yourself (although you are [indeed] present to yourself and cannot be distanced) that you are present to [being], and so [being] cannot be distanced from you in essence, just as you cannot be distanced from yourself. So it is possible for you to know in general what is present to being and what is absent from it, although being is everywhere present and again is nowhere. Those people are present to themselves who are able to go intellectually to their own essence and know their own essence and in that knowledge and in the recognition of that knowledge to grasp themselves in the unity of knower and known, and being is present to them. But all those who have gone aside from being for themselves to other things are absent from themselves, and being is absent from them.

Porphyry *Sentences* 41, pp. 52,7–53,5, Lamberz:

If something has its being in something other and has no essence on its own separately from the other, then if it turns to itself (*eis heauto strephesthai*) with a view to knowing itself without that in which it has its being, and withdraws (*apolambanein*) itself from that thing [. . .], it gets destroyed in separating itself from its being. But if something is able to know itself without that in which it resides, withdrawing itself from that, and being able to do so without being destroyed, then it cannot owe its essence (*ousiôsthai*) to the thing from which it was able to turn itself to itself (*strephein heauto eis heauto*) without getting destroyed and to know itself without that thing.

(52,16) If, then, seeing and every perceptual capacity is not perception of itself, and does not grasp itself when it separates itself from the body, nor even survive doing that, whereas intellect (*nous*) on separating itself from body then intelligizes most of all and turns to itself and does not get destroyed, it is clear that perceptual capacities acquire their activity through the body, whereas intellect is not in the body, but acquires its activity and being from itself.

An argument highly relevant to Avicenna's is found after Augustine's time in Priscian *Answers to Khosroes* and partially in Proclus and 'Philoponus'.[29] Priscian argues like Avicenna that to know something, a thing must know itself and adds that self-awareness involves turning into oneself, which bodies do not. Moreover, as in Augustine, the withdrawal from matter shows that the essence of what withdraws exists separately from matter. But, close as this is to Augustine and Avicenna, it is highly possible that this argument too began its life in Porphyry, in that Priscian at pp. 41–42 cites Porphyry's *Miscellaneous Inquiries* among many other sources as the basis of his answers to the problems raised by King Khosroes.

There is further reason to connect the discussions in Augustine (*On the Trinity* bk. 10) and Avicenna with Porphyry. As regards Augustine, Jean Pépin[30] has argued, although John Rist has denied,[31] that the preceding book of *On the Trinity*, bk. 9, borrows from Porphyry's fragmentary *Miscellaneous Inquiries* the idea of soul and body being unified '*without fusion*' to explain the relations in the Trinity. As regards Avicenna, he cites Porphyry in an adjacent chapter (*Al-Shifā: Soul = De Anima* 5.6) as the source for the view he rejects: that in thinking, the intellect becomes identical with its object.

29. Carlos Steel cites Proclus, *Elements of Theology* 16, 44, and 186, and Priscian, *Answers to Khosroes* 45,19–31 in *CAG* supplement vol. 1. See Carlos Steel, *The Changing Self*, Brussels 1978, 15. Similar is 'Philoponus' *in DA3*, 466, 19–22, translated in chapter fourteen.

30. Jean Pépin, 'Une nouvelle source de saint Augustin: le *zétéma* de Porphyre sur l'union de l'âme et du corps', *Revue des études anciennes* 66, 1964, 53–107.

31. John Rist, 'Pseudo-Ammonius and the soul/body problem in some Platonic texts of late Antiquity', *American Journal of Philology* 109, 1988, 402–15.

CHAPTER 13

Knowing self through others versus direct and invariable self-knowledge

In chapter one, we encountered an idea opposite to Descartes' suggestion in the *Second Meditation* that one knows oneself but cannot see other people, only the hats and coats that may cover automata. On the contrary, it is a pre-requisite for an infant's acquiring a concept of self that it should engage, as tends to happen around nine months, in activities of shared attention and social referencing with someone else. It is by noticing that its gaze is not aligned with the other's gaze, or that its inclinations are not aligned with the other's approval, that it comes to see itself as having a mind of its own. It would be too grand to speak of it as yet having a concept of self, but this is a prerequisite for such a concept. Moreover, it has been suggested, we saw, that the interest in alignment of attention and intention is also a prerequisite for the later learning of language.

The idea that one knows self only through others is also opposite to Augustine's view described in chapter twelve that the soul is present to itself and does not need to seek itself. But the dependence on others was favored by Plato, and so Augustine had to reject Plato.

KNOWING SELF THROUGH OTHER: PLATONISM

The idea that one knows oneself through knowing another is also found in more than one context in ancient Greek Philosophy. There is a theme in the *First Alcibiades*, ascribed by the ancients but not by all moderns to Plato. According to the *First Alcibiades*, the eye sees itself best by seeing its reflection in the eye of another (132C–133C), and this is applied to our knowledge of ourselves.

First Alcibiades 133C goes still further. It speaks of the divine and says the soul knows itself best by looking at its most divine part, wisdom. At 133C8 ff., which, however, I have put in square brackets because it may be an interpolation, it adds that the soul does so by looking at God himself.

This last idea is used by the Christian Clement of Alexandria in the late 2nd century AD, whether or not he got it from Platonism: we recognize ourselves by seeing mirrored in God our own divine element and so also coming to recognize something of God.[1]

Plotinus in a different way speaks as if moral beauty needs to be seen and loved first in another before one can take pleasure in it in oneself (5.8 [31] 2 (38–43)). Moreover, he explains at 5.1 [10] 1 (1–3) that in being ignorant of their Father, God, souls are ignorant of themselves and goes on to compare ignorance of one's human father. The comparison is powerful, because people who do not know who their parents are, or who find they have been mistaken, feel that something of themselves is missing, and the feeling is not weakened even if the real parents are also shared by other siblings.

The context in Plotinus suggests a two-way relation. Souls that separate themselves from God are in fact disregarding themselves by failing to recognize God as their Father. At the same time, things also work in the opposite direction, for this disregard for themselves causes (*aitia*) their ignorance of God.

Plato(?) *First Alcibiades* 132E–133C:

> SOCRATES: Have you, then, noticed that when someone looks at an eye, [133A] his face appears, as if in a mirror, in the eye of the person opposite. We call this the pupil [*korê* is literally a girl] because it is an image (*eidôlon*) of the one looking.
>
> ALCIBIADES: True.
>
> SOC: So an eye would see itself when gazing at an eye and looking at that part of it that is best and with which it sees?
>
> ALC: Apparently.
>
> SOC: It would not see itself, if it looked at another part of a person or at anything else other than what it happens to resemble.
>
> ALC: True.
>
> SOC: So if an eye is to see itself, it has to look at an eye and at that place in the eye where we happen to find generated the excellence of the eye—and I presume that is sight?
>
> ALC: Quite so.

1. Clement *Stromateis* 1.19, 94,4, *GCS* ed. Stählin, vol. 1, p. 60, lines 22–25.

SOC: Well then, dear Alcibiades, with a soul too, if it is to know itself, it must look at a soul, and especially at that place in a soul where the excellence of a soul is generated, namely wisdom, and at anything else that this [part] happens to resemble.

ALC: So I think, Socrates.

SOC: Can we, then, say that any part of the soul is more divine than that involved in knowing and understanding?

ALC: No.

SOC: This part of the soul, then, resembles God, and anyone who looks at it and knows everything divine, God and understanding, would also most know himself.

ALC: Apparently.

[Interpolation?]

[SOC: So as mirrors are clearer and purer and brighter than the reflection in the eye, so God turns out to be purer and brighter than the best that is in our soul?

ALC: It looks like it, Socrates.

SOC: So it is when looking at God that we would use that finest of reflectors, and among human things when looking at the soul's excellence, and that is how we would see and know ourselves most.]

AUGUSTINE'S REJECTION OF
KNOWING SELF THROUGH OTHER

But Augustine rejects the Platonic idea. Incorporeal things are not known by processes of mirroring, as Proclus agrees (chapter fourteen below). Nothing is more present to the soul than itself (*On the Trinity* 10.3.5). He thus seems to reinstate the primacy of self-knowledge over knowledge of others that Descartes has made more familiar to us. Although this addresses the problem of how we could possibly have self-knowledge, it does leave us with the problem so graphically expressed by Descartes, how we have knowledge of others.

Augustine *On the Trinity* 10.3.5:

But if the mind makes an image of itself as like what it is, then when it loves this image, it loves itself before it knows itself, because it gazes at something like itself. So it knows other minds from which it makes an image of itself and is known to itself by the generic [likeness].

Why, then, when it knows other minds, does it not know itself, since nothing can be more present to the mind than itself? But if it is as with eyes of the body, which know other eyes better than they know themselves, let the mind then not seek, since it will not find. For eyes will never see themselves, except by mirrors. But let it not in any way be thought that anything like that can be applied to the contemplation of incorporeal things in such a way that the mind knows itself as if in a mirror.

If Augustine's view does not tell us how we have knowledge of others, the question also arises how we have knowledge of God. He tells us in *Confessions* bk. 10 that God is to be found within us, and in 7.10.16 that he learned to look inwards in this way from the 'books of the Platonists', that is of Plotinus and at some stage Porphyry. So knowledge of God might seem to be through knowledge of self. This is the opposite of Clement's interpretation of Plato, according to which we know ourselves as rational beings by seeing ourselves as the image of God. But it would not be impossible for Augustine to agree to both. In fact, he has a prayer in *Soliloquiae* 2.1.1 that has been interpreted in both ways: 'Let me know myself; let me know you' (*noverim me; noverim te*). Verbeke[2] has taken this in one of the two possible directions, arguing that Augustine is treating knowledge of the self as the route to knowledge of God, not vice versa. Verbeke also sees Plotinus' discussion, mentioned above, at 5.1 [10] 1 (1−3), as influencing Augustine's *noverim me; noverim te*. But at least with Plotinus I suggested that he may have believed there was influence in both directions.

KNOWING SELF THROUGH OTHER: ARISTOTLE

Plato's discussion seems to have influenced Aristotle *Nicomachean Ethics* (*EN*) 9.9, 1169b33−1170a4, pseudo-Aristotle *Magna Moralia* (*MM*), and probably Aristotle *Eudemian Ethics* (*EE*) 7.12. The subject is why the happy person needs friends. This is especially puzzling, if happiness implies being self-sufficient,[3] a view I do not share myself, but that Aristotle treats as commonly accepted in *EN* 1.7−8, and which was to be even more emphasized by the Stoics, who sought immunity from the effects of fortune.

The answer draws on Plato's idea that self-knowledge comes about

2. G. Verbeke, 'Connaissance de soi et connaissance de Dieu chez Saint Augustin', *Augustiniana* 4, 1954, 495−515, reprinted in his *D'Aristote à Thomas d'Aquin: Antécédents de la pensée moderne*, Leuven 1990, 367−87.

3. Aristotle *EN* 9.9, 1169b33−1170a4, 1170a29−b11; *EE* 7.12; pseudo-Aristotle *MM* 2.15, 1213a10−26.

through knowledge of others, but there are four different versions, which are also different from Plato's. He had talked about our knowledge of our human nature, whereas Aristotle talks about the individual's knowledge of particular actions seen as his or her own and as good or enjoyable.

Aristotle's discussion of knowledge in the *Nicomachean Ethics* is embedded in a discussion of love, both of which consider self and other. But the discussions go in opposite directions, insofar as love for friends is based on self-love, in *EN* 8.12, 1161b18–19; 27–29; 9.4, 1166a1–2; 9.7, 1168a5–10; 9.8, 1168b5, whereas knowledge of self is based on knowledge of the other. This treatment of self-love as the basis of love for others is one of the antecedents of the Stoic theory of attachment (*oikeiôsis*) to others being a natural development from attachment to one's own person.[4]

In *EN* 9.9, 1169b3–1170a4, Aristotle argues that we can more easily look at others and at their actions than at our own and that when the actions of a friend are good and just, we can see them and take pleasure in them as our own.

A little later at 9.9, 1170a29–b14, Aristotle gives another argument, which seems incompatible with the first. For it starts from the idea that we are inevitably aware of our own existence and goodness, *without* knowledge of friends, and knowledge of a friend's existence seems to be reduced to an extra bonus. Aristotle says that it is pleasant to be aware of our own existence, since it is seen as a good, at least if one is a good person, and since a friend is a second self, his existence will be seen as good too.

Aristotle's follower in the *Magna Moralia*, attributed wrongly to Aristotle, at 2.15, 1113a13–26, argues that it is pleasant to know oneself, but for this one needs to look at a friend. For we cannot look at ourselves from our own perspective, as shown by our seeing the wrongdoing of others better than our own. So just as we use a mirror (Plato's analogy) to look at our own faces, so we can achieve the pleasure of knowing ourselves only by looking at a friend. For a friend is another self. Since the author mentions our wrongdoing, he would have done well to add the same qualification as the *Nicomachean Ethics*, that it is for the good person that self-awareness is likely to be pleasant.

Aristotle's *Eudemian Ethics* 7.12 has a different argument again. Aryeh Kosman's clarifying discussion[5] has made a very good case for saying that

4. For various antecedents, see Richard Sorabji, *Animal Minds and Human Morals*, London and Ithaca N.Y. 1993, 132–33.

5. Aryeh Kosman, 'Aristotle on the desirability of friends', *Ancient Philosophy* 24, 2004, 135–54.

the text from 1244b24 up to 1245a12 is not yet preparing to explain the value of knowledge of others, but rather building up initial perplexity about what value it could possibly have. This is plausible because the passage concludes at 1145a11–12 by suggesting that this is actually still a puzzle: 'choosing shared living, then (*dê*), might be thought stupid to one way of thinking'.

I will not here follow, though I will record, a second ingenious suggestion by Kosman, that the apparent references to having knowledge *of* oneself might be taken instead as references to *oneself* having knowledge. This understanding needs to reinterpret 1245a30–35 and to emend the preferred text at 1245a35–36 to avoid reference to self-awareness. But Aristotle's interest in *self*-perception is confirmed again at 1245b1 at the end of the quotation, when he values seeing oneself (*heauton*) immersed in the better good.

The opening puzzle in *Eudemian Ethics* 7.12 is why friendship and our knowledge of *others* should be valuable, if the really valuable thing is knowing *oneself*. There are two parts to the puzzle. First (1244b29–1245a1), if you separated the knowing, i.e., presumably separated it from *oneself*, the result would be no better than someone *else* having knowledge and life. This might so far be taken either in Kosman's way as meaning that what is desirable is *oneself* having knowledge and life, or, to suit the prevailing interpretation, as meaning that one's knowledge and life is of no value to one unless one recognizes it, i.e., has *self*-knowledge.

The second part of the puzzle at 1245a1–10 may be that the valuable thing, according to the Pythagoreans at least, is to be *known*,[6] and one is known by oneself, so long as one perceives and knows (since these are self-conscious activities). So again what need is there of another person?

The solution to the puzzle starts at 1245a30 and puts the pleasure of friendship in terms of the self-knowledge it affords. The solution draws attention to at least three facts. First, the friend is another self[7] and therefore

6. Kosman understands that our objective is not simply to be *known*, but to meet the requirement for *knowing* that Aristotle explains at *On the Soul* 3.8, 431b20–432a1. There we hear that for the mind to exercise knowledge, is for it (though not for the whole physical person) to become identical with the thing known. What the *Eudemian Ethics* passage states as our objective, when it talks of becoming perceived and wishing to be what is known, is, on this view, coming to be identical with what is known in the course of knowing it. The point will then be to intensify the puzzle as to what relevance our knowledge of *other* people could possibly have to our objective, since the mind's identity with what it knows can be achieved independently of its having knowledge of *other* people.

7. I do not join Kosman in weakening the doctrine to 'a friend is another center of consciousness', because that would be true even of an enemy, and because his construal has to

to perceive one's friend is somehow to perceive and know oneself. Second, one always perceives one's friend at the same time, and this too is pleasant. Third, if the pleasures the two of you are enjoying together are not vulgar, but divine (and Aristotle's example in *EN* 10.7 would be doing philosophy together), that will be still more pleasant, because one will see oneself immersed in the greater good.

I agree with Kosman that the references to *sunaisthanesthai* here at *Eudemian Ethics* 1244b25, 1245b22, b24, as at *Nicomachean Ethics* 9.9, 1170b3 – 14, are not simply to self-awareness, although the word often does mean that, but to something more complex: shared perceiving between friends. I take this, as I shall explain in a moment, to be not merely perceiving the same things, but being aware that each is perceiving the same things. But I think this shared perception does involve one's *self*-perception, and not merely, as Kosman argues, the activity of oneself perceiving and knowing. When Aristotle says at 1244b25, 1245b22, b24 that we share perception with our friends, I think he is referring to the phenomenon of shared attention, which, as I mentioned in chapter one, psychologists have found so important in infant development and missing from the great apes and damaged in autistic children. At around nine months, the human infant starts to be aware of divergence and convergence of gaze beetween itself and its carer. And it has been argued, as I said, by Tomasello and others that this shared attention is an essential prerequisite for learning language, since the learner and speaker have to know what each is referring to. Thus, as I interpret it, the solution as to the value of friends finishes up at 1245b1 somewhat as in the other two treatises by showing how friendship between good people enhances *self*-awareness of oneself as immersed in enjoying good things.

Aristotle *Nicomachean Ethics* 9.9, 1169b33 – 1170a4:

> If ownership is one of the pleasant things, and we can more easily look at our neighbors than ourselves, and at their actions than at our own, then to good men the actions of good men who are their friends are pleasant, because they have both these naturally pleasant features. So the man who is blessed will need such friends, if it is his policy to look at actions that are both just and his own, and the actions of a friend who is good are of that sort.

---

reinterpret the next sentence, which assumes kinship with a friend and explains that the kinship can only be partial. I don't think the sentence can be saying that it is difficult for the two friends to become one. For their becoming one would be impossible, and *panta* (or *to*) *eph' henos genesthai* means not that, but '[all the things] to converge on one'.

ps-Aristotle *Magna Moralia* 2.15, 1213a13–26:

Since, then, it is very difficult, as certain wise men have said, to know oneself, and very pleasant, since knowing oneself is pleasant, we cannot look at ourselves from our own perspective (*ex hautôn*). That we cannot is clear from the things of which we accuse others while remaining unconscious (*lanthanein*) of doing the same things ourselves, which is due to favoritism or emotion, which make many of us blind as regards judging correctly. So as when we want to see our own face, we see it by looking in a mirror, similarly when we wish to know ourselves, we can do so by looking at a friend, for a friend, as we say, is another self (*heteros egô*). If, then, it is pleasant to know oneself, and it is not possible to know without another as friend, the self-sufficing person would need friendship in order to know himself.

Aristotle, *Nicomachean Ethics* 9.9, 1170a29–b14:

If one who is seeing perceives that he is seeing, one who is hearing that he is hearing, and one who is walking that he is walking, there is something that perceives that we are engaged in activity, so as, if we are perceiving, to perceive that we are perceiving, and if we are thinking, that we are thinking. And to perceive that we are perceiving or thinking is to perceive that we are in existence (for existing was perceiving or thinking), and to perceive that one is living is one of the things that are pleasant in themselves. For life is naturally a good thing, and it is pleasant to perceive the good in oneself. Living is choiceworthy and especially for good people, because existence is for them good and pleasant, since they are pleased at consciousness within them [or shared consiousness, *sunaisthanesthai*] of what is good in itself. But as the good man is related to himself, so he is related to his friend, for the friend is another self (*heteros autos*). Consequently, as his existence is choiceworthy for each person, so, or nearly so, is his friend's existence. His existence was choiceworthy because of perceiving himself as good, and such perception is pleasant in itself. So one must have shared perception (*sunaisthanesthai*) also of one's friend's existence, and this would be achieved in shared living, and in sharing conversation and thought. For this is what shared living is thought to mean in the case of humans and not, as in the case of cattle, feeding in the same place.

Aristotle *Eudemian Ethics* 7.12, 1244b24–1245a12:

[Puzzle about the value of our knowing friends] It is evident that living is perceiving and knowing (*gnôrizein*), so that shared living is shared perceiving (*sunaisthanesthai*) and shared knowing (*sungnôriẓein*). But what is most desirable for each person is to perceive and know oneself (*to hautou, to hauton*) [so Bonitz and 2nd hand in one ms.; but Kosman: to be oneself perceiving and knowing (*to auton, to auton*); mss.: to perceive and know the same (*to auto, to auto*)].

For this reason the desire to live is innate in everyone, for living must be treated as a kind of knowing (*gnôsis*). If, then, one were to cut off knowing and not knowing (*ginôskein*) and put them on their own by themselves [sc. apart from knowing oneself; but Kosman: sc. apart from oneself knowing] (which is obscure as written in words, but in practice it need not be obscure), this would not differ at all from another person knowing instead of oneself, and that is like another person living instead of oneself.

But it stands to reason that what is more desirable is perceiving and knowing oneself [Kosman: one's own perceiving and knowing].

One must put two things together in the argument, that living is choiceworthy and so is the good, and from these two things that it is choiceworthy for such a nature to belong to themselves.

(1245a1) Now suppose one member of the [Pythagorean] pairings is always in the [column of] the desirable, and the known and the perceived is so by sharing, generally speaking, in a definite nature, so that to wish to perceive oneself [Kosman: to wish one's own perceiving] is to wish oneself to be of a certain character. Since we are each of these things not by virtue of ourselves, but by participating in capacities in perceiving or knowing (for one who perceives becomes perceived (*aisthêtos*) in the manner in which he originally perceived and in correspondence to what his perceiving corresponded to, and its manner and what it was of), it results that for this reason one wishes always to live because one wishes always to know, and this because one wishes oneself to be what is known.

(1245a11) Choosing shared living, then (*dê*), might be thought stupid to one way of thinking.

Aristotle *Eudemian Ethics* 7.12, 1245a30–b1:

[Solution] A friend means being, as the saying goes, another Heracles, another self (*autos*). But [the characteristics] are scattered and it is difficult for all of them to be realized in one person. Still, a friend is by nature what is most akin (*sungenestaton*), and one is alike in respect of body, another of soul, and of these one in respect of one part, another of another. Nonetheless, a friend means being, as it were, a separated self.

(1245a35–37) So (*oun*) necessarily to perceive one's friend (*tou philou,* mss.) is somehow to perceive oneself (*hautou,* mss.) and somehow to know oneself. [Kosman: So necessarily for one's friend (emending to *ton philon*) to perceive is somehow for oneself (reading with one codex *auton*) to perceive and somehow for oneself to know.]

(1245a37–b1) Thus it stands to reason that it is pleasant to enjoy even vulgar things together and to share living with a friend (for it is always accompanied by perception of the friend at the same time (*hama*)), but it is more pleasant to enjoy the more divine pleasures. The reason is that it is always more pleasant to see oneself (*heauton*) immersed in the better good.

Aristotle *Eudemian Ethics* 7.12, 1245b21–24:

If it is possible to share living and perceiving (*sunaisthanesthai*) with many people together, it is most desirable to share with as many as possible. But since that is very hard, the activity of shared perception (*sunaisthêsis*) has to be realized among fewer.

KNOWING SELF THROUGH OTHERS: STOICS

The theme is taken up in a different way by the Stoic Hierocles (*Elements of Ethics* 3.39–45). As pointed out by Brad Inwood,[8] the newborn chick's knowledge of its own person, which has been central to the earlier discussion, involves knowledge of others, of the weasel or hawk, which is dangerous for it, and of the bull leaping around it, which is safe—judgments for which Avicenna was later to introduce the estimative faculty. But this is not, I think, knowledge of other minds, since the chick does not have to think of the hawk as a conscious being.

Hierocles, *Elements of Ethics* col. 3, lines 39–45, Long:[9]

But domestic chicks stay quiet and do not flutter when a leaping bull circles round them, but if a weasel or hawk does so, they squawk and duck under their mother's wings as quickly as possible. And the lion makes lighter of an unarmed man, but attacks a man carrying a spear with less confidence.

8. Brad Inwood, 'Hierocles: theory and argument in the second century A.D.', *Oxford Studies in Ancient Philosophy* 2, 1984, 151–83.
9. Translated by Stephen White, work in progress.

OTHERS IN ONE'S CONCEPTION OF ONESELF

So far I have been speaking chiefly of others as *causing* one to know oneself. A different idea is that others may enter into one's very conception of oneself. We have encountered this idea too in Plotinus' point that one may not know who one is if one does not know who one's father is. Other persons may thus enter into one's very identity, if we take identity in the sense in which a persona or a woven narrative gives one an identity. This brings us closer to an idea found in modern German and French philosophy, that the self actually is a relationship among different persons. Gwen Griffith-Dickson[10] has traced this idea back to before Kant's *Critique of Pure Reason* to the German philosopher Johann Georg Hamann, who translated Hume into German for Kant. She then traces it through a sequence of German and eventually of French philosophers.

INVARIABLE SELF-KNOWLEDGE

I have pointed out that in the course of his argument at *EN* 9.9, 1170a29–30, Aristotle says, that we are always aware of our own activities, both psychological ones like seeing and hearing, but also walking. The idea that we are always aware of our psychological activities is quite common, and we have seen it in Locke and Kant in passages cited above.[11] The soul's invariable self-awareness was one of the themes we found stressed by Augustine in chapter twelve. But it is somewhat surprising that Aristotle should stress our being invariably aware of our own activities in a passage in which he is arguing that self-awareness is due to awareness of *other* persons.

This is not fully explained by the fact that the topic of self-awareness is not one topic, because there are such different objects of self-awareness. Aristotle was talking of seeing *activities* as one's own and as good or enjoyable. But there is also awareness of one's character, or motivation, or of one's essence or true nature as a human. These kinds of self-awareness are connected. We saw 'Simplicius' (Priscian?) holding that the soul's essence can be inferred from its activities. And awareness of the day's activities is connected with awareness of one's character in the Stoic practice of self-interrogation.

10. Gwen Griffith-Dickson, work in progress. She cites Feuerbach, Schleiermacher, the poet Hölderlin, Ferdinand Ebner, Martin Buber, Franz Rosenzweig, Levinas, and Lacan.
11. Chapter five above cites Locke, *Essay Concerning Human Understanding* 2.27.9, and translates Kant, *Critique of Pure Reason*, on the third paralogism, A 362–64.

But self-awareness is often recognized to be difficult whichever kind we take. The Delphic challenge to 'know thyself' is seen as difficult when taken in the manner of the *First Alcibiades* ascribed to Plato as an injunction to know one's own human nature. But equally Plotinus denies that we are always aware of our everyday activities like reading—self-awareness can actually impede them (1.4 [46] 10 (21–29)). And few, he thinks, are ever aware of the uninterrupted activity of their higher intellect (4.8 [6] 8 (1–11)). The Epicureans stressed our lack of self-knowledge of our motivation. It is because of an unrecognized fear of death that people restlessly travel, according to Lucretius (*On the Nature of Things* 3.1053–75).

Aristotle, however, often repeats the idea that we are inevitably aware of our own seeing, hearing, walking, perceiving, thinking, remembering, living, and existing.[12] Even though the claim sometimes appears in an 'if'-clause, he usually seems to rely on it. But what are his reasons? The shared attention that he finds in friendship does admittedly involve a level of self-awareness. Moreover, Stephan Eberle has drawn my attention to Aristotle's belief that we have to be aware of our own perceptions in order to judge that sweet and white belong to one single body, because he thinks we tell that by recognizing simultaneity, that is by recognizing the simultaneity of our perceiving sweet and white. This view has something in common with arguments found both in the Hindus ('I touch what I see') and in Kant's *Critique of Pure Reason* (A 108–10), which I shall cite in chapter fourteen. These arguments seem to say that a knowledge of a unitary perceiving self is required, if we are to see soft and white as belonging to a unitary external object. Aristotle's argument is given in *On Sense Perception* 7, 447b24–448a1, and he goes on to specify a second purpose for which we need to be aware of our own perception. In order to tell whether we are perceiving two similar qualities, or two dissimilar ones, we have to know whether we are using one sense or two (which is what requires self-awareness) and whether we are directing sense onto a positive quality or onto a privation (wet or cold would be examples of privation).

Aristotle *On Sense Perception* 7, 447b24–448a1:

For the soul appears to tell [that something is] one in number by nothing other than simultaneity (*hama*) and [that it is] one in kind by the sense that is dis-

12. Aristotle *On Sense Perception* 437a27–9; 448a26–8; *On the Soul* 425b12; *EN* 1170a29–b1; *EE* 7.12, 1245a7–9; *On Memory* 452b26–8; *Phys.* 244b15–245a2. I assume that the effaced mental images (*phantasmata*) of *On Dreams* 3 461a17–21 do not exist as *phantasmata* when they are effaced.

criminating and by its manner [of discrimination]. I mean that the same sense discriminates, for example, white and black, which are different in kind, and a sense the same as itself, but different from the former [sense] discriminates sweet and bitter. On the other hand, a sense discriminates each of the two opposites in a different way, but aligned opposites in the same way. For example, as taste discriminates sweet, so sight discriminates white and as sight discriminates black, so taste discriminates bitter.

There is further evidence that Aristotle thinks our distinction of sweet and white depends on our distinguishing our own *perception* of sweet from our *perception* of white. This is that he discusses the two subjects in the same breath, without explaining their connection, viz., by what faculty we are aware of our own perception and by what faculty we distinguish sweet from white. It is by the same perceptual faculty, the common one, according to *On Sleep* 2, 455a17–20, translated in chapter eleven.[13]

Aristotle has a further reason for requiring self-perception in his treatment of time.[14] For he thinks that perceiving the passage of time has to be through perceiving an inner mental process, and he requires this even in the case where we are also perceiving an external process such as the movement of the celestial clock.[15]

In *On Sense Perception* 448a26–28, he works the other way round and treats the idea of invariable self-awareness as a premiss in order to draw a conclusion about time. Having put in an 'if'-clause the idea that when we perceive, we cannot fail to notice that we exist, he uses this to argue that there cannot be any imperceptibly small times, for then we would not continuously know of our own perception and existence.

The claim that we inevitably know of our own remembering contains a difficulty, because to talk of remembering implies the correctness, not just the occurrence, of the mental activity, and concerning the correctness, we could be wrong. Aristotle realizes this in *On Memory*,[16] when he allows that a person may be remembering in spite of being in doubt whether he is doing so.

---

13.   This point is made by Stephan Eberle, 'Le problème de la perception du temps et la théorie de l'intentionnalité chez Aristote', in B. Melkevik and J.-M. Narbonne, eds., *Une philosophie dans l'histoire: hommages à Raymond Klibansky*, Laval, Quebec, 2000, 65–81.

14.   I have benefited here from Daniela P. Taormina, 'Perception du temps et mémoire chez Aristote', *De memoria et reminiscentia* 1', *Philosophie Antique*, 2, 2002, 33–61.

15.   Aristotle *Phys.* 4.11, 218b21–219a6.

16.   Aristotle *On Memory* 451a2–5.

In fact I believe it is the other tradition, so strongly expressed by Plotinus, that is right. To adapt an idea of Sartre,[17] we are often unaware of having heard the clock strike three, until someone asks us the time. If no one asks us, we may never become aware of our hearing, because our attention is distracted. Wolfgang Bernard has pointed out that 'Philoponus' makes a related point against Aristotle in the course of arguing for something else. When thinking about something else, we may see a friend, but not realize until later that we have done so (*in DA* 466,30−35).[18] Here is how Plotinus and 'Philoponus' make the point.

Plotinus 1.4 [46] 10 (21−29):[19]

> One could find many worthy activities, both theoretical and practical, when we are either contemplating or acting, which we may not be conscious (*parakolouthein*) of although we are wide awake. For the person reading does not have to be conscious that he is reading, particularly when he is reading with great concentration; nor does the person acting bravely have to be aware that he is doing so and that he is acting in accordance with bravery insofar as he is acting; there are countless other such instances. In fact, awareness is likely to take the edge off the very activities of which we are aware.

Plotinus 4.4 [28] 8 (9−16):

> In the first place it is not necessary to store up in oneself all that one sees. For when the perception is of no significance or does not concern us at all personally, but is caused involuntarily by the differences in what is seen, then it is the visual faculty alone that is affected by this, and the soul receives nothing into itself, since the perception is of no use, either in meeting some need or in bringing some other benefit from the difference perceived. But when the soul's very activity is directed exclusively elsewhere, then it would not tolerate the memory of things over and done with, since it is not aware of any perception of them even when they are occurring.

17. Sartre, *Being and Nothingness*, introduction.
18. Wolfgang Bernard, 'Philoponus on self-awareness', in Richard Sorabji, ed., *Philoponus and the Rejection of Aristotelian Science*, London and Ithaca N.Y. 1987, ch. 8.
19. The next two passages are translated by Barrie Fleet, in Richard Sorabji, *The Philosophy of the Commentators, 200−600 AD: A Sourcebook*, vol. 1, London and Ithaca N.Y. 2004.

'Philoponus' *On Aristotle On the Soul 3* 466,30–35:

When reason is busy about something, even if sight sees, we do not know that it saw, because reason is busy. And after that when reason has returned to itself, it says even now that I who am not seeing my friend did see him, as if reason took in a small imprint of what was seen, even though it was busy, [Bernard's punctuation] and now, having come to its senses, was saying that I saw him. So it is the task of reason to say that I saw.

CHAPTER 14

Unity of self-awareness

The idea of self-awareness will become important in chapters fifteen and sixteen, where I shall argue that much of our ethics and agency depends on the same person—and that includes ourselves—being the owner of different activities and experiences, and on our recognizing this. The recognition involves a sense of a unitary self. On the other side, I shall argue, Parfit recognizes only a stream of psycho-physical events without an owner in anything except in name. But he too attaches a certain importance to individual acts of self-awareness. For in seeking a unity for the stream, he bases the unity on several factors, one of them being the possibility of a single awareness of more than one of the psycho-physical events. The difficulty I shall raise is that one can be aware of events in someone else's stream as well as of events in one's own. With enough empathy, or a good enough description, one could even be aware of them as if experienced from the inside. So this does not seem to be a possible way of distinguishing streams.

There are different kinds of unity involved in different discussions. To turn to an ancient one, if perception is to compare sweet and white, to take the example of Plato and Aristotle, there must be something unitary other than taste and sight that can be aware of the objects of both senses. Aristotle does not here, unless tacitly, apply the requirement of unity to awareness of tasting and seeing, but only to awareness of sweet and white. But in a passage discussed in chapter eleven he looks for a single faculty to account for awareness of our seeing (*On the Soul* 3.2, 425b12–25). Indeed, we shall see that the Neoplatonists all looked for a unitary faculty to be aware not just of our seeing, but of our varied psychological operations, and 'Philoponus' made it explicit that there ought to be one thing apprehending all if we are

to avoid Aristotle's threat of its being as if I perceived one thing and you another (*in DA 3*, 465,7–11). They were looking for a single *faculty*. They did
not consider the option I find more plausible, that what needs to be unitary
is not the faculties, but the owner of the faculties, in other words, the person
or self. Finally, beyond these requirements of unity, there is the *sense* of a
unitary self. On the whole, the ancient texts were discussing not the *sense* of
a unitary self, but the need for a unitary subject of awareness. The same may
have been true of the original versions of the Nyaya argument that will be
outlined in chapter sixteen. But the revised version of that argument calls for
a sense of unitary ownership. For it argues that if one does not *think* of oneself as a unitary perceiver of sweet and white, one cannot think of sweet and
white qualities as belonging to one object. The sense of unitary bodies is
here made to depend on the *sense* of a unitary self.[1]

I shall come later in this chapter to the views of David Rosenthal, who
has suggested that in self-awareness there are individual thoughts about one
or more psychological states. He calls these 'higher-order thoughts' (or
'HOTs' in his abbreviation), because they are about psychological states at
a lower level.[2] This is opposed to the rival view of William Lycan that self-
awareness involves not thoughts of a higher order ('HOTs'), but higher-
order perceptions ('HOPs'). His paper is appropriately called, 'The superiority of *HOP* to *HOT*'.[3] We shall see that ancient philosophy considered
both views as well as others.

Aristotle gives a certain unity to self-perception when he makes the
'common sense' responsible for it, as explained in chapter eleven. But he
takes up the question of the unity of perception more explicitly when he
raises the question of what discriminates sweet from white, a question that
comes from Plato's *Theaetetus* (184B–186E). Plato answers that the senses
must converge (*sunteinein*) on something unitary (*mia*), the soul (184D),
and at 186A–187A, he stresses the soul's reasoning activities as needed for
these discriminations. Aristotle substitutes for soul one particular capacity

1. Jonardon Ganeri, 'Cross-modality and the self', *Philosophy and Phenomenological
Research* 61, 2000, 1–19. This develops Arindam Chakrabarti, 'I touch what I saw', *Philosophy and Phenomenological Research* 52, 1992, 103–16, which reports the views of Vâtsyâyana
around 400 AD and Uddyotakara around 600, who are in turn commenting on the *Nyayasûtra*
of Gautama 3.1.1 and 4.1.35–36 from around 190 AD.

2. David Rosenthal, 'Unity of consciousness and the self', *Proceedings of the Aristotelian Society* 103, 2002–3, 325–52.

3. William G. Lycan, 'The superiority of *HOP* to *HOT*', in Rocco W. Gennaro, ed.,
Higher Order Theories of Consciousness, Amsterdam 2004.

of the soul, the common sense, and he repeatedly stresses[4] that its role of comparing different types of sensible requires it to be unitary. Otherwise (*On the Soul* 3.2, 426b17–23) it would be as if I perceived sweet and you perceived white. The point is repeated many times by the ancient commentators.[5] It will also be encountered in chapter sixteen in the Nyaya school of Indian philosophy in the different context of the need for a unitary *self*.

But Plotinus complicates the situation, first by moving from sensibles to sensing, and second by addressing our apprehension (*antilêpsis*) not only of our sensing, but also of our thinking, our appetite, and our psychological activities generally. In his reference to thinking, he is speaking not of the intellect's automatic self-thinking, which he considers important, but rather of *us* as sometimes aware, though also sometimes not aware, of our thinking. But Plotinus does not consider self-awareness of this sort very valuable. It is a distraction, we have seen him say, if we are aware of our reading when we read (1.4 [46] 10 (6–29)). He therefore tends to assign the double awareness of perceptions and thoughts to a lowly faculty, the imagination (*phantasia, phantastikon;* 4.3 [27] 30 (5–16); 1.4 [46] 10 (6–21)). Presumably, Plotinus thinks imagination can perform this double job because of the point, made in the adjacent chapter, 4.3 [27] 31 (1–20), that there are two faculties of imagination, one concerned with intelligibles, one with sensibles. An earlier treatise refers apprehension of appetite to inner sense (*hê aisthêtikê hê endon dunamis*), which is the probable origin of Augustine's use of the corresponding Latin phrase, or discursive reason (4.8 [6] 8 (10–11)) and of our psychological activity generally to the perceptual faculty (5.1 [10] 12 (5–14)), which is the faculty in which Aristotle had located *phantasia*. Plotinus describes self-consciousness in this last passage in terms of turning (*epistrephein*) the apprehension inwards and making it attend (*prosokhê*) within. But in the two passages that ascribe our awareness of thought to imagination, he compares mirroring, and speaks of thought bending back (*anakamptein*) and being thrust back again (*apôsthênai palin*).

Proclus objects to the appeal to mirroring, at least for apprehending the soul's essence. He says at *Commentary on Euclid Book 1* 141,2–19, that mirroring in the imagination by projecting (*proballein*) patterns there merely shows you the outward form (*morphê*). In order genuinely to see oneself

4. Aristotle *On the Soul* 3.1, 425a30–b1, 3.2, 427a9–12; *On Sense Perception* 7, 449a6–20; cf. *On the Soul* 3.7, 431a14–20; *On Sleep* 2, 455a12–22.

5. See the ancient commentators ad loc. and, e.g., Alexander *in Sens.* 36,13–19; *On the Soul* 60,27–61,3; Plotinus 4.7 [2] 6 (18–19); Philoponus (*in DA* 13,7–20,136, 16–17; and 'Philoponus' *in DA 3*, 465,10.

(*heauton*), one would need to stand in the relationship exemplified by the self-thinking intellect, which is both thinker and thing thought: one would need to become both seer and seen. This would require a procedure of turning (*strophê*) inwards.

Second, for self-awareness of *activities*, Proclus makes it harder to find a unitary faculty by objecting that there are not merely two or three, but *many* different types of mental activity and we need a single thing to exercise consciousness (*parakolouthein*) of all of them (*Commentary on Plato's Parmenides* 957,28–958,11 Cousin). In cognition, there are the five senses, the common sense, and reason. Among desires, there are appetite (*epithumia*), anger (*thumos*), and deliberate choice (*proairesis*), to which a unitary vital faculty can give the nod (*sunepineuein*), having enabled us to say 'I have appetite', 'I am angry', and 'I exercise deliberate choice'. But prior to (*pro*) both cognitions and desires, there is another unitary faculty conscious (*parakolouthein*) of all these activities, which says, 'I am perceiving', 'I am reasoning (*logizomai*)', 'I have appetite', 'I will (*boulomai*)'. It both knows the activities and distinguishes among them. It is set over (*epi* with dative) the common sense, and is prior to (*pro*) opinion (*doxa*), appetite, and will (*boulêsis*).

In another passage, Proclus gives a unifying role to *logos*, reason, which can use faculties both higher and lower than itself in order to judge about objects (*in Tim.* 1,254,31–255,20), and Philoponus also gives this role to reason (*in DA* 14,33–35). This echoes Plato's stress at *Theaetetus* 186A–187A on reasoning as needed for the discrimination of sweet and white.

The subject had also been advanced by Proclus' teacher, Plutarch of Athens (not of Chaeroneia), as we learn from the commentary on Aristotle *On the Soul* bk. 3 (464,20–465,31) ascribed to Philoponus, but thought by some to be by a pupil of Philoponus, and by others to be by the still later Stephanus. 'Philoponus' starts by saying that in Plutarch's view it was the lowest faculty of the rational soul, namely opinion (*doxa*), that was responsible for knowing the activities of the senses. But he finishes by saying that this was an interpretation of Plutarch by certain newer interpreters whom he rejects. For he has nowhere found Plutarch giving this view, but considers that Plutarch followed Alexander in holding the common sense responsible, a view that 'Philoponus' considers wrong. Why the discrepancy? Could these divergent readings of Plutarch be explained if Plutarch, unlike Aristotle, located the common sense wholly or partly in the rational soul as its lowest part?

He could have done so, if he included the common sense within *phan-*

tasia. For he is reported by 'Philoponus' at 515,12–15 as having been like Plotinus (3.6 [26] 4 (18–23), 4.3 [27] 31) in recognizing a higher kind of *phantasia* that is the lower boundary of discursive reason. Moreover, Plotinus, at least in the first of these two passages, equates the higher *phantasia* with opinion (*doxa*), so Plutarch might have done the same. The net result would be that both reports about Plutarch could be right: Plutarch might have made the common sense responsible, as 'Philoponus' says, but also, in a passage unnoticed by 'Philoponus', equated the common sense with *doxa*, so that the newer interpreters were right as well. We shall be reminded shortly that there was a Platonist tradition, including Plutarch's pupil, Proclus, of treating human sense as imbued with rationality. This is an alternative to Blumenthal's suggestion that Plutarch changed his mind.[6]

The newer interpreters, starting perhaps with Proclus, made a contribution of their own because they postulated an extra part of the rational soul that they called the 'attentive' (*prosektikon*). Because the human being is unitary, this part needs to apprehend all mental and even biological activities, or it would be, as Aristotle said, as if you perceived one thing and I another. But the part gets different names, being called the *prosektikon* insofar as it ranges over cognitive activities and conscience (*suneidos*) insofar as it ranges over the vital desires. *Suneidêsis* was a name for both conscience and consciousness. Opinion could not do this work, because it could not apprehend activities higher than itself.

On the next page (466,18–29), 'Philoponus' endorses the role of the *prosektikon* and explains that *sight* could not know what it sees, because it would have to turn back (*epistrephein*) on itself, and such turning back would require it to be separable from body. This last explanation goes back at least as far as a commentator earlier than Proclus or 'Philoponus'. Porphyry, in *Sentences* 41, explains that sight, unlike intellect, cannot know itself, since by having its essence (*ousiôsthai*) in body, it is prevented from turning back (*strephesthai*) on itself. For bodies cannot penetrate themselves, a point which is further stressed by 'Simplicius' (*in DA* 173,3–7).

There is a final twist to the story because Aristotle's appeal to the common sense comes to be reinstated, but in a form that Aristotle himself would entirely repudiate. Common sense is turned into a rational, instead of a perceptual, faculty. It was suggested above that this development might have started with Plutarch of Athens. It is certainly found in Priscian and in 'Sim-

6. H. J. Blumenthal, 'Plutarch's exposition of the *De Anima* and the psychology of Proclus', in H. Dörrie, ed., *De Jamblique à Proclus*, Entretiens 21 Foundation Hardt Vandoeuvres—Geneva 1975, 123–47.

plicius' *On Aristotle On the Soul* 3, whose authorship is still disputed, but which is also assigned by Carlos Steel and Fernand Bossier to Priscian. In *On Theophrastus' On Sense Perception* 21,32–22,23 Priscian says that Aristotle's successor, Theophrastus, agrees with Aristotle that it is the common sense that is conscious (*sunaisthanesthai*) that we see. Instead of repudiating the view, Priscian defends it, by saying that the common sense is more separable from bodies than are the individual senses, and so can turn back (*epistrephesthai*) into itself.

'Simplicius' agrees (*in DA* 187,27–188,35, 173,3–7). Only humans can perceive that they perceive, because only the rational can turn back (*epistrephein*) on itself. And rationality, as already hinted by Iamblichus, penetrates human sense perception, so that what perceives is to some extent separable from bodies. In the case of sense perception, this separability is especially true of the *common* sense, which therefore has consciousness (*sunaisthêsis*) of our seeing. But it falls short of intellect and reason in that it recognizes not substance, nor power, but only activities, and in that it recognizes individuals. Other things cannot turn back on themselves at all (*anepistrophon*).

The interpenetration of sense by reason, though repudiated by Aristotle, I believe,[7] had a Platonist history. Plato himself considered imagination (*phantasia*), which Aristotle viewed as perceptual, as a kind of opinion (*doxa*), which Aristotle viewed as rational (*Sophist* 263E–264D; *Republic* 603A). In *Theaetetus* 190E–196C, Plato again mixes Aristotle's distinction of rational and perceptual faculties, when he treats opinion (*doxa*) as a kind of recognition (*anagnôrisis*) and recognition as a fitting together of perception with memory imprints, two functions that Aristotle regards as perceptual. Moreover, Plato further shifts to talk of fitting perception to thought (*dianoia*), which Aristotle classes as rational, and again describes perception and memory as both giving us knowledge, using the whole gamut of words for knowledge, at least some of which Aristotle reserved for the rational: *epistasthai, eidenai, gignôskein*.

Further, there was a Platonist tradition that *doxa* and *dianoia* are needed to supplement perception, starting with Plato *Theaetetus* 186B–187A and continuing.[8] Proclus had gone further and made *doxa* penetrate sense perception (*in Tim.* 1.248,25–29) and called it a rational (*logikê*) sense percep-

---

7. But contrast Charles Kahn, 'Aristotle on thinking', in M. C. Nussbaum and A. O. Rorty, eds., *Essays on Aristotle's de Anima*, Oxford 1992, 367–72.

8. Alcinous *Didaskalikos* ch. 4, 156,8–11, 154,40–155,5; Plotinus 5.3 [49] 3(1–9), 4.3 [2] 23 (21–24, 33–34); Proclus *in Tim.* 1,249,13–27, 1,292,27–293,5; cf. *Platonic Theology* Saffrey-Westerink vol. 3, 23,25–24,2; Priscian *On Theophrastus' On Sense Perception* 19,9–13.

tion (1. 251,16–17), and before him Iamblichus had contrasted our rational perception as perception in a different sense from the irrational, according to the report of 'Simplicius' in a passage just mentioned above, *in DA* 187,37.

The scope of the *prosektikon* is expanded by the head of Priscian's school, Damascius, when he makes it aware also of recollection.[9] Otherwise Damascius confirms many of the points made above.

A final point is that St. Augustine, writing in Latin, agrees with the Neoplatonists that we cannot sense (*sentire*) by sight that we are seeing. Rather, he uses the phrase from Plotinus (4.8 [6] 8 (10–11)), 'inner sense' (*interior sensus*), and says that it perceives both corporeal objects and the senses, while all these things, including inner sense, are known by reason (*On Free Choice of the Will* 2.4.10 (41); *City of God* 22.29). When Augustine says (*Confessions* 10.40.65), 'I, that is my capacity (*vis*) of introspection, I understand 'that is' as 'or rather'.

Plotinus 4.3 [27] 30 (5–16):

Perhaps there might be a reception into the imagination (*phantastikon*) of the reason (*logos*), which is conscious (*parakolouthein*) of the intellect's thought content (*noêma*). For that thought content (*noêma*) has no parts and remains hidden within, without yet having proceeded (*proelthein*) forth, as it were. But reason (*logos*) unfolds it and brings it from being a thought content into the imagination (*phantastikon*) and displays the thought content as if in a mirror. And that is how there is apprehension (*antilêpsis*) and retention (*monê*) and memory of it. And that is why, even though the soul is always moved towards thinking (*noêsis*), our apprehension (*antilêpsis*) [of the thinking] is when it comes to be in the imagination. The thinking is one thing, and the apprehension of it another. We are always thinking, but we do not always apprehend it. And this is because what receives [the thinking] receives not only thinking but also, on its other side, perceiving.

Plotinus 1.4 [46] 10 (6–29):[10]

It seems that apprehension (*antilêpsis*) exists and occurs when the thought turns back (*anakamptein*) and when that which is active in the soul because of its life is thrust back again (*apôsthênai palin*), so to speak, as happens in a mirror when the surface is smooth, clear, and held still. In such cases when the

9. Damascius *Lectures* series 1 *on Plato's Phaedo*, §269; 271–72; *Lectures* series 2, §21–22, Westerink.

10. Translated by Barrie Fleet, in Richard Sorabji, *The Philosophy of the Commentators, 200–600 AD: A Sourcebook*, vol. 1, London and Ithaca N.Y. 2004.

mirror is there, the image (*eidôlon*) occurs, but when it is not, or is not in the same condition, the object of which there might have been an image is still actually there. In the same way with the soul, when that part of us which acts like this, and in which the likenesses of the reason and the intellect are imaged, is peaceful, then they are envisaged and known as it were perceptually (*aisthêtôs*) alongside the prior knowledge (*protera gnôsis*) that the intellect (*nous*) and the reason (*dianoia*) are active. But when it is disrupted because the harmony of the body is upset, the reason and intellect think without an image; then thinking takes place without imagination (*phantasia*). Consequently something like this might be concluded: that thinking does take place accompanied by imagination, although thinking is not the same as imagination. One could find many worthy activities, both theoretical and practical, when we are either contemplating or acting, which we may not be conscious (*parakolouthein*) of, although we are wide awake. For the person reading does not have to be conscious that he is reading, particularly when he is reading with great concentration; nor does the person acting bravely have to be aware that he is doing so and that he is acting in accordance with bravery insofar as he is acting; there are countless other such instances. In fact, awareness is likely to take the edge off the very activities of which we are aware.

Proclus *Commentary on Plato's Parmenides* col. 957,28−958,11 Cousin:

(1) For indeed hearing knows audibles in one way, the common sense knows all sensibles before these audibles in a different way, and before this common sense again, reason knows in a different way both these things and all the things that perception does not know.

(2) Moreover again, appetite (*epithumia*) desires some things, anger (*thumos*) aims at others, and deliberate choice (*proairesis*) moves [the soul] to others [reading: *alla*]. But moving the soul to all of these, there is a certain unitary vital power through which we say, 'I have appetite' and 'I am angry' and 'I deliberately choose'. That power gives the nod alike (*sunepineuein*) to all these [desires] and lives with all of them, being a desiderative power directed to every kind of desideratum.

(3) And indeed prior to (*pro*) both of these [(1) and (2)], there is something unitary in the soul, which often says 'I am perceiving', 'I am reasoning (*logizesthai*)', 'I have appetite', and 'I will (*boulesthai*)'. It is conscious of (*parakolouthein*) all these activities and cooperates with them. Otherwise, we would not know them all, nor could we say how they differ, unless there were in us some unitary thing without parts which knew them all and which is set over (*epi*, with genitive) the common sense, prior to (*pro*) opinion (*doxa*),

prior to appetite, and prior to will. It knows their cognitions, has gathered their desires into a partless unity (*amerôs*), and in the case of each says 'I' and 'I am active'.

'Philoponus' in *DA* 3, 464,24–465,31:[11]

Plutarch said it was the function of the rational soul to know the activities of the senses. For he says that this happens by virtue of the inferior part of the rational soul, which is opinion (*doxa*). For opinion, the most common part of the soul and the inferior, joins the rational to the non-rational. For, as we have often come to know, it is always by the inferior parts of themselves that the first are joined to the second. So that is how it is now. He says, then, that it belongs to opinion to do these things and lay hold of the activities of the senses.

(464,30) But more recent interpreters neither tremble at Alexander's frown nor pay heed to Plutarch, but pushing Aristotle himself to one side they have devised a newer interpretation. They say that it belongs to the attentive (*prosektikon*) part of the rational soul to lay hold of the activities of the senses. For the rational soul, according to them, does not have only five powers— intellect (*nous*), discursive thought (*dianoia*), opinion (*doxa*), rational wish (*boulêsis*), and choice (*proairesis*); they add another sixth power to the rational soul, which they call 'attentive'. This attentive part, they say, stands over what happens in a human being and says 'I exercised intellect', 'I thought', 'I opined', 'I became angry', 'I experienced appetite'; and in general this attentive power of the rational soul ranges over all the powers, the rational, the non-rational, and the vegetative. If, they say, the attentive power is to range over all, let it go over the senses too and say 'I saw', 'I heard'. For it is proper to what apprehends (*antilambanesthai*) the activities to say this. If it is the attentive part, then, that says this, it follows that this is what apprehends the activities of the senses. For there ought to be one thing apprehending all, since the human being is one. If *one* laid hold of these and *another* of those, it would be, as he [Aristotle *On the Soul* 3.2, 426b17–21] himself says elsewhere, as if you perceived this and I that. It must then be one thing, and that is the attentive part. This attentive part roves over all powers, cognitive and vital. But if it is roving over the cognitive, it is called 'attentive', which is why, when we want to rebuke someone who is wool-gathering in his cognitive activities, we say 'Pay attention (*prosekhe*) to yourself!' Whereas if it is going through the vital powers it is called 'conscious' (*suneidos*), which is why the tragedy [Euripides *Ores-*

11. Both 'Philoponus' passages are translated by William Charlton, in *'Philoponus' on Aristotle On the Soul* 3.1–8, London and Ithaca N.Y. 2000.

tes 396] says 'Conscience (*sunesis*), since I am conscious (*suneidenai*) in myself of having done terrible things'. The attentive part, then, is what lays hold of the activities of the senses.

(465,17) And Plutarch, they say, did ill to hold opinion responsible. For there ought to be one thing that apprehends the activities of all the powers, and opinion does not lay hold of the activities of intellect. It does not say 'I exercised intellect' or 'I thought'. Even if it says 'I opined' or 'I became angry', still, it cannot contemplate the activities of the better powers. But saying this they are not accusing Plutarch. For I nowhere found him saying that the power which perceives the activities of the senses belongs to opinion, but in this he agrees with Alexander, and he too holds the common sense responsible. Both are convicted of speaking wrongly, since they say that the common sense lays hold of the activities of each sense. For the common sense lays hold of nothing that is not a sense object. Every sense object is in a body, but the activity is not in a body. Hence it is not a sense object. And if it is not a sense object, it does not fall under the common sense.

'Philoponus' *in DA* 3, 466,18–29:

Besides, it is absurd that the same sense should know that it sees. For it must be by turning (*epistrephein*) back on itself after having seen the color that it gets to know that it sees. But if it turns on itself, it also has an activity which is separate [sc. from matter], and what has a separate activity has a separate essence, and on that account is eternal and incorporeal. So someone who says in an ambiguous way that the rational soul is immortal will be shouting out plainly that the non-rational soul is immortal; which is absurd. The senses are not eternal, and for that reason do not turn back on themselves. And if they do not turn back on themselves, they do not apprehend their own activities. For a thing's turning on itself is nothing other than its apprehending its own activities. So Aristotle does not speak rightly but, as we said, it belongs to the attentive part (*prosektikon*) of the soul to get to know the activities of the senses.

Priscian *Metaphrasis* 21,32–22,23 (reporting Theophrastus):[12]

Following this, about how we perceive that we perceive, he [Theophrastus] sets out his argument on the same lines as Aristotle, wanting the common sense to be that which has this extra awareness, since it is conscious (*sunaisthane-*

---

12. Translated by Pamela Huby, in *Priscian on Theophrastus on Sense Perception*, London and Ithaca N.Y. 1997.

sthai) of both the activity of each [sense] and its inactivity. For the opposites are of the same [sense]. But the common sense is neither the same as the particular ones nor entirely different. For it is by way of the synthesis of all [the senses] and their concentration into an undivided one; hence in a way each [sense] is conscious (*sunaisthanetai*) that it perceives, not as having been divided off but as joined together in the one. For it belongs to a power already separate from bodies to revert (*epistrephesthai*) into itself and know itself, and each is more corporeal insofar as it has been divided up, and it goes up more to what is apart by means of its indivisible unity with the others. For in fact this indivisible unity is appropriate to the forms which are apart from bodies.

(22,9) But if, as he himself well claims, it belongs to the same [sense] to be aware of opposites, and for this reason of [its own] inactivity also, on the one hand even each [sense] will grasp what is separate in a way from its own organs—for [otherwise] sight would not perceive that the sense organ's not being affected was darkness, for it [sight] appears to be active even when [that] is not affected—and, on the other, to a greater extent the common [sense], which is aware also of the inactivity of the senses themselves. Hence, also the common [sense], but not each [individual one], will be conscious of itself and of its own activity; and if of its activity, then also of its inactivity; and if of its inactivity, it would at the same time be both inactive and active, in that it was conscious [in this way]. Therefore it is inactive, on the one hand, as being divided off and by itself, and, on the other, it is active insofar as it transcends its own special activity and inactivity. So that [it is active] in respect of being (*kata*) the common [sense], connected with (*kata*), which also is each [sense], not as each [individual one], nor [all] as divided off, but as united in (*kata*) the one union of all [the senses], of which it is the function to be aware of the objects of all the senses in the same [center] and undividedly, being active in accordance with the different concepts (*logoi*). Hence also what is aware is in number one and indivisible, but in its being (*tôi einai*) divisible, in that it is active in accordance with different concepts (*logoi*).

'Simplicius' *in DA* 187,27–188,3: [13]

On the other hand, perceiving that we perceive seems to me to be a special characteristic of humans only: for it is a rational soul which has the function of turning to itself (*to pros heautên epistreptikon*). It is also shown in this way that our rationality penetrates as far as sense perception, if it is the case that human

13. The three 'Simplicius' passages are translated by Henry Blumenthal, in *'Simplicius' on Aristotle On the Soul* 3.1–5, London and Ithaca N.Y. 2000.

sense perception is able to cognize itself. This is so because in a way what is perceiving cognizes itself, when it cognizes itself while it perceives. And for this reason it turns to (*epistrephein pros*) itself and belongs to itself, and its being separate from bodies already shows through more, insofar as every body having different parts of itself in different places would never be able to turn its attention (*sunneuein eis*) to itself. For this sort of activity is gathered together and becomes undivided, while every body is divided. Therefore our power of sense perception is rational.

(187,36) Indeed, even the body itself is provided with organs in a rational way and, which is what Iamblichus says, ours is a power of sense perception in a different sense from the irrational power of sense perception, that is our power which turns to (*sunagesthai*) itself is sense perception in a different sense from that which inclines (*neuein*) as a whole to the body. But it does not turn to itself like intellect or reason. For it is not able to cognize its substance or its power, nor on the whole is it stimulated by itself: it is cognitive only of its activity, and at the time when it is active. And it is active when it is being moved in some way by the sense object.

'Simplicius' *in DA* 188,25–35:

(188,25) And one could say in addition that the argument which posits other senses apart from the five is an artificial creation, both because of what has already been said, by which completeness was shown to be present in these ones, and because every sense is primarily something that perceives a sense object and not a sense. For if it perceives a sense, it will merely happen to perceive the sense object of that sense and will have a special sense object of its own, just like each of the five senses. What then? Is this to be granted to the sense that is known as the common sense as a special privilege? Perhaps the common sense alone cognizes nothing at all, but operates alongside each of the five. And so, cognizing sight and color, with which sight is concerned, it will cognize them alongside sight. And so cognizing itself is not an attribute of the common sense alone but of each one, even if it belongs in a purer way to the common sense, since in its case being separate shows through more.

'Simplicius' *in DA* 173,3–7:

It is proper particularly to intellect, and in the second place to reason, to have the capacity to cognize itself, and to the life that is separate from bodies (because body, on account of its being divided with different parts of itself in different places, does not turn back to itself (*anepistrophon*)), so that it belongs to the kind of sense perception that is like reason (*logoeidês*), if not quite, but is in a way free from any body.

MODERN CONTROVERSY

The controversy continues today on how we are aware of our own perceptions, by perception or thought. I have mentioned the view of David Rosenthal, who has suggested that in awareness of our psychological states there are individual thoughts about one or more psychological states and who calls these thoughts higher-order thoughts, or HOTs, because they are about psychological states at a lower level. And I have mentioned William Lycan's rival view that awareness involves higher-order *perceptions*, or HOPs.

ALTERNATIVES

Both these views are opposed to views that regard self-awareness as being due to something more *direct* than a higher-order awareness,[14] and among views maintaining directness we can again distinguish different versions. One instance of direct self-awareness is provided by Aristotle's view, endorsed by Plotinus, that thinking thinks itself (*On the Soul* 3.4, 430a2−4; cf. 429b9; *Metaphysics* 12.7, 1072b19−21; cf. 12.9, 1074b38, 1075a5). In this self-thinking, there is no higher-order thought, because the acts of thinking involved are identical, and not at different levels. Another direct view is offered by Plotinus' pupil, Porphyry, late in the 3rd century AD, when he speaks of one being present to oneself (*Sentences* 40, p. 49,10−11, Lamberz), and this, I have said, may be where Augustine got the idea of the soul being present to itself, early in the 5th century (*On the Trinity* 10.3.5, 10.7.10, 10.9.12, 10.10.16), as a result of which the soul knows itself directly (10.4.6). This Neoplatonist idea is compatible with yet another one recorded above in connection with Proclus (*Commentary on Euclid Book 1* 141,2−19), but also found in Porphyry (e.g., *Sentences* 41), and reflected in the same work of Augustine (14.6.8). According to this view, one turns into oneself, so as to find oneself directly. In Indian philosophy, it has been said, theories of di-

14. Although higher-order awareness is not considered direct, Rosenthal thinks that self-awareness gives an *illusion* of direct presence, and Lycan that it is an advantage of the appeal to higher-order perception, that perception, like self-awareness, gives this illusion, whereas thinking, in his view, does not. I do not know where Plotinus' candidate, the imagination, should be placed in this assessment.

rect self-awareness are accepted by far more schools than theories of higher-order awareness, the latter being approved by few but the Nyaya school that is discussed in chapter sixteen.[15]

Thus HOT and HOP are only two views among many. Moreover, even among those who agree in postulating an *indirect* higher-order awareness of one's own psychological activities, there are other alternatives besides the two canvassed in the recent literature, perception and thought. Plotinus, we saw, postulated imagination, and the 'newer interpreters' postulated the faculty of attention, to which I shall return, as giving us awareness of our psychological activities.[16]

Proclus created a problem for the idea that *perception* is what makes us aware of our psychological activities when he pointed out that we need to be aware not just of perception, for which some perceptual faculty might seem an appropriate monitor, but of many types of desire and reasoning as well. For these other objects of awareness one would need special reasons if one is to retain perception or a perceptual faculty like imagination, as monitor. One strategy, we saw, was to impregnate perception with reason. Alternatively, Plotinus and Plutarch of Athens recognized a higher kind of imagination related to reason. Plotinus may have had an additional ground for thinking the mirror of imagination adequate for awareness of our thoughts and perceptions, given that he thought such awareness was an optional extra and not necessarily required in ordinary mental functioning like reading.

Admittedly, Aristotle had sided with the HOP against the HOT view, but only for awareness of *perception*. His reason is partly, we have seen, in order to avoid certain infinite regresses (*On the Soul* 3.2, 425b12–28). He invokes in particular the so-called common sense, rather than one of the five particular senses (*On Sleep* 2, 455a15–22), as giving us awareness of *perception*. As regards awareness of *thought*, he takes the very differently motivated view that thought is aware of *itself*. This is neither a HOP not a HOT view, because self-thinking is a direct awareness, for the reason explained above, that no act of thinking is considered to be at a higher level, but there is an identity between the acts of thinking mentioned.

15. Bimal Matilal, *Perception: An Essay on Classical Indian Theories of Knowledge*, Oxford 1986, ch. 5.

16. In chapter thirteen, we encountered the idea in Plato and Aristotle that we get various kinds of self-awareness best from our awareness of another person. The examples are recognizing what one's true self is, finding something to be personally proud of, and having a more intense and expanded awareness of one's own mental states. I shall not make use of this here, because it leaves open whether the expanded awareness that results is or is not a form of HOT or HOP.

If there is any threat of an infinite regress in awareness of perception (which I do not believe), Aristotle's HOP solution, which makes perception aware of seeing, is not a very promising model for other cases because it could not be applied generally to other psychological states, for example to disgust. It is no more disgust at one's disgust than pleasure at one's disgust that makes one aware of one's disgust. Either attitude to the disgust already presupposes awareness of it.

THE IMPORTANCE OF ATTENTION

Before I give my own view, let me consider for a moment those late Greek interpreters who ascribed our self-awareness to a general ability to *attend,* because I think attention does need to be taken into account. It is not unreasonable to think of attention as a single generic faculty, even though it will have very different mechanisms, according to the type of object to which it is directed. But one reason why it is valuable to pick out attention as a general faculty is that attention has a global quality which takes it beyond any one mode of cognition. Thus there are circumstances in which attention is heightened by an alarm or impaired by damage quite generally, and not in respect of just one type of cognition such as seeing or thinking. Indeed, attention is more general still, because attention to our own psychological states is only one instance of attention. Plotinus is right when he points out that we attend little, indeed we can attend only selectively, to *what* we are perceiving (4.4 [28] 8 (9–16)), just as we attend little (1.4 [46] 10 (6–29)), to the *fact* that we are perceiving. The appeal to attention has the further advantage that, like the appeal to thought, but unlike the appeal to perception, it avoids Proclus' problem concerning the great variety of psychological states of which we may be aware, very different types of desire as well as of cognition. Attention is something that can be directed to a great variety of objects. I have found attention playing many roles in ancient Greek thought.[17] Inattention was cited by Aristotle to explain going against one's better judgment. Switching attention was recommended by Epicurus as a way of reducing emotional upset. But inattention can also heighten emotion, for example when one does not attend to the fact that one is only watching a play, not reality. The Stoics spoke of attending to themselves (*prosokhê*) in moral self-interrogation. Strato may have thought that all per-

---

17. Some of these examples can be found in the index to Richard Sorabji, *Emotion and Peace of Mind,* Oxford 2000.

ception required attention. But attention is often invoked only in passing, and so I think the 'newer interpreters' approved by 'Philoponus' did well to pick it out as sufficiently important to be separated out as a distinct capacity.

Attention to what one is perceiving or hearing is not an extra bit of perceiving or hearing. We saw this at the end of the last chapter beautifully established by 'Philoponus', who pointed out that I may only realize that I saw my friend after my friend is no longer there to be seen. I gave the further example of realizing that I heard the clock strike three only after it had finished sounding. What I do in this case is either attend to what I perceived or, on another view, attend to some representation lingering in the imagination of what I perceived. I do not do some extra perceiving, and it is not enough either that I should merely do some thinking.

We find further evidence that attending is not necessarily a piece of extra perceiving or thinking when we consider attention not to the clock striking but to our own hearing. Somebody whose ears have been blocked for a time, and then unblocked, may be aware both of the *fact* that they are hearing again and to the *quality* of their hearing. Those people reported by Plato in *Republic* 531A who tried to discover the smallest change of pitch that could be detected were interested in the quality of their hearing. What they needed was not to do some extra hearing, but to attend to the sounds, and equally to their detection of the sounds, to find how many changes they could detect. They had to count the detectable changes and compare them with seen physical changes going on in the musical instrument or felt changes in the vocal cords in order to tell what they might be missing. This did not involve extra hearing. It did involve some thinking, but the thinking was concerned with data acquired by attending to what was detectable. The story would be different again if we considered an impressionist painter attending to the quality of his or her experience of light and how it might be represented in the available materials.

CONCLUSION ON SELF-AWARENESS

What I now want to suggest, turning to my own view, is that we have asked a wrong question in asking what supplies awareness of our psychological states and of our perceiving in particular. It is a wrong question because there is no single answer to it. If there is unity in one's self-awareness, the unity is supplied by the single owner of that awareness, not by the owner's using a single faculty. The need for a single owner is something I shall argue in chapter fifteen, when I discuss the alternative view that there is only an ownerless stream of consciousness. David Rosenthal was asking, in the work I referred to above, what gives the sense of a unitary self. My own answer to his important question rests on my argument in chapter fifteen that there is in normal cases a unitary self and that our very survival requires us to be aware of it, so that it is not surprising that natural selection has structured us to be so aware. The particular mechanism, on this view, becomes a less urgent question, although I do not believe that it depends on our using a single faculty.

Even if we confine ourselves to awareness of *perceiving*, that is not a single thing. It may be awareness of fact or quality. Further, there are different mechanisms in different contexts by which we have this awareness. In awareness of perceiving, extra perceiving is often not needed. Certain types of thinking may have a special relevance to awareness of perceiving. But thought, in the examples given, comes in only after attention has been directed to some particular experiences. That initial attention to experience is not very naturally called 'thinking'. This is not to say that 'attending' would give us a complete account of what happens. Attending to how small a change you can detect involves some attention to experience, but it also involves some thinking. I am suggesting that the 'newer interpreters' were right to insist on the central role of attending, but that whether thinking is also involved, and what thinking, will depend on exactly what we want to be aware of.

If we turn to awareness of our *thinking*, this too may be awareness of the *fact* of thinking or of its *character*. Here the need for extra perception may be still less, and the need for extra thinking greater. Attending will be required, but if one is to be aware of the *character* of one's thought, one may be required to ask oneself questions about one's thoughts, and recall how they happened. Admittedly, in this case, the term 'thinking' is wide enough for this questioning and recalling to count as a form of thinking. But higher-order thinking cannot serve, any more than can higher-order perceiving, as the sole mechanism of self-awareness.

PART VI

Ownerless streams
of consciousness rejected

CHAPTER 15

Why I am not a stream of consciousness

MY VIEW

My view in chapter one was that talk of *me* is, roughly speaking, talk of *this person*, and that a person is something that has psychological states and does things; for short that *owns* psychological states and actions. The importance of ownership will only become clear when I reach the subjects of agency and ethics. On the usual view, which Parfit rejects, I am also the same person over time. Let me now summarize Parfit's rival view, but only after saying that I find it the best challenge to normal views, worked out in depth with originality, clarity, and honesty.

PARFIT'S TWO REDUCTIONIST VIEWS

Parfit is more interested in the idea of *this stream of psycho-physical events,* not his own phrase, but he speaks of a mental sequence, a series of experiences, and *this* sequence (of events).[1] In his book of 1984, revised 1987, *Reasons and Persons,*[2] he takes it that the idea of a person who *has* experiences is deducible from the idea of a sequence of psycho-physical events, and so does not require separate mention (pp. 210, 212–13, 216, 225–26). Persons are thus *reduced* to the stream of psycho-physical events. But while granting with one hand that there are thinkers who *have* thoughts and subjects who *have* experiences, he takes the concession away with the other by saying that

1. Derek Parfit, 'Experiences, subjects, and conceptual schemes', *Philosophical Topics* 26, 1999, 266–67, 229.
2. Derek Parfit, *Reasons and Persons*, Oxford 1984, revised 1987. Page references are to the 1987 edition.

this is true because we talk in this way (223, 225–26). It seems, then, to be just a way of talking, a *façon de parler*, and he concludes explicitly (225) that 'we could fully describe our thoughts without claiming that they have thinkers. We could fully describe our experiences, and the connexion between them, without claiming that they are had by a subject of experiences. We could give what I call an *impersonal* description'.

In a later article of 1999, he withdraws his earlier claim, which he now labels 'F', that 'reality could be fully described in impersonal terms: that is, without the claim that people exist'.[3] He says, 'F, as I shall admit here, was a mistake'. The idea that thoughts, experiences, and acts are *had by*, or *performed by*, something is now agreed to be an extra idea, but we can imagine someone operating instead with the idea of thoughts, experiences, and acts merely *occurring in* a body (261). Parfit thinks that such a person would lack our concept of a person, but would be no worse off (221, 256, 262–63) and in a way better off (264). He would be like someone who lacked the concept of a river, but had the concept a continuous flowing of water in a certain pattern (228). Parfit distinguishes the ownership relations of *had by, done by,* from the *components* of a person (259), and he sees our existence as *consisting* in 'the existence of a body and the occurrence of various interrelated mental processes and events'. He thus sees himself as still maintaining some kind of 'reductionism', in that persons can be 'reduced' to these latter things as *components,* even though ownership, which is part of the concept of a person, is no longer included as something deducible. This seems to be a weaker form of reductionism, in that the account is an account not of a person, but only of a person's *components*. And it might be added that the components are themselves under-described, in that it is omitted that the mental processes and events are *owned*.

THE IMMATERIAL EGO ALLEGED TO BE
THE ALTERNATIVE TO THE STREAM

A refrain in Parfit's case is that if you think that personal identity must be a determinate relation (1999, p. 217), and often if you reject reductionism ((1984) 1987, p. 210), this will be because you believe in an immaterial subject of experiences such as Descartes' ego. I should say that my own view is different. I do believe, for reasons that will become clear when I talk about

3. Parfit, 'Experiences, subjects, and conceptual schemes', 218.

agency and ethics, that there needs to be an owner of experiences, and not just because we talk that way, but the only owner I know of is embodied, the embodied person, and therefore quite unlike Descartes' immaterial ego.

DOES THE REDUCTION ELIMINATE OWNERSHIP IN ALL BUT NAME?

The basic difficulty for Parfit's reductionism, I believe, is that it treats talk of experiences being *had* and actions being *done*, for short talk of an owner, as a *façon de parler* that adds no information, or at least (1999) no information of importance.[4] I shall argue that Parfit's reader gets the illusion that agency and ethics have been accommodated, only insofar as he or she does not hold in mind that, in retaining talk of ownership, Parfit has in his book robbed the idea of all content. He says:

> A Reductionist can admit that, in this sense, a person is *what has* experiences, or the *subject of experiences*. This is true because of the way in which we talk. ((1984) 1987, p. 223)
>
> We can refer to and describe different thoughts and the relations between them, without ascribing these thoughts to thinkers. Because we talk in this way, Descartes could truly claim, 'I think, therefore I am'. ((1984) 1987, p. 226)

In his 1999 paper, as I have said, Parfit goes further. He acknowledges that the idea of ownership is not after all included, not even as a way of talking, in his account of an embodied stream of consciousness. This seems to me to acknowledge that the idea of ownership has actually been *eliminated* from that account, rather than being reduced to something else. It is not the person, but only the components of the person, that are now treated as reducible. But already the earlier claim that talk of ownership could be dropped without loss looks to me like elimination of all but a name.

This seems to me to have serious consequences for the possibility of talking about agency and ethics. I shall shortly propose a test. Let us omit the talk of an owner, since it adds nothing, and see if we can say all we need to say without it. Before I come to agency and ethics, however, I want to raise some questions about the account of experiences and of the links be-

---

4. A fuller consideration and endorsement of this criticism is in Quassim Cassam, 'Kant and reductionism', *Review of Metaphysics* 43, 1989–90, 72–106.

tween them. I shall start with the links, which are intended to make the idea of ownership redundant.

LINKS IN PARFIT'S STREAM

What are the links that hold together the sequence or stream? Parfit mentions four *direct* psychological links, then contemplates strengthening them with a requirement that there be *enough* such links, then weakens them by requiring only that there be overlapping chains of the strengthened links, so that the linkage is *indirect* ((1984) 1987, pp. 205–7). These seemingly complicated maneuvers are designed to avoid various objections that I need not rehearse here. The direct links are described as providing direct connectedness, and this may be the most important linkage (206). The overlapping chains are described as giving psychological continuity, which may be equally important (301). What matters is that there should be one and/or the other (216–17). Only four illustrations are offered of direct connectedness (205–7), memory and intention, or (220, 260–61) quasi-memory and quasi-intention, and the persistence of beliefs and desires.

The reference to the quasi-intention and quasi-memory already acknowledges a difficulty. It is meant to substitute reference to a sequence of activities that, unlike memory and intention, includes no reference to the same owner of activities at different times. But I think that the same difficulty attends Parfit's other two links. What is it for a desire or belief to persist other than its having the same content and belonging to the same owner over a period of time? I believe Parfit should have spoken of quasi-persistence of desire and belief.

Parfit adds some physical as well as psychological requirements. The psychological states are causally dependent on one or (in certain science fiction cases) more bodies, and correspondingly the stream may be one of mental and physical events ((1984) 1987, pp. 216–17).

There is also a further psychological link. A single state of awareness can be an awareness of many different experiences and thereby bind these experiences together (250–51). This would become especially important, Parfit argues, if there were cases in which a single owner could not play the role of individuating the streams of experience because one owner had two different streams of experience, as might happen if the brain had been split into two. But I think that even in this case, the experiences surveyed would be seen as linked by belonging to one owner, while there might be no recognition of there being a rival owner.

It may be possible to build up the links still further by drawing on the ideas of Sydney Shoemaker, who does not agree with Parfit, but who has been concerned with links for the different purpose of analyzing psychological states in terms of the functional roles that link them to each other and to other states. Shoemaker has suggested to me in personal communication that there are at least three ways in which some beliefs are linked to others and in which belief and desire are linked to intention or action. First, beliefs and desires can *cause* later intentions and actions (or beliefs cause other beliefs). Second, they can *rationalize* them, in the sense of providing a reason to have them. Third, it may be *built in* to how my desires are realized that, other things being equal, in combination with other states, they are likely to generate further intentions or other states in me.

One more type of linkage is suggested by John Locke's treatment of personal identity. We saw in chapter five that in his *Essay Concerning Human Understanding,* he thinks of the self as both surveying several of its activities in one overview (2.27.9), in the way that Parfit thinks of one act of awareness surveying other acts, and also thinks that the self feels *concern* as regards the activities it surveys (2.27.17–18 and 26). Someone might, then, suggest that one act of awareness in the stream might unite various other events in the stream by being a feeling of *concern* about them.

REPLIES: HOW TO LINK A SINGLE STREAM WITHOUT APPEAL TO AN OWNER

There are two kinds of linkage problem: how to link together a stream and how to distinguish different streams. Parfit's quasi-memory and quasi-intention involve a causal link between present experience and past or future activities. The link of quasi-persistence of desires and beliefs is not discussed, but one (controversial) view would be that this persistence involves the persistence of some state in the brain. In fact, Parfit generalizes this last type of approach. What unifies a stream, on this view, is not its belonging to one owner, but its occurring in one body or brain. Here is how he puts the idea in 1999.

> (261) As these remarks suggest, though this impersonal scheme differs from ours, this difference is not metaphysically deep. And this difference is in part merely grammatical. In our scheme, all thoughts, experiences, and acts are claimed to be *had by* or *done by* either some persisting body or embodied brain, or some distinct entity that has this body and brain. In my imagined

scheme, these thoughts, experiences, and acts might instead be claimed to *oc-cur in* this persisting body or embodied brain. Is this an important difference? If we moved from *had by* to *occur in*, would we be moving to an incoherent or radically defective scheme?

(262) As before, I do not see the importance of this distinction. If my imagined beings thought of their experiences as either directly dependent on or as occurring in their brains, but they did not ascribe these experiences to their brains, or to any other entities, how much would they be missing? They would, I agree, be missing certain truths, since it is true that all thoughts have thinkers, and that all experiences have subjects. But this is like the truth that, for every continuous flowing of water in a certain pattern, there is a river which does the flowing. And that truth does not have to be recognized in any adequate understanding of such flowings of water. The same may apply to the truth that, for every stream of thoughts and experiences, there is an entity that thinks these thoughts and has these experiences. This impersonal scheme, I have claimed, is metaphysically no worse than ours.

There is, however, a difficulty for Parfit's substitution of occurrence in a single brain or body in place of belonging to a single owner. We have already seen that in teletransportation he allows the possibility of one stream inhabiting a succession of bodies and brains. Which bodies or brains are relevant? Presumably those that house a single stream identified as single independently of the bodies and brains. Even more radically, we shall find in chapter sixteen that the Buddhists deconstructed not only the self but also the body into a stream, and that one of their Nyaya opponents insisted that one deconstruction implied the other. Parfit has turned the self into a stream, but not the body. If the Nyaya argument is right, this will not be legitimate.

There is yet another difficulty: a person's activities are linked together in a far greater variety of contexts than the few that Parfit considers, and normally the linkage involves the idea of same owner, so that, if we drop that idea, all these cases would need to be re-described. Parfit himself, we shall see below, discusses a person's deserts, commitments, compensation, and relief. Marya Schechtman stresses the persistence and the interconnection of a person's activities very well in her book, *The Constitution of Selves*. She points out first[5] that duration is required for talking, listening, walking, acting, having beliefs, desires, goals, intentions, thinking, being inconsistent, and vacillating. Second,[6] she gives examples of how one experience is

---

5. Marya Schechtman, *The Constitution of Selves*, Ithaca N.Y. 1996, 9; cf. p 137.
6. Ibid., 100–114, 137, 143–56.

pregnant with others. The individual words of a spoken sentence are understood as a combined whole. The adult is more consoled than the child through foreseeing that the setback is temporary. The case in which experiences are taken in isolation is that of the victim of Alzheimer's disease, not that of the normal person.[7]

What I am adding is that pregnant interconnection often involves the idea of the same owner. The range of contexts in which we think of persistence in terms of same owner is greater still.

Parfit's examples of direct psychological connections allow for memories of, and intentions, desires, and beliefs about quite trivial matters. I am struck that the Indian philosophical literature about streams of consciousness is interested in aspirations, talents, habits, and virtues, in other words psychological characteristics that might be thought to be more fundamental to a sense of individuality. And persistence in these cases too tends to involve the idea of same owner.

REPLIES: HOW TO DISTINGUISH DIFFERENT STREAMS WITHOUT APPEAL TO DIFFERENT OWNERS

A further problem is how to distinguish different streams without appeal to different owners. The trouble with the links canvassed on behalf of Parfit's theory is that they can cut across different streams. There is, for example, a difficulty about the idea that a single act of awareness might be an awareness of many experiences in one stream, because it might also include awareness of experiences in another stream too, and in the case of a sufficiently sympathetic person, the experiences of the other person might be viewed as if from the inside.

The same problem would apply to the idea that a stream might be held together by a single feeling of concern for many of the acts and experiences in the stream. For that runs into the parallel difficulty that one can feel equal concern for events in the life of others, of one's children for example.

The same problem of streams interacting affects the claim that desires and beliefs cause and rationalize intentions and acts in the same stream.

7. This is not the only example in which a philosophical theory describes as normal what is actually found only in sickness. Remembering through reading information off mental images, or through random association of ideas, was a feature of the sick patients of A. R. Luria. Luria, *The Mind of a Mnemonist*, London and New York 1969; id., *Man with a Shattered World*, London 1972.

Might not the master's desire for a cup of tea indirectly help to cause the devoted servant to make the tea, and in the ordinary sense of the words give him a reason to do so? Can this case be distinguished without appeal to difference and sameness of persons, when the project was to appeal only to difference and sameness of streams?

It might be replied that the causing and rationalizing would be indirect because via the servant's recognition of, and belief in, the master's desire. But then is not indirectness found in the case of a single person's desires and intentions? To take an example from Aristotle's *Nicomachean Ethics*, my desire for health is too remote to cause my actions directly. I have to make inquiries involving other people, and deliberate what are good means and the best means for me: Diet or exercise? Perhaps light or dry food is good for health, but which food is light or dry? Should I turn to a diet of fish? As I come to believe of each means in the chain that it is a good one for me, I come to desire it, and this process of deliberation goes on until I reach something in my power. A diet of fish may be in my power, and in that case it becomes a policy decision, or *proairesis*. There will still be some more reasoning to do in order to fulfill the policy before I actually act. The point is that desire for health is not a *direct* cause of my action, if indeed I ever get around to acting at all, which notoriously people fail to do in matters of health. It also does not *directly* give me a reason to eat fish. Nor can it be said, I think, of such a remote desire that it is built into how the desire is realized that, other things being equal, in combination with such and such other states, it is likely to have such and such a consequence.

This is where appeal might be made to Parfit's suggestion that the master's desire for tea can easily be distinguished from my own desire for health, without appeal to differences between persons, through appeal to the difference between human bodies or brains on which the desires depend. But, as I have said, this route is not open to Parfit, because he believes that the same stream may be surgically transplanted into new human bodies or be teletransported many times into new brains.

A final question is why it even appears that there is a single someone who does things and experiences things. Since this appearance of a single owner is an illusion if there is only an embodied stream of linked events, why should such an illusion arise? [8] In sum, I doubt if links within streams can be used to replace the idea of an owner.

8. An admirably circumspect attempt to answer this question, on the basis that the sense of a unitary owner may or may not be illusory, is offered by David Rosenthal, 'Unity of consciousness and the self', *Proceedings of the Aristotelian Society* 103, 2002–3, 325–52. But my own reaction is to think the attempt shows how unanswerable the question is.

REPLIES: AGENCY AND MOTIVATION
REQUIRE CONTINUING OWNERS

Let us return to the test of omitting the idea of the *same owner* of different acts and experiences, since reductionism takes it to add nothing except a way of talking, or nothing important. Could we then still say what we need to say about agency and ethics? I shall, as in chapters one and two, focus particularly on the omission of the first-person idea of *me* and *me again*, because this is the omission that touches us most personally. But for agency and ethics, I believe, we also need to be able to talk from a third-person perspective about *him* or *her* as the same owner of acts and experiences.

Taking the omission of 'I'-thoughts, then, only as a special case of the omission of thoughts about ownership, let us recall from chapter one that intention involves 'I'-thoughts in the form of beliefs and desires that *I* shall do something. Intention is very central to agency, and agency very central to our idea of self. Without owners, there might still be illusory 'I'-thoughts, and hence illusory intentions, just as there might be illusory ethical judgments, but not genuine ones.

Intending is relevant also to meaning, if meaning is a kind of intending, as argued by Paul Grice,[9] and meaning, both pre-linguistic and linguistic, is central to human life. Linguistic meaning for Grice involves not only the intentions of individual speakers, but whole communities of speakers with repertoires of agreed practices for carrying out their intentions.

So much for intending, but second, in chapter one I spoke of some of the social games played by infants: shared attention, social referencing, and 'look at me'. The first two are considered by some psychologists as essential prerequisites for the subsequent acquisition of language. All involve me as an infant seeing the world as related to me, even if neither concept nor word for me is yet available. I also pointed out that many emotions, even though not all, involve thoughts about good or harm for me and mine.

But third, if 'I'-thoughts are unavailable, except as an illusion, might there be analogical substitutes? Might there, for example, instead of an intention, be a desire contained in a stream that some horrible accident should be averted by an action performed later in the same stream? But now the question arises of what would be the point of such a desire? If there are no sufferers and no beneficiaries, because there are no owners, the importance

---

9. Paul Grice, 'Meaning', *Philosophical Review* 66, 1957, 377–88; id., 'Utterer's meaning and intentions', *Philosophical Review* 78, 1969, 147–77; id., 'Utterer's meaning, sentence meaning, and word meaning', *Foundations of Language* 4, 1968, 1–18.

of averting a horrible accident will be reduced, which is not to say that it will be non-existent. It is still better that the world should contain less suffering. But another question about the point of the suggested desire is why it should matter at all which stream contains the averting action. There will be no benefactors, any more than there will be beneficiaries, but only at best averting actions. The questions about the point of things begin to show why ownership is important and not just a dispensable way of talking.

It might be replied, fourth, that it could matter which stream contained the averting action if there was a belief linked in the same stream to the desire, the belief being to the effect that no other stream would be able to contain an averting action. But this brings us back to some of the earlier problems about linkage, even though we are now talking about linking simultaneous, rather than successive, states, a belief and a desire. What links between beliefs and desires can be specified within a stream that do not also cut across streams? Further, if there are not persisting owners, what is meant by the *same* belief or desire continuing over a long period?

Parfit himself recognizes the complaint about pointlessness (*Reasons and Persons*, 307–12). But he still puts it in terms of whether 'we' would have reason to be concerned about 'our' futures, rather than whether there would be any reason for the *stream* to contain desires about *its* future contents. The complaint is an old one, as he notes, having been directed against Locke by Butler and Reid, against Hume by Sidgwick, and having been much used by modern opponents of reductionism whom he lists, and to whom I would now add Marya Schechtman.[10] But Parfit focuses on those who make the complaint out of a belief in human soul as the basis of 'me'-talk, whereas the complaint requires no such grounding. In any case, Parfit's view is that the objection can neither be refuted nor proved, even when it is accompanied by the postulate of a soul. So a fortiori he would have to leave the pointlessness objection unrefuted when not so accompanied.

I have conceded that in the absence of owners there might still be illusory desires involving the *mistaken* belief in an owner. Might not such an illusory desire motivate subsequent action? But now it needs to be asked what likelihood there would be that such illusory desires would arise.

It might be proposed that some desires could have a selective advantage in the unintentional workings of natural selection. Natural selection might

10. Marya Schechtman, *The Constitution of Selves*, Ithaca N.Y. ch. 3, discusses together a whole set of complaints that Parfit labels 'extreme' (307–11, 323–29, 336–45), to the effect that reductionism does not explain the importance we attach to identity in self-concern, compensation, and responsibility as well as survival.

favor desires for aligning gazes between bodies, or vocal sounds between bodies, because of their selective utility. More fully, if there are bodies that reproduce, natural selection might favor those bodies that housed streams containing desires about the later state of the same body (or, if it can be defined, of the same stream). This would depend on bodies not themselves being mere streams, as the Buddhists suppose. Certainly, some illusory desires might be favored by natural selection and so provide motivation, but this will account for only that small proportion of desires that have selective value.

REPLIES: ETHICS REQUIRES OWNERS

The biggest value expected from Parfit's view comes in the field of ethics. The more we take in that there are streams of consciousness, but no owners or selves, the less selfish we should surely become, and the less afraid of the supposed loss of self at death. Parfit claims to be allied in this with ancient Buddhism (*Reasons and Persons*, p. 273 and appendix J), and we shall see in chapter sixteen that there is one such tradition among others in Buddhism.

Parfit, recognizing that he has treated personal identity as unimportant, expects that his ethics will have to be modified in a utilitarian direction, so as to take account of the total quantity of good or harm produced, rather than the distribution of good or harm to this individual or that. As agreed by some Buddhists, reducing the present quantity of suffering may matter more than relieving the individuals who have suffered longest. But Parfit has treated as unimportant not only the idea of personal identity but even the idea of an owner, and that leaves me wondering which ethical concepts remain applicable at all.

First, what about deserving credit or blame? We are not now being allowed, except as a way of talking, to think of a *person* as deserving credit or blame. Rather it would be the *act* that deserved credit or blame, and the resulting stream. But this would have to be in the different sense that it would be more admirable, or less so, just a sunset may be admirable, without anybody *deserving* credit or blame.

Second, Parfit assumes, in chapter 15 of his book, the applicability of moral talk about deserving punishment, commitment, compensation, and relief. But I doubt that these moral concepts will have any application, once it is recognized, as it is in Parfit's later paper, that talk of 'this sequence of psycho-physical events' does *not* include the concept of 'I'. Correspondingly, in the later paper (1999, pp. 266–67), Parfit recognizes that there is a question of whether sense can be made of rights, duties, moral responsibility, feeling sorry for someone, and normative reason. But in chapter 15 of the book, Parfit still takes it that talk of 'this sequence' *does* include the concept of 'I', albeit a modified concept, and he allows himself to talk of later and future *selves* (*Reasons and Persons*, 305, 327). That is why he assumes, wrongly I believe, that the moral concepts he mentions are applicable.

Could we, third, substitute for the idea of deserving punishment the idea of using punishment to deter? Deterrence would be difficult to effect if, in the absence of owners, there is no one who would suffer from deterrent measures, and no one who would benefit from their being applied.

Returning, fourth, to commitment, compensation, and relief, the last two need sufferers, and the first needs a promisee. Parfit again brings these in with reference to later selves. But in the absence of owners, except as a way of talking, there will be no selves.

Fifth, we shall encounter in chapter sixteen the attempts of the ancient Buddhists to give some account of karma and the idea of reward and punishment for deeds in a past life, without relying on the idea of a continuing self. We shall see that the Nyaya school of the Hindus thought this impossible.

Sixth, in his later paper of 1999, Parfit recognizes that it is a question whether we can 'feel sorry for a series of experiences'. Compassion for suffering is indeed very central to Buddhism. We shall see below how one Buddhist, Śāntideva, dealt with them. What sort of compassion and suffering will be available in the absence of enduring owners? Many forms of suffering, such as disappointment, bereavement, and remorse, seem to presuppose one and the same subject having different experiences over time. If pangs as of disappointment or remorse could occur in the absence of enduring subjects, they would presumably be real pangs, but based on an illusion of enduring sufferers. Admittedly, momentary pangs of *physical* pain, if they can be divorced from pangs of psychological distress and worry, would not presuppose more than a momentary owner, or perhaps any owner at all, if we agree with Lichtenberg, whom I shall discuss in chapter seventeen. Such pangs would not in the same way depend on illusion, and they might last as long as the phenomenological experience lasted without interruption. But would not the very brevity and even more the lack of an enduring owner make the suffering, and any consequent help, less important? For not only is suffering ephemeral, but there is no enduring being that suffers. Moreover, there would only be pangs of compassion rather than any enduring sympathizer, so that compassion too would seem to lose its significance. And there would be no possibility of a sympathizer forming an intention to help.

If I am right that the replacement of continuing owners with embodied streams of consciousness rules out so much of agency, motivation, and ethics, except insofar as a few types of illusory thought might occur and provide illusory surrogates, then I believe there is an onus on the proponent of streams to explain why we should pay such a heavy price. What was the incentive in the first place for agreeing to the idea that there are only embodied streams of consciousness, with owners either as a mere *façon de parler* or as an additional idea of no value? The supposed benefit was to get rid of the idea of a disembodied owner such as Descartes' ego. This was what John Locke sought to do when he said, quite correctly, that the soul would not help us to determine questions of personal identity. But he did not himself throw out the idea of an owner. To throw out, except as a *façon de parler*, the idea of an *embodied* owner, as well as the idea of a disembodied owner, seems to me to be throwing out the baby with the bath water. I think that the proposal seemed reasonable only because of the historical background to it: the reasonableness of Locke's refusal to appeal to a disembodied owner, and the thinness of what was left, if the idea of an embodied owner was not then emphasized. Locke himself emphasized certain psychological relations between events, including memory, concern, and appropriation. This was followed by Hume's founding a tradition that questioned the existence or value of a self or owner over and above the events and their relations. I think it may be necessary to take account of the historical background, if we are to see how the jettisoning of ownership came to seem reasonable and thus to recover a sense of how devastating it would in fact be.

CHAPTER 16

The debate between ancient Buddhism and the Nyaya school

I think there is great value in looking at another culture to which the question of a continuous self has been much more central, the culture of India. Among various Buddhists and Hindus we will find the idea that reductionism can be applied to bodies as well as minds. We will find the question of whether there are any basic entities at all to which a reduction can be made. We will find the idea that, although all suffering matters, compassion may require one to think of an *individual's* suffering. We will encounter the argument that even understanding one single sentence, or having the very idea of a body, may require having the idea of a self. I think the controversy on this subject between Buddhists and Hindus is much more sophisticated than what is found in the ancient Greeks, as well as extending beyond the point which discussion has so far reached in current anglophone philosophy.

Parfit, as I have said, claims that his reductionist view is like that of Buddhism (*Reasons and Persons*, 1987, p. 273 and appendix J), and there is one strand that seems similar. But even this strand includes some views very unlike Parfit's. Furthermore, there are different schools in Buddhism and I shall distinguish three. First, there were the Personalists, who retained the idea of person, but not by way of Parfit's reduction of a person to a stream of psycho-physical events. Then there were two further groups, one being the followers of Nâgârjuna, who seem to have been more extreme than Parfit, as he recognizes.[1] They seem to eliminate the self, and, although I have complained that this may be the *effect* of Parfit's position, his *intention* was rather to retain the self, but to say it consisted of nothing but events in a

---

1. Derek Parfit, 'The unimportance of identity', in Henry Harris, ed., *Identity*, Oxford 1995, 13–45, at 17.

stream. Since the school of Nâgârjuna seems to eliminate even the events in the stream, it does not wish, like Parfit, to reduce the person to them, but to render the self 'empty'. But a final twist, the claim of the emptiness of emptiness, we shall see, makes the 'eliminativist' description not entirely straight-forward.

Included in the remaining group there are two further Buddhist think-ers, of whom the first, Nâgasena, speaks as if he was, like Parfit, seeking to *reduce* the self to a psycho-physical stream. This is how Mark Siderits understands him.[2] The second, Vasubandhu, though he is commenting on Nâgasena, seems to waver somewhat between reducing and eliminating the self.

The Buddha of our era, who is considered the most recent Buddha of a series, is dated to c. 563 – 483 BC. The Buddhist doctrine that there is no con-tinuing self of the kind we tend to believe in is expected, as with Parfit, both to reduce fear of the loss of self at death, and to make us less selfish in ethi-cal attitudes and conduct.

The Personalist movement in Buddhism started very early, perhaps in the 3rd century BC.[3] But because the reports by Vasubandhu and others are nearly all hostile and may be foisting their own concepts on the Personalists, it is hard to make out what they said. According to Vasubandhu, they refer to fleeting mental and physical bundles on which they say the self depends. But they use a 'neither-nor' formula, which we shall find in others too. The self is neither discrete nor not-discrete from the bundles. One must not say that it is, nor that it is not, visible form. In fact it is ineffable.

NÂGASENA: REDUCTION OF SELF?

An early Buddhist work of a non-Personalist kind, written in Pali and closer in spirit to Parfit's reductionism, was *The Questions of Milinda*. Milinda is Menander, who was the Greek king of Bactria, in what is now Afghanistan, in the 2nd century BC. He is represented as learning about Buddhism by questioning the Buddhist monk, Nâgasena, who explains to him the doc-

2. This view is argued by Mark Siderits, 'Buddhist Reductionism', *Philosophy East and West* 47, 1997, 455–79, on the basis of a particular account of what reductionism is.

3. Matthew Kapstein, *Reasons, Traces, and Identity in Indian and Buddhist Thought*, Il-ford 2001, 81–88, with translation of Vasubandhu's report at 350–75 (see esp. 351–55); James Duerlinger, 'Vasubandhu's philosophical critique of the Vastiputriya's theory of persons', *Journal of Indian Philosophy* (3 parts), 1997–2000: 25, 307–35; 26, 573–605; 28, 125–70.

trine of no-self and its implications for shedding selfishness and fear of death.[4] The text may have been put together three centuries after Menander with a mixture of new material and old. It cannot be certain that such a conversation really took place, since the arguments are stock ones, but it is possible. The self is compared with a chariot. Each is said to be a 'conceptual construct', a designation, appellation, convention, and mere name. This is reminiscent of Parfit's 'way of talking'. As the chariot is a construct that depends on its most basic constituents, namely, axle, wheels, chassis, pole, so the self is a construct that depends on its most basic constituents. These are said to be five bundles, namely physical form, along with sensation, conceptualization, motivation (*saṃskâra*), and consciousness. These seem to be elementary and fleeting constituents, which succeed each other to form streams. It is said that no person is apprehended, as opposed to being constructed. Milinda is represented as objecting that without enduring persons, Nâgasena must lack parents, teacher, or superiors to ordain him, and that there cannot be agency, or punishment for his murder. Nâgasena replies that over time, there is neither the same self nor another self. Or rather I am the same person as I was because of the body, but the body is itself to be compared with the flame of a lamp.[5] On that analogy, a person is neither the same nor another at different times.

It looks as if Nâgasena is not merely denying a particular conception of self, such as the *atman* of his Hindu opponents, but is denying self as more ordinarily conceived and as the Greek Menander might conceive it.

VASUBANDHU: REDUCTION OF SELF
VEERING TOWARDS ELIMINATION?

The other Buddhist philosopher I mentioned as having much in common with Nâgasena is Vasubandhu in the 4th century AD, in his *Treatise on the Negation of the Person*, which is part of a longer work. James Duerlinger sees him too as reducing the self to bundles of fleeting events,[6] and Vasubandhu

---

4. Translated by I. B. Horner, *Sacred Books of the Buddhists*, vols. 22–23, London 1964; and by T. W. Rhys Davids, Oxford 1890. Extracts also translated in Christmas Humphreys, *Buddhism*, Harmondsworth 1951; short extracts translated in Kapstein, *Reasons, Traces, and Identity*, 88–90, 116–17.

5. *Questions of Milinda*, all included in the short extracts in Kapstein.

6. Vasubandhu, *Treatise on the Negation of the Person*, translated by Kapstein, *Reasons, Traces, and Identity*, 350–75; and by James Duerlinger, *Indian Buddhist Theories of Persons*, London 2003, 71–111. Duerlinger sees him as a reductionist, 'Reductionist and nonreduc-

does say that 'self' and 'person' refer to the bundle continuum alone,[7] that the person is like a heap or stream,[8] and that the Buddha's use of 'I' for his previous incarnation, Sunetra, denotes being a continuum like a fire,[9] all of which sounds like a reduction of the person to bundles. Vasubandhu, like Nâgasena, and again in the same spirit as Parfit, holds that the self is a conceptual construction, construct, convention, or name, and the same is true of pots and water.

He seems to go a little further in the direction of eliminating the self, if he is rightly translated at one point as saying, 'There is no self',[10] and, as we shall see, saying 'there is noone called Caitra', and denying the need for a doer when there is doing. But in this I think he is simply being consistent, if I was right in chapter fifteen that to say something is only a name and adds no information, so that it could be omitted without loss, is in effect to eliminate it.

Elsewhere in the longer work, *Abhidharmakośabhâṣyam*, Vasubandhu explains more about the basic elements to which selves, pots, and water are reduced. Things exist only relatively if their existence depends on their not being broken up physically, like a pot, or by mental analysis into color, smell, etc., like water. By contrast, physical matter exists absolutely, because it survives being broken up physically into atoms and having smell etc. mentally separated off from it. Sensations also exist absolutely. We have seen sensation and physical form listed in the *Questions of Milinda* as two of the basic five bundles, which were treated as fleeting events, and it may indeed be easier to think of physical form as a fleeting event than physical matter.

The talk of existence being relative, *saṃvṛti*, or in the Pali of *Questions of Milinda*, *sammuti*, is often translated in terms of its being conventional. But when it comes to selves, it is easier in English to understand the idea of self being relative than of its being conventional, given that conventions hold between persons and hence, in my sense at least, between selves.

Not only does physical matter exist absolutely, but it is also said to be absolutely true. Things are absolutely true only in the manner in which they

---

tionist theories of persons in Indian Buddhist philosophy', *Journal of Indian Philosophy* 21, 1993, 79–101.

7. As translated by Kapstein, *Reasons, Traces, and Identity*, 350, 357.

8. As translated ibid., 360.

9. As translated ibid., 366.

10. Ibid., 350. James Duerlinger, however, sees him as a reductionist, 'Reductionist and nonreductionist theories of persons in Indian Buddhist philosophy', *Journal of Indian Philosophy* 21, 1993, 79–101.

are perceived with the benefit of transworldly knowledge.[11] Vasubandhu seems to think here that what is merely relatively true, e.g., 'There is a jug, there is water', is true. But if the relative truth that there is a self is true, I am not sure how this squares with the claim already noticed from elsewhere in the work that there is no self or with the absolute truth, if it is one, that there is no self.

Vasubandhu explains in his *Treatise on the Negation of the Person* why we say that somebody remembers, cognizes, goes, or does something. Remembering consists of one event causing and resembling a later one. It is not that a person, call him Caitra, remembers. Rather, there is a continuum that we call 'Caitra' and that, in Vasubandhu's view, causes an act of remembering. There is no such thing as *owning* an act of remembering over and above causing it, and the *continuum* is the cause. There is no one called Caitra.[12] Similarly, if it is said that Devadatta cognizes or goes, the going is like a case of a moving flame coming to be elsewhere.[13] In general, when there is doing, do not look for a doer. Doing might consist merely in recollection, interest, consideration, willful effort, vital energy, action.[14]

Karma, and reward or punishment for past deeds in a later life, after the original deeds are exhausted, depends on the stream that is viewed as a seed that will eventually bear fruit.[15] But, as is revealed for example by a later Buddhist, Kamalaśīla, in the 8th century AD, the Buddhists' Hindu opponents in the Nyaya school continued to object that such karma would depend on there being a continuing self.[16] We shall encounter in chapter seventeen another application of the idea of *saṃskāras*, or enduring traces in the stream, by which the effects of karma were meant to persist in the stream. But without a self of some sort, by which I do not mean an incorporeal *atman*, I find it hard to see how the consequences of activities in a stream would count as reward or punishment.

11. *Abhidharmakośabhāṣyam* VI. 4, auto-commentary on his *Treasury of the Abhidharma*, translated into French from a Chinese version by Louis de la Vallée Poussin, and from French into English by Leo M. Pruden. Conventional truth is also distinguished by an author, Abhayâkaragupta, of about 1100 AD, whose treatise survives only in a Tibetan version, translated into English by Matthew Kapstein, in *Reasons, Traces, and Identity*, 396 ff. For conventional truth in the rival school of Nâgârjuna, see below.

12. Kapstein, *Reasons, Traces, and Identity*, 367–68.

13. Ibid., 368–69.

14. Ibid., 373.

15. Ibid., 374–75.

16. Kamalaśīla, *Tattvasamgrahapanjika*, a commentary on his teacher's *Compendium of the Quiddities*, a relevant passage translated by Kapstein, *Reasons, Traces, and Identity*, 39–40.

Vasubandhu *Treatise on Negation of the Person,* translated Kapstein:

(p. 350) For [our opponents] have not determined that the conceptual construction 'self' refers to the bundle-continuum alone.

(p. 357) In a sûtra, moreover, the Transcendent Lord has determined that 'the denomination "person" [applies] to the bundles alone'.

(p. 366, of the Fortunate Lord's saying) 'I indeed was he' denotes being one continuum. E.g., 'that very fire, burning, has approached'.

(p. 367) If, then, there is no self whatsoever, then how is it that among instantaneous mental events there occurs memory or recognition of objects experienced long before?

Owing to a distinctive mental event, following from an act of concept formation directed upon the object of memory.

What sort of distinctive event is it from which memory immediately follows?

From one endowed with an act of concept formation, etc., which has a resemblance to and connection with the enjoyment of that [object], and whose force is not destroyed by peculiarities of the support [i.e., the body], grief, distraction, etc. For even though it may resemble that [object], a distinctive mental event not caused by it has not the capacity to produce memory, and even if it follows from it, that [mental event] which resembles another [object] has not the capacity to produce memory.

(pp. 367–68) What, then, does the remembering?

It has been stated what does it, namely, the specific mental event that is the cause of the memory. What, then, is spoken of as 'Caitra remembers' is spoken of owing to a perceived state of being caused by that continuum called' Caitra', namely, that 'Caitra remembers'.

(p. 368) There being no self, whose is the memory?

What's the meaning of the genitive case of the pronoun 'whose'?

Possessive. E.g., who is the possessor of what? E.g., Caitra of a cow. . . .

But then the cause must be the possessor, and it [memory] the result. Wherefore the cause has the power [to determine] the effect; and through the effect what has it is the cause. Thus what is the cause of the memory is its [possessor]. Thus having taken as one the continuum of the assemblage of conditions called 'Caitra', it is spoken of as the possessor of the so-called 'cow'. Thinking of him as being thus a cause of the production of its movement and change, there is nonetheless no one called 'Caitra', nor is there a cow. Hence, even in that case, there is no being-a-possessor above and beyond being-a-cause.

(pp. 368–69) And how does Devadatta go? The instantaneous conditions in an unbroken continuum—which is regarded by childish persons who grasp it as a unified lump of existence, as the so-called 'Devadatta'—are the cause of its own coming-into-being elsewhere. E.g., 'going' designates the passage of the continua of flames and words. Similarly, too, there being causes of consciousness, they are spoken of as 'Devadatta cognises'. The Sublime also speak using such denominations for the sake of convention.

(p. 373) Therefore, no doer characterised in that manner is apprehended. That which is the dominant cause of something is called its doer. But the self is not found to be a cause with respect to anything. Therefore, there cannot thus be a self. For from recollection there is interest; from interest consideration; from consideration willful effort; from willful effort vital energy; and from that, action. So what does the self do here?

Vasubandhu *Abhidharmakośabhâsyam* VI. 4, auto-commentary on his *Treasury of the Abhidharma,* translated into French from a Chinese version by Louis de la Vallée Poussin, and from French into English by Leo M. Pruden:

The blessed one proclaimed the Four Noble Truths, but he also declared Two Truths, relative truth and absolute truth. What are these two truths?

4. 'The idea of a jug ends when the jug is broken; the idea of water ends when, in the mind, one analyses the water. The jug and the water, and all that resembles them exist relatively. The rest exist absolutely.'

If the idea of a thing disappears when this thing is broken into pieces, then this thing has relative existence; for example, a jug: the idea of a jug disappears when it is reduced to pieces. If the idea of a thing disappears when this thing is dissipated, or broken to pieces, by the mind, then this thing should be regarded as having relative existence; for example, water. If we grasp and remember the *dharmas,* such as colour, etc., in the water, then the idea of water will disappear.

These things,—jug, clothes, etc., water, fire, etc.,—are given their different names from the relative point of view or conforming to conventional usage. Thus if one says, from the relative point of view, 'There is a jug, there is water', one is speaking truly and one is not speaking falsely. Consequently this is relatively true.

That which differs is absolute truth. If, when a thing is broken to pieces or dissipated by the mind, the idea of this thing continues, then this thing has absolute existence; for example, physical matter: one can reduce physical matter into atoms, one can remember smell and other *dharmas* in the mind, but the idea of the unique nature of physical matter persists. The same holds for sensations, etc. And as this absolutely exists, it is absolutely true.

The ancient masters say: Things are absolutely true in the manner in which they are perceived, either by transworldly knowledge or by the worldly knowledge acquired after transworldly knowledge. They are relatively true in the manner in which they are perceived by any other defiled or non-defiled worldly knowledge.

QUERIES ON THE BUDDHIST REDUCTIONISM

I have already expressed some uncertainties about the reductionist views in Buddhism, making confessions of uncertainty, not objections, since I depend on the translations and interpretations of others. One uncertainty was about how the conventionally true can be true, and I was worried because the elimination of self, towards which Vasubandhu sometimes seems to veer, was something I found difficult to square even with ideas that Vasubandhu seeks to retain, like reward and punishment.

I am also unclear why a whole should be thought, if that is the intention at least of Nâgasena, to be *nothing but* its parts. Certainly, it cannot be said that the chariot is nothing but its parts. A rival viewpoint was Aristotle's, that the whole chariot and its form is something over and above its parts and the matter. Either may be needed to explain the other; either may outlast the other. The structure and function of the chariot is something extremely important, which does not belong to the parts. Otherwise we should all be Shakespeares, since we can, like Shakespeare, produce the letters of the alphabet. But the arrangement makes all the difference. Admittedly, in the *Questions of Milinda* the suggestion is canvassed that the person might be the parts *combined* with physical form and other bundles.[17]

There is the further question how physical form, sensation, conceptualization, motivation, and consciousness *give rise to* particular thoughts and desires.

17. *The Questions of Milinda*, trans. Rhys Davids, 42–43, as pointed out to me by Alex Catlin, but that is not the view finally endorsed.

NÂGÂRJUNA REJECTS REDUCTION:
THE SELF IS EMPTY

These queries are all avoided by a more extreme Buddhist school which denies that reduction of the self is possible. So far I would welcome the disavowal of reduction, but there is a cost. Reduction is avoided at the cost of making no attempt to retain persons. Nâgârjuna, the source of the Madhyamika school, therefore goes well beyond Vasubandhu and Parfit. He dates from around 150 AD and his follower and commentator Candrakîrti from around 600 AD. In some ways they offer the same denials as the other Buddhists. The self and a carriage exist not under meditational analysis, but only in the context of everyday experience.[18] Although the Buddha spoke of I and mine when teaching, he had no philosophical thesis of a real, substantial self.[19] In fact, I and mine are 'empty'.[20] The self is merely a name, and it would be wrong to reify.[21] Like Vasubandhu, Candrakîrti speaks in some contexts of merely conventional truth.[22] The self is not, is not there, and there is no self.[23]

Like Vasubandhu,[24] Candrakîrti says that the self is not identical with the fleeting psycho-physical bundles, but is not other than them either,[25] although he allows dependence on them. For good measure, the two next most tempting relations are explicitly ruled out: ownership and location. The self neither *owns* nor *contains* the psycho-physical bundles. It is like a carriage, which is also not related to carriage parts by any of these relations.

But in his next point Candrakîrti goes further than Vasubandhu. Not only does he refuse to relate the self in the expected way to the fleeting bundles, but he disallows any ultimate parts to which the self could be re-

18. Candrakîrti *Introduction to the Middle Way* (*Madhyamakâratâva*) VI 167.

19. Ibid., VI 44.

20. Ibid., VI 165.

21. *Commentary on Nâgârjuna* XIV 344–45.

22. Nâgârjuna *Vigrahavyâvartanî*, ed. and translated in E. H. Johnstone and Arnold Kunst, *The Dialectical Method of Nagarjuna*, Delhi 1978, verse 28; Candrakîrti *Introduction to the Middle Way* (*Madhyamakâratâva*), VI 80, translated from the Tibetan version by C. W. Huntington and Geshé Namgyal Wangchen, in Huntington, *The Emptiness of Emptiness*, Honolulu 1989, and in Padmaka Translation Group, Shambala 2002.

23. *Commentary on the Catusataka of Âryadeva* (200AD), 10.3.

24. As translated by Kapstein, *Reasons, Traces, and Identity*, 352.

25. Candrakîrti *Introduction to the Middle Way* (*Madhyamakâratâva*) VI 150–51, discussed in Kapstein, *Reasons, Traces, and Identity*, 101–2.

duced. He affirms that the carriage has no parts and that meditational analysis burns up not only the carriage, but also its supposed parts.[26] The burning implies that there are no irreducible parts to reduce anything to.

There are no irreducible parts, because Candrakîrti introduces a requirement that goes beyond Vasubandhu's demand that a thing should be able to survive division and mental subtraction of its qualities.[27] For Candrakîrti, a thing needs to be free from causal dependence on anything else, in order to have its own nature, and this causal independence will make it eternal. But nothing in the ordinary world meets this stringent requirement, and that is why irreducible parts are denied. This is already a huge divergence from Vasubandhu, and I am not sure what justifies so stringent a requirement. But after illustrating the view as so far described with quotations, I shall go on to show that it diverges far more radically still from Vasubandhu's.

Candrakîrti *Introduction to the Middle Way* (*Madhyamakâratâva*) VI 150–51:[28]

> Consequently, the basis of clinging to an 'I' is not an entity. It is not different from the psycho-physical aggregates, it is not the essence of the aggregates, it is not the receptacle of the aggregates and it does not possess them. [The self which is the basis of clinging to an 'I'] is established in dependence on the aggregates.
>
> [The self is in this respect similar to a carriage]. One does not consider a carriage to be different from its own parts, nor to be identical, nor to be in possession of them, nor is it 'in' the parts, nor are they 'in' it, nor is it the mere composite [of its parts]; nor is it the shape of those parts.

Candrakîrti *Introduction to the Middle Way* (*Madhyamakâratâva*) VI 161:

> When the carriage does not exist, then the 'possessor of the parts' does not exist, and neither do the parts. Just as, for example, when a carriage has burned, its parts no longer exist, so when the fire of discrimination burns the possessor of parts, the parts themselves [are incinerated].

26. Candrakîrti *Introduction to the Middle Way* (*Madhyamakâratâva*) VI 161.

27. I am very grateful to Probal Kumar Sen for drawing my attention to the different criteria of the two thinkers.

28. All translations of Candrakîrti *Introduction to the Middle Way*, are from C. W. Huntington and Geshé Namgyal Wangchen in Huntington, *The Emptiness of Emptiness*.

NÂGÂRJUNA'S SCHOOL:
EMPTINESS OF EMPTINESS

So far, I have applauded Nâgârjuna for disavowing reduction, but regretted his abandonment of persons. But next we find that his philosophy takes yet another twist. For the remark that all things, including the self, are empty is declared itself to be empty. (The translation below puts the point in terms of being void and devoid). Nonetheless, the remark may perform a function, for emptiness and lack of intrinsic nature do not stop a pot or a statement from performing a function, whether the function be carrying water or establishing the lack of intrinsic nature.[29] We may compare how even an artificial model of a woman could create an effect, namely desire in a male based on an illusion, and an artificial model of a man might be used to dispel the illusion created by the artificial model of a woman.[30] The function of Nâgârjuna's remark is not to offer a proposition or conclusion (*pratijñâ*).[31] Speech can make non-existence known, without issuing a denial.[32] Candrakîrti, like Nâgârjuna, recognizes that there is also an emptiness of emptiness (*śûnytâśûnyatâ*), since emptiness is not a being, but is empty of any essence of emptiness.[33] But he gives one of Nâgârjuna's responses, that he is not offering a conclusion (the Tibetan may reflect *pratijñâ* in the lost Sanskrit),[34] and elsewhere he quotes a sûtra that fills this out. Emptiness is not to be taken as a view (*drishti*), but as a medicine that is to be expelled along with what it expels.[35]

This treatment of emptiness as a medicine, not a statement, makes the idea of emptiness once again easier to accept. It also explains how Nâgârjuna can think of himself as taking a middle path between postulating eternal entities and a nihilistic denial of any entities. He does not deny entities, because a medicine is not a denial. A further advantage of treating emptiness as a medicine will emerge shortly, when we see that it may also explain the oscillation of attitudes recommended by a later figure, Sântideva, although

---

29. *Vigrahavyâvartanî* 22.

30. Ibid., 28

31. Ibid., 29.

32. Ibid., 64.

33. Candrakîrti *Introduction to the Middle Way* (*Madhyamakâratâva*) VI 185–86.

34. Ibid., VI 173.

35. *Prasannapadâ*, 248–49, quoting the *Ratnakûṭasûtra*, translated by M. Sprung, London 1979, and in C. W. Huntington Jr., *The Emptiness of Emptiness*, 57–58.

it will turn out to create a fresh difficulty of its own. But first let us illustrate what has been said so far.

Nâgârjuna *Vigrahavyâvartanî* 22:[36]

Likewise it follows that my statement also, being dependently originated, is devoid of an intrinsic nature, and hence void.—But things like a cart, a cloth, etc., though devoid of an intrinsic nature, because of being dependently originated, are occupied with their respective functions, e.g., carrying wood, grass and earth, containing honey, water and milk, and protecting from cold, wind and heat. Similarly this statement of mine, though devoid of an intrinsic nature, because of being dependently originated, is engaged in the task of establishing the being-devoid-of-an-intrinsic-nature of the things.

Nâgârjuna *Vigrahavyâvartanî* 27:

Or suppose that in an artificial woman, void of an intrinsic nature, some man should have the false notion that it is really a woman, and as a result of that false notion, should feel desire for her. The Tathâgata or a disciple of the Tathâgata would then create an artificial man, [and] the latter would dispel the false notion of that man, through the power of the Tathâgata or of the disciple of the Tathâgata. Likewise by my void statement, comparable to the artificial man, is prevented the idea of an intrinsic nature in all things which are devoid of an intrinsic nature and comparable to the artificial woman.

Nâgârjuna *Vigrahavyâvartanî* 29:

If I had any proposition (*pratijña*), then this defect would be mine. I have, however, no proposition.

Candrakîrti *Prasannapadâ* 248–49, quoting a sûtra:[37]

Kâśyapa, emptiness is the exhaustion of all philosophical views. I call incurable whoever holds emptiness as a philosophical view (*drishti*). Kâśyapa, it is as if a physician were to give medicine to a sick man, and when the medicine had

---

36. All translations of Nâgârjuna *Vigrahavyâvartanî*, are from E. H. Johnstone and Arnold Kunst.

37. Translated in C. W. Huntington, *The Emptiness of Emptiness.*

cured all the original problems, it remained in the stomach and was not itself expelled. What do you think, Kâśyapa, would this man be cured of his disease?—No, indeed, Blessed One, if the medicine cured all the original problems and remained in the stomach, unexpelled, the man's disease would be much worse. The Blessed One said: thus it is, Kâśyapa, that emptiness is the exhaustion of all philosophical views.

ŚÂNTIDEVA'S OSCILLATING PERSPECTIVE

The teaching that the emptiness of all things, including self, is a medicine, not a doctrine, could throw a different light on the oscillation of attitudes recommended by a very striking later figure, assigned by some but not by all to the school of Nâgârjuna, the saintly Śântideva in the early 8th century.[38] He treats it as an illusion that there are beings or persons who suffer. But he seems to be qualifying that treatment, when he says in the same breath that it is a necessary illusion for his purposes, including the practice of compassion.[39] The recognition of illusion is intact in the preceding chapter when he says that we should realize that, since there are not persons in reality, this in turn means that all pains should be equally objects of compassion, because there is no difference between mine and yours.[40] It seems there are benefits both from illusion and from seeing through it, and he deliberately oscillates in his perspective for different purposes. The paradox of Buddhist recognition of self alongside virtual denial will recur in the next chapter, where Buddhism will be seen to express belief in a particularly strong kind of individuality lasting through incarnations.

A small question should be raised about Śântideva's claim that compassion involves suffering.[41] This would not follow automatically, for, as Max Scheler argues in his book, *Sympathy*,[42] sympathy and compassion concerning a pain do not require the compassionate sympathizer to have a pain. The

38. Śântideva *The Bodhicaryâvatâra*, trans. Kate Crosby and Andrew Skilton, Oxford 1995, with introduction by Paul Williams; see also Paul Williams, *Altruism and Reality*, Richmond, Surrey, 1998, ch. 5.

39. Śântideva *The Bodhicaryâvatâra* ch. 9, para. 75. I do not think he means that it is necessary only because we have failed to transcend compassion, since I presume that compassion would not be eschewed by Śântideva while suffering lasts, but I thank Alex Catlin for mentioning this interpretation.

40. Ibid. 8.102–3.

41. Ibid. 8.104–5.

42. Max Scheler, *The Nature of Sympathy*, translated from the German, London 1954.

sympathizer may well be more effective as a helper if he is not himself distracted by suffering. Moreover, it has been said (although I have not seen this borne out) that infants have to pass through the stage of being distressed at the distress of others before they can express genuine sympathy.[43]

Śântideva engages in exercises that put the illusion of others to use and imagines himself in the position of another while imagining also that other's unflattering view of himself.[44] The exercises would reinforce the idea of the unimportance of self and eventually perhaps of its illusoriness. He also thinks that those who can think of the suffering of others as being as important as what they hold dear will be freed from fear and fulfilled.[45] This combination of spiritual exercises with analytic philosophy is perfectly familiar from later Greek philosophy, as has been especially brought home by Pierre Hadot, for example in his book translated from French as *Philosophy as a Way of Life*.[46] The analysis on its own may not succeed in changing your feelings, although Parfit reports that he is less afraid of death on the basis of his intellectual conclusion. The combination of an intellectual conclusion with spiritual exercises has been thought in many cultural milieux to change your way of life and thought more effectively.

If Śântideva's teaching is meant to be combined with Nâgârjuna's teaching that the denial of a continuous self is not a statement, but a medicine, then Śântideva will not after all view selfhood as really an illusion and acceptance of it as merely a useful pretence. Rather, each of the opposite attitudes will be a medicine, with neither representing a matter of fact. This interpretation offers the advantage that there will have been no statement or denial that there is a self. Nonetheless, this combination of Śântideva's teaching with Nâgârjuna's raises a difficulty of its own. The emptiness of all things is offered by Nâgârjuna as a medicine designed to serve a purpose rather than as a statement of fact. But if there is to be a possibility of serving a purpose, such as effecting a change of attitude of the kind Śântideva seeks, then there must be the possibility of the purpose, the change of attitude, being effected as a matter of *fact*. Not everything said can be a medicine rather than a statement of fact, and yet it is not clear that Nâgârjuna has left room for statements of fact about the ordinary world if we are to regard all things as empty.

43. M. L. Hoffman, 'Empathy, its development and prosocial implications', in C. B. Keasey, ed., *Nebraska Symposium on Motivation* 25, University of Nebraska 1977.

44. Śântideva *The Bodhicaryâvatâra*, 8.

45. Ibid. 8.107–8.

46. Pierre Hadot, *Philosophy as a Way of Life*, trans. Michael Chase, Oxford 1995.

Śântideva *The Bodhicaryâvatâra*, 8.102–3, 9.75:

(8.102–3) Without exception, no suffering belongs to anyone. They must be warded off simply because they are suffering.

   If one asks why suffering should be prevented, noone disputes that! If it must be prevented, then all of it must be. If not, then this goes for oneself as for everyone.

   (9.75) If you argue: for whom is there compassion if no being exists?, [our response is] For anyone projected through the illusion which is embraced for the sake of what has to be done.

NYAYA REPLIES TO THE BUDDHISTS ON SELF

Hindu philosophers of the Nyaya school introduced objections of their own to the Buddhists. Many of their attacks on the Buddhist view appeal to me, with a qualification to be mentioned. Some of them highlight the interrelations of different psychological activities in one person. For example, the Nyaya philosopher Vâtsyâyana, commenting around 400 AD on Gautama's *Nyâyasûtra*, a work of about 150 AD, draws attention to desiring to possess or avoid something of a type remembered. This, he argues, requires a single person to be the former experiencer, the present desirer, and the future attainer. We have seen on the other side the Buddhist Vasubandhu instead analyzing memory not in terms of the same person, but of causation and resemblance holding between a past experience and a present one. We saw him give as an example of the sequence involved in wanting something of a kind remembered: recollection, interest, consideration, willful effort, vital action, without reference to a self.[47]

   Perhaps the most remarkable argument in Vâtsyâyana[48] is that I touch the very same thing that I see. There is a contrast here with Parfit, who turns

---

47. Vasubandhu *Treatise on the Negation of the Person*. Vâtsyâyana comments on Gautama's *Nyâyasûtra*, 1.1.10, translated with comments on Vasubandhu by Uddyotakara (c. 600 AD), in Kapstein, *Reasons, Traces, and Identity*, 373, 378–83.

48. Vâtsyâyana and Uddyotakara commenting on *Nyâyasûtra* 3.1.1 and 4.1.35–36. See the excellent discussions by Arindam Chakrabarti (who requires both or neither), in 'I touch what I saw', *Philosophy and Phenomenological Research* 52, 1992, 103–16; and by Jonardon Ganeri (who introduces the 'thinks' version of the argument and includes translations of Vâtsyâyana), in 'Cross-modality and the self', *Philosophy and Phenomenological Research* 61, 2000, 1–19.

selves into streams but whose account of the streams depends on bodies and brains remaining intact and not stream-like. Vâtsyâyana, by contrast, argues that if there are only visual sensations and tactual sensations, without a perceiver who has both, then there is no opportunity to think of the sensations as being of visual and tactual qualities that belong to the same object. The question of their belonging to the same object can arise only for a perceiver who perceives both. Jonardon Ganeri gives a cautiously epistemological version of the argument that takes us back to the topic of self-awareness and is reminiscent of Kant (*Critique of Pure Reason*, A108–110): if one does not *think* of oneself as a unitary perceiver, one cannot *think* of the sweet and white qualities as belonging to one object. Presumably, Buddhists would not mind this, because they give the same status to selves and bodies anyhow. But it is very startling to find an argument that they are obliged to do so. In fact, there is evidence that in the English-speaking tradition, Berkeley agreed that if we make objects perceived into bundles, we must do the same with the minds or spirits that perceive them.[49] And it is the view of David Hume[50] that identity over time is an illusion produced by the association of ideas, equally in the case of selves and of bodies.

It might be asked if it would not be as good for there to be perceptions of qualities as co-existing in the same *location*, rather than as belonging to a single object. But recognition of the shared location would still require a single perceiver of both qualities, and the location would need to be judged either by the direction and distance of the qualities from the single perceiver or by their direction and distance from other entities perceived by the single perceiver. Still less satisfactory, I believe, would be the suggestion that the perceptions need to follow a single route, rather than belong to a single observer.[51] If you had one perception and I another, there would not yet be any reason to ascribe the qualities perceived to one thing.

Nyâyasûtra 3.1.1–3 with Vâtsyâyana's comment:[52]

[The self is a substance] because a single object is grasped by touch and sight. [If you say] 'no, for there is restriction of each sense to its proper object', [we

49. A. C. Lloyd, 'The self in Berkeley's philosophy', in John Foster and Howard Robinson, eds., *Essays on Berkeley*, Oxford 1985.

50. Hume, *A Treatise of Human Nature* 1.4.6.

51. See Simon Blackburn, 'Has Kant refuted Parfit?' in Jonathan Dancy, ed., *Reading Parfit*, Oxford 1977, 180–201, at 187–91.

52. Translations of Vâtsyâyana from Jonardon Ganeri, 'Cross-modality and the self', *Philosophy and Phenomenological Research* 61, 2000, 1–19.

reply] this is not a refutation because the existence of the self follows too from that very restriction.

A certain object is grasped by sight, and that same object is also grasped by touch. And it is thought, 'that which I saw with my visual sense I now touch with my haptic sense', and 'that which I touched with my haptic sense I now see with my visual sense'. Here two perceptions of a single object are integrated qua having a unitary agent; not qua ones whose agent is a mere aggregation.

Nyâyasûtra 1.1.10 with Vâtsyâyana's comment:

There can be no [integration] in the case of a mere thought-series, each thought having a different object, as in the case of different bodies. . . .

The phrase 'as in the case of different bodies' is to be explained thus. Just as even for the no-self theorist, a thought-series where each thought has a fixed object but is in a different body is not integrated, so too the objects of [the thoughts of] a single body ought not to be integrated, as there is no difference [between the two cases].

Nyâyasûtra 4.1.35 – 36 with Vâtsyâyana's comment:

Compare: '[Not all objects are mere aggregates], because a single object can arise with many characteristics. Since the indicative function [of words] is subject to restrictions, there is no refutation [of this idea]'.

The commentator adds: 'When one thinks "that pot which I saw I now touch", or "that which I touched I now see", one does not grasp an aggregate of atoms, and an aggregate of atoms is not being grasped, what is grasped is nothing but a single thing'.

Immanuel Kant *Critique of Pure Reason*, trans. Norman Kemp Smith, London 1929, extracts from A 108, 110:

(A108) There can be no modes of knowledge, no connection or unity of one mode of knowledge with another, without that unity of consciousness which precedes all data of intuitions, and by relation to which representation of objects is alone possible. This pure unchangeable consciousness I shall name *transcendental apperception*.

(A110) The objective reality of our empirical knowledge rests on the transcendental law, that all appearances, in so far as through them objects are to be given to us, must stand under those *a priori* rules of synthetical unity whereby the interrelating of these appearances in empirical intuition is alone possible.

The Buddhist Kamalaśīla in the 8th century AD records a list of Nyaya arguments for the self, which suggests that a huge range of examples had been assembled by them.

Kamalaśīla, *Tattvasamgrahapanjika,* a commentary on his teacher's *Compendium of the Quiddities,* passage translated at Kapstein, *Reasons, Traces, and Identity,* 35:

> If everything is affirmed to be instantaneous, then how do you go about estab-
> lishing causal connection, etc., which are well known to the world and to sci-
> ence? The 'etc.' here refers to the whole mass of objections raised by the Nyaya
> opponents concerning: inductive knowledge of cause and effect, recognition
> of what had been previously experienced, desire for something on the basis of
> prior experience of another [similar] thing, bondage and liberation, memory,
> resolution of doubt, recovery of what had been entrusted to another, famil-
> iarisation or absence of astonishment when it is the case that the [astonishing]
> thing had been seen before.

Finally, the verses of the Nyaya philosopher Jayanta Bhaṭṭa in the 10th century AD are currently being translated into English by Arindam Chakra-barti. He tells me that the arguments for a self include appeals to some of the things already discussed: navigating, wanting, recognizing an old friend, and commerce with people more generally, and the self-healing of the body. Chakrabarti already has translated in an earlier article Jayanta's appeal to linguistic communication and the understanding of a single sentence, which reveals the level of detail of his argument:

Jayanta Bhaṭṭa, extract from *Nyaymanjari:*[53]

> The successive hearing of different phonemes, a successive understanding of
> the word meanings with the help of remembered conventional semantic rules,
> a recollection of all those previously apprehended meanings through the men-
> tal trace they left at the time of listening to the last syllable, a synthesising of all
> the singly understood meanings according to the rules of syntactical relevance

53. Translated by Arindam Chakrabarti, 'The Nyaya proofs for the existence of the soul', *Journal of Indian Philosophy* 10, 1982, 211–38, at 225.

among them, all these would be impossible without one abiding subject who runs through the whole process and holds it together to yield a single understanding of the sentence.

There is an aspect of the Nyaya defense of self that I would not support and that is the view that it is incorporeal, an *atman* or soul. As Stephen Phillips[54] has pointed out, the Naiyâyika Udayana around 1000 AD argues for an incorporeal self against materialists on the basis of the newborn's desiring the breast and knowing how to get it as implying prior experience of these things and its retention after the destruction of the previous incarnation's body. There is, therefore, no body available to do the retaining, even if, which Udayana denies, a body could be a locus of conscious experience.

ANCIENT GRAECO-ROMAN THOUGHT

Are there analogies with Graeco-Roman thought? Analogies have been sought for the idea of emptiness of emptiness. But denial followed by the denial of denial was applied by the Neoplatonist mystics only to the supreme God, whereas Nâgârjuna goes in the very opposite direction, applying the idea of emptiness to everything *except* the transcendent. Second, the enlightenment that follows, when theses are given up and mere appearances are acted on, has been compared to Skepticism, and the Pyrrhonian skeptics did claim to achieve tranquility by giving up the search for something more than appearance. They even had the same analogy of a laxative,[55] but it is put to a different use. The recognition that every statement has its opposite purges the Greek Pyrrhonian skeptic of any *assent* to how tings appear and even of assent to the appearance that every statement has its opposite. But he is purged only of *assent*, not of *appearances*, which indeed he is urged to follow. So the analogies are not close on further inspection, and they do not warrant the conclusion that the school of Nâgârjuna was either skeptic or mystic.[56] A third analogy is that the Greeks were very interested in the idea of streams, but as a theory about the nature of the universe. They did less to

54. Stephen Phillips, 'Self as locus /substratum (*adhikarana*) of psychological continuities and discontinuities', paper to American Philosophical Association 2005, which he has been kind enough to show me.

55. Diogenes Laertius *Lives* 9.76. I am grateful to Alex Mourelatos for the point.

56. See Mark Siderits, 'Matilal on Nâgârjuna', in P. Bilimoria and J. N. Mohanty, eds., *Relativism, Suffering, and Beyond: Essays in Memory of Bimal K. Matilal*, Delhi 1997, 69–92.

work out the implications for life. Was there any historical interconnection between the discussions? I have mentioned *The Questions of Milinda*, which remains the closest connection.

I have traced in chapter two the history of claims about discontinuity in Graeco-Roman thought. It started in the 5th century BC with the comic playwright Epicharmus and the Presocratic philosopher Heraclitus. Epicharmus was echoed later by the Growing Argument, which postulated a new person with each change of size, and was answered by a Shrinking Argument, so I claimed in chapter four. Aristotle raised further problems about identity through growth, as discussed in chapter three. Heraclitus' belief in perpetual flux was developed and reduced to absurdity in Plato's *Theaetetus*. But Plato entertained a considerable degree of flux in people, especially in one of his discussions in the *Symposium*. I resisted the idea that the Cyrenaic philosopher Aristippus denied a continuing self. But I did think that a superficial acquaintance with Buddhism might have influenced the poorly integrated passages in Seneca and Plutarch that use the denial of a continuing self to counter the fear of annihilation at death.

The continuity of individuals is made by Augustine to depend on God's continuing every moment to exert his sustaining power, and, in Islamic thought, the Mutakallimun represented God as re-creating the world at every indivisible atom of time.[57]

The Buddhist view was known to Avicenna, if the story is true that an eager student came up to him and said, 'Master, Master, have you heard this one? We have no continuous self.' Avicenna said nothing. 'Master, Master', persisted the student, 'Why are you not answering me?' Avicenna replied, 'I only answer the person who asked the question'.

I have mentioned only a few types of human attitude and moral concept that seem to me to depend on the idea of a continuing owner. But I think this dependence may hold for a large range of human attitudes and moral concepts—though not for all. To name just a few other moral concepts that would call for investigation, there are loyalty, ownership, remorse, reliability, rights, determination, forgiveness, resentment, and freedom.[58]

57. References in Richard Sorabji, *Time, Creation, and the Continuum*, Ithaca N.Y. 1983, ch. 17, 'The origins of occasionalism'.
58. On the last three, see Peter Strawson, 'Freedom and resentment', *Proceedings of the British Academy* 48, 1962, 187–211.

PART VII

Mortality and loss of self

CHAPTER 17

How might we survive death?

The earliest written suggestion in Western writing that we might be annihilated at death is said to be on the inscription for those who fell at the battle of Potidaea in Greece in 432 BC.[1] For hundreds of years before that, the Homeric bards had been singing of at least a shadowy after-life. Not that a Homeric after-life would comfort everybody. It was pretty gloomy, with a very dimmed form of consciousness, and it allowed for punishment of the wicked. The possibility of annihilation is not necessarily what people fear about death. They may rather fear illness or pain, or the interruption of their projects and relationships, or subsequent punishment. Indeed, around 300 BC, the philosopher Epicurus sought to remove the fear of punishment after death by saying that we need not worry, because we were a bunch of atoms and would have disintegrated. Plutarch, the Platonist, we saw, had to respond to him that disintegration was exactly what other people feared.[2] But perhaps only 50 percent of a Western audience is likely to be horrified at the thought of annihilation. In India, the proportion is much less, because so many people believe that they will be reincarnated, even if only as animals. It is the fear of annihilation that I will consider and certain suggested ways in which it might be avoided. I shall mention three familiar suggested ways in this chapter, and a less familiar way in the next.

1. So John Burnet, 'The Socratic doctrine of the Soul', *Proceedings of the British Academy* 14, 1915–16, 235–59.
2. Kirk Sanders informs me that he plans to argue that Epicurus addressed this fear too.

REINCARNATION

One way of surviving is thought to be reincarnation, rebirth in a different body. This belief is partly concerned with moral responsibility. Your present woes are due to sins in a past incarnation and your present sins will bring woes in a future one. It was not, however, typically treated by Buddhists or Hindus as a source of solace, since reincarnation renews suffering, and often their goal was escape. In just the same way, few Stoics apart from Seneca in one of the earlier and less demanding letters in his series (36,10–11) suggest that solace might be found in the idea of the eternal recurrence of the world's history, which brings the same people back. Even Seneca suggests a sterner message when he returns to the subject in *Letter* 71,15. However, in the Hindu epic, the *Bhagavadgîtâ*, ch. 2, part of the *Mahâbhârata*, Krishna does tell Arjuna that he can kill family members in war because they will be reincarnated. This is a supplement to the main consideration, that he is obliged by his inherited role or persona as a warrior.

Reincarnation takes different forms according to whether it depends on a continuing soul, or a continuing stream. For Platonists, reincarnation took place through the same soul inhabiting a new body. In Platonism, Buddhism, and Hinduism, reincarnation is not immediate. Plato's Socrates in the *Phaedo* and *Phaedrus* envisages an intervening period in which the soul will be disembodied, while the Neoplatonists supply the soul with a tenuous physical vehicle, and some Hindu schools with a set of sheaths, in the intervening period. Buddhism expected the stream to continue, but did not regard it as a self, unless merely as a way of talking.

Does the idea of reincarnation provide a possible way to avoid annihilation? Only if it is the very same person as before who is reincarnated. I suggested in chapter six that Plotinus' discussion in 5.7 [18] 1 (1–11) of Pythagoras being reincarnated as Socrates might see them as the same soul, but not the same individual. But I found that problematic. How could Pythagoras continue if the soul that was his self had been borrowed by a different individual, and if he could continue, how would he feel about that soul being taken in a different moral direction by someone else? It would be easier if Pythagoras and Socrates were regarded as the same individual. But Plotinus does not do the work, I thought, needed to make it plausible that they could be. Can the work be done?

One problem about its being in Plotinus' terms the same individual or, as I would prefer to say, the same person is that the next incarnation will at best be in the body of a human baby, and in less favorable scenarios in that of a gnat or lower. Some Indian thinkers regarded reincarnation in animal form as an unusual punishment for a human, and among the Neoplatonists, Iamblichus tried to argue that Plato did not intend this.[3] But even reincarnation as a baby in a new environment, let alone class, culture, or race, seems to involve the loss of many mental and physical characteristics. Can the psychological connection, then, be strong enough?

Another problem about its being the same person is that some psychological links seem too weak, at least in isolation. If the grown child displays an apparently accurate memory of a past life, and if that is not better explained as an admittedly mysterious case of clairvoyance, there would still be questions to ask. Should mere memories provide reassurance to the remembered person on their deathbed? Having their life remembered, even as if it had been experienced from the inside, does not seem enough on its own to suggest that the person whose life is remembered has survived. It does not help that Empedocles is said to have been able by great concentration of mind to remember twenty past lives.[4] What Indian philosophy does, however, is to give a much fuller account of psychological linkages.

I think it makes a great difference that according to some versions of Buddhism, the most recent incarnation of the Buddha and aspirant Bodhisattvas could remember a forward-looking aspiration in earlier lives to progress towards Buddhahood and to postpone escape from reincarnation until all suffering is removed. As I mentioned in chapter nine, A. R. Luria found with his brain-damaged patients that forward-looking projects are more important to a person than recollections.[5] The prospect and memory of progress through successive lives towards an aspiration that is central to you should both give a sense of its being you in other lives and be potentially cheering. The idea would not fit with the denials or virtual denials of a continuous self that we found associated with Buddhism in the last chapter. In fact, it suggests a particularly strong individuality lasting between incarnations. The same idea is found in Jainism, if the most recent divine incarnation, Tirthankar Mahavir Swami, recalled its being declared seven incarnations earlier that he was to be so incarnated.

I am indebted to Stephen Phillips for informing me not only about this, but also about the Buddhist and Hindu belief in *saṃskāras,* or impressed traces, by which continuity between incarnations is thought to be main-

---

3. We shall in chapter nineteen encounter problems about the idea of surviving as a cricket, and for the moment I shall ignore it.

4. Porphyry *Life of Pythagoras* 30.

5. A. R. Luria, *The Man with a Shattered World*, New York 1972, London 1973.

tained. *Saṃskâras* are invoked in other contexts too besides that of rebirth. In the Nyaya school, a long-term belief is thought of as a *saṃskâra*, or imprint, that is implanted by a cognition and can in the right circumstances awaken memory. *Saṃskâras* can impress the stream postulated by Buddhists or the five sheaths posited among Hindu schools, for example by Advaita Vedanta, sheaths of subtle bodies that are in principle sheddable in turn by the soul. The deepest sheath impresses the others, and it is hard, though not impossible, to get rid of habits and talents that have become ingrained through many incarnations. A baby may be born with a musical ear, even though the musical talent may not become apparent until it has grown. In the *Bhagavadgîtâ* (ch. 6), Krishna encourages Arjuna to learn discipline, because in another incarnation, he will, though not at once, recover the same level of ability, and be able to progress from there.

> There he regains a depth of understanding from his former life and strives further to perfection, Arjuna. Carried by the force of his previous practice, . . .[6]

Later commentators explain this by *saṃskâras*. In the Saṃkhya Yoga of Patanjali, pleasure, pain, and action all leave marks. Such marks make it possible to remember the last ten rebirths or birth as a cat 100 cycles of the universe ago, provided the conditions are right to stimulate memory.[7]

Some of the difficulties of reincarnation are offset by the appeal to aspirations, talents, habits, and virtues, things that are much more central to a person than the ordinary intentions and memories to which the tradition of Locke and Parfit appeals.

I think that with this strengthened idea of reincarnation, we can see how Socrates might be considered to be Pythagoras, and not merely the borrower of his soul. On the other hand Ram Prasad has warned that in some Hindu thinkers the soul, *atman*, is so impersonal a consciousness that it is something borrowed by one distinct person after another.[8]

DISEMBODIED SURVIVAL

Another remedy suggested is that we might survive without bodies. Although Christianity believes in an embodied resurrection, in Augustine

6. Trans. Barbara Stoler Miller, New York 1986.
7. Patanjali, *Yoga-Sûtra* 2.15, 3.18, 4.9.
8. Ram Prasad, 'The great divide', *Prospect Magazine* 119, Feb. 2006.

(*City of God* 13) and in earlier Church Fathers from the 2nd century AD,[9] we find the complication of an intervening period of existence before the final resurrection. This was said, e.g., by Augustine (*On the Literal Interpretation of Genesis* 12.32–33), to be a period of disembodiment, and it is more fully described as such by Thomas Aquinas in the 13th century. So even Christians need to consider the possibility of disembodied survival.

Can we perhaps imagine this? Suppose that as you sit alone in your room, you notice your foot seems to be disappearing from view and that you cannot feel it either. Gradually the disappearance spreads up your legs and then the rest of your body, leaving your clothes a crumpled heap. Last to go is your voice, and then you could no longer have any direct effect on what was going on. But would you have ceased to exist, or would you not rather be surveying in helpless horror the scene that you had vacated?

Even though this may seem imaginable, the disembodied scenario faces more criticisms than any other. It would, of course, go against all the scientific evidence we have access to, since we see that impairments of the brain are correlated with impairments of experience and activity, so that it would go outside the available empirical evidence to suppose that total destruction of the brain could go with the recovery of psychological experience and activity. In chapter one, I referred to the major role that one's body plays in one's conception of oneself. If we are to become disembodied, we should have to think of embodiment as a mere stage, analogous to that of a caterpillar, which will become a chrysallis and then a butterfly.

But apart from empirical difficulties, there are some major philosophical problems. One is whether there can be any mental activity at all in the absence of a body. Another is whether mental activities could be linked into a stream in the absence of a body, since the stream of consciousness discussed in chapter fifteen depended on relation to a body and brain. We need to ask also whether there could be an *owner* of such activities. In chapter fifteen, it was argued that the stream did not amount to a person or self, and that we needed an embodied owner. Could there be any owner in the absence of embodiment? Could there be the same owner as formerly lived on earth? And could different owners be distinguished? Finally, we need to consider whether the experiences and activities that would remain open to a disembodied owner would make for a life that would be for us at all desirable. These four problems are not entirely distinct from each other.

---

9. Our fathers exist (Justin Martyr *Apologia* 1.63), but are asleep (Irenaeus *Adversus Haereses* 4.5.2).

(i) *Disembodied mental activities.* To take the first, concerning disembodied mental activities, in the second half of the 20th century, there were many different kinds of philosophical attack on the idea of psychological experience and activity as something separable in principle from the body. Psychological experiences and activities were analyzed by Gilbert Ryle as dispositions towards bodily behavior.[10] Later, there were various identity theories that attempted to show how psychological states might be identical with brain states.[11] While these proposals recommended physicalistic accounts of psychological experience and activity, Wittgenstein presented a still more famous attack on what he called 'private language', which argued against the very possibility of divorcing psychological experience and activity from what could be observed by other people. Psychological experience and activity stand in need of publicly observable criteria.[12]

More recently, a functionalist view has been found attractive,[13] although it is admitted to be still at a sketchy stage.[14] It suggests that different psychological states might be defined by their functional role as something (which may be a brain state) that plays a specified role in a network of causally related stimuli (which may be bodily), and behavior (which may be bodily) and other psychological states. Sometimes the relations are justificatory rather than causal. The analysis in terms of function or role allows mental states to be physical, and that was the main intention, but it does not insist on physicality, in case they should turn out to be non-physical after all.

Why the stress on the physical? Wittgenstein's reasons were different from the others. His view was that social ways of life are the basic phenomenon. But Ryle was particularly attacking Descartes' conception of soul and body, which he characterized as postulating a ghost in a machine. He rejected not only Descartes' soul as the non-physical *subject* of psychological states, but also the idea that might have seemed more tempting, that psychological states are themselves non-physical events.

10. Gilbert Ryle, *Concept of Mind*, London 1949.

11. These are best represented in anthologies of the time such as John O'Connor, *Modern Materialism: Readings on Mind-Body Identity*, New York 1969; C. V. Borst, *The Mind/Brain Identity Theory*, London 1970.

12. Ludwig Wittgenstein, *Philosophical Investigations*, pt. 1, translated by G. E. M. Anscombe, Oxford 1953.

13. See, e.g., Hilary Putnam, 'Philosophy and our mental life', in his *Mind, Language, and Reality: Philosophical Papers 2*, Cambridge 1975, 291–303; Sydney Shoemaker, in Sydney Shoemaker and Richard Swinburne, *Personal Identity*, Oxford 1984, sec. 6, pp. 92–97; id., 'Qualia and consciousness', *Mind* 100, 1991, 507–24.

14. Shoemaker, *Personal Identity*, 101.

One functionalist author has said clearly and engagingly why he is attracted to the idea that psychological states may be neurophysiological states, citing the explanatory success of the physical sciences.[15] I am inclined to think that the sciences often offer *psychological* explanations, but that when they offer *physical* ones, they often do so by restricting the range of facts explained. Science may seek physical explanations of the chemical and electrical activities involved in, say, a chain of practical reasoning and action, or the physical agitation involved in emotion. The physical explanations will not necessarily explain why the reasoning or action takes the course it does, so much as *how* it does so, nor explain the occurrence of the thoughts involved in the emotion, so much as the physical states of agitation that belong in a causal network with the thoughts. If the facts explained are different, it is not excluded, but equally not suggested, that the states explained will be the same.

Nonetheless, the belief that there might be disembodied psychological states travels in the opposite direction by going, as I have said, against all the empirical evidence to which we have access. It would need to trade on the limitations of our empirical evidence and on the conceptual possibility not having been excluded by the philosophical objections.

I believe that only a limited range of experiences and activities would be candidates for disembodiment. I suggested in the little thought experiment above that you could not have an effect on what was going on, put on your coat, for example, and summon help, but I suggested you might remember (without a brain) what you had been doing a moment ago, might feel horror at the change, and might still see the scene that you had vacated. Would even seeing be possible?[16] Such seeing would not be of a kind known to science, since you would not have any receptors capable of receiving light rays. But we are asking what might be possible beyond what is known to science. Might not the experience be the same as that of ordinary vision, and equally informative? The experience of seeing involves a point of view, with things seen as being to the right or left, nearer or further away. This experience can be imagined as continuing, so that even though you no longer had a body occupying space, your visual experience would be as from a sizeless point in space. But as the scene before you seemed to shift, would this be a case of your gaining information about what was happening next door, or merely imagining it?

15. Ibid., 139; cf. 69.
16. Discussion of this sort of question can be found, for example, in Terence Penelhum, *Survival and Disembodied Existence*, London 1970.

Normally you know that you have gone next door from a number of clues. The psychologist J. J. Gibson, as explained in chapter one, showed that your eye sockets provide a stable frame to your field of vision and your nose a stable protrusion, with which you can contrast the flow of the scene that you are approaching, and so monitor your progress. But without eye sockets or nose, you would have lost these clues. The only remaining visual clue customarily associated with your approach is the fact that the center point in the scene towards which you are moving is the slowest to flow towards the sides of your visual field. You might check on whether this was happening. I hope I have said enough to indicate that even something as straightforward as seeing could be problematic, if no spatial characteristics are retained. But now let us consider some non-visual checks on the seeing.

Tactual clues are in normal circumstances useful for checking whether you have really moved next door, if you can check on whether you have had the expected muscular sensations throughout your limbs of moving next door. But in the new circumstances, if sensations were felt over an extended area, you would have to be thought of as spread out over a whole area, not merely as occupying a sizeless viewpoint. We are having to imagine the restoration to you of some aspects of a body, although, if the area was only tactile, but not itself tangible, we would perhaps be imagining you as a spatially extended being, but not yet as a bodily one.

To confirm that you had really moved to view next door, you might also try relying not on your tactual experience of moving next door, but on the testimony of other people who were still embodied about what was happening next door. But could you communicate with other people? I have already supposed that your voice would go. But could you both hear others and cause them to hear in their minds sounds like that of your voice by means not known to science? Does hearing voice mean that we would still be communicating in English or Greek, separated into linguistic groups, rather than in the mentalese postulated by Augustine *On the Trinity* 15.10.19 – 20? And would our thoughts contain traces of our cultural identity as Sikhs or Mexicans, or would cultural identity disappear, as it seems to in Augustine's heaven of heavens in *Confessions* 12 –13? How much would that leave of us? But this question of selfhood or persona already takes us far beyond our first question. Moreover, checking and converstation raise issues of continuing identity, because it has to be the same individual who checks the tactual experience against the visual and who puts (or receives) the question and gets (or gives) the answer.

Tactual sensations might be important to something else, namely, whether there could be disembodied shock and horror at the disappearance of your body, and in general disembodied emotion. I believe that emotions involve bodily agitation, which is usually sensed, as well as typically involving judgments. As the ancient Stoics said, the emotions typically involve the judgment that harm or benefit is at hand, although the Stoic Posidonius, at least as interpreted by Galen, correctly pointed out that this judgment may sometimes be disowned, or even be absent. What I think cannot in normal circumstances be bypassed is the physiological disturbance, sensed or not, since a merely intellectual appreciation of benefit or harm does not constitute emotion. This physiological requirement, if correct, would seem to rule out disembodied emotion right away. But could there be an analogue of emotion, if there were still tactual sensations, like those of physiological disturbance, related in a causal network with thoughts of harm and benefit?

I have spoken of emotion and of perception, and as regards the latter, it turned out that having the same continuing individual owner was important for tactual and conversational checking on whether the visual experience of moving next door corresponded to reality. It would also be important for agency in general, and our agency, like our body, forms an important part of our normal concept of self. But except for such basic actions as raising one's arm, most actions require a sequence of steps. This is true even of the manipulation of thoughts, such as trying to recall, or reasoning something out. So we need it to be the same individual at different stages in the sequence.

I have so far imagined one's disembodied self having an effect on the minds of others but not on their bodies, but if one could by will power move sound waves or alarm bells, one could summon help after all. This might seem to come close to restoring a body, but not if there were no sensations reporting the normal resistance of other bodies to one's own body, or limitations to the reach of one's powers to cause motion. It might further seem that, since a physical scene has been imagined as producing by non-physical means mental experience of the scene, it would be only symmetrical to imagine that the mind could by non-physical means produce physical effects.[17] But accepting the asymmetry may be preferable to seeking explanations of why physical communication from the disembodied is not observable everywhere all the time. There will be another asymmetry if the disembodied communicate mentally with each other, but not with the embodied.

17. My thanks to Markus Glodek for the comment.

(ii) *Disembodied activities linked into streams.* I come now to the second question, whether experiences and activities could link up, so as to form individual streams of consciousness. In chapter fifteen, we found two kinds of problem about embodied streams of consciousness. First, what links a stream together? Second, what distinguishes different streams? The links suggested for holding a stream together might turn out, contrary to all intention, to link together the streams of different persons, when, for example, one person's desire caused and gave reason for another's action. Derek Parfit was seen to rely on the relationship with a particular body to give unity to the stream and to distinguish it from other streams. But now body is being supposed absent. Would all the right sequences of events link with each other to form a single stream. Would it be distinct from other streams? And would there be no isolated experiences that failed to link into any stream?

Linkages might be increased, but problems of differentiation intensified, if we accepted certain holistic views that make it more appropriate to think of a network of psychological activities rather than of a linear stream. One such view is the functionalism already mentioned that defines one psychological activity by its role in a network of other activities. Another holistic view [18] is that our psychological attitudes need to be taken as an interlinked whole, because, for example, the leaving behind of one's umbrella can be interpreted as revealing any of an indefinite number of attitudes: expectation of good weather, a desire to get wet, a desire that someone else shall not get wet, or an absent-minded preoccupation. What our actual attitude was can only be told from, and depends upon, what our other psychological states are. So perhaps psychological states do form holistic networks in normal circumstances. But if I was right in chapter fifteen that, without identifiable owners, many acts and experiences would become either impossible or pointless, holism would be restricted in its application, unless we can find owners.

Let us take an example of a sequence of disembodied events that we might well think important. Could there be exchanges of a conversational type between different streams of consciousness? It was seen in chapter fifteen that there are problems about linguistic communication even between embodied streams if they are ownerless. For communication normally involves intentions with their innumerable 'I'-thoughts, which would be illu-

18. In, e.g., W. V. O. Quine, *Word and Object,* Cambridge Mass. 1960, ch. 2; Donald Davidson, 'Mental events', in L. Foster and J. W. Swanson, eds., *Experience and Theory,* Amherst 1970.

sory in the absence of owners. But could there be some type of desire other than intention, which was a desire that one stream, rather than one person, should produce beliefs in another stream, and would that provide an analogue of linguistic communication?

For thoughts of any complexity to be transferred, a common language would be needed. Would these be known human languages, or should we have to resort to the neutral mental nouns and verbs postulated by Augustine and still being discussed?[19] The possession of languages involves long-term abilities, and the beliefs induced might also be long-term dispositions activated only from time to time. So we should need the long-term abilities and dispositions to be recognizable as the same at different times. Could they be the same except by belonging to the same owner?

(iii) *Disembodied owners.* We can no longer postpone the question of whether there could be an owner of disembodied consciousness, and whether that could be the same owner as was previously embodied. In the case of embodied consciousness, the continuing owner would be clearly identifiable, the embodied organism. But what identifiable entity could serve as the continuing owner if an embodied organism was not available to do the job? In chapter three there was doubt whether the same owner could survive the sudden replacement of one owner by another in teletransportation. But now we are imagining there to be no embodied owner at all.

The idea of a non-physical soul as owner seems problematic because it is not independently identifiable, unlike an embodied owner. It is also not experienceable unlike a non-physical psychological activity, despite the claim of Augustine, discussed in chapter twelve, that nothing is so present to itself as soul. To postulate a soul is to postulate one particular kind of disembodied owner, but that is precisely what we are trying to explore: what sense can we make of the idea of a disembodied owner? A soul has the extra puzzling feature that during the period of embodiment it would have been only one of two owners, since the embodied person was then an owner as well. So in seeking a disembodied owner, I shall not depend on the idea of a soul.

Different from a soul would be a momentary owner of momentary activities. But that would not offer continuing survival, and in any case is put in question by Lichtenberg's reply to Descartes in the 18th century. Descartes seeks in his *Second Meditation* something of which he can be infallibly

19. The modern discussion is inspired by the work of Noam Chomsky. See Jerry Fodor, *The Language of Thought*, New York 1975.

certain, and argues that he cannot be wrong if he judges, 'I am', or 'I think'. But he cannot have infallible certainty of more than the momentary existence of this I, since with regard to any past or future history of it, he would be fallible. This is why Lichtenberg objects that it would be better for Descartes to say 'thought occurs', or 'it thinks' by analogy with English, 'it thunders', rather than to speak of an 'I' who does the thinking.[20]

It begins to look as if the evidence for a single continuing owner would now have to be the same as the evidence for a single continuing stream of consciousness, with all the problems that raised. Let us return to the example of disembodied conversation and consider whether the evidence could build up sufficiently to suggest that there was both a single stream of consciousness and a single owner of it, distinct from the owners of other streams.

Would the imagined participants in a disembodied conversation be distinguished by the content of what was said? That would require very distinctive thoughts. Or would there be preserved the very strong sense we have in embodied life of the difference between self-generated and other-generated events? I mentioned this in chapter one in connection with our recognition that we are moving towards the ball or that the ball is moving towards us. The same phenomenon is found, except in those who hear self-produced inner 'voices', in our distinction between our own utterances and those of others. Another thing that would help is if there was such a thing as hearing in what Augustine calls our 'inner ears' (*interioribus auribus*)[21] what sounded like a familiar voice. If all these conditions were met, would that give unity to a stream of communications, distinctness from the answering stream of communications and at the same stroke the idea of two distinct *producers* of the communications who thereby fulfilled the ownership role? There would remain the question of whether the producers of earlier conversations were the same as the producers of later conversations or other activities.

I have ruled out a number of possibilities, but left open whether sense could be made of disembodied visual experience, or of disembodied conversation, both of which would require continuing owners. The example of conversation is relevant to the fourth question, whether the activities and life available to disembodied beings would be something to be desired.

(iv) *Desirability of disembodied life.* Conversation would spare people from solitude. But we need to reflect how different continuation of oneself

20. G. C. Lichtenberg, *Schriften und Briefe*, Sudelbücher II, Darmstadt 1971, 412.
21. Augustine *City of God* 16.6.

might be from that with which we are familiar, if we are to assess its desirability. The ancients were right to think that we should need to *prepare* for something so very different. Plato expresses this view in the 4th century BC, when he makes Socrates suppose in the *Phaedo* that he himself will continue disembodied after his execution. For he also makes him think that what he will principally be doing after death is *thinking*, and also enjoying his thoughts, and that philosophy can prepare you now for this very different sort of existence by occupying you with thinking, not with the seeing and feeling that is so dependent on a body. Notoriously, Cleombrotus misunderstood Socrates' description of philosophy at 64A as practicing death, and took it that the philosopher was to commit suicide. Hence the discussion of suicide in the late Neoplatonist treatises on the nature of philosophy.

Plato's pupil Aristotle speaks of those who are thought to go after death to the Isles of the Blessed, and although he does not believe that this happens, he thinks the same would be true of such people and of the gods.[22] Would they have money, so as to practice generosity and justice? Would they face dangers, so as to need courage? Would they have passions, so as to need self-control? No, rather they would be exercising *thought*.

Plato was followed by many Christians. Even though they believed that we will be resurrected with a body, many of them felt that the appropriate, even if not the inevitable, occupation for the next life would be one of contemplation. At the end of the 4th century AD, Saint Augustine in his *Confessions*, as noticed in chapters five and nine, described the members of the heaven of heavens as having no memory of this life including their friends, but as being rapt in contemplation of God, even if in *City of God* (19.5) he believes that somehow the life of the saints must be social. He is disgusted in his controversy with Julian at the idea that there could be eating in heaven (*Against Julian* 5.5.22), and he held, as observed in chapter six, that there will be no genetic relationships after death, not even those of parent and child. Christ himself said that in heaven there would be no marriage, nor giving in marriage. Another 4th-century Christian, Gregory of Nyssa, however, as we have also noticed, offers the much more enticing view that life after death could be endlessly fascinating because there would be an infinite amount to find out about God.

The Christian ascetics living in solitude in the desert earlier in the same century had pushed human possibilities to the limit in trying to get rid of all emotion, although Augustine disapproved of this, in the hope of coming

---

22. Aristotle *Protrepticus* frag. 12, Ross, Walzer; *EN* 10.8, 1178b8–23.

closer to the state suited to the next life.[23] What I am suggesting is that if there were a disembodied after-life, it might require you to prepare yourself for a life with very different activities from those of the one we know.

Avicenna's view was particularly interesting, because he was disturbed by the suggestion that the next life might after all be rather the same as this one. It was seen in chapter twelve that he argued that it is soul not body that constitutes my essence, and that his Flying Man argument for this conclusion had much in common with the Cogito argument of Augustine. His view of life after death involved the continuation of disembodied soul, and his ideal was akin to the Neoplatonist one of a life of thinking. But he was worried by the physical character of some descriptions of the next life in the Koran, including descriptions of very physical rewards. His solution was that these descriptions were offered for the benefit of those who could not attain to the spiritual and intellectual kind of life beyond death to which he aspired. Such people would indeed be given a very different kind of after-life, a dream world based on their own imaginations, but with a kind of coherence missing from an ordinary dream. That dream world could incorporate, in a dream form, the kind of physical rewards that the Koran describes.[24] Avicenna is then describing the next life as either one of thinking or one of dreaming.

It is no accident that philosophers and theologians alike have so often settled on thinking or contemplation as the activity most easy to conceive as happening and to ascribe to an owner when no body is available. And it is no accident that they have also thought that we would have to prepare ourselves to enjoy an eternity of this very special range of activities, and no accident that Plato called philosophy a preparation for death. It is not easy to abandon our delight in all the varied activities of human life even if it be for pleasures that we may not know of. But if we do not prepare ourselves for the very different kind of life that might be available, that life, if it were to happen, might be a kind of hell. Of course, if there were no memory of the past life, there would be no regret, but with neither memory, nor similar activities, the question would be intensified of whether the same individual was still there.

Let us then recall instead a final possibility, which is in fact the possibility endorsed by ancient Christianity, that of resurrection with a body.

23. Richard Sorabji, *Emotion and Peace of Mind*, Oxford 2000, chap. 23.
24. Jean (= Yahya) Michot, *La destinée de l'homme selon Avicenne: le retour à Dieu et l'imagination*, Leuven 1986.

RESURRECTION

Resurrection with a body, like disembodied survival, is not something expected by science. Resurrection is thought to depend on a God, who is both benevolent and thinks us important. It is one of the striking features of Christianity that we are told that every hair of our head is numbered. If there is a God who cares about our individuality so much, that would for many people be very comforting. It was, of course, easier for those who accepted Plato and Aristotle to think of ourselves as being important. Although Plato and Aristotle did not believe that every hair of our head was numbered, they did think that the earth was at the center of the universe, and that humans were the most important species, not merely a product of evolution eventually to be superseded in its turn. They both knew of rival views. The ancient atomists had said that the earth was merely a speck in an infinite sea of worlds. And other predecessors had proposed theories of evolution and natural selection, which Plato and Aristotle consciously rejected. Plato even went so far as to reverse the evolution of humans out of apes. Rather, he suggested, animals evolved out of humans, but not by natural selection; rather by natural disselection. Animals were the reincarnations of humans who had led animal-like lives.

The idea of resurrection eliminates the problems we have just been looking at. The familiar range of experiences would be available to embodied persons, if that was thought appropriate, and there would be no puzzzle about what kind of owner the experiences could belong to. Even so, we encountered some problems in chapter three. It was not clear that the reassembly of our particles scattered through the universe, after having passed through other people, would give us back the very same bodies, or the very same persons. But the alternative, that we would be given new matter, imprinted with a photographic likeness of our former selves, raised the same questions of whether that would provide a mere replica of the former bodies and persons.

CHAPTER 18

Could we survive through time going in a circle?

THE POSSIBILITY IN PRINCIPLE

In the next two chapters, I shall ask whether survival of a different sort might be provided by natural instead of supernatural means, if time went round in a circle. And I shall also ask whether it is irrational to feel horror at the thought of not continuing to exist, or whether this represents a confusion.

We usually think of time as a straight line, but could time go around in a circle? [1] How could that be imagined? Think of yourself as standing on an old-fashioned clock face at the position of 3 o'clock. Then 12 o'clock would be behind you, and yet it would also lie in front of you. You could think of 12 o'clock as representing your birth. In that case, your birth would lie in two directions from you, both behind and in front. That would not mean that you had two births. There are not two 12 o'clocks on the clock face. It is merely that your birth lies in two directions, in the past but also in the future. This would seem to guarantee life with no permanent end. On your deathbed, you could reflect that in due course, your birth, your one and only birth, would be occurring.

That is what it would be like. But what on earth could induce anyone to think that it was actually the case? Suppose that there were only a finite number of distinguishable events in the history of the universe. We would then expect there to be a first event and a last event. But suppose further that every event seemed to have a preceding cause and a following effect, so that

1. I hope I have here improved, though I have also shortened, the argument I gave in *Matter, Space, and Motion*, Ithaca N.Y. 1988, ch. 10. Extra details can be found there.

none looked like a first or a last event. Would that mean that time had gone in a circle? Not necessarily. An alternative conclusion would be that history was repeating itself exactly, and that exactly similar events were recurring in an exactly similar cycle. In that case, only the events would be coming back round in a circle. Time itself would still be a straight line, and the similar events would be happening again further along the line. If there was never a last event, the cycle of events would, presumably be repeating itself without end, an infinite number of times.

But some people would think even one exact repetition impossible. How, they would ask, could the events be different if there was nothing to differentiate them, given that they were exactly alike? The obvious answer would be that the *time* was different. Some would ask, how could the time be different if there was nothing to differentiate the time, given that it was characterized by exactly similar events? But others would say that times can be different, even if there is nothing further to differentiate them.[2] I am inclined to agree with that, and consequently so far I do not see a reason to say that time itself, as opposed to the events, was forming a circle.

On the other hand, presumably, if events were happening again in exactly the same way as before, that could not be a mere coincidence, especially, if they happened in an exactly similar way an infinite number of times. In that case, something must be *forcing* them to recur in exactly the same way. What then if we found good evidence that there was no forcing[3] because there were quantum jumps that were not necessitated by anything? This is in fact the view of quantum physics. Nothing makes it inevitable that a small lump of radioactive material will emit radiation in the next sixty seconds. If it does, that is undetermined and not inevitable. We should need to be sure that there were no other sources of necessity, for example that God was not constrained to make history recur in exactly the same way, because his good nature did not allow him to accept anything less than the best possible history. If we had good reason to believe that no necessity was operating, we could not stomach the consequence that history was by mere chance repeating itself exactly again and again. Now we should need another hypothesis. And this is where circular time would come in.

The situation now would be that there is no first event lacking a pre-

2. As argued by R. W. Adams, 'Primitive thisness', *Journal of Philosophy* 76, 1979, 5–26.

3. This type of empirical evidence for a single circle rather than repetition is suggested by Susan Weir, *An Inquiry into the Possibility and Implications of a Closed Temporal Topology*, Ph.D. diss., Bristol 1985.

decessor nor a last event lacking a successor. Yet this is not because history is repeating itself infinitely many times, nor because there is an infinite number of distinguishable events—we started by postulating a finite number. With infinity of either kind ruled out, we need a different explanation of there being no first event or last. The best explanation would be that time was circular. A circle of time would contain no first time and no last time, and that would now be the best explanation of there being no first or last event, despite the series of events being finite. A large circle of millions of years would be the least problematic, as we shall see. Although we should die, we should also be able always to have our birth in the future.

Every event in circular time, including your birth, would be both past and future. Does that make a nonsense of the distinction between past and future? No, if you sail around the globe, starting from London, although you leave London behind, London will always be ahead of you also. And circular time would be like spherical space in this regard.

But do not the notions of past and future refer to the direction of time from past to future, and would there be any direction, if all events lie equally in the past and the future? Yes, there would still be one single direction, because for any three events there would be a particular order in which they could be *reached*. If a tree is planted, sprouts, and gives shade, all three events are equally past and future, yet from the planting, the shading can only be *reached via* the sprouting. You cannot *reach* these events in a different order, such as planting, then shading, then sprouting. Reaching is a mobile notion, unlike the static notion of lying. All events *lie* equally in the past and future. To bring out the directionality, we need to appeal to *reaching*. (Some people appeal instead to one-way processes like entropy, but I do not believe that that helps, since entropy *presupposes* direction in time).

There would also be a set order of explanation. The planting would be needed for the shading, *because* it was needed for the sprouting. Explanation would also retain its directionality.

What if there were no empirical evidence, such as evidence of determinism or indeterminism, to favor the single circle account or its rival? This would not be fatal to the description in terms of circular time, but it would alter the force of the description in a way suggested by Quine.[4] We might then have two legitimate descriptions, but they would be descriptions of one situation, two descriptions without a difference. Before agreeing that this was actually the case, however, we should need to be sure that there was no relevant evidence waiting to be found.

4. W. V. O. Quine, 'Comments on Newton-Smith', *Analysis* 39, 1979, 66–67.

OUR ACTUAL SITUATION

So far I have said only that the universe might have been so constructed as to allow time to be circular. But is there any chance that the actual universe we live in really is like this? The great mathematician Gödel thought so.[5] Relativity theory implies, he said, that if one could reach a high enough velocity in a space rocket, and if the matter in the universe is distributed in a certain way, then as a space traveler you would loop back in your personal time to the past long before your birth. In that case, your birth would lie in your personal future, so that we should have the same result: that you could look forward to your birth always being in your future. Gödel's case is different from the one I have described in that, following relativity theory, he is talking of your personal time. Those not in the space rocket with you would have a different time, and their time would not loop. It would be best if you jumped in a discontinuous or incommensurable leap backwards in personal time. If instead your personal time in the space rocket slid smoothly backwards, we would get the funny situation that when in your space rocket you had glided backwards for five minutes of your personal time, you would also in that same personal time be on the ground five minutes before launch. We should have to wonder whether there would be enough atoms to make up both of you, the one still on the ground and the one already aloft.

But what about the shared time of those of us who do not travel at these velocities in space rockets? Does modern physics rule out the possibility of our time being circular, with its theory that everything started from a big bang? No: why should it rule out circularity? For modern physics admits that it has nothing to say about whether anything occurred before the big bang. That bang might merely have been the most recent bang in an alternating series of explosions and implosions. Such a universe, though the merest speculation, has been called a ping-pong universe. Could not a ping-pong universe form a great circle of time punctuated by pings and pongs, none of them looking like the first or last?

With any universe in circular time, the physics would need to be different, because everything that was done in the past would need to be undone in time for it to be done in the future. Your atoms, scattered at your one and only death, would need to be assembled in time for your one and only birth.

5. Kurt Gödel, 'A remark about the relationship between Relativity Theory and Idealistic Philosophy', in P. A. Schilpp, ed., *Albert Einstein: Philosopher-Scientist*, New York 1951, 555–62.

That should not be difficult, given a large circle of time. But the case of a ping-pong circle would create a special difficulty. No atoms survive in the intense chaos of a big bang. Since you have only one birth in circular time, your future birth needs the very same atoms as it needed before. But after a big bang, your atoms could only be re-identified as similar atoms, similarly placed, not as the very same atoms. There would be no independent way of establishing more than exact similarity. There is a tension here between the needs of the circular hypothesis that only one set of atoms can be involved in your one and only birth and the lack of any independent way of giving sense to the idea that the very same atoms have survived through a big bang. Does this mean that after all, although time might have been circular, the big bang has in fact ruled this out? Or could the case for time being circular give sense on its own to the claim that the very same atoms were in play, despite the senselessness of the idea of tracing them through a big bang? I am supposing that the situation might be best described in terms of the very same atoms, despite the atoms not being traceable in principle.

THE CRAZY FORTY-YEAR CIRCLE

But now I want to introduce a complication. Can we imagine a small time circle, say, one of forty years? We know that we are not living in a universe with a forty-year time circle, but would such a universe even be possible in principle? Now, if you died at age thirty-nine, you would only need to wait one year in order to be born. Or you could last all forty years, if you dwindled down into the very seeds from which you were born. This would fulfill the prediction of the Presocratic philosopher Alcmaeon, to be quoted below, that we should be immortal if we could join our beginning to our end.

This already shows that the physics of a forty-year cycle would need to be very different indeed, if everything done was to be undone in time for its future doing. You would need to shed your childhood atoms in time for them to be available to the baby, so atoms would be racing hither and thither. You could also kill your parents, but they would need to be resuscitated in time to give birth to you.

There might seem to be a new danger that in a forty-year cycle, an event might cause itself, either causally explaining itself, or causally guaranteeing itself, or being a causally necessary prerequisite for itself. Suppose I plant a tree, and that helps to bring about the shade in my house. Might the shade motivate me to do the planting? And in that case would not the planting *indirectly* have caused the planting? I think not. Certainly, it does not *follow* that if, A (planting) explains B (shading), and B (shading) explains C (planting), A (planting) has to explain C (planting). We should need in the new situation to treat causal guarantees and causal prerequisites in the same way as we treat explanations and be ready just to refuse to allow that an event is ever causally related to itself.

But what would the psychological demands of a forty-year cycle be like? You need not worry that it would be tedious to live the same life over again almost at once, because you would not be living it again. In a time circle, you live only once, even though your life is both past and future. It might be tedious, if you were born with memory of your life, and not only tedious, but also a source of terror and guilt at what you knew was going to happen. It would also interfere with deliberation if you already knew the outcome. Even stranger, if when planting a tree, you remembered planting it, then presumably you could in principle remember remembering. But all these ills could be cured at one blow, if we assume that birth wipes out memory, just as we silently assumed this in the case of a long time circle, or at least that it wipes out most memory. The long and the short circle are not in principle different in this regard.

One psychological demand would be severe if you realized that time was circular and that all progress would be undone. This is what Augustine thought revolting about the different hypothesis that history will repeat itself exactly. Christ's crucifixion and attempt to redeem us would then have been pointless. In circular time too, we should have to accept, if we understood our situation, that any achievement would be undone. The best psychological attitude for coping with this would be to try to enjoy the *process* of bringing something about and not set our hearts on the *outcome* of the process. This was recommended in any case by the ancient Stoics and Epicureans, who told you to live in the present, not in the future. The unending future offered by this short circle would, if recognized, call for a lot of psychological adjustment.

But now let me imagine something even stranger. Suppose that you neither died nor dwindled after forty years of the forty-year circle. We should now have to distinguish your personal time from the universal time of forty years. Your personal time would be the fifty years that you remember of your life, although the universe has actually lasted only 40 years, with you, as we shall see, reduplicated in ten of them. You could last to a personal age of fifty years, provided that you moved out of the way to make room for your younger self to be born, and provided you shed the particles making up your body in time for your younger self to pick them up. Buildings and trees could not have a personal time of more than forty years, because they cannot, except by perishing, move out of the way of each other and transfer their particles. You and your baby self could converse with each other.

We should have to extend our concept of a person. There would be a strong case for saying that the elder was the same person as the younger. For the body would have traced a single path through space and time. By a single path, I mean that if relays of detectives had followed the body of the baby from infancy, later members of the team would find that they finished up dogging the footsteps of the older person, and they would encounter no such splitting as jeopardized talk of the same person in chapter four. The older person would also remember doing what the younger person did. He or she would have all the normal links with the younger person so that there would be good reason to allow that he or she was the same person. But on the other hand, if there is only one person, it would change our concept of person to allow that a person could be in two bodies in different places and in two different states of mind at the same time. This would normally be taken as establishing two persons. There might be painful decisions to make, as there sometimes are in linear time in connection with brain-damaged persons, as to whether there were two persons or one. For purposes of marriage, one might marry one, and not the other. For purposes of medical history, one should consider both as one.

You would now have more than one vantage point simultaneously both on the external world and on yourself. And in your two minds you would see your baby self and your older self both from the inside and from the outside. You could also remember your younger vantage point. The possibility mentioned before of killing your parent could now be extended. The older self could kill the younger, provided that the younger was resuscitated in time to be the killer. The world would be the richer because it would contain juxtaposed developments that went beyond the first forty years of your personal time. The world would be richer still if you lived to ninety years of personal time. Then there could be three juxtaposed selves. Whenever you died there would be at least one self surviving and possibly more.

IRREVOCABILITY AND INEVITABILITY

But circular time does not require anything as complicated as a forty-year circle, much less a forty-year circle in which people live to a personal time of fifty years. So the idea of circular time does not stand and fall with these possibilities. I want to finish by looking at two further questions. I said that in circular time the universe would need to be indeterministic. That is, the events in it should not have been inevitable all along. But since every event in circular time would be past, would not every event be irrevocable, and therefore inevitable? There is a counter-argument: since every event in circular time would be future, would it not remain forever open what was going to happen? Which conclusion should we believe? The case for irrevocability says that if I consider planting a tree, in order to give shade to my house in the future, that future, in circular time, is also past, and so the shading or nonshading of my house is already irrevocable. So, for that matter, is the planting or nonplanting.

But the shading would not be irrevocable, I believe, and I think we can see this by considering what we mean by irrevocability. I believe irrevocability needs to be defined in terms of 'were' and 'would'. To say that the shading is irrevocable is to say that even if I *were* to refrain from planting, it *would* make no difference to my house having been shaded. But if that is what irrevocability means, it is not true that the past shading is irrevocable. For if I *were* to refrain from planting, it might very well make a difference. My house might well not have been shaded.

There is another mistake that we must avoid. It concerns the difference between 'will not' and 'cannot'. If my house has already been shaded because of tomorrow's tree-planting, it follows that I *will not* refrain from planting. It does not follow that I *cannot* refrain from planting.

If we want to deploy the word 'cannot', we shall have to deploy it at a different point in the sentence. It *cannot* be the case that my house has been shaded by my tomorrow's planting and that I refrain from planting tomorrow. But now we must guard against a further mistake. It concerns the difference between the impossibility of a certain combination, and the impossibility of refraining. What is impossible here is the *combination* of planting with refraining from planting, and it tells us nothing relevant that that *combination* is impossible. What has not been shown is that the *refraining* itself is impossible.

It may be wondered if there are other sources of inevitability. Certainly, we need not be bugged by some interfering memory that we did or didn't plant, which would inhibit our deliberating what to do. For as mentioned before, memories need not all be preserved. Nor need there be causes compelling us to plant. Causal factors will compel, if they are themselves irrevocable, and if furthermore they necessitate. I do not think that either is true of our case. I have just been claiming that things would not be irrevocable. I have also argued elsewhere[6] that what is caused is not in every case necessitated.

BACKWARDS CAUSATION

Let me come to my last subject. Circular time seems to have committed me to backwards causation. I could plant a tree tomorrow in order to shade my house yesterday. And backwards causation has been said to be impossible. The most powerful objection to backwards causation that I know is the 'sabotage' objection of Michael Dummett.[7] But the objection is addressed to backwards causation in linear time and I believe it is inapplicable to circular. I have some additional doubts about it in any case, and I also have some qualifications to make to the claim that in circular time causation runs backwards.

In a way, causation in circular time is no more backwards than forwards, since the planting is past and the shading future as much as the other way round. In addition, as stated above, as between the three events of planting, sprouting, and shading, the order of reaching and the order of explanation is in the usual direction. Nonetheless, let us consider the sabotage objection.

The sabotage objection is that after yesterday's shading, sabotage could have prevented tomorrow's planting, so (it is alleged) tomorrow's planting cannot be the cause. Why can it not be the cause? There have been several suggestions on this, but let me take the simplest two. Once the shading has happened, it is irrevocable, so the planting cannot be needed, as is shown by the fact that if we were to sabotage the planting, the shading would still have taken place. Alternatively, it will have been shown that the planting does not add to the probability of the shading.

To these two versions of the sabotage objection, there are several answers. First, as I have said, in circular time, the shading is not irrevocable, nor, to speak in terms of 'were' and 'would', can it be assumed that the shading *would* still have taken place, even if we *were* to sabotage planting. Hence the planting might well be needed. Actually, in circular time, nothing would

6. Richard Sorabji, *Necessity, Cause, and Blame*, London and Ithaca N.Y. 1980, ch. 2.

7. Michael Dummett, 'Can an effect precede its cause?', *Proceedings of the Aristotelian Society*, supp. vol., 28, 1954, 27–44; 'Bringing about the past', *Philosophical Review* 73, 1964, 338–59.

become irrevocable: it would be either irrevocable or revocable at all times. I have argued above for the latter: irrevocability.

But second, suppose that shading *would* still have taken place. This would not show that planting had not in fact been its cause, but only that planting was not a necessary prerequisite, because other causes of tree-shade would have been available in case of need, such as windblown seedlings or underground suckers.

It would also show that planting does not increase the probability of tree-shade. But that can be freely admitted. The planting could still have been the cause, even if it made shading *less* probable, as well it might, for the seedlings and suckers might be a more reliable method of securing tree-shade, and the planting might have been obstructing these more reliable methods. Admittedly, it could be debated whether they would have produced exactly the same shade or merely another instance of shade. This would depend on how we count shadows.

There has been another reply to the sabotage objection, which does not, however, tempt me. It has been suggested that the sabotage of planting might turn out to be frustrated, however hard the saboteurs tried. Would that show that planting really was the cause? I am not tempted either by the reply that has been suggested to this reply, that it would rather show that the planting was the *effect* of the shading. Although the mechanism of such causation would be unfamiliar, it has been said, at least the causation would be in the normal direction, from past to future.

This exchange seems to me mistaken. For one thing, in circular time, the frustration of sabotage would be no more forwards causation than backwards. Further, in circular time, even if yesterday's shading was causing tomorrow's planting, that would not, given the circularity, prevent tomorrow's planting *also* causing yesterday's shading. Indeed, that double direction of causation might be confirmed. For if, in circular time, shading could not be sabotaged after planting any more easily than planting after shading, the failure of sabotage ought to show, if it shows anything at all, that each causes the other.

But does it show anything at all? The mechanism of such causation is admitted to be unfamiliar. And it would be even more unfamiliar if there were, say, three possible causes of shading, namely planting, seedlings, and suckers. By what possible mechanism could shading frustrate sabotage on all three causes and guarantee that at least one of the three would occur? If that really happened, rather than conclude that shading was the cause, we might rather conclude that nature allowed such things as shading only when paired with a cause. And that conclusion would leave intact the claim that tomorrow's planting could cause yesterday's shading.

I do not think that circular time involves backwards causation of any unacceptable kind.

CONCLUSION CONCERNING MORTALITY

I can now draw a conclusion about surviving death. I believe that circular time is in principle possible. There is no reason to assert, but also no way to deny, that our universe, despite its inclusion of at least one big bang, might involve a huge circle of time. As we would have no knowledge of this, we cannot enjoy, if this is what we want, more than the possibility that our dying breath will not be our last. In principle it would have been possible for there to be a universe with a forty-year time cycle. In such a universe, we might dwindle and regrow, rather than die, or be dead only very briefly. But it would be an extremely bizarre universe, and it would take much psychological effort to make it tolerable.

GREEK ANTECEDENTS FOR CIRCULAR TIME

There are several passages that have been, or might be, thought to anticipate the idea of circular time. But often it turns out that no more is meant than that *events* come round in a circle, as for example the seasons do. That does not put in doubt the idea that *time* is best represented by a straight line.

In one passage, reported by Simplicius (*Commentary on Physics* 732,26 – 733,1), Aristotle's pupil Eudemus is only reducing to absurdity the idea first found in the Pythagoreans that the universe will repeat its history exactly in cycles. He uses Aristotle's definition of time as the countable aspect of motion in respect of before and after to provide a refutation: since everything countable would be the same, the time would not after all be different, and there would be no repetition. He does not go on from there to argue that time would be circular.

Proclus considers two cases, when he explains the reference in Plato's *Parmenides* (141A–B) to becoming younger. When I reach the age of ten, my nine-year-old self becomes younger than my ten-year-old self. But for Plato in *Timaeus* 39D the motions of the planets are time, and eventually, the planets will get back to their original alignments (*sunapokatastasis*) (Proclus *in Tim.* 3.84,1). Thus the planets and their souls are, in a fuller sense than me, getting younger by approaching the beginning of time, and time, at least measured time, will start again. But I understand this as a case of *measured* time, not of time itself, going in a circle. In that case it is not different in principle from the idea of the *seasons* coming round in a circle, although Proclus will be talking of giant seasons and a giant year.

A. A. Long has made the very interesting suggestion that the Stoics were postulating a single circle rather than endless repetition, in their theory of eternal recurrence, which was considered in chapter three above.[8] This would have an advantage of enabling them to maintain for events and for times, as well as for individuals, the idea that when A and B are indistinguishable (do not differ in their properties), they are one and the same.[9] But I think there are two obstacles. First, Ricardo Salles has pointed out that the reports on the Stoics use the idea of events occurring again (*palin;* Alexander *Commentary On Prior Analytics* 180, 33−36) and indeed many times (*pollakis;* Nemesius *On the Nature of Man* 111,20−23). So it does not look as if the principle just cited, the principle known as identity of indiscernibles, was applied by the Stoics to events and times.[10] Second, if the Stoics had intended the idea of a single circle, they would have had to work out a drastically altered physics and set of attitudes to life. They would have to reconsider their views on freedom, causation, and responsibility. I see no trace of this in them, and they would have met with positive difficulties. For one thing, they were determinists, and it was indeterminism that I suggested would be needed for the hypothesis of a single circle.

Despite this, I have argued that there is one passage that tries to express a more rigorous idea of circular time and to draw conclusions for mortality, despite its inappropriate use of concepts like beginning, end, revert, and again, and despite rejecting the conception it describes. The pseudo-Aristotelian *Problemata* formulates an argument according to which we are earlier, as well as later, than the people of Troy, because things are circular. Unfortunately, the argument supports the idea of our being earlier by postulating a beginning and suggesting that we might be nearer to it than are

8. A. A. Long, 'The Stoics on world-conflagration and everlasting recurrence', *Southern Journal of Philosophy* vol. 23, supp., ed. R. Epp.

9. The Stoic interest in this principle, the identity of indiscernibles, was applied to times by Jonathan Barnes, 'La doctrine du retour éternel', in Jacques Brunschwig, ed., *Les stoïciens et leur logique*, Paris 1978, 3−20, esp. 12.

10. Ricardo Salles, 'The individuation of times in orthodox Stoicism', in his ed., *Metaphysics, Soul, and Ethics: Themes from the Work of Richard Sorabji*, Oxford, 2004.

the people of Troy. The pseudo-Aristotelian author then has no difficulty, in the closing sentence, in dismissing the argument by pointing out that a circle contains no beginning. And he looks for no other way in which the circular hypothesis might be true. What is very interesting, however, is that he compares a remark of Alcmaeon, the philosopher of the 5th century BC who was at least a friend of Pythagoreans, if not a Pythagorean himself. Alcmaeon says that people die because they are not able to join beginning to end. This remark has been considered hard to understand.[11] It has been taken to mean either that the soul will eventually be unable to complete its circling motions[12] or that the body will be eventually unable to complete its physiological cycles.[13] But interesting as are the parallels about soul circles and physiological circles, when they are viewed as mere parallels, it needs to be considered that Alcmaeon may be making a fresh point here, and one of very considerable interest. Humans would be immortal if they could only join their beginning to their end, that is, if they could dwindle into the very seeds from which they came. Of course, the seeds would have to be the very same ones in order that the ensuing life might be the same life—their own. Alcmaeon need not have worked out what would make that possible, but merely assumed that it was impossible. But the pseudo-Aristotelian author connects Alcmaeon's idea with that of circular time. And the discussion of circular time above has provided a set of hypotheses under which the immortality that Alcmaeon regards as impossible would actually come about. For people in the forty-year circle envisaged above could dwindle into the very seeds from which they came, and in doing so, they would secure a kind of immortality. Here is the passage.

Ps-Aristotle *Problemata* 17.3, 916a18–39:

> How should we take 'earlier' and 'later'? In the sense that the people in the time of Troy are earlier than us, and the people before them are earlier than them, and as you go higher the people are always earlier? Alternatively, if there is a

11. Charles Kahn, 'Anaximander and the arguments concerning the *Apeiron* at *Physics* 203b4–15', in H. Diller and H. Erbse, eds., *Festschrift Ernst Kapp*, Hamburg 1958, 19–29, at p. 26; G. S. Kirk, J. E. Raven, and M. Schofield, eds., *The Presocratic Philosophers*[2], Cambridge 1983, 347; Jonathan Barnes, *The Presocratic Philosophers*, vol. 1, London 1979, 115.

12. J. Burnet, *Early Greek Philosophy*[4], 1930, repr. Cleveland 1957, 195; A. E. Taylor, *A Commentary on Plato's Timaeus*, Oxford 1928, 262–63; cf. W. K. C. Guthrie, *A History of Greek Philosophy*, vol. 1, Cambridge 1962, 356.

13. Kahn, 'Anaximander and the arguments concerning the *Apeiron* at *Physics* 203b4–15'; Charles Mugler, 'Alcméon et les cycles physiologiques de Platon', *Revue des Études Grecques* 71, 1958, 42–50.

beginning, middle, and end of the universe, and a man too, when he grows old and comes to his limit, reverts again to his beginning, and things nearer the beginning are earlier, what prevents us from being closer to the beginning part? If we are, we will also be earlier. Just as in motion there is a circle for the heavens and for every star, what prevents the formation and destruction of perishable things being such that the same things [reading: *t'auta*] are always being formed and destroyed? They also say that human affairs form a circle like that.

Now it is simple-minded to think that those being born are always numerically the same people, but we could more readily accept that they are the same in kind. Thus [sc. on their mistaken view] we ourselves would be earlier, and someone could posit that the order of the series was such as to turn back again to the beginning and to make things continuous and to remain forever in an identical state. In fact, Alcmaeon says that people die simply because they are not able to join beginning to end—a clever remark, if you take him to be speaking impressionistically and do not want to make the saying precise.

Now if there is a circle, and a circle has neither beginning nor end, people could not be earlier by being closer to a beginning, neither we earlier than they, nor they than us.

In this chapter and the previous one, I have surveyed some ways in which we might survive death. In the next, I shall ask whether it is irrational to be dismayed if we do not.

CHAPTER 19

If we do not survive death, is it irrational to feel dismay?

FINITE LIFE NOT POINTLESS

In the last two chapters, I have discussed four ways in which we might be expected to survive death: reincarnation, disembodiment, resurrection, and time going round in a circle. All turned out to have their difficulties, though I did not exclude them all as impossible methods. Nonetheless, if we do not survive, is it irrational to feel dismay at that prospect? I certainly do not accept the view that annihilation would make life pointless. If there is no point in a life of four score years, it will not gain point by being prolonged, even indefinitely. But I want to consider the opposite view: that fear of annihilation, so far from being justified, is irrational. Of various reasons that have been, or might be, suggested for rejecting dismay, I shall mention some only briefly.

NO-SELF AND COMPASSION

By far the most space has been given in chapter fifteen to the view that there is no continuous self (eliminativism) or that, if there is, it is no more than an embodied stream of psycho-physical events (reductionism). Both views were found among ancient Buddhists and one of them in Derek Parfit. If persuasive, this would make the fear of death irrational. On the eliminativist view, death does not threaten loss of a continuing self, because there is no such self to lose. At the intellectual level, I sided against these views. But the Buddhists related the intellectual level to the practice of spiritual exercises of compassion. In the case of Śântideva, it was held necessary for Buddhist purposes to retain the illusion of self and others, the latter to serve as objects of compassion. In the exercises, one would imagine exchanging places with others, and picture oneself from their unflattering point of view. These exercises surely would increase the sense of the unimportance of the distinction of self and other and help lead to Śântideva's view that there is no difference between the suffering of self and that of other. This in turn he expects to lead to fulfillment and loss of fear for oneself. It seems likely that it would both strengthen belief in the metaphysical view that there is no distinction between self and other and reduce the concern for self and the related fear of death. But Śântideva's exercises on compassion are not for anyone to adopt, since they follow his renunciation of sex and embracement of solitude.

Derek Parfit also recognized the link between denying that there is more than a continuing stream and the recognition that there is not such a separation between streams as is normally assumed by those who believe in separate persons.[1] But he operated at an entirely intellectual level, without the spiritual exercises. In this respect, ancient Greek thought, especially in late Antiquity, is closer to Buddhism in combining intellectual thought with spiritual exercise, as I have mentioned. Spiritual exercise would surely be important for producing the kind of conviction needed for producing real freedom from fear and selfishness.

SELF CONTINUOUS WITH OTHERS

The idea that self is not so independent of others can also be found elsewhere. The Stoics emphasized in their ethics that we are only parts of a whole, like mutually supporting stones in an arch. The Neoplatonist Plotinus took this further, being attracted by the idea, but also resistant to it, that we all share the same soul. But the strongest sense I have ever got of the unity of all things was from an exhibition of American Indian poems, sayings, and customs in the Museum of Indian Arts and Culture in Santa Fe. According to the presenters, hunters thought of themselves as needing to conduct a ceremony before it would be permissible to draw energy from the victim to themselves. Grinders of grain saw the grinding as making the very grinding stones happy. Dancers felt that everything was joining them in

---

1. Derek Parfit, *Reasons and Persons*, Oxford, 1984, corrected edition 1987, 332–39. As in previous chapters, page citations refer to the 1987 edition.

their dance. At death they saw themselves as returning to the earth from which their ancestors had sprung. The sense of unity would not be accessible to our culture but might surely reduce the sense of personal loss if they expected to lose such individuality as they had had. Admittedly, other customs suggest that they did indeed retain a strong sense of individuality, for example the custom whereby the first person to make a baby laugh had to give a party for it.

IS THE FLOW OF TIME REAL?

There are entirely different approaches. Fear of annihilation at death depends on the assumption that time flows. What is future becomes present and then past, and there is a constant flow in which it makes no difference whether we think of the future as traveling towards us, or of ourselves as traveling towards the future. The fear, for those who feel it, is that possibly their future will sooner or later all be over and forever past. If time does not really flow, the fear is incoherent. For it can be formulated only in such terms as 'future', 'will', 'soon', 'over', and 'past'. Let us then consider these terms.

These terms belong to the same group as was mentioned in chapter one, a group that includes the word 'I', but I am now especially interested in the temporal members of the group. The temporal members include also other tenses, 'was' and 'is', along with 'now', 'today', 'tomorrow', 'yesterday', 'ago', 'still to come', etc. These terms are to be contrasted with temporal terms like 'the year 2006', 'before the battle of Hastings', 'after the battle of Hastings', or 'simultaneously with the battle of Hastings'. What is before the battle of Hastings, or 2006 years after the birth of Christ, is *changelessly* so. By contrast, what is past, or future, or soon is *not* always so, but has become, or will become, or cease to be so. Hence terms like 'past' and 'future' reflect the *flow* of time.

These flow-related terms, like the term 'I', have a unique ability to guide our emotions and actions. It does not frighten me if I know that December 12, 2006, is the day I die, unless I can also know that December 12, 2006, is *today* and not a hundred years hence. There are also, as I have said, non-temporal words that guide actions and emotions in the same way, such as 'I', 'you', 'here', 'this', and 'that'. It does not frighten me to know that today is the day that Richard Sorabji dies, unless I can know that *I* am Richard Sorabji.

Have these words anything else in common? One suggestion is that they can all be paraphrased by a certain demonstrative use of the word 'this'. To think of the present is to think of *this* time, or of the time of *this* occurrence, where '*this*' can pick out any suitable occurrence, but one always conveniently available to the thinker will be the thinker's thought. To think of the past or future is to think of what is earlier or later than *this* time, or than the time of *this* occurrence. Similarly, to think in terms of 'here' is to think in terms of *this* place.

Admittedly, some references to presentness will be indirect and require a correspondingly indirect paraphrase. If I think that my life *will* be past at some time, this reference to pastness does not mean that my life will be earlier than the time of *this* thought of mine. Rather, I imply that at some time someone else would be right to think of me, 'His life is earlier than *this* thought', where '*this*' refers to the *thinker's* new thought. A converse admission is that some uses of the term 'present', although paraphrasable in terms of 'this', introduce a changeless truth, and correspondingly do not guide emotion and action, e.g., 'His death is past, present, or future'.

We are now in a position to consider the claim that the flow-related terms express a mere illusion. One objection has been that every event, for example the battle of Hastings in 1066, is all three—past, present, and future—and that this involves a contradiction. But the battle is these only at different times. And no regress need start, since, if I am asked to specify the different times, I need not call them past present and future, but can simply give examples, such as the years 1000, 1066, and 2006. Examples are enough, for I am not giving a general account of what is meant by 'past', 'present', and 'future', having already done that in terms of the word 'this'.

A second objection is that although we need to make judgments of pastness and futurity, there are no facts about pastness and futurity corresponding to the judgments, because what makes the judgments true can be expressed in terms of being earlier or later than a given thinker's thought. But it seems to me that the person who does not know that the day of his death is *today* is best described as not knowing a certain very important fact.

A third objection is that there might well have been no conscious beings in the universe, and at least in that case, there would have been no past, present, or future. For my account of the three terms 'past', 'present', and 'future' introduces the demonstrative word, 'this', which only confirms how egocentric the three terms are. In a universe without conscious beings who could think in demonstrative terms, the word 'this' would have no application. I believe that this objection is mistaken in at least two ways. For one thing, if we think that in that universe, there might have been no people up to *now*, this reference to our now does not smuggle us illegitimately into the imagined scene, but only relates the imagined scene to the time of us who are imagining it from the outside. Second, if we have the thought that in that universe, as in ours, events would come to be past and over, we would be imagining what could have been said, if within that person-less universe there had after all been a person. That person *would* have been able to think, 'So and so is over', i.e., to think, 'So and so is earlier than *this* time'. Once again, this is not illegitimately to smuggle an *actual* observer into the observer-free scene.

A final objection is that relativity theory gives a complete account of time without making use of any of the terms related to flow. But the answer is that the account given by relativity theory is incomplete insofar as it does not cover the temporal notions that physicists need in order to carry out their experiments, and one of these notions is '*now*'.

The fear of annihilation would indeed have been incoherent, if the flow of time had been unreal, but I have not been able to see how it can be unreal.

IMMORTALITY BORING?

There has been another reason for regarding the fear of annihilation as irrational. It has been said that immortal life would be boring, and the fictional case of Elina Makropoulos has been cited. Having taken an elixir at the age of 42 that maintained her with the attributes of a 42-year-old, she decided at 342 years to die because her life was so boring.[2] But in the story told that way, there are several mistakes. First, even if immortal life was boring, that tells us nothing about whether annihilation is not also an evil to be feared.

But worse, Makropoulos' mistake was to rule out progress by remaining with the attributes of a 42-year-old. The very antithesis of this is the view mentioned earlier of Gregory of Nyssa in the 4th century AD, who looked forward after death to a life of perpetual progress on the grounds that there would be an infinite amount to discover, in his view to discover about God. Gregory of Nyssa thus cleverly avoids both boredom and satiety. Why indeed should there not be an infinite number of things that it would be worthwhile coming to understand, and an infinity of interactions between persons in which it would be worth engaging? None of this is to deny

2. Bernard Williams, 'The Makropoulos case: reflections on the tedium of immortality', in his *Problems of the Self,* Cambridge 1973, ch. 6.

that a community in which everyone was immortal would have to be very different from any we know. There could not be careers, marriages, or families as we know them.

It needs to be admitted that the right choice for Makropoulos would be a difficult one to achieve. Psychological maturing is desirable, physical aging is not, as illustrated by the ancient Greek myth of Tithonus. Eos, the Dawn, gained immortality for him, but forgot to ask for eternal youth. Eventually, she turned him into a cricket and carried him in a basket, so that at least she could hear his voice. Crickets were thought to be immortal because of their annual shedding of skin. The story provides a salutary reminder that it cannot but affect our psychology whether our bodies remain like those of a forty-five-year-old human, or shrivel to become like those of a cricket. This is despite Plotinus' attempt to resist such a conclusion in connection with his spherical bodies discussed in chapter six.

ESCAPE FROM TIME PREFERABLE?

Another view is that everlasting life is to be avoided because it is a life set in time, whereas the truly happy life escapes from time. This is the view, for example, of Plotinus in the 3rd century AD and of the mystical tradition that he influenced. It would incidentally exclude boredom for another reason: that there would be neither passage of time, nor sense of it. Plotinus took the sense of timelessness that mystics experience as evidence of what reality was really like, not as an illusion from which one returned to reality. Influential as his idea has been, I confess that I have not been able to understand it. The kind of life to which we aspire would have to involve consciousness, and I have not been able to see what it would be for consciousness not to occur in time. In Plotinus' view, although this was contested, the timeless consciousness of our higher soul is uninterrupted; it is only our attention to it during life that is intermittent.

CONTENTLESS CONSCIOUSNESS IS ALL THERE IS

There is a strand in Indian philosophy that would challenge the assumption I have just expressed, that the life to which we aspire would have to involve consciousness, if that is consciousness *of* things, as we normally understand it to be. Yoga is not just a practical but also a metaphysical system, and the Sâṃkhya Yoga of Patanjali, as amplified in a commentary of the 4th century AD, adumbrates a view of consciousness and self that was developed more fully by the Advaitans from Śaṅkara in the 8th century AD onwards. Everything is reducible to one thing, *brahman*. One's self is one's consciousness, but these are really *brahman*. Moreover, that consciousness is not consciousness of things, but only of itself. Consciousness of other things due to embodiment is not real, and to understand this is liberation. Here the contentlessness of consciousness that in Greek thought was raised as a worrying possibility is viewed as the true reality to be embraced.

This understanding is reached through a series of exercises. First, one thinks of self as one's body. Then, with exercises, one comes to see it as one's breath; then as one's external perceptions; then as inner awareness; then as intellect. But all these are only physical sheaths of decreasing materiality. The first three sheaths remind one of the three vehicles of the soul postulated by Neoplatonists: fleshly, pneumatic, and luminous. When all five sheaths have been rejected, one recognizes the self, which is consciousness, but not consciousness of anything.[3]

The Nyaya opponents of the Advaitans raised an objection to such self-consciousness, curiously like that which Plato had also raised, when, much earlier and quite independently, he considered self-consciousness of this kind. If there is no consciousness of anything else, self-consciousness will not have anything to be conscious of—it will have no content. Seeing was an example used by Śaṅkara to illustrate his type of self-consciousness, but it had also been used as an example on the other side by Plato. We might put the difficulty by saying that seeing needs to be directed to qualities like color, light, and shade. If there was no seeing of color, light, and shade, sight could not see itself operating, for there would be no content for it to get hold of. Another Indian system, Mimamsa, concluded that in liberation there is no kind of consciousness at all. But the Advaitans tried to insist that the idea of such consciousness was coherent, although they conceded that the consciousness could not be experienced.[4]

Such a bald summary of vast systems of thought and controversy cannot hope to do justice to them. But all I need say for our purposes is that the

3. My account is derived from conversations with Arindam Chakrabarti, but any errors are my own.

4. I take this information from Ram Prasad, *Knowledge and Liberation in Classical Indian Thought*, London 1991, 172, with translation from Śaṅkara, *Brhadâranyaka upanisadbhâsya*, Poona 1914, I. iv.10, 161–62.

fear of annihilation depends on the fear of losing all consciousness and self-hood as we know it. If we could understand how consciousness and selfhood are very different from what we suppose, we might well find that our fear of annihilation is misconceived.

PAST NON-EXISTENCE IS NO EVIL

I come finally to the view that I find most useful at the intellectual level, al-though I supect that it cannot be as effective as the route of spiritual exer-cise. It is that we do not feel horror at our past non-existence before our birth, so it must be irrational to feel horror at the prospect of future non-existence, since the two are mirror-images of each other. This argument was cited on his death-bed by the philosopher David Hume to Boswell, the bi-ographer of Dr. Johnson, but it did not relieve Boswell of his fear. The argument is sometimes attributed to Lucretius, who put his Epicurean phi-losophy into Latin verse in the 1st century BC. But it is common to many schools, appearing in the pseudo-Platonic *Axiochus,* in Cicero, in the Stoic Seneca, in Pliny the Elder, in Teles, and in the Platonist Plutarch.[5] Here is what Lucretius says in book 3 of *On the Nature of Things,* lines 972−77 (cf. 832−42):

> Again, look back and see how the ancient past of everlasting time before we are born has been nothing to us. Nature then shows us this as a mirror of future time after our final death. Does anything appear horrible there, does anything seem sad? Does it not stay steadier than any sleep?

Lucretius may, however, only be repeating the point he made at lines 834−42 about actual suffering: that we did not experience any suffering in that past, and equally will not in that future. Similarly in several of the other authors, the point is quite clearly about lack of sensation (*anaisthêsia*) be-fore and after life. There is one text that is definitely speaking about non-

5. Pseudo-Plato *Axiochus* 365D; Cicero *Tusculan Disputations* 1.37.90; Seneca *Letter* 54.4−5; Plutarch *Consolation to His Wife* 610D; Plutarch(?) *Consolation to Apollonius* 109F; Cicero *On Ends* 1.49; Cicero *On the Republic* 6.23; Pliny *Natural History* 7.188, 190; Sen-eca *On Consolation to Marcia* 19.5; Seneca *Letters* 77.11; Teles *On Freedom from Emotion ap.* Stobaeus 4.44.83, ed. Wachsmuth, Hense, vol. 3, *Florilegium,* p. 990, line 21−991,3. I owe the last six references to a list in James Warren, *Facing Death: Epicurus and His Critics,* Ox-ford 2004.

existence rather than non-sensation, and that text is different in another way too, because it is addressing not fear, but grief at the death of another. James Warren mentions a much earlier antecedent in the philosopher Teles of the late 3rd century BC,[6] classified by some as a Cynic, but I shall quote Plutarch, because he is so eloquent, as he is elsewhere (*Amatorius*) on marriage.

Plutarch *Consolation to His Wife* 610D:

> Try in your thought to move and restore yourself repeatedly to the time when this child was not yet born, and we had no complaint against fortune. Then match this present time to that one, seeing that our circumstances have become the same again. If we make things before she was born less a cause of complaint, we shall seem to be regretting her birth.

This text is indeed about the child's non-existence, not her non-sensation. But although Plutarch tries to counteract it, there is, of course, an asymmetry for the bereaved in reflection on her past and future non-existence, even though there is no asymmetry for the child herself. For after her death, the parents will be missing, for example, the new charms every day, which before her birth they could not even imagine. For pure symmetry, we need to think about our *own* past and future non-existence.

One attempt at reply to the argument about asymmetrical horror would urge that it is conceptually impossible to feel horror at past non-existence, and so our differential dislike of future non-existence is logically inevitable. I do not agree with this, although there is a merely verbal truth, that we do not use the word 'fear' in relation to past evils. But that is why I used the word 'horror'. Whether horror at past non-existence ever occurs in actual fact is a different question. The closest I have found is the case of Nabokov, who in his autobiographical work, *Speak, Memory,* describes someone who was horrified to see a home movie taken a few weeks before he was born:

> He saw a world that was practically unchanged—the same house, the same people—and then realised that he did not exist there at all and that nobody mourned his absence. He caught a glimpse of his mother waving from an upstairs window, and that unfamiliar gesture disturbed him, as if it were some mysterious farewell. But what particularly frightened him was the sight of

6. Teles *On Freedom from Emotion ap.* Stobaeum 4.44.83, ed. Wachsmuth, Hense vol. 3, *Florilegium,* 990,21−991,3.

a brand-new baby carriage standing there on the porch, with the smug, encroaching air of a coffin; even that was empty, as if, in the reverse course of events, his very bones had disintegrated.

I am not sure that even here we have an exact mirror-image of horror at the prospect of future non-existence. For his horror was at his not existing and not being missed *in that particular environment* — one where he felt he should have belonged. There is no sign that he would have felt horror at his absence in the more remote past. For something closer to this, we might consider the horror that some people feel when they think of the infinitude of time and feel their own brief existence dwarfed by it. Here the infinity of past time before their existence is just as effective a source of horror as the infinity of future time, although the horror is not at the past non-existence, but at something else that partly depends on the past non-existence. The horror evoked by reflection on past non-existence could even be greater than that at future non-existence, when one reflects that a tiny turn in events could have brought it about that one never came into existence at all, whereas at least this horrifying possibility is excluded when one thinks about future non-existence.

Here too the horror is at something else that depends on past non-existence. But whether or not there are actual examples of straightforward horror at past non-existence, the important point is that such horror is, as far as I can see, conceptually possible.

A second attempt to answer the 'asymmetrical horror' argument would object that an attitude cannot be dismissed as irrational merely because it is not based on a *further* reason. Probably those who feel horror merely at the prospect of future non-existence have no *further* reason for their fear. But then, if we are to avoid an infinite regress, we must just see some things as preferable to others, *without* further reason, and to do so is not in itself either rational or irrational. But this reply misses the point of the 'Lucretian' argument, which is that our preference for past over future non-existence is a preference between things that are mirror-images of each other. In other cases where we prefer one thing to another without further reason, the choice is at least between things that are not alike.

The only qualification I had to offer when I first considered the 'asymmetrical horror' argument was that our greater dislike of *future* non-existence is not surprising because it is simply one example of a much more general preference. Take the analogy of friendship. There was a time before we got to know our friend, but we do not normally think this fact an evil unless there are special circumstances. But we do think a permanent separation in the future to be an evil. The analogy is still closer. For we do not, except in a very intimate friendship, think it an evil if our future associations are intermittent. In the same way, many of those who fear annihilation would not mind an intermittent future existence, interrupted by periods of suspended animation, just so long as their existence did not come to a permanent end.

There is indeed a very general tendency to give a preference to one direction or the other in time. Thus we are not interested merely in the *quantity* of good things in our lives, but also in the *order* in which they come. Any sensible person would prefer a life of promotion to a life of demotion, even if the life of demotion started at the top, and included the same total quantity of advantages. Gregory of Nyssa has been cited as someone attracted by a future of perpetual progress in understanding. He was not attracted by a future of perpetual regression albeit containing the same total quantity of understanding. We must discount complicating factors such as the thought that the progress is due to one's own efforts and the regression to one's lack of effort. But when such allowances have been made, I think that preferences concerning temporal order and direction will turn out to be so widespread that we would hardly be human without them.

Moreover, something has caused this to be the case: natural selection. Animals that minded past pain or danger more than future would not fare well in the evolutionary process. This provides a causal explanation of some of our preferences, although it does not identify our reason for having the preference. Indeed, we may have no further reason.

When I first offered these arguments in *Time, Creation, and the Continuum* in 1983, I intended to concede that all these preferences were irrational, but to say on the other side that none was surprising, because the type of preference was so widespread. Since then, Derek Parfit's book, *Reasons and Persons*, has expressed a seemingly opposite conclusion, that the bias between future and past is not irrational.[7] But in fact, I think we were doing exactly the same thing, namely arguing that the bias between future and past is not confined to the context of death, but is a very widespread human phenomenon. I concluded merely that we should not find any instance of something so widespread surprising. But I still called all the instances irrational, because it is not self-evident why mere position in the past or future should be important. I could, however, just as well have said that natural selection has caused us to treat position in the future or past as a *reason* for different

7. Parfit, *Reasons and Persons*, 174–86, esp. 186.

reactions, so that the preference in the particular case of death is *in a way* rational.

There is one context in which it may seem that we set aside our fear. Someone may say, 'I would like to have been a contemporary of Aristotle'. It would not change his or her mind to reply, 'But in that case, you would be dead by now'. Why not? Although the imagined you would be past caring by now, the you that entertains the wish is the actual you, and the actual you would normally be appalled at the thought of being already dead. Have you after all achieved the desirable state of treating non-existence after death with equal indifference? Rather, I think the indifference is due to the fact that the death you are asked to contemplate is not the cessation of your actual present life. What you would be appalled by is the thought that your present life might already have come to an end.

When I call the state of equal indifference desirable, I do not, like Derek Parfit,[8] think it would be better if on *other* matters too one could feel indifferent as between past and future, but only as regards horror at non-existence.

If natural selection has *made* us feel this preference in the case of death, how can it reduce our fear to learn that the preference is irrational, or at least something that we are caused by evolutionary forces to treat as having a reason? I do not think it can remove the fear, because those who feel the fear have had the fear programmed into them. So I am not surprised that Boswell was not comforted. With fears that are not so strongly programmed, I believe that philosophy can often help. But even here, I think that philosophy can still do something. By making us see that the fear is, in the sense I explained, irrational and merely the product of evolutionary forces, it can help us to take our own agitation less seriously. It makes fear worse if we feel that the fear is justified. The 'Lucretian' argument that the fear is not justified does not remove it, but it can keep it in check and prevent it from growing.

What I see as the ideal attitude is to think that what matters is not the location of our life in the flowing series of past, present, and future, but the quality of our life. However variously different people may assess quality, it is quality, not location, they should be concerned with. And even though something stops many of us from feeling that way, I stick to the thought that that would be the rational way to think.

8. Ibid., 174–77.

WESTERN

BC 8th cent.?	Homer
5th cent.	Epicharmus, comic playwright Presocratic philosophers: Heraclitus Alcmaeon
4th cent.	Plato in Athens Aristotle, his pupil in Athens Epicurean school founded in Athens 307
3rd cent.–4th	Aristotle's pupils: Theophrastus Eudemus of Rhodes
3rd cent.	Stoic school founded in Athens 300 Stoics: Chrysippus, 3rd head c. 232–206 Cynic(?): Teles, fl. c. 235
2nd cent.	Greek King Menander, subject of Buddhist *Questions of Milinda,* compiled after his time Stoics: Panaetius head c. 129–109
1st cent.	Epicurean: Lucretius, expositor in Latin in Rome Cicero, Roman statesman, expositor of Greeks in Latin Stoic: Posidonius in Rhodes
AD 1st cent.	Stoics: Seneca, in Rome Epictetus, exiled from Rome Platonists: Plutarch of Chaeroneia Pythagorean *Table of Cebes*

2nd cent.	Stoics: Hierocles
	Marcus Aurelius, Roman Emperor
	Aristotelians: Alexander of Aphrodisias
	Sceptic: Sextus Empiricus
3rd cent.	Neoplatonists: Plotinus in Rome
	Porphyry, his pupil
	Christian: Origen
4th cent.	Neoplatonist: Iamblichus, Porphyry's pupil
	Christian bishops: Methodius
	Gregory of Nyssa
	Independent Platonizer: Themistius
4th to 5th cent.	Christian: Augustine
5th cent.	Neoplatonists: Plutarch of Athens
	Proclus
6th cent.	Neoplatonists: Simplicius
	Priscian
	Christian Neoplatonists: Philoponus
	Boethius
c 980–1037	Islam: Avicenna
c 1126–c 1198	Islam: Averroës
c 1224–1274	Christian: Thomas Aquinas

INDIAN

Buddhist

BC 5th cent.	The Buddha, incarnation of Gautama
3rd cent.	Personalists
2nd cent.–1st AD	*The Questions of Milinda*, Reductionist
AD 4th cent.	Vasubandhu, Reductionist
AD c. 150	Nâgârjuna, empty self
AD c. 600	Candrakîrti, empty self
AD 8th cent.	Śântideva, empty self

Nyaya school, replying to Buddhists

AD c. 100	Nyâyâ-sûtra
c. 400	Vâtsyâyana
c. 600	Uddyotakara
8th cent.	Nyaya arguments going back to 2nd cent. reported by Buddhist Kamalaśîla
10th cent.	Jayanta Bhaṭṭa

SELECT BIBLIOGRAPHY OF
SECONDARY LITERATURE

1. OPPONENTS AND FRIENDS OF THE SELF

Opponents

Ludwig Wittgenstein, *Philosophical Investigations*, Oxford 1953, para. 413, criticizing William James.

Elizabeth Anscombe, 'The first person', in S. Guttenplan, ed., *Mind and Language*, Wolfson College lectures, repr. in her *Collected Philosophical Papers*, vol. 2, Cambridge 1991.

Norman Malcolm, 'Whether "I" is a referring expression', in Cora Diamond and Jenny Teichman, eds., *Intention and Intentionality*, Ithaca N.Y. 1979, 15–24.

A. J. P. Kenny, 'The Self', the Aquinas Lecture, Marquette University, Milwaukee, Wisconsin, 1988–89.

A. J. P. Kenny, 'Body, soul, and intellect in Aquinas', in James Crabbe, ed., *From Soul to Self*, Wolfson College lectures, London 1999.

Daniel Dennett, 'Why everyone is a novelist', *Times Literary Supplement*, 16–22 September 1988, p.1016.

Daniel Dennett, *Consciousness Explained*, Boston 1991.

Friends of the Self

Marya Schechtman, *The Constitution of Selves*, Ithaca N.Y. 1996.

Thomas Nagel, *The View from Nowhere*, Oxford 1986.

Peter Strawson, *Individuals*, London 1959.

2. HISTORY OF CONCEPTS OF THE SELF

General

Charles Taylor, *Sources of the Self*, Cambridge 1989.

James Crabbe, ed., *From Soul to Self*, London 1999.

Raymond Martin and John Barresi, *Naturalization of the Soul*, London 2000.

Antiquity in general

Michel Foucault, *The History of Sexuality*, vol. 3, *The Care of the Self*, translation of *Le souci de soi*.

Michel Foucault, *L'Herméneutique du sujet*, Paris 2001.

Christopher Gill, *Personality in Greek Epic, Tragedy, and Philosophy: The Self in Dialogue*, Oxford 1996.

Christopher Gill, 'Is there a concept of person in Greek philosophy?' in S. Everson, ed., *Psychology: Companions to Ancient Thought*, vol. 2, Cambridge 1991, 166–93.

Christopher Gill 'The structured self in Hellenistic and Roman thought', in Paulina Remes, ed., *Philosophy of the Self in Ancient Thought*, forthcoming.

Christopher Gill, *The Structured Self in Hellenistic and Roman Thought*, in preparation.

Richard Sorabji, 'Soul and self in ancient philosophy', in James Crabbe, ed., *From Soul to Self*, London 1999, 8–32.

A. A. Long, 'Finding oneself in Greek philosophy', *Tijdschrift voor Filosofie* 54, 1992, 255–79.

Myles Burnyeat, 'Idealism and Greek philosophy: what Descartes saw and Berkeley missed', *Philosophical Review* 91, 1982, 3–40.

Homer

R. B. Onians, *The Origins of European Thought*, Cambridge 1954.

Bruno Snell, *The Discovery of the Mind*, Cambridge Mass. 1953.

R. W. Sharples, 'But why has my spirit spoken with me thus?': Homeric decision-making', *Greece and Rome* 30, 1983, 1–7.

Richard Gaskin, 'Do Homeric heroes make real decisions?', *Classical Quarterly* 40, 1990, 1–15.

J. Pépin, Héraclès et son reflet dans le néoplatonisme', *Le Néoplatonisme*, Paris 1971, 167–92.

Plato

Theodor Heckel, *Der innere Mensch*, Tübingen 1993.

M. M. McCabe, *Plato's Individuals*, Princeton 1994.

A. A. Long, 'Platonic souls as persons', in Ricardo Salles, ed., *Metaphysics, Soul, and Ethics in Ancient Thought: Themes from the Work of Richard Sorabji*, Oxford 2005, 173–91.

Aristotle

D. M. Balme, 'Aristotle's biology was not essentialist', *Archiv für Geschichte der Philosophie* 62, 1980, 1–12, repr. in Allan Gotthelf and James Lennox, eds., *Philosophical Issues in Aristotle's Biology*, Cambridge 1987.

A. C. Lloyd, *Form and Universal in Aristotle*, Liverpool 1981.

Epicureans: Lucretius

A. A. Long, 'Lucretius on nature and the Epicurean self', in K. Algra, M. Koenen, and P. H. Schrijvers, eds., *Lucretius and His Intellectual Background*, Amsterdam 1997, 125–39.

James Warren, 'Lucretian palingenesis recycled', *Classical Quarterly* 51, 2001, 499–508.

James Warren, *Facing Death: Epicurus and His Critics*, Oxford 2004.

Stoics

David Sedley, 'The Stoic criterion of identity', *Phronesis* 27, 1982, 255–75.

A. A. Long, 'Representation and the self in Stoicism', in S. Everson, ed., *Psychology: Companions to Ancient Thought*, vol. 2, Cambridge 1991, 101–20, repr. in his *Stoic Studies*, Cambridge 1996.

Troels Engberg-Pedersen, 'Stoic philosophy and the concept of the person', in Christopher Gill, ed., *The Person and the Human Mind*, Oxford 1990, 109–35.

Gretchen Reydams-Schils, 'Roman and Stoic: the self as a mediator', *Dionysius* 16, 1998, 35–61.

Stoics on family love

Brad Inwood, 'L'oikeiôsis sociale chez Epictète' in K. Algra, P. van der Horst, and D. Runia, eds., *Polyhistor: Studies in the History and Historiography of Ancient Philosophy*, Leiden 1996, 243–64.

Gretchen Reydams-Schils, *The Roman Stoics: Self, Responsibility, and Affection*, Chicago 2005, ch. 4.

A. A. Long, *Epictetus*, Oxford 2002, 77–78 and ch. 9.

Stoics on oikeiôsis

See under 'Identity in ethics' (below).

Stoics on personae

See under 'Identity in ethics' (below).

Stoics on eternal recurrence

See under "Personal identity over time and survival' (below).

Stoic 'Shrinking Argument' and fusion

See under 'Personal identity over time and survival' (below).

Augustine

Phillip Cary, *Augustine's Invention of the Inner Self*, Oxford 2000.

John Rist, *Augustine*, Cambridge 1994, ch. 4.

Ronnie Rombs, 'St. Augustine's inner self: the soul as "private" and "individuated"', *Studia Patristica*, forthcoming.

Plotinus

E. R. Dodds, 'Tradition and personal achievement in the philosophy of Plotinus',
Journal of Roman Studies 50, 1960, p. 1–7.
A. H. Armstrong, 'Form, individual, and person in Plotinus', *Dionysius* 1, 1977,
repr. in his *Plotinian and Christian Studies*, Aldershot 1979.
Gerard O'Daly, *Plotinus' Philosophy of the Self*, Shannon, Ireland 1973.
W. Himmerich, *Eudaimonia: die Lehre des Plotin von der Selbstverwirklichung des
Menschen*, Würzburg 1959.
Arthur Madigan, 'Plotinus on personal individuality: the early period', in Wil-
liam J. Carroll, J. J. Furlong, and C. S. Mann, eds., *The Quest of the Individual:
Roots of Western Civilization*, New York 1990.

Porphyry

Riccardo Chiaradonna, 'La teoria dell' individuo in Porfirio e *l'idiôs poion* stoico',
Elenchos 20, 2000, 303–31.
Jaap Mansfeld, *Heresiography in Context*, Leiden 1992, 92–98.

Late Neoplatonists

Carlos Steel, *The Changing Self: A Study of the Soul in Later Neoplatonism: Iamblichus, Damascius, and Priscianus*, Brussels 1978.

3. RISE OF INDIVIDUALISM

Colin Morris, *The Discovery of the Individual 1050–1200*, London 1972.
Thomas Greene, 'The flexibility of the self in Renaissance literature', in Peter De-
metz, Thomas Greene, and Lowry Nelson Jr, eds., *The Disciplines of Criticism*,
New Haven Conn. 1968, 241–64.
Robert Rehder, *Wordsworth and the Beginnings of Modern Poetry*, London and
Totowa N.J. 1981.
Diskin Clay, 'Missing persons, or the selfless Greeks', in William J. Carroll, J. J.
Furlong, and C. S. Mann, eds., *The Quest of the Individual: Roots of Western Civ-
ilization*, New York 1990.
Charles Taylor, *The Malaise of Modernity*, Concord Ontario 1991.

4. MODERN PSYCHOLOGY

Self-perception

Ulrich Neisser, 'Five kinds of self-knowledge', *Philosophical Psychology* 1, 1988,
35–59.
Ulrich Neisser, ed., *The Perceived Self*, Cambridge 1993.

Ulrich Neisser, 'The ecological self and its metaphors', *Philosophical Topics* 26, 1999, 201–15.

Colwyn Trevarthen, 'The self born in intersubjectivity: the psychology of an infant communicating', in Neisser, *The Perceived Self.*

Michael Tomasello, 'On the interpersonal origins of self-concept', in Neisser, *The Perceived Self.*

Michael Tomasello, *The Cultural Origins of Human Cognition,* Cambridge, Mass. 1999.

S. Feinman, 'Social referencing in infancy', *Merrill-Palmer Quarterly* 28, 1982, 445–70.

José Luis Bermúdez, *The Paradox of Self-Consciousness,* Cambridge Mass. 1998.

Brian O'Shaughnessy, *The Will,* Cambridge 1980, vol. 1, ch. 7, on awareness of our bodies.

John Barresi and Chris Moore, 'Intentional relations and social understanding', *Behavioral and Brain Sciences* 19, 1996, 107–54.

José Luis Bermúdez, Anthony Marcel, and Naomi Eilan, *The Body and the Self,* Cambridge Mass. 1998.

Richard Sorabji, *Animal Minds and Human Morals,* London and Ithaca N.Y. 1993, p. 43, quoting:

Andrew Whiten and Richard W. Byrne, 'The manipulation of attention in primate tactical deception', in their, ed., *Machiavellian Intelligence: Social expertise and the Evolution of Intellect in Monkeys, Apes, and Humans,* Oxford 1988, 349–61.

O.-J. Grusser, 'Interaction of efferent and afferent signals in visual perception: a history of ideas and experimental paradigms', *Acta Psychologica* 63, 1986, 3–21.

Memory

A. R. Luria, *Man with a Shattered World,* London 1973.

Autism

Charlotte Moore, *George and Sam,* London 2004.

Peter Hobson, *The Cradle of Thought,* London 2002.

Simon Baron-Cohen, H. Tager-Flusberg, and D. Cohen, eds., *Understanding Other Minds: Perspectives from Autism,* Cambridge 1993.

Simon Baron-Cohen, 'Precursors to a theory of mind: understanding attention in others', in A. Whiten, ed., *Natural Theories of Mind: Evolution, Development, and Simulation of Everyday Mindreading,* Oxford 1991.

Linguistic communication

Paul Grice, 'Meaning', *Philosophical Review* 66, 1957, 377–88.

Paul Grice, 'Utterer's meaning and intentions', *Philosophical Review* 78, 1969, 147–77.

Michael Tomasello, *The Cutural Origins of Human Cognition,* Cambridge Mass. 1999, Chs. 3 and 4.

José Luis Bermúdez, Anthony Marcel, and Naomi Eilan, *The Body and the Self*, Cambridge Mass. 1998.

5. IDENTITY IN ETHICS

Symposium on Derek Parfit's Reasons and Persons, Ethics 96, July 1986.
Robert Adams, 'Should ethics be more impersonal?', in Jonathan Dancy, ed., *Reading Parfit*, Oxford 1997.
Susan Wolf, 'Self-interest and interest in selves', *Ethics* 96, 1986, 704–20.
Christine Korsgaard, 'Personal identity and the unity of agency' *Philosophy and Public Affairs*, 18, 1989, 101–32.
Marya Schechtman, *The Constitution of Selves*, Ithaca N.Y. 1996.
Richard Sorabji, *Emotion and Peace of Mind*, Oxford 2000, ch. 16.
Richard Sorabji, 'Soul and self in ancient philosophy', in James Crabbe, ed., *From Soul to Self*, London 1999.
Gretchen Reydams-Schils, 'Roman and Stoic: the self as mediator', *Dionysius* 16, 1998, 35–62.

Stoics on oikeiôsis

S. G. Pembroke, '*Oikeiôsis*', in A. A. Long, ed., *Problems in Stoicism*, London 1971, 114–49.
Brad Inwood, 'Hierocles: theory and argument in the second century A.D.', *Oxford Studies in Ancient Philosophy* 2, 1984, 151–83.
Brad Inwood, 'L'oikeiôsis sociale chez Epictète' in K. Algra, P. van der Horst, and D. Runia, eds., *Polyhistor: Studies in the History and Historiography of Ancient Philosophy*, Leiden 1996, 243–64.
Richard Sorabji, *Animal Minds and Human Morals*, Ithaca N.Y. 1993, chs. 10–11.
Gretchen Reydams-Schils, 'Human bonding and oikeiôsis in Roman Stoicism', *Oxford Studies in Ancient Philosophy* 22, 2002, 221–51.
Troels Engberg-Pedersen, *The Stoic Theory of Oikeiosis*, Aarhus 1990.

Personae in Stoics, Indian, Chinese, and modern thought

Phillip De Lacy, 'The four Stoic personae', *Illinois Classical Studies* 2, 1977, 163–72.
Christopher Gill, 'Personhood and personality: the four-*personae* theory in Cicero *De Officiis* I', *Oxford Studies in Ancient Philosophy* 6, 1988, 169–99.
Francesca Alesse, *Panezio di Rodi e la tradizione stoica*, Naples 1994, esp. 267–78.
Aditya Adarkar, 'Karna's choice: courage and character in the face of an ethical dilemma', in T. S. Rukmani, ed., *The Mahabharata: Whatever Is Not Here Is Nowhere Else*, New Delhi 2005, ch. 9.
Roger T. Ames, 'The focus-field in classical Confucianism', in his (ed.) *Self as Person in Asian Theory and Practice*, Albany N.Y. 1994, 187–212.
Charles Taylor, *The Malaise of Modernity*, Concord Ontario 1991.

Charles Taylor, *Sources of the Self,* Cambridge 1989.

Bikhu Parekh, *Rethinking Multiculturalism,* Basingstoke 2000 (on cultural identity).

Epictetus on self as invulnerable proairesis

Robert Dobbin, 'Prohairesis in Epictetus', *Ancient Philosophy* 11, 1991, 111–35.

Richard Sorabji, 'Epictetus on *proairesis* and self', in Theodore Scaltsas and Andrew Mason, eds., Proceedings of conference on Epictetus held at Larnaca, Sept. 2001, forthcoming.

Plutarch and life-narrative

Alasdair MacIntyre, *After Virtue,* London 1981, 2nd ed. 1985.

Marya Schechtman, *The Constitution of Selves,* Ithaca N.Y. 1996.

Galen Strawson, 'Against narrativity', *Times Literary Supplement,* 13 Oct. 2004.

6. PERSONAL IDENTITY OVER TIME AND SURVIVAL

Parfit

Derek Parfit, *Reasons and Persons,* Oxford 1984, corrected 1987.

Derek Parfit, 'Experiences, subjects, and conceptual schemes', *Philosophical Topics* 26, 1999, 217–270.

Derek Parfit, 'The unimportance of identity', in Henry Harris, ed., *Identity,* Oxford 1995, 13–45.

Derek Parfit, 'Personal identity', *Philosophical Review* 80, 1971, 3–27.

Jonathan Dancy, ed., *Reading Parfit,* Oxford 1997.

Mark Johnston, 'Human concerns without superlative selves', in Dancy.

Sydney Shoemaker, 'Parfit on identity', in Dancy.

John McDowell, 'Reductionism and the first person', in Dancy.

Ethics 96, 703–872, is devoted to discussion with Parfit.

Susan Wolf, 'Self-interest and interest in selves', *Ethics* 96, 1986, 704–20.

Marya Schechtman, *The Constitution of Selves,* Ithaca N.Y. 1996.

Marya Schechtman, 'Personhood and personal identity', *Journal of Philosophy* 87, 1990, 71–92.

Ernest Sosa, 'Surviving matters', *Nous* 24, 1990, 297–322.

David Lewis,'Survival and identity', expanded in his *Philosophical Papers,* vol. 1, from the earlier version in A. Rorty, ed., *The Identities of Persons,* Berkeley 1976, 17–40.

John Perry, 'Can the self divide?' *Journal of Philosophy* 69, 1972, 463–88.

Quassim Cassam, 'Kant and reductionism', *Review of Metaphysics* 43, 1989–90, 72–106.

Ray Martin and John Barresi, eds., *Personal Identity,* Oxford, forthcoming.

Other modern treatments

C. B. Martin, 'Identity and exact similarity', *Analysis* 18, 1958, 83–87.
Graham Nerlich, 'Sameness, difference, and continuity', *Analysis* 18, 1958, 144–49.
Elizabeth Anscombe, 'Were you a zygote?', *Royal Institute of Philosophy*, supp. vol. 1984, 111–15.
Bernard Williams, *Problems of the Self*, Cambridge 1973.
David Wiggins, *Identity and Spatio-temporal* Continuity, Oxford 1967.
Robert Nozick, *Philosophical Explanations*, Oxford 1981, ch. 1.
Sydney Shoemaker and Richard Swinburne, *Personal Identity*, Oxford 1984.
Sydney Shoemaker, *Self-knowledge and Self-identity*, Ithaca N.Y. 1963.
John Perry, ed., *Personal Identity*, Berkeley 1975.
Amelie Rorty, ed., *The Identities of Persons*, Berkeley 1976.

Survival after death

For Christians, Avicenna, and Averroës see below under 'Christian resurrection', 'Avicenna', 'Averroës'.
Terence Penelhum, *Survival and Disembodied Existence*, London 1970.
Sydney Shoemaker and Richard Swinburne, *Personal Identity*, Oxford 1984.

Does survival matter?

Ernest Sosa, 'Surviving matters', *Nous* 24, 1990, 297–322.
Bernard Williams, 'The Makropoulos case: reflections on the tedium of immortality', in his *Problems of the Self*, Cambridge 1973.
Tom Nagel, *Mortal Questions*, Cambridge 1979, Ch. 1.
Richard Sorabji, *Time, Creation, and the Continuum*, London and Ithaca N.Y. 1983, ch. 12.

Aristotelian tradition on persistence

Inna Kupreeva, 'Alexander of Aphrodisias on mixture and growth', *Oxford Studies in Ancient Philosophy* 27, 2004, 297–334.
Richard Sorabji, *The Philosophy of the Commentators 200–600 AD*, vol. 3, *Logic and Metaphysics*, London and Ithaca N.Y. 2004, ch. 6, 176–81.

Stoic identity and individuation

Eric Lewis, 'The Stoics on identity and individuation', *Phronesis* 40, 1995, 89–108.
David Sedley, 'The Stoic criterion of identity', *Phronesis* 27, 1982, 255–75.

Stoic eternal recurrence

A. A. Long, 'The Stoics on world-conflagration and everlasting recurrence', *Southern Journal of Philosophy*, vol. 23, supp., ed. R. Epp, 1985.
Jonathan Barnes, 'La doctrine du retour éternel', in Jacques Brunschwig, ed., *Les stoïciens et leur logique*, Paris 1978, 3–20.

Stoic 'Shrinking Argument' against the 'Growing Argument'

David Sedley, 'The Stoic criterion of identity', *Phronesis* 27, 1982, 255–75.

John Bowin, 'Chrysippus' puzzle about identity', *Oxford Studies in Ancient Philosophy* 24, 2003, 239–51.

Terry Irwin, 'Stoic individuals', *Philosophical Perspectives 10: Metaphysics,* 1996, 459–80.

Michael Burke, 'Dion and Theon: an essentialist solution to an ancient puzzle', *Journal of Philosophy* 97, 1994, 129–39.

Richard Sorabji, *The Philosophy of the Commentators 200–600 AD*, vol. 3, *Logic and Metaphysics*, London and Ithaca N.Y. 2004, ch. 6, pp. 184–85.

Platonism: is the true self individual?

Richard Sorabji, 'Is the true self an individual in the Platonist tradition?', in M. O. Goulet-Cazé, ed., *Le Commentaire entre tradition et innovation*, Paris 2000.

Richard Sorabji, *The Philosophy of the Commentators 200–600 AD*, vol. 3, *Logic and Metaphysics*, London and Ithaca N.Y. 2004, chs. 17–18.

Christian resurrection

H. Crouzel, 'Les critiques addressés par Méthode et ses contemporains à la doctrine origénienne du corps ressuscité', *Gregorianum* 53, 1972, 679–716.

H. Crouzel, 'La doctrine origénienne du corps ressuscité', *Bulletin de littérature ecclésiastique* 81, 1974, 175–200; 241–66.

Jon F. Dechow, *Dogma and Mysticism in Early Christianity: Epiphanius of Cyprus and the Legacy of Origen*, Macon, Ga. 1988, ch. 12.

Henry Chadwick, 'Origen, Celsus, and the resurrection of the body', *Harvard Theological Review* 41, 1948, 83–102.

Ph. Lyndon Reynolds, *Food and the Body*, Leiden 1999, chs. 13–14.

A. van Roey, 'Un traité cononite contre Jean Philopon sur le resurrection', in *Hommage à Maurits Geerard*, Wetteren 1984.

Richard Sorabji, 'Philoponus', in his, ed., *Philoponus and the Rejection of Aristotelian Science*, London and Ithaca N.Y. 1987, ch. 1, 'John Philoponus', pp. 32–33.

Carolyn Bynum Walker, *Fragmentation and Redemption*, New York 1992.

Richard Sorabji, *The Philosophy of the Commentators 200–600 AD*, vol. 3, *Logic and Metaphysics*, London and Ithaca N.Y. 2004, ch. 6, pp. 181–83.

Avicenna

Jean (= Yahya) Michot, *La destinée de l'homme selon Avicenne: le retour à dieu et l'imagination*, Leuven 1986.

Thérèse-Anne Druart, 'The human soul's individuation and its survival after death: Avicenna on the causal relation between body and soul', *Arabic Sciences and Philosophy*, 10, 2000, 259–73.

Averroës

Richard Taylor, 'Personal immortality in Averroës' mature philosophical psychology', *Documenti e studi sulla tradizione filosofica medievale* 9, 1998, 89–110.

Locke and Berkeley

Raymond Martin and John Barresi, *Naturalization of the Soul*, London 2000.

A. C. Lloyd, 'The self in Berkeley's Philosophy', in John Foster and Howard Robinson, eds., *Essays on Berkeley*, Oxford 1985.

7. BUDDHISM VS. NYAYA ON NO-SELF

Matthew Kapstein, *Reasons, Traces, and Identity in Indian and Buddhist Thought*, Ilford 2001.

Roy Perrott, 'Personal identity, minimalism, and Madhyamaka', *Philosophy East and West* 52, 2002, 373–85.

Paul Williams, introduction to Śântideva, *The Bodhicaryâvatâra*, Oxford 1995.

Jonardon Ganeri, 'Cross-modality and the self', *Philosophy and Phenomenological Research* 61, 2000.

Jonardon Ganeri, 'Self-intimation, memory, and personal identity', *Journal of Indian Philosophy* 27, 1999, 469–83.

Jonardon Ganeri, *The Concealed Art of the Soul*, in preparation.

Arindam Chakrabarti, 'I touch what I saw', *Philosophy and Phenomenological Research* 52, 1992, 103–16.

Arindam Chakrabarti, 'The Nyaya proofs for the existence of the soul', *Journal of Indian Philosophy* 10, 1982, 211–38.

James Duerlinger, 'Reductionist and nonreductionist theories of persons in Indian Buddhist philosophy', *Journal of Indian Philosophy*, 21, 1993, 79–101.

James Duerlinger, *Indian Buddhist Theories of Persons*, London 2003.

Steven Collins 1994, 'What are Buddhists doing when they deny the self?', in Frank E. Reynolds and David Tracy, eds., *Religion and Practical Reason*, SUNY Press 1994, 59–86.

Mark Siderits 'Buddhist reductionism', *Philosophy East and West*, 47, 1997, 455–78.

Mark Siderits, 'Matilal on Nâgârjuna', in P. Bilimoria and J. N. Mohanty, eds., *Relativism, Suffering, and Beyond: Essays in Memory of Bimal K. Matilal*, Delhi 1997.

Mark Siderits, *Personal Identity and Buddhist Philosophy*, Aldershot 2003.

Paul Williams, *Altruism and Reality*, Richmond, Surrey 1998.

C. W. Huntington Jr., with Geshé Namgyal Wangchen, *The Emptiness of Emptiness*, Honolulu 1989.

Jay L. Garfield, *The Fundamental Wisdom of the Middle Way*, Oxford 1995.

Claus Oetke, 'Some remarks on theses and philosophical positions in early Madhyamaka', *Journal of Indian Philosophy* 31, 2003, 449–78.

Tom J. F. Tillemans, 'Metaphysics for Madhyamikas', in Georges B. J. Dreyfus and Sara L. McClintock, eds., *The Svatantrika-Prasangika Distinction*, Boston 2003, 93–123.

8. CIRCULAR TIME

Kurt Gödel, 'A remark about the relationship between Relativity Theory and Idealistic Philosophy', in P. A. Schilpp, ed., *Albert Einstein: Philosopher-Scientist*, New York 1951, 555–62.

Paul Horwich, *Asymmetries in Time*, Boston Mass. 1987, Ch. 6, 'Time travel'.

Murray Macbeath, 'Who was Dr. Who's father?' *Synthese* 51, 1982, 397–430.

Michael Dummett, 'Can an effect precede its cause?', *Proceedings of the Aristotelian Society*, supp. vol. 28, 1954, 27–44'.

Michael Dummett, Bringing about the past', *Philosophical Review* 73, 1964, 338–59.

Richard Sorabji, *Matter, Space, and Motion*, London and Ithaca N.Y. 1988, ch. 10, 'Closed space and closed time'.

9. DIFFERENTIATION OF INDIVIDUALS, INDIVIDUALS AS BUNDLES

Differentiation

See also 'Platonism: is the true self individual?' (above).

Allan Bäck, 'The Islamic Background: Avicenna (b. 980; d. 1037) and Averroës (b. 1126; d. 1198)', in Jorge J. E. Gracia, ed., *Individuation in Scholasticism*, Albany N.Y. 1994, ch. 3.

Jorge J. E. Gracia, *Introduction to the Problem of Individuation in the Early Middle Ages*, Munich 1984, ch. 2, 'Formulation of the issues: Boethius'.

Richard Sorabji, *The Philosophy of the Commentators 200–600 AD*, vol. 3, *Logic and Metaphysics*, London and Ithaca N.Y. 2004, ch. 5.

A. C. Lloyd, *Form and Universal in Aristotle*, Liverpool 1981, 67.

Bundles

Richard Sorabji, *Matter, Space, and Motion*, London and Ithaca N.Y. 1988, ch. 4.

Jaap Mansfeld, *Heresiography in Context*, Leiden 1992, 92–98.

Riccardo Chiaradonna, 'La teoria dell' individuo in Porfirio e l'*idiôs poion* stoico', *Elenchos* 20, 2000, 303–31.

10. INFALLIBLE SELF-KNOWLEDGE: COGITO AND FLYING MAN

Augustine's Cogito

P. Courcelle, *Connais-toi toi même*, Paris, 1974, vol. I.

E. Booth, 'St. Augustine's "notitia sui" related to Aristotle and the early Neoplatonists', *Augustiniana*, vol. 27, 1977, 70–132, 364–401; vol. 28, 1978, 183–221; vol. 29, 1979, 97–104.

Étienne Gilson, 'Les sources gréco-arabes de l'augustinisme avicennisant', *Archives d'histoire doctrinal et littéraire du Moyen Âge* 4, 1929, 1–149, at 39–42.

É. Gilson, *Introduction à l'étude de Saint Augustin*, Paris 1929, pp. 56–59.

Dominic O'Meara, 'Scepticism and ineffability in Plotinus', *Phronesis* 45, 2000, 240–51.

Avicenna's Flying Man

Th.-A. Druart, 'The soul and body problem: Avicenna and Descartes', in her, ed., *Arabic Philosophy and the West*, Washington 1983, 27–49.

É. Gilson, 'Les sources gréco-arabes de l'augustinisme avicennisant', *Archives d'histoire doctrinal et littéraire du Moyen Âge* 4, 1929, 1–149.

Ahmad Hasnawi, 'La conscience de soi chez Avicenne et Descartes', in J. Biard and R. Rashed, eds., *Descartes et le Moyen Âge*, Paris 1997, 283–91.

D. Hasse, *Avicenna in the Latin West*, London 2000, 80–92.

M. Marmura, 'Avicenna's "Flying Man" in context', *Monist* 69, 1986, 383–95.

Christopher J. Martin, 'Flights of fancy: Avicenna's arguments for the incorporeality of the soul and their interpretation', in preparation.

Jean (= Yahya) Michot, 'La réponse d'Avicenne à Bahmanyâr et al-Kirmânî', *Le Muséon*, 1997, 143–221.

S. Pines, 'La conception de la conscience de soi chez Avicenne et chez Abú 'l-Barakât al-Baghdâdî, *Archives d'histoire doctrinale et littéraire du Moyen Âge*, 29, 1954, 21–56, repr. in *The Collected Works of Shlomo Pines*, vol. 1, Jerusalem and Leiden 1986.

Meryem Sebti, *Avicenne: L'âme humaine*, Paris 2000.

G. Verbeke, Introduction to Avicenna Latinus, *De Anima*, ed. S. Van Riet, Louvain 1972.

11. SELF-AWARENESS

See also 'Infallible self-knowledge: Cogito and Flying Man' (above).

Antiquity in general

A. C. Lloyd, 'Nosce Teipsum and Conscientia', *Archiv für Geschichte der Philosophie* 46, 1964, 188–200.

Puzzles as to the possibility of self-knowledge

Ian Crystal, *Self-intellection and Its Epistemological Origins in Ancient Greek Thought*, Aldershot 2002.

Ian Crystal, 'Plotinus on the structure of self-intellection', *Phronesis* 43, 1998, 264–86.

On Plato

Julia Annas, 'Self-knowledge in early Plato', in Dominic O'Meara, ed., *Platonic Investigations: Studies in Philosophy and the History of Philosophy*, vol. 13, Washington, D.C. 1983, 111–38.

Voula Tsouna (McKirahan), 'Socrate et la connaissance de soi: quelques interprétations', *Philosophie antique* 1, 2001, 37–64.

On Aristotle

Victor Caston, 'Aristotle on consciousness', *Mind* 111, 2002, 751–815.

John Sisko, 'Reflexive awareness *does belong* to the main function of perception', *Mind* 113, 2004, 513–21.

Victor Caston, 'More on Aristotle on consciousness: reply to Sisko', *Mind* 113, 2004, 523–33.

Aryeh Kosman, 'Aristotle on the desirability of friends', *Ancient Philosophy* 24, 2004, 135–54.

Knowledge of self through other

Ulrich Neisser, ed., *The Perceived Self*, Cambridge 1993.

Colwyn Trevarthen, 'The self born in intersubjectivity: the psychology of an infant communicating', in Neisser, *The Perceived Self*.

Michael Tomasello, 'On the interpersonal origins of self-concept', in Neisser, *The Perceived Self*.

Michael Tomasello, *The Cultural Origins of Human Cognition*, Cambridge, Mass. 1999.

José Luis Bermúdez, *The Paradox of Self-Consciousness*, Cambridge Mass. 1998.

Aryeh Kosman 'Aristotle on the desirability of friends' *Ancient Philosophy* 24, 2004, 135–54.

Charles Kahn, 'Aristotle on Altruism', *Mind* 90, 1981, 20–40.

Brad Inwood, 'Hierocles: Theory and Argument in the second century A.D.', *Oxford Studies in Ancient Philosophy* 2, 1984, 151–83.

G. Verbeke, 'Une anamnèse métaphysique chez Plotin', in D. O'Brien and M. O. Goulet-Cazé, eds., *Sophiês Maiêtores "Chercheurs de sagesse"*, hommage à Jean Pépin, Paris 1992, 297–316, at 297–99.

G. Verbeke, 'Connaissance de soi et connaissance de Dieu chez Saint Augustin', *Augustiniana* 4, 1954, 495–515, reprinted in his *D'Aristote à Thomas d'Aquin: Antécédents de la pensée moderne*, Leuven 1990, 367–87.

E. Booth, 'St. Augustine's "notitia sui" related to Aristotle and the early Neoplatonists', Augustiniana, vol. 27, 1977, 70–132, 364–401; vol. 28, 1978, 183–221; vol. 29, 1979, 97–104.

Dan Zahavi, *Self-Awareness and Alterity*, Evanston Ill. 1999, 160–69.

Knowledge of self and knowledge of God

P. Courcelle, *Connais-toi toi même*, Paris, 1974, vol. I.

E. Booth, 'St. Augustine's "notitia sui" related to Aristotle and the early Neo-platonists', *Augustiniana*, vol. 27, 1977, 70–132, 364–401; vol. 28, 1978, 183–221; vol. 29, 1979, 97–104.

K. Kremer, 'Selbsterkenntnis als Gottserkenntnis', *International Studies in Philosophy* 13, 1981, 41–68.

J. Pépin, *Idées grecques sur l'homme et sur dieu*, Paris 1971, 192–93.

Gerard Verbeke, 'Connaissance de soi et connaissance de Dieu chez Saint Augustin', *Augustiniana* 4, 1954, 495–515, reprinted in *his D'Aristote à Thomas d'Aquin: Antécédents de la pensée moderne*, Leuven 1990, 367–87.

Unity of self-awareness

David Rosenthal, 'Unity of consciousness and the self', *Proceedings of the Aristotelian Society* 103, 2002–3, 325–52.

William C. Lycan, 'The superiority of *HOP* to *HOT*', in Rocco W. Gennaro, ed., *Higher Order Theories of Consciousness*, Amsterdam 2004.

Self-awareness, modern psychology

See also 'Modern Psychology', 'Knowledge of self through other', and 'Unity of self-awareness' (above).

Ulrich Neisser, ed., *The Perceived Self*, Cambridge 1993.

José Luis Bermúdez, *The Paradox of Self-Consciousness*, Cambridge Mass. 1998.

Plato

Julia Annas, 'Self-knowledge in early Plato', in Dominic O'Meara, ed., *Platonic Investigations: Studies in Philosophy and the History of Philosophy*, vol. 13, Washington, D.C. 1983, 111–38.

Voula Tsouna, 'Socrate et la connaissance de soi: quelques interprétations', *Figures de Socrates, Philosophie Antique* 1, 2001, 37–64.

Aristotle

See also 'Knowledge of self through other' (above).

Victor Caston, 'Aristotle on consciousness', *Mind* 111, 2002, 751–815.

John Sisko, 'Reflexive awareness *does belong* to the main function of perception', *Mind* 113, 2004, 513–21.

Victor Caston, 'More on Aristotle on consciousness: reply to Sisko', *Mind* 113, 2004, 523–33.

Stephan Eberle, 'Le problème de la perception du temps et la théorie de l'intentionnalité chez Aristote', in B. Melkevik and J.-M. Narbonne, eds., *Une philosophie dans l'histoire: hommages à Raymond Klibansky*, Laval, Quebec 2000, 65–81.

Daniela P. Taormina, 'Perception du temps et mémoire chez Aristote', *De memoria et reminiscentia* 1', *Philosophie Antique*, 2, 2002, 33–61.

Epicureans

David Glidden, 'Epicurus on self-perception', *American Philosophical Quarterly* 16, 1979, 297–306.

Stoics

See also under 'Stoics on *oikeiôsis*' (above).

David Hahm, 'A neglected Stoic argument for human responsibility', *Illinois Classical Studies* 17, 1992, 1–26.

A. A. Long, 'Hierocles on *oikeiôsis* and self-perception', in his *Stoic Studies*, Cambridge 1996, 250–63.

Plotinus

See also 'Puzzles as to the possibility of self-knowledge', 'Knowledge of self through other' (above)

A. H. Armstrong, 'The background to the doctrine "that the intelligibles are not outside the intellect"', in *Les Sources de Plotin*, Fondation Hardt, *Entretiens* 5, Geneva 1957, 393–425.

W. Beierwaltes, *Selbsterkenntnis und Erfahrung der Einheit: Plotins Enneades 5.3*, Frankfurt 1991.

W. Beierwaltes, 'Das wahre Selbst', in his *Das wahre Selbst*, Munich 2001, 84–122.

Ian Crystal, 'Plotinus on the structure of self-intellection', *Phronesis* 43, 1998, 264–86.

Lloyd Gerson, 'Introspection, self-relativity, and the essence of thinking according to Plotinus', in John J. Cleary, ed., *The Perennial Tradition of Neoplatonism*, Leuven 1997, 153–73.

Jens Halfwassen, *Geist und Selbstbewusstsein: Studien zu Plotin und Numenius*, Akademie der Wissenschaften und der Literatur Mainz, Abhandlungen, Stuttgart 1994.

C. Horn, 'Selbstbewusstsein in der Antike: neue Untersuchungen zu Plotins Schrift 5.3', *Philosophische Rundschau* 44, 1997, 33–43.

Gerard O'Daly, *Plotinus' Philosophy of the Self*, Shannon 1973, esp. pp. 44, 53, and 70–81.

Pauliina Remes, *Plotinus' Philosophy of the Self: Unity, Reason, and Awareness*, Ph.D. diss., University of London, 2001.

F. M. Schroeder, 'Synousia, synaesthesis, and sunesis: presence and dependence in the Plotinian philosophy of consciousness', *Aufstieg und Niedergang der römischen Welt* 2.36.1, 1987, 677–99.

F. M. Schroeder, 'Conversion to consciousness in Plotinus Enneads 5.1 [10] 7', *Hermes* 114, 1986, 186–95.

G. Verbeke, 'Une anamnèse metaphysique chez Plotin', in D. O'Brien, M. O. Goulet-Cazé, eds., *Sophiês Maiêtores "Chercheurs de sagesse", Hommage à Jean Pépin*, Paris 1992, 297–316, at 297–99.

Dominic O'Meara, 'Scepticism and ineffability in Plotinus', *Phronesis* 45, 2000, 240–51.

Neoplatonism

See also 'Puzzles as to the possibility of self-knowledge', 'Knowledge of self through other', 'Infallible self-knowledge: Cogito and Flying Man' (above).

John Dillon, 'Damascius on procession and return', in John Cleary, ed., *The Perennial Tradition of Neoplatonism*, Leuven 1997, 369–79.

Lloyd Gerson, 'Epistrophê pros heauton: History and Meaning', *Documenti e Studi sulla tradizione filosofica medievale* 8, 1997, 1–32.

A. C. Lloyd, *The Anatomy of Neoplatonism*, Oxford 1990, 130–35.

K. Oehler, *Die Lehre vom noetischen und dianoetischen Denken bei Platon und Aristoteles: Ein Beitrag zur Erforschung der Geschichte des Bewusstseinsproblems in der Antike*, Munich 1962.

Wolfgang Bernard, 'Philoponus on self-awareness', in Richard Sorabji, ed., *Philoponus and the Rejection of Aristotelian Science*, Ithaca N.Y. 1987, ch. 8.

H. J. Blumenthal, 'Plutarch's exposition of the De Anima and the psychology of Proclus', in H. Dörrie, ed., *De Jamblique à Proclus*, Fondation Hardt, *Entretiens* 21, Geneva 1975, 123–47.

Ilsetraut Hadot, 'Aspects de la théorie de la perception chez les néoplatonciens', *Documenti e Studi sulla tradizione filosofica medievale* 8, 1997, 1–53, esp. 31–53.

Peter Lautner, 'Rival theories of self-awareness in late Neoplatonism', *Bulletin of the Institute of Classical Studies* 29, 1994, 107–16.

Peter Lautner, 'Can self-reflection be a generative principle? Atticus and Porphyry on Timaeus 37B3–6', in J. Finamore, ed., *The Ancient World* 32, 2001, 71–84.

Peter Lautner, 'Plutarch of Athens on koinê aisthêsis and phantasia', *Ancient Philosophy* 20, 2000, 425–46.

A. C. Lloyd, 'Nosce Teipsum and Conscientia', *Archiv für Geschichte der Philosophie* 46, 1964, 188–200.

Carlos Steel, 'Conversion vers soi et constitution selon Proclus', in A. Charles-Saget, ed., *Retour repentir et constitution de Soi*, Paris 1998, 161–75.

L. G. Westerink, *The Greek Commentators on Plato's Phaedo*, vol. 2, *Damascius*, Amsterdam 1977, 162–63.

Augustine

See also 'Knowledge of self and knowledge of God' (above).

P. Courcelle, *Connais-toi toi même*, Paris 1974, vol. I.

E. Booth, 'St. Augustine's "notitia sui" related to Aristotle and the early Neoplatonists', *Augustiniana*, vol. 27, 1977, 70–132, 364–401; vol. 28, 1978, 183–221; vol. 29, 1979, 97–104.

Brian Stock, Sather Classical Lectures 2001, University of California, Berkeley, forthcoming.

Gerard Verbeke, 'Connaissance de soi et connaissance de Dieu chez Saint Augustin', *Augustiniana* 4, 1954, 495–515, reprinted in his *D'Aristote à Thomas d'Aquin: Antécédents de la pensée moderne*, Leuven 1990, 367–87.

INDEX LOCORUM

Compiled by Michael Griffin